PHILADELPHIA

KARRIE GAVIN WITH MOLLY GAVIN

Contents

Discover Philadelphia 24
Planning Your Trip............. 26
Top 10 for Kids................. 29
The Three-Day Best of
  Philadelphia 30
Best Cheesesteaks 31
Fun and Free Philly 32

Sights....................33

Restaurants...............88

Nightlife 140

Arts and Culture 165

Sports and Activities 187

Shops 216

Hotels....................244

Excursions 265

Background 297

Essentials...............330

Resources..............345

Index....................350

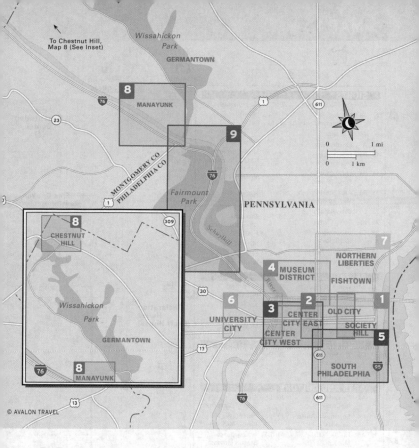

Maps

MAP 1: **Old City and Society Hill** 4-7

MAP 2: **City Center East** 8-9

MAP 3: **City Center West** 10-11

MAP 4: **Museum District** 12-13

MAP 5: **South Philadelphia** 14-15

MAP 6: **University City** 16-17

MAP 7: **Northern Liberties and Fishtown** 18-19

MAP 8: **Chestnut Hill and Manayunk** 20

MAP 9: **Fairmount Park** 21

MAP 10: **Greater Philadelphia** 22-23

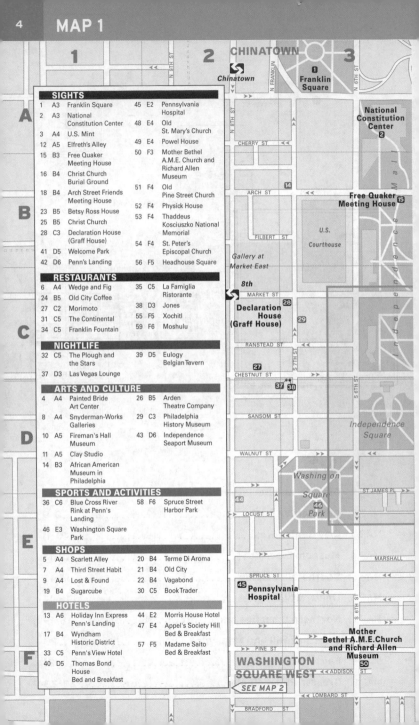

CHINATOWN

Chinatown

❶ **Franklin Square**

National Constitution Center ❷

Free Quaker Meeting House ❶❺

U.S. Courthouse

Gallery at Market East

8th

MARKET ST

Declaration House (Graff House) ❷❽

❷❾

Independence Square

Washington Square Park ❹❻

ST JAMES PL

MARSHALL

SPRUCE ST

❹❺ **Pennsylvania Hospital**

Mother Bethel A.M.E.Church and Richard Allen Museum ❺⓪

WASHINGTON SQUARE WEST

SEE MAP 2

		SIGHTS			
1	A3	Franklin Square	45	E2	Pennsylvania Hospital
2	A3	National Constitution Center	48	E4	Old St. Mary's Church
3	A4	U.S. Mint	49	E4	Powel House
12	A5	Elfreth's Alley	50	F3	Mother Bethel A.M.E. Church and Richard Allen Museum
15	B3	Free Quaker Meeting House			
16	B4	Christ Church Burial Ground	51	F4	Old Pine Street Church
18	B4	Arch Street Friends Meeting House	52	F4	Physick House
			53	F4	Thaddeus Kosciuszko National Memorial
23	B5	Betsy Ross House			
25	B5	Christ Church	54	F4	St. Peter's Episcopal Church
28	C3	Declaration House (Graff House)	56	F5	Headhouse Square
41	D5	Welcome Park			
42	D6	Penn's Landing			

		RESTAURANTS			
6	A4	Wedge and Fig	35	C5	La Famiglia Ristorante
24	B5	Old City Coffee			
27	C2	Morimoto	38	D3	Jones
31	C5	The Continental	55	F5	Xochitl
34	C5	Franklin Fountain	59	F6	Moshulu

		NIGHTLIFE			
32	C5	The Plough and the Stars	39	D5	Eulogy Belgian Tavern
37	D3	Las Vegas Lounge			

		ARTS AND CULTURE			
4	A4	Painted Bride Art Center	26	B5	Arden Theatre Company
8	A4	Snyderman-Works Galleries	29	C3	Philadelphia History Museum
10	A5	Fireman's Hall Museum	43	D6	Independence Seaport Museum
11	A5	Clay Studio			
14	B3	African American Museum in Philadelphia			

		SPORTS AND ACTIVITIES			
36	C6	Blue Cross River Rink at Penn's Landing	58	F6	Spruce Street Harbor Park
46	E3	Washington Square Park			

		SHOPS			
5	A4	Scarlett Alley	20	B4	Terme Di Aroma
7	A4	Third Street Habit	21	B4	Old City
9	A4	Lost & Found	22	B4	Vagabond
19	B4	Sugarcube	30	C5	Book Trader

		HOTELS			
13	A6	Holiday Inn Express Penn's Landing	44	E2	Morris House Hotel
17	B4	Wyndham Historic District	47	E4	Appel's Society Hill Bed & Breakfast
33	C5	Penn's View Hotel	57	F5	Madame Saito Bed & Breakfast
40	D5	Thomas Bond House Bed and Breakfast			

SEE MAP 7

BENJAMIN
FRANKLIN
BRIDGE

Pier 12 N

Pier 11 N

To
4 Painted Bride
Art Center

FLORIST ST

RACE ST

5

676 30

**U.S.
Mint**
3

6

7

CHERRY

QUARRY ST

8

9

19

10

11

12 Elfreth's
Alley

13

**Betsy Ross
House**
23

OLD CITY

ARCH ST

**Arch Street Friends
Meeting House**

16

17

CUTHBERT

**Christ Church
Burial Ground**

18

FILBERT ST

26

COMMERCE ST

20

21

22

24

25

CHURCH

**Christ
Church**

N. AMERICAN ST

DISTANCE ACROSS MAP
Approximate: 1.3 mi or 2 km

0   100 yds

0   100 m

5th

MARKET ST

30 2nd

33

LUDLOW ST

31

34

RANSTEAD ST

35

95

36

S. RANK ST

ELBOW LN

TROTTERS ALV

S. STRAWBERRY ST

32

LETITIA ST

S. FRONT ST

S. COLUMBUS BLVD

CHESTNUT ST

39

Penn's
Landing
42

**U.S.
Customs
House**

IONIC ST

**PENN'S
LANDING**

Delaware River

40 SANSOM WALK

41
**Welcome
Park**

WALNUT ST

DOCK ST

43

THOMAS ST

*Rose
Garden*

S. COLUMBUS BLVD

International

INDEPENDENCE SQUARE

Sculpture

DOCK ST

38TH PARALLEL PL

*City
Park*

Garden

Boat Basin

48
**Old St. Mary's
Church**

49
**Powel
House**

LOCUST ST

**SOCIETY
HILL**

47

SPRUCE ST

S. 4TH ST

S. 3RD ST

**Physick
House**

S. 2ND ST

CYPRESS ST

52

DELANCEY ST

58

**Thaddeus Kosciuszko
National Memorial**

53

51
**Old Pine Street
Church**

PINE

54 **St. Peter's
Episcopal
Church**

55 56 **Headhouse
Square**

95

59

STAMPER ST

SOUTH STREET

SEE MAP 5

FRONT ST

57

GASKILL ST

MARKET ST

1 Independence Visitor Center

5th

2 President's House

A

LUDLOW ST

3

N 5TH ST

S 5TH ST

11

RANSTEAD ST

9 Liberty Bell Center

B

10

12

CHESTNUT ST

Independence Hall
19

21 Second Bank of the United States

C

Philosophical Hall and Library Hall **20**

S 6TH ST

N 5TH ST

S 4TH ST

Independence Square

D

Curtis Center and *Dream Garden* Mosaic
24

WALNUT ST

Philadelphia Contributionship **25**

0   50 yds
0   50 m
DISTANCE ACROSS MAP
Approximate: 0.5 mi or 0.8 km

Washington Square Park

E

ST JAMES PL

Rose Garden
34

SEE MAP 2

33 Athenaeum

SIGHTS							
1	A1	Independence Visitor Center	20	C2	Philosophical Hall and Library Hall	24	D1	Curtis Center and *Dream Garden* Mosaic	28	D4	Bishop White House
2	A1	President's House	21	C3	Second Bank of the United States	25	D3	Philadelphia Contributionship	29	D5	Merchants' Exchange Building
4	A4	Franklin Court	22	C4	Carpenters' Hall	26	D4	Todd House	33	E1	Athenaeum
9	B1	Liberty Bell Center	23	C4	First Bank of the United States				35	E4	Old St. Joseph's Church
19	C2	Independence Hall									

4 MARKET ST
5 **6**
7
5 MARKET ST
6 2nd

Franklin Court
4

8

ELBOW LN

S 3RD ST

TROTTERS ALY

S BANK ST
S STRAWBERRY ST
N 2ND ST

13 **14**

16

15
CHESTNUT ST
17

18

RESTAURANTS

5	A4	High Street on Market	13	B4	Buddakan
6	A4	Fork	17	B5	Amada
7	A5	Gianfranco Pizza Rustica	31	D6	Positano Coast by Aldo Lamberti
8	A5	Farmicia	32	D6	City Tavern Restaurant
11	B3	The Bourse	36	E5	Zahav

First Bank of the United States
23

U.S. Customs House

22
Carpenters' Hall

S 3RD ST
N 2ND ST
SANSOM WALK

Todd **26** House
Bishop White House
28
Merchants' Exchange Building
29

32

27
WALNUT ST
30
DOCK ST
31

THOMAS ST

Old St. Joseph's Church
35

DOCK ST

WILLINGS ALLEY
S 3RD ST

36 SEE MAP 5

© AVALON TRAVEL

ST. JAMES PL

NIGHTLIFE

| 18 | B6 | Khyber Pass Pub |

ARTS AND CULTURE

| 3 | A2 | National Museum of American Jewish History | 27 | D4 | Polish American Cultural Center and Museum |
| 14 | B4 | National Liberty Museum | 30 | D5 | Landmark Theatres |

SPORTS AND ACTIVITIES

| 34 | E3 | Rose Garden and Magnolia Garden |

HOTELS

10	B2	Hotel Monaco	16	B5	Apple Hostels of Philadelphia
12	B3	Franklin Hotel at Independence Park			
15	Bb	Best Western Independence Park Hotel			

1

2

3

Hahnemann University Hospital

Race-Vine

SEE MAP 4

❶
❷

SPRING ST

CHINATOWN

RACE ST

A

◀ SEE MAP 3

611

❸

N 10TH ST

N 11TH ST

CHERRY ST

❹

Arch Street United Methodist Church

Chinatown Friendship Gate

❶❷ ❶❸

B

❺

Thomas Paine Plaza

3

❻

❼ Masonic Temple

ARCH ST

N JUNIPER ST

N 13TH ST

❽ ❾

CUTHBERT ST

N 12TH ST

Reading Terminal Market

❶❶

ARCH ST

CUTHBERT ST

FILBERT ST

❶❶

N BROAD ST

JOHN F KENNEDY BLVD

❶❶

❶❹

Dilworth Park

15th

City Hall

3

City Hall

City

Hall

Juniper

❶❼

13th

❶❽

Gallery at Market East

11th

MARKET ST

C

❶❺

Macy's

CENTER CITY EAST

LUDLOW ST

❷❶

St. Stephen's Episcopal Church

AVE OF THE ARTS

❶❻

❶❾

CHESTNUT ST

❷❶ ❷❷

❷❹
❷❺
❷❼

❸❽

Thomas Jefferson

D

◀◀

SANSOM ST

❷❻

❷❽
❷❾

❸❷

❸❷ ❸❻

❸❼

University Hospital

MORAVIAN ST

❸❶

❸❷
❸❸

❸❹

WALNUT ST

❸❾ ❹❶

❹❶

❷❸

Walnut-Locust

CHANCELLOR ST

❸❺

CHANCELLOR ST

❹❽

❹❾

Thomas

Jefferson

University

9th

ST JAMES ST

❹❻

12th

❹❼

❺❻

LOCUST ST

E

❹❷

611

Library Company of Philadelphia

❹❸

❺❶

❺❶ ❺❷

LATIMER ST

S CAMAC ST

S JUNIPER ST

S 12TH ST

S QUINCE ST

BACH PL

◀ SEE MAP 3

❹❹

SPRUCE ST

❺❸

❹❺

❺❹

❺❺

Kimmel Center

❺❼

S BROAD ST

S WATTS ST

S JUNIPER ST

S 13TH ST

S CAMAC ST

S 12TH ST

CYPRESS ST

CYPRESS ST

CLINTON ST

❻❷

PINE ST

❺❾

❻❶

PINE ST

F

ANTIQUE ROW ❻❶

SEE MAP 5

WAVERLY ST

❺❽

4

Chinatown

Franklin Square SEE MAP 7

FRANKLIN ST

RACE ST

CHERRY ST

N 8TH ST

N 7TH ST

SEE MAP 1

U.S. Courthouse

FILBERT ST

N 6TH ST

Independence Visitor Center

Independence Mall

8th

Liberty Bell

Independence Square

JEWELER'S ROW

Washington Square

Pennsylvania Hospital

S 8TH ST

S 7TH ST

S 6TH ST

S 5TH ST

SEE MAP 1

PINE ST

ADDISON ST

ADDISON ST

SIGHTS

6	B1	Arch Street United Methodist Church	15	C1	City Hall
7	B1	Masonic Temple	20	C3	St. Stephen's Episcopal Church
10	B2	Reading Terminal Market	43	E1	Library Company of Philadelphia
13	B3	Chinatown Friendship Gate			

RESTAURANTS

1	A3	Vietnam Restaurant	36	D2	1225 Raw Sushi and Sake Lounge
3	A3	Ray's Café and Tea House	45	E1	Vetri
23	D1	XIX	47	E2	Vedge
26	D2	Lolita	53	E2	Valanni
29	D2	Barbuzzo	54	E2	Mercato
30	D2	Capogiro	56	E2	Garces Trading Company
31	D2	Sampan			

NIGHTLIFE

2	A3	Yakitori Boy	46	E2	Voyeur
12	B3	Trocadero Theatre	49	E2	The Bike Stop
32	D2	Vintage	51	E2	U Bar
35	E2	Woody's	52	E2	Tavern on Camac
37	D2	Fergie's	59	F2	Dirty Frank's

ARTS AND CULTURE

4	B1	Pennsylvania Academy of the Fine Arts	42	E1	Academy of Music
9	B2	Fabric Workshop and Museum	44	E1	Wilma Theater
			57	F1	Kimmel Center
11	B3	Space 1026	58	F1	Philadelphia Theatre Company and Suzanne Roberts Theatre
40	D2	Forrest Theatre			
41	D3	Walnut Street Theatre			

SPORTS AND ACTIVITIES

| 14 | C1 | Dilworth Park | 48 | E2 | 12th Street Gym |
| 21 | D1 | Lucky Strike Lanes | 61 | F2 | Mama's Wellness Joint |

SHOPS

8	B2	AIA Bookstore and Design Center	28	D2	Verde
17	C1	Macy's	33	D2	Modern Eye
19	C2	Mitchell & Ness	34	D2	Midtown Village
22	D1	West Elm	38	D2	Lapstone and Hammer
24	D2	Grocery	39	D2	Ten Thousand Villages
25	D2	Open House	60	F2	Giovanni's Room
27	D2	Duross & Langel			

HOTELS

5	B1	Le Méridien	50	E2	The Independent Hotel
16	C1	The Ritz-Carlton of Philadelphia	55	E2	Alexander Inn
18	C2	Loews Hotel	62	F3	Clinton Street Bed & Breakfast

0   100 yds

0   100 m

DISTANCE ACROSS MAP
Approximate: 4.2 mi or 6.9 km

© AVALON TRAVEL

30th

SEE MAP 6

Schuylkill River

MARKET ST
LUDLOW ST
LUDLOW ST
RANSTEAD ST
CHESTNUT ST
IONIC ST
SANSOM ST
MORAVIAN ST
WALNUT ST
LOCUST ST
LATIMER ST
RITTENHOUSE SQUARE
MANNING ST
SPRUCE ST
FITLER SQUARE
CYPRESS ST
DELANCEY ST
PANAMA ST
Fitler Square
PINE ST
LOMBARD ST
NAUDAIN ST
RODMAN ST
SOUTH ST
GRAYS FERRY AVE
KATER ST
BAINBRIDGE ST
PEMBERTON ST
FITZWATER ST
CLYMER ST
CATHARINE ST
WEBSTER ST
KAUFFMAN ST
CHRISTIAN ST

SIGHTS
| 5 | A5 | Comcast Center |

RESTAURANTS
4	A4	Mama's Vegetarian	50	C4	Audrey Claire
12	B3	Fuji Mountain	51	C4	Metropolitan Bakery
13	B3	Vic Sushi Bar			
15	B3	Vernick	53	C5	Parc
18	B4	Tinto	56	C5	The Black Sheep
26	A5	Di Bruno Bros.	57	C5	Tequilas Restaurant
31	B5	LeBus	58	C5	Monk's Café
43	B5	Rouge	65	E2	Ants Pants
45	B6	Oyster House	68	E6	Jamaican Jerk Hut
49	C4	Seafood Unlimited			

NIGHTLIFE
3	A3	First Unitarian Church	59	C6	Good Dog
			60	C6	McGlinchey's
16	B3	The Bards	61	D4	Pub and Kitchen
19	B4	Village Whiskey	64	E2	Grace Tavern
24	B5	Franklin Mortgage & Investment Co.	66	E3	Ten Stone
			67	E6	Bob & Barbara's
28	B5	Tria	69	F3	Sidecar Bar & Grille
34	B5	a.bar			

ARTS AND CULTURE
| 2 | A3 | Mutter Museum | 54 | C5 | Curtis Institute of Music |
| 14 | B3 | Adrienne Theatre | | | |

SPORTS AND ACTIVITIES
| 1 | A2 | Schuylkill River Trail | 40 | B5 | Dhyana Yoga |
| 8 | A5 | One Liberty Observation Deck | 51 | C4 | Rittenhouse Square |

SHOPS
6	A5	Knit Wit	33	B5	Head Start Shoes
7	A5	Buffalo Exchange	35	B5	Kiehl's
10	A5	The Shops at Liberty Place	36	B5	Bluemercury Apothecary and Spa
11	A5	Children's Boutique	37	B5	Rescue Rittenhouse Spa
17	B4	Balance Health Center	38	B4	Urban Outfitters
			39	B5	Joan Shepp
20	B4	Boyd's	41	B5	Theory
21	B4	Toppers Spa and Salon	42	B5	Apple Store
22	B4	Born Yesterday	44	B5	Rittenhouse Row
25	B4	Anthropologie	47	B6	Ublq
27	B5	Benjamin Lovell Shoes	48	B6	The Shops at the Bellevue
32	B5	Joseph Fox Bookshop	63	D5	Omoi Zakka Shop

HOTELS
9	A5	Westin	55	C5	Rittenhouse 1715
23	B4	Rittenhouse Hotel	62	D4	La Reserve Center City Bed and Breakfast
29	B5	Sofitel			
30	B5	Hotel Palomar			
46	B6	Roost Apartment Hotel			

© AVALON TRAVEL

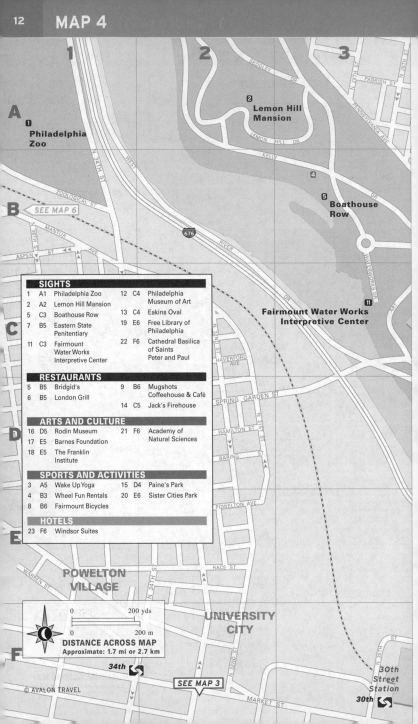

Philadelphia Zoo

Lemon Hill Mansion

Boathouse Row

SEE MAP 6

Fairmount Water Works Interpretive Center

SIGHTS
1	A1	Philadelphia Zoo	12	C4	Philadelphia Museum of Art
2	A2	Lemon Hill Mansion	13	C4	Eakins Oval
5	C3	Boathouse Row	19	E6	Free Library of Philadelphia
7	B5	Eastern State Penitentiary	22	F6	Cathedral Basilica of Saints Peter and Paul
11	C3	Fairmount Water Works Interpretive Center			

RESTAURANTS
5	B5	Bridgid's	9	B6	Mugshots Coffeehouse & Café
6	B5	London Grill	14	C5	Jack's Firehouse

ARTS AND CULTURE
16	D5	Rodin Museum	21	F6	Academy of Natural Sciences
17	E5	Barnes Foundation			
18	E5	The Franklin Institute			

SPORTS AND ACTIVITIES
3	A5	Wake Up Yoga	15	D4	Paine's Park
4	B3	Wheel Fun Rentals	20	E6	Sister Cities Park
8	B6	Fairmount Bicycles			

HOTELS
23	F6	Windsor Suites

POWELTON VILLAGE

UNIVERSITY CITY

0 200 yds
0 200 m
DISTANCE ACROSS MAP
Approximate: 1.7 mi or 2.7 km

34th

SEE MAP 3

30th Street Station

30th

© AVALON TRAVEL

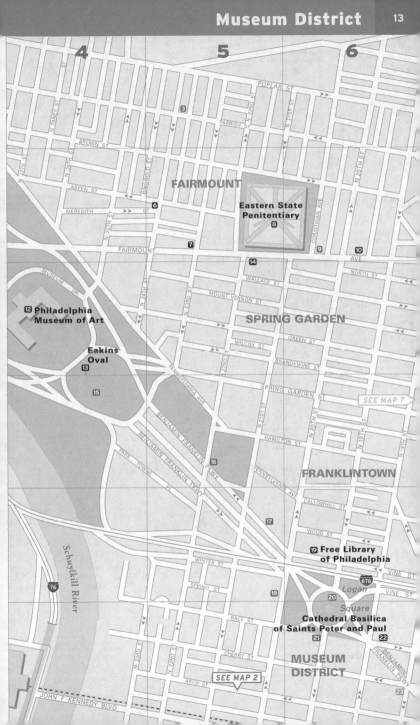

4   **5**   **6**

POPLAR ST

3

PARRISH ST

N 21ST ST

N 20TH ST

N TANEY ST

BROWN ST

ASPEN ST

RINGGOLD ST

FAIRMOUNT

CORINTHIAN AVE

MEREDITH

6

Eastern State Penitentiary
8

FAIRMOUNT

N 25TH ST

7

9

10

AVE

14

WALLACE ST

NORTH ST

N 24TH ST

MOUNT VERNON ST

MUSEUM DR

12 **Philadelphia Museum of Art**

SPRING GARDEN

N 23RD ST

WILCOX ST

GREEN ST

Eakins Oval
13

BRANDYWINE ST

N 22ND ST

15

SPRING GARDEN ST

SEE MAP 7

PENNSYLVANIA AVE

HAMILTON ST

N 21ST ST

N 20TH ST

N 19TH ST

N 18TH ST

BENJAMIN FRANKLIN PKWY

16

PENNSYLVANIA AVE

FRANKLINTOWN

PARK TOWNE

CALLOWHILL ST

17

WOOD ST

19 **Free Library of Philadelphia**

Schuylkill River

WINTER ST

VINE ST

676

76

SPRING ST

Logan

VINE ST

18

20

Square

N 23RD ST

N 22ND ST

RACE ST

Cathedral Basilica of Saints Peter and Paul

21

22

CHERRY ST

MUSEUM DISTRICT

BENJAMIN FRANKLIN PKWY

SEE MAP 2

ARCH ST

23

JOHN F KENNEDY BLVD

SEE MAP 2 **1**

Philadelphia's
Magic Gardens

RODMAN ST

2

SEE MAP 1 **3**

1

SOUTH ST

2

9

KATER ST

4

3

6

7
8

BAINBRIDGE ST

A

S CLIFTON ST

S WAMOCK ST

S ADLER ST

FITZWATER ST

19

22

S 6TH ST

21

23

B

CATHARINE ST

S 10TH ST

S 9TH ST

S 8TH ST

25

CATHARINE ST

S 12TH ST

CHRISTIAN ST

20

24

26

E PASSYUNK AVE

SEE MAP 3

S 11TH ST

31

S 7TH ST

CARPENTER ST

HALL ST

MONTROSE ST

32

C

KIMBALL ST

LEAGUE ST

30

WASHINGTON AVE

ELLSWORTH ST

D

33

ANNIN ST

ANNIN ST

FEDERAL ST

WHARTON

S 11TH ST

S 10TH ST

S 9TH ST

E PASSYUNK AVE

S 6TH ST

S 7TH ST

E

WHARTON ST

36

37

Passyunk
Square

SEARS ST

SEARS ST

EARP ST

S 12TH ST

REED ST

45

F

To
39 The Dolphin Tavern

WILDER ST

DICKINSON ST

To
41 Marra's Pizza
42 Bing Bing Dim Sum
43 South Philly Barbacoa
44 Fountain Porter

40

CROSS ST

GREENICH ST

CROSS ST

GASKILL ST

4 14

SOUTH STREET

5

6

SIGHTS

| 1 | A1 | Philadelphia's Magic Gardens | 35 | D6 | Gloria Dei (Old Swedes' Episcopal Church) |

RESTAURANTS

3	A2	Chapterhouse Café	26	B3	John's Water Ice
7	A3	Beau Monde	28	B4	Hungry Pigeon
14	A4	Marrakesh Restaurant	29	B5	Dmitri's
15	A4	Jim's Steaks	30	D1	Nam Phuong
16	A4	Famous 4th St. Delicatessen	31	C2	Anthony's Italian Coffee House
19	B1	Hawthornes Café	37	E2	Pat's King of Steaks
20	B2	Isgro Paticceria	38	E5	Federal Donuts
22	B2	Sam's Morning Glory Diner	41	F2	Marra's Pizza
23	B2	Ralph's	42	F2	Bing Bing Dim Sum
24	B2	Sabrina's Café	43	F2	South Philly Barbacoa

NIGHTLIFE

4	A3	The Good King Tavern	33	D1	Devil's Den
8	A3	L'Etage	36	E2	Garage
11	A4	Tattooed Mom	39	F1	The Dolphin Tavern
18	A4	Theatre of Living Arts	40	F1	Pub on Passyunk East (POPE)
32	C3	Royal Tavern	44	F2	Fountain Porter

ARTS AND CULTURE

| 25 | B3 | Fleisher Art Memorial | 45 | F6 | United Artists Riverview Stadium 17 |
| 34 | D5 | Mummers Museum | | | |

SHOPS

2	A2	Via Bicycle	13	A4	Philadelphia AIDS Thrift
5	A3	South Street	17	A4	Brickbat Books
6	A3	Anastacia's Antiques	27	B4	Moon and Arrow
9	A3	Repo Records	45	F2	East Passyunk Avenue
10	A4	Garland of Letters			
12	A4	Retrospect Vintage			

HOTELS

| 21 | B2 | Bella Vista Bed & Breakfast |

FABRIC ROW

MONROE ST

FITZWATER ST

S 6TH ST
S LEITHGOW ST
S 5TH ST
S 4TH ST
S 3RD ST

CARPENTER ST

S 2ND ST

Gloria Dei (Old Swedes' Episcopal Church) 35

WASHINGTON AVE

Jefferson Square Park

34

95

MANTON ST

38

TITAN ST

E MOYAMENSING ST
S 2ND ST
S FRONT ST

SEARS ST

S 3RD ST

REED ST

45

WATER ST
S COLUMBUS BLVD

| 0 | | 100 yds |
| 0 | | 100 m |

DISTANCE ACROSS MAP
Approximate: 1.7 mi or 2.7 km

95

PENNSPORT

© AVALON TRAVEL

GREENWICH ST

SIGHTS

6	C6	30th Street Station	26	F3	Woodlands Cemetery and Mansion
13	D4	University of Pennsylvania			

RESTAURANTS

2	C3	Distrito	20	E2	Green Line Cafe
5	C6	JG Domestic	23	F1	Vientiane Café
15	D5	White Dog Café	24	F1	Dahlak
19	E2	Marigold Kitchen			

NIGHTLIFE

8	D3	Rotunda	16	D5	New Deck Tavern
11	D3	Cavanaugh's	18	D6	World Café Live

ARTS AND CULTURE

3	C4	International House	14	D4	Institute of Contemporary Art
9	D3	Rave Motion Pictures University City 6	22	E5	University Museum of Archaeology and Anthropology

SPORTS AND ACTIVITIES

7	C6	Cira Green	17	D5	University of Pennsylvania Arena
10	D3	Neighborhood Bike Works	21	E2	Clark Park

HOTELS

1	B5	Cornerstone Bed & Breakfast	12	D4	The Hilton Inn at Penn
4	C4	International House	25	F2	Gables

0   200 yds

0   200 m

DISTANCE ACROSS MAP
Approximate: 2.3 mi or 3.7 km

Lee Park

40th

LUDLOW ST

CHESTNUT ST

SANSOM ST

WALNUT ST

LOCUST ST

LOCUST WALK

SPRUCE ST

WEST PHILADELPHIA

PINE ST

OSAGE ST

LARCHWOOD AVE

BALTIMORE AVE

40th

HAZEL AVE

CEDAR AVE

Clark Park

BALTIMORE AVE

Woodlands Cemetery and Mansion

FAIRMOUNT AVE

WALLACE

MOUNT VERNON ST

HARVERFORD ST

BRANDYWINE ST

BARING ST

POWELTON AVE

FILBERT ST

© AVALON TRAVEL

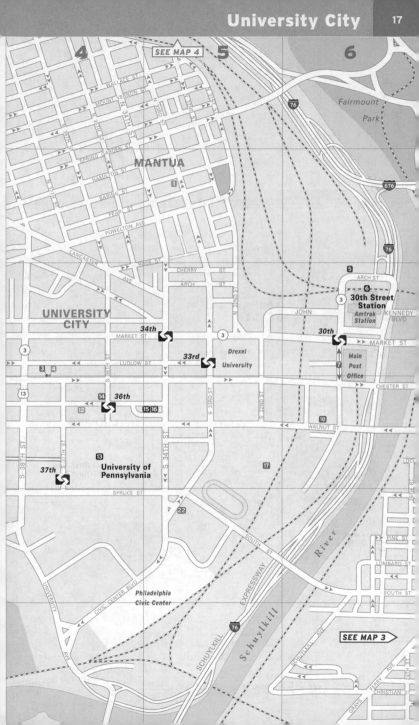

SEE MAP 4

MANTUA

WALLACE ST
MOUNT VERNON ST
SPRING GARDEN ST
HAMILTON ST
BARING ST
PEARL ST
POWELTON AVE

Fairmount
Park

LANCASTER AVE
HAUS ST
CHERRY ST
ARCH ST

UNIVERSITY
CITY

34th
MARKET ST
33rd
LUDLOW ST
36th
12
14
15 16
37th
13 University of
Pennsylvania
SPRUCE ST

Drexel
University

ARCH ST
30th Street
Station
Amtrak
Station
JOHN

KENNEDY
BLVD

30th
MARKET ST

Main
Post
Office
CHESTER ST

18
WALNUT ST

17

22

Philadelphia
Civic Center

SCHUYLKILL EXPRESSWAY

Schuylkill

River

SCHUYLKILL AVE

PINE ST
LOMBARD ST
SOUTH ST

SEE MAP 3

76

CHRISTIAN

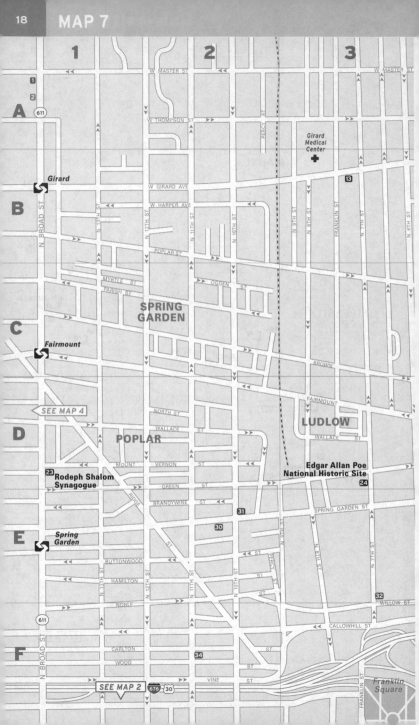

OLD KENSINGTON

W THOMPSON ST

National Shrine of St. John Neumann

W GIRARD AVE

Girard

FISHTOWN

GEORGE ST

WILDEY ST

NORTHERN LIBERTIES

POPLAR ST

Spring Garden

```
0          200 yds
0          200 m
```

DISTANCE ACROSS MAP
Approximate: 1.7 mi or 2.8 km

SEE MAP 1

© AVALON TRAVEL

Norman Porter Company 3
Philadelphia Record Exchange 6
Pizza Brain 8
Loco Pez 9

SIGHTS

14	B4	National Shrine of St. John Neumann
23	D1	Rodeph Shalom Synagogue
24	D3	Edgar Allan Poe National Historic Site

RESTAURANTS

4	A6	Wm. Mulherin's Sons
7	A6	La Colombe
8	A5	Pizza Brain
11	A6	Pizzeria Beddia
13	B3	Tiffin
16	B5	Bar Ferdinand
20	C5	Standard Tap
25	D4	Honey's Sit 'n Eat
26	D5	North Third

NIGHTLIFE

9	A5	Loco Pez
10	A6	Frankford Hall
12	A6	Johnny Brenda's
17	B6	Barcade
21	C6	The Barbary
22	C6	Punch Line Philly
27	D5	700 Club
30	E2	Union Transfer
31	E2	W/N W/N
32	E3	Electric Factory
33	E4	Silk City
35	F6	Morgan's Pier

ARTS AND CULTURE

1	A1	New Freedom Theatre
2	A1	The Legendary Blue Horizon
34	F2	Vox Populi and Khmer Gallery

SPORTS AND ACTIVITIES

19	C5	North Bowl

SHOPS

3	A5	Norman Porter Company
6	A5	Philadelphia Record Exchange
15	B5	The Schmidt's Commons
18	C5	Jinxed
28	D5	Art Star
29	D5	R.E. Load Baggage, Inc.

HOTELS

5	A6	Wm. Mulherin's Sons

MONTGOMERY COUNTY
PHILADELPHIA COUNTY

CHESTNUT HILL

Wissahickon

GERMANTOWN

Park

MANAYUNK

FAIRMOUNT PARK

RESTAURANTS

| 3 | C2 | McNally's Tavern | 7 | C3 | Paris Bistro and Jazz Café |
| 4 | C2 | Osaka Japanese Restaurant | 9 | C3 | El Poquito |

SPORTS AND ACTIVITIES

| 1 | A1 | Morris Arboretum | 10 | D2 | Wissahickon Ice Skating Rink |
| 2 | C1 | Wissahickon Park | | | |

SHOPS

| 5 | C2 | Hideaway Music | 6 | C3 | Germantown Avenue |

HOTELS

| 8 | C3 | Chestnut Hill Hotel | | | |

CHESTNUT HILL

Wissahickon Park

Wissahickon Creek

Chestnut Hill West

Wyndmoor

THOMAS MILL RD.

0 — 200 yds
0 — 200 m

DISTANCE ACROSS MAP
Approximate: 1.7 mi or 2.8 km

Pastorius Park

Highland

To Wissahickon Ice Skating Rink

© AVALON TRAVEL

MANAYUNK

Manayunk

Schuylkill River

0 — 200 yds
0 — 200 m

DISTANCE ACROSS MAP
Approximate: 1.2 mi or 1.9 km

RESTAURANTS

| 2 | E1 | Jake's and Cooper's Wine Bar | 6 | E2 | Bayou Bar & Grill |
| 5 | E2 | The Couch Tomato Café | 8 | F2 | Manayunk Brewery and Restaurant |

SPORTS AND ACTIVITIES

| 7 | E2 | Human Zoom |

SHOPS

| 1 | E1 | Main Street Music | 4 | E2 | Manayunk |
| 3 | E2 | Salon L'Etoile & Spa | | | |

© AVALON TRAVEL

1 A3 Laurel Hill Cemetery
2 (Schuylkill River area marker)
3 Strawberry Mansion

SIGHTS

1	A3	Laurel Hill Cemetery	6	D1	Belmont Mansion
3	C3	Strawberry Mansion	8	D3	Mount Pleasant
4	C3	Woodford Mansion	15	F3	Cedar Grove
5	C3	Laurel Hill Mansion	16	F3	Smith Civil War Memorial

ARTS AND CULTURE

12	F1	Mann Center for the Performing Arts	14	F2	Please Touch Museum

SPORTS AND ACTIVITIES

7	D2	Fairmount Park	11	E3	Sedgley Woods Disc Golf Course
9	E2	Philadelphia Horticulture Center	13	F2	Shofuso Japanese House And Gardens
10	E3	Smith Memorial Playground and Playhouse			

HOTELS

2	B2	Chamounix Mansion

0   300 yds
0   300 m

DISTANCE ACROSS MAP
Approximate: 1.2 mi or 1.9 km

Laurel Hill Cemetery

Mount Vernon Cemetery

Strawberry Mansion **3**

Woodford Mansion **4**

Laurel Hill Mansion **5**

East Park Reservoir

Mount Pleasant **8**

Belmont Mansion **6**

FAIRMOUNT PARK

Fairmount Park

River

Cedar Grove **15**

Memorial Hall **14**

Smith Civil War Memorial **16**

Centennial Lake

Concourse Lake

12

9

13

7

10

11

© AVALON TRAVEL

1 **2** **3**

276

A 476 Plymouth
Meeting

73

PENNSYLVANIA

Chestnut
Hill

309

Conshohocken

GERMANTOWN AVE

Elkins

B 76

23

MONTGOMERY CO
PHILADELPHIA CO

3
Fairmount

Germantown

611

Manayunk

Schuylkill

Wissahickon Valley

Park

5

C To
Villanova

Bryn Mawr

76

River

HENRY AVE

1

West
Manayunk

23

PHILADELPHIA

Narberth

30

CITY LINE AVE

Fairmount

LEHIGH
AVE

D Havertown

DARBY RD

1

LANCASTER AVE

Park

GIRARD
AVE

3

E Springfield

Upper
Darby

CHESTNUT ST

WALNUT ST

676 30

S. BROAD AVE

Drexel Hill

BALTIMORE PIKE

13

Darby

LINDBERGH BLVD

7

611

95

76

18

F 13

To
Delaware

Glenoden

To Union
and PPL Park

BARTRAM
AVE

SASSYPUNK

ESSINGTON AVE

S. 26TH AVE

PENROSE
AVE

10

Franklin
Delano
Roosevelt
Park

11
12
13
14
15

16

17

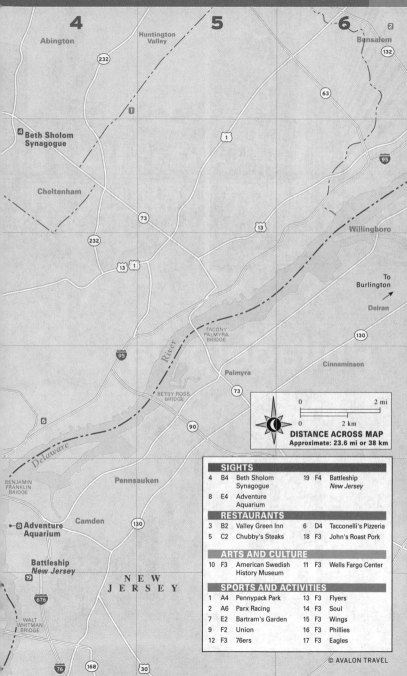

4 Abington

Huntington Valley

5

6 Bensalem

232

132

1

63

4 Beth Sholom Synagogue

1

95

Cheltenham

73

13

Willingboro

232

13 1

To Burlington

TACONY PALMYRA BRIDGE

Delran

130

Palmyra

95

Cinnaminson

73

BETSY ROSS BRIDGE

River

0   2 mi
0   2 km

DISTANCE ACROSS MAP
Approximate: 23.6 mi or 38 km

6

90

Delaware

BENJAMIN FRANKLIN BRIDGE

Pennsauken

8 Adventure Aquarium

Camden

130

Battleship New Jersey

19

676

N E W
J E R S E Y

WALT WHITMAN BRIDGE

76

168

30

© AVALON TRAVEL

SIGHTS

4	B4	Beth Sholom Synagogue	19	F4	Battleship *New Jersey*
8	E4	Adventure Aquarium			

RESTAURANTS

3	B2	Valley Green Inn	6	D4	Tacconelli's Pizzeria
5	C2	Chubby's Steaks	18	F3	John's Roast Pork

ARTS AND CULTURE

10	F3	American Swedish History Museum	11	F3	Wells Fargo Center

SPORTS AND ACTIVITIES

1	A4	Pennypack Park	13	F3	Flyers
2	A6	Parx Racing	14	F3	Soul
7	E2	Bartram's Garden	15	F3	Wings
9	F2	Union	16	F3	Phillies
12	F3	76ers	17	F3	Eagles

Philadelphia

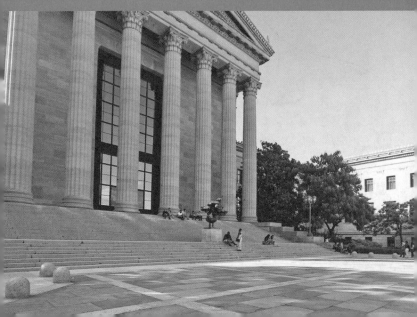

I n 2015, Philadelphia became America's first UNESCO World Heritage City for its significant role in the birth of the United States. As you explore Philly's streets (some paved and some still cobblestone), you'll find that the historical roots of this city are alive and well, even as it continues to evolve into a modern metropolis. New skyscrapers, restaurants, and galleries still mingle with the well-preserved homes and churches of the founding fathers.

Center City has blossomed into a world-class downtown; revitalized commercial corridors and parks, restaurants with famous chefs, and new museums and music venues continue to generate buzz and drive Philadelphia to the top of international travel destination lists. In the colorful neighborhoods beyond Center City, you'll discover family-run greasy spoons where you'll be called "hon" and dive bars where Quizzo and karaoke rival the 76ers, Eagles, Phillies, and Flyers as serious competitive sports. It is these contrasting highbrow and lowbrow vibes that make Philly so special.

Many visitors come to see the Liberty Bell and Independence Hall or to jog up the famed Art Museum steps à la *Rocky*. But while you're here, indulge in the activities that locals enjoy, too: relax in Rittenhouse Square; have lunch in Reading Terminal Market; stroll along the Schuylkill River Trail; catch a play or a concert on the Avenue of the Arts; and after jogging up the grand steps of the Philadelphia Museum of Art, go inside that magnificent building to see works that rival many of Europe's best museums.

Philadelphia has become a thriving, modern city while remaining true to its historical roots and hometown pride. There has been no better time to visit…and you just may find that you want to stay awhile.

Clockwise from top left: Arch Street; Independence Hall; the Liberty Bell; the Philadelphia Museum of Art.

Planning Your Trip

Where to Go

Old City

Most first-time visits to Philadelphia begin in Old City, home to **Independence National Historical Park**, "the nation's most historic square mile." This is where you'll find **Independence Hall**, the **Liberty Bell**, the **National Constitution Center**, and many other historic attractions. Old City also has a wealth of dining, shopping, hotels, and nightlife.

Society Hill

A tranquil neighbor to Old City, Society Hill boasts many of the finest and oldest homes and cathedrals in the city. Bordered by leafy **Washington Square Park** to the west and the **Penn's Landing** waterfront strip to the east, it is a lovely place to soak up American history.

Center City East

Broad Street is known as **Avenue of the Arts** in the blocks south of **City Hall**, which are home to the city's biggest theater and opera houses, and it divides the downtown business district into East and West. Center City East is home to **Reading Terminal Market, Chinatown, Midtown Village, Antique Row**, and **Washington Square West**, which is the center of the local gay culture.

Center City West

The skyscrapers, hotels, restaurants, bars, and shops are the biggest and

The Friendship Gate marks the entrance to Chinatown in Center City East.

University of Pennsylvania

generally the most upscale on the west side of Broad Street in Center City West. The action centers around tree-lined **Rittenhouse Square** and the chic **Rittenhouse Row** shopping district, also home to many restaurants, hotels, and bars.

Museum District

Lined with flowers, sculptures, and flags from around the world, the **Benjamin Franklin Parkway** is the broad diagonal street connecting **City Hall** to the **Philadelphia Museum of Art.** Home to the **Franklin Institute, Rodin Museum, Academy of Natural Sciences,** and the **Barnes Foundation,** the Museum District is considered the cultural center of the city. Just north in the **Fairmount neighborhood** is the spooky **Eastern State Penitentiary.**

South Philadelphia

South Street, known for its eclectic mix of tattoo parlors, independent record stores, and dive bars, forms the northern border of South Philly. The **Italian Market** embodies the area's diverse mix of Italian and Asian influences. Farther south, **East Passyunk Avenue** has eclectic restaurants and funky boutiques alongside centuries-old family-run pizza joints and tchotchke shops.

University City

The **University of Pennsylvania** and **Drexel University** are just blocks apart in University City, the section of West Philly nearest to Center City. While the area is dominated by student life, there are also museums, restaurants, shopping, and bed-and-breakfasts for all ages to enjoy.

Northern Liberties and Fishtown

For many years considered the up-and-coming neighborhoods to the north of Old City, "No-Libs" and Fishtown have officially come up. Boutique shopping and **Edgar Allan Poe's house** draw a sprinkling of visitors by day, but the area—with its excellent restaurants and nightlife—truly comes alive at night.

Chestnut Hill and Manayunk

A short drive from Center City along I-76 or Kelly Drive, Manayunk and Chestnut Hill are well worth the trip. **Main Street** is Manayunk's trendy strip of boutiques, bars, and restaurants, and **Germantown Avenue** is Chestnut Hill's upper-crust shopping district. While you're in the northwest part of the city, take a hike in peaceful **Wissahickon Park** and visit the historic homes in nearby **Germantown.**

Fairmount Park

The largest urban park system in the nation boasts miles of hiking, biking, and jogging trails. The **Schuylkill River Trail** is a paved loop that spreads out on both sides of the river. In addition to endless recreational opportunities, the park is home to historic sights, gardens, and the **Philadelphia Zoo.**

Greater Philadelphia

Greater Philadelphia is the area just outside the Philadelphia city limits, including suburbs and the surrounding counties. For the purposes of this guidebook, there are also some destinations included on this map that are part of the city but do not lie within the primary neighborhood map areas.

When to Go

To enjoy the mildest weather and avoid the largest crowds, visit in **spring** or **fall.** To be assured that all attractions are open, visit **May-October,** as a small selection of tourist sites are only open seasonally. If you don't mind longer lines for popular attractions and hotel rates that rise along with the temperature, the city comes alive in **summer** with festivals, fireworks, and parades—especially during the week of Independence Day. And if you don't mind bundling up, **winter** offers the lowest hotel rates, fewest crowds, and, if you're lucky, perhaps a beautiful snowfall.

spring flowers near Liberty Bell Center

Top 10 for Kids

- Join in a real archaeological dig at the **Academy of Natural Sciences** (page 178).

- Take the RiverLink Ferry across the Delaware to the **Adventure Aquarium** (page 86) in Camden, New Jersey.

- Tour the **Betsy Ross House** (page 50), with an audio tour and scavenger hunt designed just for kids.

- Take a ride in a paddleboat or play boardwalk games at the riverfront **Spruce Street Harbor Park** (page 191). There's even a beer garden to keep the adults entertained.

- Walk through the giant human heart model and visit the IMAX theater at **The Franklin Institute** (page 179).

- Ride the carousel and play mini-golf at the historic-themed course in **Franklin Square** (page 53).

- Take part in interactive exhibits at the **National Constitution Center** (page 43).

- Visit the hands-on petting zoo and Treehouse and ride in the Zooballoon at the **Philadelphia Zoo** (page 74).

- Discover one of the world's best interactive kids' museums, the **Please Touch Museum** (page 184).

- Play in Fairmount Park's sprawling indoor and outdoor **Smith Memorial Playground and Playhouse** (page 207).

a tiger at the Philadelphia Zoo

The Three-Day Best of Philadelphia

Day 1

▶ Any first-time visit to Philadelphia should begin in **Old City,** where Philly's most famous historic sights are conveniently located within a few square blocks dubbed **Independence National Historical Park.**

▶ Have breakfast at **the Continental** and then head to the **Independence Visitor Center.** Here, you'll find information and maps, watch a short historical film, sign up for tours, buy tickets for tour buses, and reserve your free timed ticket for Independence Hall.

▶ Spend the rest of the morning at the **National Constitution Center** or take a **mural tour** in an open-air trolley.

▶ Eat lunch at **The Bourse** food court, then spend the afternoon visiting the **Liberty Bell** and **Independence Hall.** If time allows, stop at nearby **Franklin Court** or the **Betsy Ross House.**

▶ Old City is filled with restaurants and nightlife, so you have plenty to choose from. Try **Amada** for exquisite tapas, **Zahav** for modern Middle Eastern cuisine, or continue to immerse yourself in history with dinner at historic **City Tavern Restaurant.**

▶ Finish the night in the present by catching a show at **Union Transfer** or bar hopping on **Fishtown's** Frankford Avenue.

Day 2

▶ Spend the day in the **Museum District.** Walk along the picturesque **Benjamin Franklin Parkway,** and take your pick from the many museums while stopping for photo ops along the way.

▶ Don't miss the world-class **Philadelphia Museum of Art,** and before you run up those famous steps, snap some pictures with the **Rocky statue.** Visit the stunning, newly relocated **Barnes Foundation,** or if you prefer science to art, go to the **Franklin Institute** or the **Academy of Natural Sciences** instead.

▶ Have lunch at **Sabrina's Café** and stroll behind the art museum to see **Fairmount Water Works Interpretive Center** and **Boathouse Row.**

▶ If time allows, walk a few blocks north to the **Eastern State Penitentiary** and have dinner at **London Grill** or one of the other restaurants and bars lining Fairmount Avenue.

Day 3

▶ Begin your day with breakfast at **Reading Terminal Market.** A few blocks away, explore **City Hall,** and on weekdays take a tour or ride the

Best Cheesesteaks

Luckily, you're never far from a great cheesesteak in Philly, and it's true that they are simply not as good anywhere else. They're served in every neighborhood, at diners and in bars, out of food trucks and storefront windows, and in restaurants serving upscale twists on the classic. Just remember you're in Philly, so it's just a cheesesteak, not a Philly cheesesteak.

- **Pat's King of Steaks** and **Geno's Steaks** (page 118), the famous dueling spots in South Philly, are worth a visit for the cultural experience.

- **Jim's Steaks** (page 118), a Philadelphia landmark and regular stop for visiting celebs, serves superior steaks.

- Locals claim that no-frills **John's Roast Pork** (page 138), in business since 1930, serves the best sandwiches in town.

- Add a side of cheese fries or onion rings at **Chubby's Steaks** (page 138), and order a beer to wash it all down.

Pat's King of Steaks

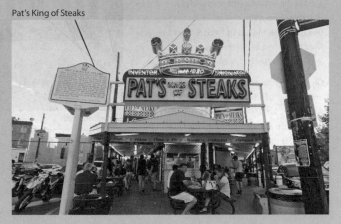

elevator to the base of the **William Penn statue** at the top of City Hall for a spectacular view of the city.

► Next, tour the **Masonic Temple** across the street or the nearby **Pennsylvania Academy of the Fine Arts.**

► Grab lunch at one of the many area food trucks or at **Di Bruno Bros.** market and take it to **Rittenhouse Square** for a picnic. Spend the afternoon strolling and shopping on **Rittenhouse Row,** or visit the nearby **Mutter Museum.**

► In the evening, catch a show at any of the lovely theaters on the **Avenue of the Arts.** Have dinner at one of the many restaurants in Rittenhouse Square or head to **Chinatown.** Or—if you somehow haven't yet, have a **cheesesteak** already! Venture into South Philly for a one-of-a-kind experience at **Pat's King of Steaks.**

Fun and Free Philly

Sights

- With the exception of the National Constitution Center, all of the sights operated by **Independence National Historical Park** are free, including the **Liberty Bell Center, Independence Hall, Franklin Court, Carpenters' Hall, Bishop White House,** the **U.S. Mint,** and **Edgar Allan Poe's house.** The **Independence Visitor Center** also has a free mini-museum and film to help visitors get acquainted with the area.

- Most of the historic cathedrals and places of worship throughout the city are open to the public free of charge, including **Arch Street Friends Meeting House, Old Pine Street Church,** and **Mother Bethel A.M.E. Church.**

- On the Avenue of the Arts, free themed tours are offered of the **Kimmel Center** and the **Academy of Music,** two of the city's most beautiful theaters, and the Kimmel Center offers free performances.

Carpenters' Hall

Museums

- Pay whatever you wish (zero is a number too) at the **Barnes Foundation** and the **Philadelphia Museum of Art,** including the **Perelman Building,** on the first Sunday of each month.

- The **University Museum of Archaeology and Anthropology** is free during the last hour of each day.

- The **Fairmount Water Works Interpretive Center** and the **Institute of Contemporary Art** are always free.

- At the **Rodin Museum,** an $8 donation is suggested but not required.

Galleries

- Most of the city's art galleries are free, including the **Morris Gallery** and ground floor of the **Pennsylvania Academy of the Fine Arts,** which presents rotating exhibitions of regional artists.

- The best time to visit the smaller galleries, mostly located in Old City and Northern Liberties, is on the **First Friday** of the month, when they are open to the public, many with the added lure of snacks and wine, which are also free.

Sights

Old City 36

Society Hill 55

Center City East.................61

Center City West................ 66

Museum District................ 67

South Philadelphia 75

University City.................. 76

Northern Liberties.............. 78

Fairmount Park 79

Greater Philadelphia........... 86

Highlights

★ **Most Momentous Building:** Both the Declaration of Independence and the Constitution were debated and drafted in **Independence Hall,** where our nation was officially born (page 40).

★ **Most Iconic Philadelphia Landmark:** The Liberty Bell is practically synonymous with Philly. Learn about its history and the many freedom movements that claim it as their symbol at the **Liberty Bell Center** (page 42).

★ **Most Modern Old City Attraction:** Offering a refreshing contrast to the many historic buildings in its vicinity, the world-class **National Constitution Center** highlights the history and meaning of the U.S. Constitution through high-tech interactive exhibits (page 43).

★ **Most Complicated Sight:** Many of the men who fought for our nation's independence on the premise that "all men are created equal" also owned slaves. The **President's House** explores this paradox at the site of the nation's first White House (page 48).

★ **Most Beautiful Office Building:** Philadelphia's **City Hall** is the largest municipal building in the nation and arguably the most breathtaking. This impressive work of architecture is crowned by a 37-foot-tall figure of William Penn—the largest statue atop any building in the world (page 61).

★ **Most Secretive Sight:** A tour of the **Masonic Temple,** considered one of the three most impressive Masonic temples in the world, reveals a lot about the magnificent building and a little about the world's oldest, most mysterious fraternal order (page 64).

★ **Most Historic Market:** Where else but the **Reading Terminal Market** can you eat delicious international fare and shop for unique goods in a former railroad station more than 100 years old (page 64)?

★ **Spookiest Sight:** Take a tour of **Eastern State Penitentiary** to learn about its famous residents and encounter their creepy ghosts—if you're lucky, you may even meet Al Capone (page 68).

★ **Best Art Museum—Inside and Out:** Before entering the world-renowned **Philadelphia Museum of Art,** take in the stunning Greek Revival building and survey the city from the top of the "Rocky steps" (page 71).

★ **Best Place to See Animals and Get High:** The **Philadelphia Zoo** is the nation's oldest zoo, but it is regularly updated with all-new cutting-edge attractions, including the Zooballoon—a hot-air balloon that rises high above the city, offering breathtaking views (page 74).

Millions of visitors from the United States and abroad come each year to soak in the rich history of our nation's birthplace—and for good reason. Our nation was formed largely out of events that took place on local ground, including Revolu-tionary War battles and the drafting of the Declaration of Independence and the Constitution. In 2015, Philadelphia became the first U.S. municipality to earn the designation of World Heritage City for its historical significance, joining the ranks of Paris, Jerusalem, and Prague.

The largest concentration of sights can be found in Independence National Historical Park, rightfully dubbed America's most historic square mile. Many of the city's most famous attractions—including the Liberty Bell and Independence Hall—are conveniently located within this compact and attractive area, where tour guides in colonial garb and horse-drawn carriages make it easy to imagine the Philadelphia of our founding fathers. Even the least patriotic among us find it hard not to feel a surge of national pride after spending time in this part of town.

The past decade has brought still more life to Independence Park with the addition of the interactive multimedia National Constitution Center; the Liberty Bell Center, a mini-museum to house the Liberty Bell; and a major renovation of Franklin Square. The President's House monument and the National Museum of American Jewish History both opened in 2010, bringing even more diverse stories of early Philadelphia and U.S. history than ever before.

While Old City is the nexus of action for tourists, you're never far from history anywhere in Philadelphia, with markers of the city's long life

Previous: the Philadelphia Museum of Art; City Hall at twilight.

apparent from South Philadelphia to Germantown. As you explore, look for the National Historic Landmark symbols on homes, churches, cemeteries, hotels, and even some of the buildings that now house modern shops and restaurants.

In addition to the 300-plus-year-old sights, you will see 19th-century architectural gems like City Hall and the Masonic Temple sharing the skyline with ultramodern skyscrapers like the Cira Centre and the Comcast Center. Extending out from Center City, the Benjamin Franklin Parkway, often called the museum or cultural district, is a sight in its own right. Inspired by Paris's Champs-Élysées, it connects City Hall with the world-renowned Philadelphia Museum of Art, which expanded in 2007 with the addition of the Perelman Building across the street. On or near the parkway, you can also visit The Franklin Institute, the Academy of Natural Sciences, the Rodin Museum, and the world-renowned Barnes Foundation that relocated from suburban Merion to the parkway in 2012.

Fairmount Park extends on both sides of the Schuylkill River and into the northwest section of the city. In addition to its vast recreational opportunities, Fairmount Park is home to the Philadelphia Zoo, historic homes, gardens, and sculptures. Still more historic homes—including stops on the Underground Railroad and sites of Revolutionary battles—are open for tours in Germantown. Meanwhile, local institutions like Reading Terminal Market have remained popular for more than a century, helping connect Philadelphia's history with the present. In a place that has done an extraordinary job of preserving its past while keeping up with the times, there is no shortage of interesting sights to see.

Old City Map 1

INDEPENDENCE NATIONAL HISTORICAL PARK

Operated by **National Park Services** (215/965-2305, www.nps.gov/inde), Independence National Historical Park includes many of the most important sights in the heart of Old City, including the Liberty Bell and Independence Hall. Because this is a government organization dedicated to preserving American history, all of the sites, with the exception of the National Constitution Center, are free. Major sites are open daily 9am-5pm, some with extended hours in summertime, whereas hours of more minor sites change seasonally, and some close completely in winter. Smartphone users can download the official National Park Service's Independence app for up-to-date information on special events and programs taking place throughout the park.

Start your day at **Independence Visitor Center** (800/537-7676, www.phlvisitorcenter.com) to find information, sign up for tours, and pick up the free timed-entrance tickets required for Independence Hall

CityPass or Philadelphia Pass?

Purchasing a **CityPASS** (888/330-5008, www.citypass.com/philadelphia) is a convenient and economical option if you're planning to visit most or all of the attractions that are included. It buys you one day of hop-on, hop-off service on the Philadelphia Trolley Works and Big Bus Company, which connect all of the other attractions, and admission to The Franklin Institute, the Adventure Aquarium, as well as your choice of admission to either the Philadelphia Zoo or the National Constitution Center, and your choice of the Please Touch Museum or Eastern State Penitentiary. Good for a total of four attractions and valid for nine days, the passes are available at the Independence Visitor Center, online, or at any of the participating attractions. At a cost of $59 for adults and $39 for kids 2-12, visiting three of the six attractions makes the pass worthwhile, and visiting all six will save almost half of the full admission prices.

Another option is the **Philadelphia Pass** (877/714-1999, www.philadelphiapass.com), which includes admission to more than 40 popular attractions, including all of those offered with the CityPASS, as well as discounts at other sights, tours, shops, and restaurants. This may be a better choice if you're short on time and planning a whirlwind tour, but you'll have to move quickly since it is only valid for one, two, three, or five consecutive days. Prices range $59-109 for adults and $49-99 for kids 2-12 depending on how many days you purchase. The more days, the more you can save, with the five-day pass getting you access to most of the city's sights for just $22 per day. Purchase online in advance and the pass can be sent to you or you can print out an email confirmation and pick it up at Independence Visitor Center. An extra perk of either of these passes is skipping the lines at most attractions.

Keep in mind that these passes are economical when you're planning to pay for admission to several of the sights included, but if it is just an easy means of transportation you're looking for, the **PHLASH** buses (484/881-3574, www.phillyphlash.com, $2 per trip) are a convenient option. Offering continuous weekend service May-October every 15 minutes 10am-6pm, the big purple buses cover a lot of ground, stopping at 22 attractions across the city.

March-December. Come early in summertime as it's first come, first served, and tickets are often gone for the day by lunchtime. Beyond the national park, there are many additional attractions in the surrounding blocks of Old City and Society Hill.

The area is easily explored on foot, but if you prefer, take the **PHLASH** (484/881-3574, www.ridephillyphlash.com, $2 per trip). The big purple bus offers continuous service May-October daily 10am-6pm with 22 stops at major attractions within the park and throughout the city.

BISHOP WHITE HOUSE

Reverend William White (1748-1836) was the first Episcopal bishop of Pennsylvania and founder of the American Episcopal Church. For nearly 50 years he lived in this home conveniently located between the two churches where he served as rector—Christ Church and St. Peter's Church. Many prominent 18th-century figures, among them George Washington and Benjamin Franklin, visited him here. Restored to its 1787 appearance, the elegant Federal-style mansion offers a glimpse into the life of an upper-class 18th-century Philadelphia family. It contains White's library, personal items, and an early version of a flush toilet, or privy—one of the very first in a Philadelphia home. Tours are limited to 10 people at a time on a first-come, first-served basis in combination with a tour of the Todd House.

MAP 1 DETAIL: 309 Walnut St., 215/965-2305, www.nps.gov/inde; tour only, June-Sept. daily, times vary; call ahead; tickets required, available at Independence Visitor Center ranger desk on the morning of your visit; free

CARPENTERS' HALL

Before the meeting of the Second Continental Congress at Independence Hall, the First Continental Congress met in 1774 at Carpenters' Hall. George Washington, John Adams, Samuel Adams, and Patrick Henry were among the group, which included delegates from 12 colonies who met to discuss their discontent with their ruler, King George. They were particularly disgruntled about the "taxation without representation" imposed on the colonies. The meeting resulted in one of the earliest formal acts of rebellion against British rule—a trade embargo—and was the precursor to the Second Continental Congress, which met two years later and declared war. The Georgian-style building was designed by Robert Smith and built in 1770 to serve as headquarters for the Carpenters' Company of Philadelphia. Founded in 1724, the Carpenters' Company exists today as the nation's oldest trade guild. Over its long history, it has also been home to Franklin's Library Company, the American Philosophical Society, the First and Second Banks of the United States, and a hospital for American forces during the Revolutionary War. Inside you'll find a scale model of the building, the original Windsor chairs used by members of the Continental Congress, and a banner carried during the 1788 parade celebrating the ratification of the Constitution.

MAP 1 DETAIL: 320 Chestnut St., 215/925-0167, www.ushistory.org/carpentershall; Mar.-Dec. Tues.-Sun. 10am-4pm, Jan.-Feb. Wed.-Sun. 10am-4pm; free

DECLARATION HOUSE (GRAFF HOUSE)

When bricklayer Jacob Graff Jr. decided to rent out rooms in the modest home he built for himself in 1775, he never could have anticipated what would happen under his roof. Thomas Jefferson—a Virginia delegate to the Continental Congress and future president of the United States—was his boarder, and it was in these rooms that he drafted the Declaration of Independence. A small exhibit on the 1st floor contains rough drafts of the seminal document and a small theater for viewing the short film *The Extraordinary Creation*. The film reveals important details—like Jefferson's original version called for the abolishment of slavery, but it was eliminated because the committee, including Benjamin Franklin and John Adams, didn't feel people were ready for the change. Upstairs, you can see

Jefferson's bedroom and parlor, which include reproduction furnishings of his desk and swivel chair.

MAP 1: 701 Market St., 215/965-2305, www.nps.gov/inde; June-Aug. daily 12pm-5pm; free

FRANKLIN COURT

Philadelphia's favorite son—a printer, diplomat, inventor, publisher, author, statesman, and postmaster—founded the Library Company, Pennsylvania Hospital, Philosophical Society, the University of Pennsylvania, and much, much more, so it's fitting that an entire court occupying a large portion of a city block is dedicated to him. This is where Ben Franklin's home stood for the final 5 years of his life after he returned from nearly 20 years of working as a commissary in France and England. On the spot, a "ghost structure" made of steel designed by world-famous architect Robert Venturi for the bicentennial, outlines the area. Remains of the original foundation, underground kitchen, and privy pit (toilet) can be seen through viewing pits in the ground, and flagstones around the house have been carved with bits of correspondence between Ben and his wife, Deborah, mostly discussing renovations to their home while he was away.

At the opposite end of the court, a row of homes built by Franklin in the late 1780s has been transformed into the **Franklin Court Museum Shop** and the **B. Free Franklin Post Office and Museum.** Note that the post office is the only one in the country that does not display an American flag— the flag had not yet been created at the time it was founded. The court also contains an archaeological display called *Fragments of Franklin Court* and a **Printing Office and Bindery.** The **Underground Museum** showcases interactive exhibits. As you will learn at the site, Franklin—like most major public figures—was highly praised and highly criticized. But there is no doubt he left quite a mark on Philadelphia, and the world.

MAP 1 DETAIL: 314-322 Market St., 215/965-2305, www.nps.gov/inde; daily 9am-5pm; free

FREE QUAKER MEETING HOUSE

The Revolutionary War raised a major dilemma for many Quakers— whether to uphold their religious values or fight those darn Brits. Since one of the most important tenets of the religion is pacifism, those who decided to join the fight for independence were often excommunicated from their meeting houses. So in 1783, those ousted for their political beliefs founded one of their own. The simple brick Georgian structure designed by Samuel Wetherill had 200-plus members at one time, including Betsy Ross and Constitution-signer Thomas Mifflin, who became known as the fighting Quakers. After the war, most returned to their former meeting houses, and by 1834 services were no longer held here. It has since been a school, an apprentice library, a plumbing warehouse, and headquarters for the Junior League of Philadelphia. Take a peek at the two original benches and original window and the five-pointed-star tissue pattern that Betsy

Ross is believed to have used to make the first American flag. Descendants of the original group still hold annual meetings here.

MAP 1: 500 Arch St., 215/965-2305, www.nps.gov/inde; Mar.-May Sat.-Sun. 11am-4pm; free

★ INDEPENDENCE HALL

Independence Hall is the centerpiece of Independence National Historical Park. Just in case you slept through grade school history classes, this is where the Declaration of Independence and the Constitution were debated, drafted, and signed, and where the United States' independence from England became official. The principles that our nation was founded on were formed inside these walls.

Originally called the State House, the classic Georgian structure was designed by Andrew Hamilton and Edmund Woolley and built in 1732-1756. Of the many restorations it has undergone, the most notable were those by Greek Revival architect John Haviland in 1830 and by the National Park Service in 1950; the latter greatly restored the building to its late 18th-century appearance. The furniture is largely reproduction pieces, since most of the original furniture was burned during the winter of 1777-1778, when Philadelphia was briefly occupied by the British Army. Independence Hall was the meeting place for the Second Continental Congress in 1775-1783, except during that brief British occupation. The most important decisions were made in the 1st-floor **Assembly Room,** home to George Washington's famous "Rising Sun" chair. This is where he was appointed commander in chief of the Continental Army (1775), the Declaration of Independence was adopted (July 4, 1776), the design of the American flag was agreed upon (1777), the Articles of Confederation were adopted (1781), and the U.S. Constitution was drafted (1787). Original copies of the Articles of Confederation, Declaration of Independence, and the Constitution are on display in the **Great Essentials Exhibit** in the west wing. You can also see the Syng silver inkstand that the founding fathers dipped their ink into to sign the Declaration of Independence and the Constitution.

Independence Hall is actually the center of a trio of matching Georgian buildings that housed the three branches of early government, and it makes sense to visit all of them together. On the corner of Chestnut and 5th Streets sits **Old City Hall.** Built in 1790 by master carpenter David Evans, it was home to the United States Supreme Court 1791-1800. Once the capital moved to DC, this building became Philadelphia's City Hall until 1870.

On the corner of Chestnut and 6th Streets is **Congress Hall,** where the two branches of Congress met (1790-1800). The House of Representatives was on the 1st floor and the Senate on the 2nd floor. Built in 1787, Congress Hall was the site of the presidential inaugurations of George Washington (second term) and John Adams. It is also where the Bill of Rights was ratified. On the 2nd floor, there are many symbolic designs, including a 19th-century fresco of an eagle holding an olive branch signifying peace and a plaster medallion on the ceiling with an oval sunburst with 13 stars to

Top: Independence Hall. Bottom: the Liberty Bell Center.

honor the 13 original states. The carpet features 13 state shields and cornucopias wishing for abundance in the new land and is a reproduction of the original made in the 1790s by William Sprague, who was founder of the first woven carpet mill in Philadelphia, credited with bringing the carpet industry to the United States.

MAP 1 DETAIL: Chestnut St. btwn. 5th and 6th Sts., 215/965-2305, www.nps.gov/inde; daily 9am-5pm, extended hours in summer; tours start every 15-30 minutes, last tour at 4:30pm; free, timed-ticket required Mar.-Dec., reserve at Independence Visitor Center the day of visit (tickets go fast in summer so come early) or in advance online or by phone ($1.50 charge)

INDEPENDENCE VISITOR CENTER

Just across the street from the Liberty Bell and steps from Independence Hall and the Constitution Center, the visitor center should be the first stop on any visit to historic Philadelphia. You can pick up maps, sign up for tours, check out the latest schedule of events, and ask the helpful park rangers questions. Visit the free mini-museum and watch the short film *Independence* for an introduction to the history of the area. Automated kiosks provide loads of information and allow you to book tickets to area attractions, not just within the historic area, but across the Philadelphia region as well. The center has a gift shop, café, and wireless Internet, and it is also where you go to reserve your free timed tickets to Independence Hall and sign up for tours of the Todd and Bishop White Houses.

MAP 1 DETAIL: 6th and Market Sts., 800/537-7676, www.phlvisitorcenter.com; daily 8:30am-7pm Memorial Day-Labor Day, daily 8:30am-6pm during remainder of year; free

★ LIBERTY BELL CENTER

You have to see the Liberty Bell if you're visiting Philadelphia; it's just one of those things. Don't set your hopes too high—it is just a bell, after all, and not a very well-made one at that. But the real attraction here is not the 2,080-pound piece of metal; it is what it has come to symbolize for people. The iconic symbol of United States' independence and the birth of democracy, the bell has also been adopted as a symbol for other groups' fights for freedom, including freedom from slavery and the women's rights movement. In fact, the abolitionists were the ones who began calling it the Liberty Bell.

There is some debate over the details of the bell's history, but it goes something like this: Originally built for the tower of the State House (now Independence Hall), it was cast in London and arrived in Philadelphia in 1752. It was built to commemorate the 50-year anniversary of William Penn's Charter of Privileges, a document that had established unprecedented freedoms to the people of Pennsylvania and whose principles form a basis for some of the content of the National Constitution that would follow.

As for the cracks, the first occurred during its first ring in a test run. It was recast two years later by two local guys, John Stow and John Pass, who took the opportunity to carve their own names into it, which can be seen today. The bell purportedly was rung for several important events, including the first public reading of the Declaration of Independence in 1776. No one is sure when it rang for the last time, but some claim it was for George Washington's birthday in 1846, at which point the cracks were so bad that the bell was rendered useless.

Housed in Independence Hall for more than 200 years, it was moved to Liberty Bell Pavilion in 1976 for the bicentennial. In 2003, it was moved again to its current home in the Liberty Bell Center, a modern glass-enclosed mini-museum and multimedia gallery containing documents, images, and a short History Channel film exploring facts and myths surrounding the bell available in nine languages. The bell's strategic position offers an uninterrupted view of Independence Hall, making it one of the most photographed spots in the city. On the bell, Pennsylvania is spelled "Pensylvania," which was one of several acceptable spellings at the time. It is engraved with the message "Proclaim Liberty throughout all the Land unto all the Inhabitants thereof."

MAP 1 DETAIL: 501 Market St., 215/965-2305, www.nps.gov/inde; daily 8:30am-7pm Memorial Day-Labor Day, daily 8:30am-6pm during remainder of year; free

MERCHANTS' EXCHANGE BUILDING

This magnificent Greek Revival building designed by William Strickland (also responsible for the Second Bank of the United States and the steeple atop Independence Hall) was essentially the first stock exchange building in the country. Merchants came here to barter or sell their wares—previously done on the streets and in coffee shops and taverns. Now headquarters for the National Park Service, it holds a small exhibition on the building's history. Built 1832-1834, the tower is based on the Choragic Monument of Lysicrates in Athens. At the dedication speech in 1832, solicitor John Kane aptly predicted: "The building which we have founded shall stand among the relics of antiquities, another memorial to posterity of the skill of its architect—and proof of the liberal spirit, and cultivated taste, which, in our days, distinguish the mercantile community."

MAP 1 DETAIL: 143 S. 3rd St., 215/965-2305, www.nps.gov/inde; Mon.-Fri. 8am-4:30pm; free

★ NATIONAL CONSTITUTION CENTER

The only national museum entirely dedicated to telling the story of the U.S. Constitution, this modern structure sits just across from Independence Hall, where the seminal document was drafted. The museum opened July 4, 2003, and immediately became one of the area's most popular attractions, bringing in more than a million visitors a year. Inscribed on the outside of the two-story building are the first three words of the Constitution, "We the People."

A visit begins with *Freedom Rising,* a live-actor Hollywood-style show complete with film, lights, dramatic voice-overs, and inspirational music that runs twice an hour. It's actually quite entertaining and educational.

Sightseeing Tours

Taking a guided tour can be a fun and educational way to start your visit to Philadelphia. Options range from your basic history tour to a bar crawl led by guides in colonial garb. Old City, with lots of sights within close proximity of one another, is usually best explored on foot, but to cover farther-reaching areas of the city—or when hot summer temperatures make it unpleasant to do much walking at all—there are also bike, bus, trolley, carriage, boat, and even kayak tours to choose from.

On Foot

- Guided 75-minute **Constitutional Walking Tours** (215/525-1776, www.theconstitutional.com, Apr.-Nov., $19 pp, $12.50 child 3-12, $55 family of four) start at Independence Visitor Center (6th and Market Sts.) and cover about 20 sites, including the Betsy Ross House, Christ Church, and the National Constitution Center. For $15, download the tour to your MP3 player and go at your own pace. Note that the price of the tour does not include admission tickets.

- On a 90-minute **Candlelight Ghost Tour** (215/413-1997, www.ghost-tour.com/Philadelphia.html, Mar.-Oct. daily 7:30pm, additional times in summer, Oct., and Dec., $17 adult, $10 child 4-12) of Independence Park and Society Hill, you'll hear tales of ghosts believed to roam "America's most historic and most haunted city," with stops including Independence Hall and St. Peter's Cemetery. The same company offers a Haunted Trolley Tour, also 90 minutes, which covers more ground with less time at each site ($30 adult, $20 child 4-12). Walking tours depart from Signers Garden (5th and Chestnut Sts.), and trolley tours depart from outside the Bourse (11 S. 5th St.). Purchase tickets at the Independence Visitor Center, Omni Hotel Gift Shop (415 Chestnut St.), or online.

- A variety of unique tours depart from **Historic Philadelphia Center** (Chestnut and 6th Sts., 215/629-4026, www.historicphiladelphia.org, Apr.-Oct., times vary). On the **Tippler's Tour** ($45 adult, $40 senior, military, and student), adults enjoy a drink at four different bars while learning about the role of the local watering holes in colonial Philadelphia. The **Independence After Hours Tour** ($85 adult, $55 child 12 and under, $80 senior, military, and student) includes a three-course dinner at City Tavern with colonial townspeople and Revolutionary-era reenactments between courses, followed by a walk to Independence Hall, where you'll "sneak" inside to watch the founding fathers debate the Declaration of Independence.

- For a free tour of Independence Park, **Twilight Tours** (mid-June-Labor Day, daily 6pm, free) are offered by **Friends of Independence National Historical Park** (143 S. 3rd St., 215/597-7919, www.friendsofindependence.org). The volunteer-led walking tours meet at Signers Garden (6th and Chestnut Sts.) and last about an hour.

- **Philadelphia Society for the Preservation of Landmarks** tours

(1608 Walnut St., 215/546-1146, www.preservationalliance.com, prices and tours vary) are a hit with those interested in an in-depth tour focusing on architecture and history and featuring off-the-beaten places that most visitors and many locals never see.

On Wheels

- **Philadelphia Trolley Works and 76 Carriage Company** (215/389-8687, www.phillytour.com) operates narrated tours on open-air Victorian trolleys, double-decker London-style buses (Big Bus Company), and horse-drawn carriages (76 Carriage Company). Bus and trolley tours depart from the Independence Visitor Center (5th and Market Sts.) and allow you to hop off at any of 21 stops around the city, including Independence National Historical Park, Chinatown, City Hall, Eastern State Penitentiary, Philadelphia Museum of Art, Philadelphia Zoo, The Franklin Institute, and Penn's Landing. An all-day pass costs $30 (adult), $28 (senior), or $10 (child 4-12), and a two-day pass is $35, $32, or $12, respectively. Carriage rides through Old City and Society Hill depart from 5th and Chestnut Streets and cost $40-100 for four people, depending on the length of the tour, and an extra $25 for each additional rider. Avoid taking a carriage ride on the hottest summer days—the horse will be even hotter than you are. Check the website for the full variety of specialty tours offered by this company.

- Tours on Segways (those two-wheeled, self-balancing electric scooters) are offered by **Wheel Fun Rentals** (215/523-5827, www.philadelphia.segwaytoursbywheelfun.com, $70-100). Choose from the 3-hour all-encompassing tour of downtown Philadelphia or a 1.5-hour Old City Historic Tour. Both tours depart from the Independence Visitor Center.

On Water

- **Schuylkill Banks River Tours** (Schuylkill River at Walnut St., 215/309-5523, www.schuylkillbanks.org) offers three seasonal boat tours: a general river tour; a trip to Bartram's Garden with time to explore; and a kayak tour led by a certified instructor.

- **Patriot Harbor Lines** (211 S. Columbus Blvd., Penn's Landing and Schuylkill River at Walnut St. 800/979-3370, www.phillybyboat.com, May-Oct.) offers a variety of themed tours of both the Schuykill and the Delaware Rivers on a reproduction of a classic 1920s commuter yacht. The Walnut to Walnut Cruise will give you a good lay of the land.

- Not exactly a tour, but more of a party on water, the *Spirit of Philadelphia* (Pier 3, S. Columbus Blvd., Penn's Landing, 866/455-3866, www.spiritofphiladelphia.com, prices vary) is a large ship with two floors offering lunch, dinner, late-night cruises, and special theater and holiday cruises along the Delaware River. The staff entertains with Philadelphia facts and dance routines before the dance floor opens to everyone.

The 360-degree theater is surrounded by a circular exhibit space, where you can learn anything you ever wanted to know about the Constitution; the events, people, and ideas that led to its creation; and the ideals from it that remain central to the function of government today.

You will see photographs, artifacts, and an original copy of the Constitution, and you can participate in interactive and multimedia exhibits that both kids and adults will enjoy. Try on judicial robes, take a photograph of yourself projected onto a screen so it looks like you're taking the oath of office, and vote for your favorite president. In Signers' Hall, choose for yourself whether to sign or dissent to the Constitution and snap pictures with life-size bronze figures of the founding fathers.

MAP 1: 525 Arch St., 215/409-6600, www.constitutioncenter.org; Mon.-Sat. 9:30am-5pm, Sun. noon-5pm; $14.50 adult, $13 senior and youth, $8 child, free children 4 and under and active military

PHILOSOPHICAL HALL AND LIBRARY HALL

Property of the American Philosophical Society, Philosophical Hall is the only privately owned building on Independence Square. Founded in 1743 by Benjamin Franklin to "promote useful knowledge," it is the oldest learned society in the country. The word "philosophy" once had a much broader context, and the society was intended to encourage thinking about all sorts of topics, including science, nature, machinery, industry, and government. Its esteemed list of past and present members includes Benjamin Franklin, Charles Darwin, Madame Curie, Albert Einstein, Toni Morrison, Nelson Mandela, more than a dozen U.S. presidents, and 200 Nobel Prize winners. The Federal-style building was constructed in 1786-1789 by Samuel Vaughan and remodeled in 1949 by Sydney Martin. It houses one of the nation's first museums, founded in 1784 by Charles Willson Peale—artist, naturalist, and Philosophical Society member—and features rotating exhibits exploring art, science, and early U.S. history, including scientific specimens and instruments, patent models, portraits, maps, rare books, and millions of manuscripts.

Just across the street, Library Hall houses many of the society's most important collections, including original journals of Lewis and Clark, a copy of the Declaration of Independence in Jefferson's handwriting, and first editions of Sir Isaac Newton's *Principia* and Charles Darwin's *On the Origin of Species.* The building is a reproduction of the original Library Hall, built in 1790 by architect William Thornton and is the original home to the Library Company of Philadelphia. Founded by Benjamin Franklin, it was the first public library in the country and served as Library of Congress when Philadelphia was the capital. While only researchers who contact the library in advance have access to the materials, there are rotating exhibits in the entrance hall that are open to the public when the library is open.

MAP 1 DETAIL: 105 S. 5th St., 215/440-3400, www.amphilsoc.org; Philosophical Hall: call for hours; Library Hall: Mon.-Fri. 9am-5pm; free

Top: the National Constitution Center. **Bottom:** the President's House.

"The President's House: Freedom and Slavery in the Making of a New Nation" is the newest addition to Independence Park. It opened in late 2010 just next to the Liberty Bell. An oversight committee took great care in planning and debating the details of the site with the dual and often conflicting goals of honoring the earliest executive branch of government while evoking critical thought about the complex paradoxes that existed around the practice of slavery in our nation's early history. Many of our founding fathers, the same men who fought for American independence and democracy based on the premise that "all men are created equal," owned slaves, and this site that stands on the ground inhabited by the nation's first White House sets out to explore this contradiction.

While it's extremely modest by modern standards, George Washington once called the three-story brick mansion owned by financier Robert Morris that occupied this spot "the best single house in the city." During the first 10 years of our nation, before the capital relocated to Washington, DC, George Washington (1790-1797) and John Adams (1797-1800) lived and worked here. Future presidents Thomas Jefferson, James Madison, James Monroe, and John Quincy Adams were among other famous dignitaries who spent time here. Adams did not have slaves, but George and Martha Washington had at least nine, including a cook and Martha's personal servant. While many slave owners in the northern states chose to emancipate their slaves much earlier as the consciousness around the immorality of the practice shifted in the years leading to the Civil War, George Washington did not free his slaves until after his death, as stipulated in his will.

Archaeologists have discovered over 10,000 artifacts to help recreate the history and layout of the house, including the location of the slave quarters. At the open-air site, visitors will see structural fragments of the home, learn about events through illustrated glass panels, timelines, and video reenactments, and can visit an area for silent reflection. One of the display panels reads: "It is difficult to understand how men who spoke so passionately of liberty and freedom were unable to see the contradiction, the injustice, the immorality of their actions. We cannot ignore the past; we can only honor the memory and lives of those who endured bondage in a land where freedom rings for some, not all."

MAP 1 DETAIL: 6th and Market Sts., 215/965-2305, www.nps.gov/inde; open-air site daily 24 hours, interactive exhibits daily 8am-10pm; free

SECOND BANK OF THE UNITED STATES

Designed by William Strickland and built in 1819-1824, this is considered one of the finest examples of Greek Revival architecture in the United States. Based on the Parthenon, the building served as a model for countless other U.S. financial institutions. The bank was chartered in 1816 during a time of massive currency fluctuations to provide credit for government and businesses—think of the Fed today. In 1832, President Andrew Jackson vetoed a bill to recharter the bank because he feared it was creating an unconstitutional monopoly. While it has greatly evolved over the years, the banking system of today operates under many of the same structures and ideas.

Today, the building is owned by the National Park Service and houses the portrait gallery *People of Independence*. The 185 paintings of colonial and federal leaders, scientists, explorers, and officers include George Washington, Alexander Hamilton, Thomas Mifflin, Thomas Jefferson, Robert Morris, and the Marquis de Lafayette. Charles Willson Peale (1741-1827), the most famous portraitist of the 18th century, painted 85 of them. If you've ever wondered what the founding fathers looked like, this is a good place to find out.

MAP 1 DETAIL: 420 Chestnut St., 215/965-2305, www.nps.gov/inde; daily 11am-5pm; $2

TODD HOUSE

From 1791 to 1793, future first lady Dolley Payne lived in this Georgian home with her husband, lawyer John Todd. Todd died during the 1793 yellow fever epidemic, leaving young Dolley to care for their son. She quickly attracted the attentions of many men, including a lawyer from Virginia, James Madison. They were married; he became president of the United States and she became one of the favorite first ladies in history. The parlor of the house is believed to be where Madison—17 years her senior—first wooed young Dolley. On the tour, you can see a reproduction of John Todd's law office and leather fire buckets hanging from the ceiling. The home exemplifies a middle-class American home in the late 18th century.

MAP 1 DETAIL: 4th and Walnut Sts., 215/965-2305, www.nps.gov/inde; tour only, call ahead; free; tickets available at Independence Visitor Center (corner of 6th and Market Sts.), first come, first served, combined with tour of the Bishop White House

MORE OLD CITY SIGHTS
ARCH STREET FRIENDS MEETING HOUSE

The oldest and largest Quaker meeting house in the world fittingly occupies a piece of land donated by Quaker founder William Penn. In 1793, Penn donated the site to the Religious Society of Friends to be used as a Quaker burial ground with a large wall surrounding it to keep cats and dogs out of the graves. Constructed in 1804 by architect Owen Biddle, the building sits at a slight elevation to accommodate the layers of graves underneath. The modest, symmetrical brick structure reflects the early Quaker values of simplicity.

There are three distinct sections inside. The east wing is the most interesting to visitors, with dioramas depicting the major events in the life of William Penn as well as the Drinker dollhouse, a reproduction of the 18th-century home of a Philadelphia Quaker, Elizabeth Drinker. The west wing was used for women-only meetings, some of which were attended by famous abolitionist Lucretia Mott. Today, men and women attend worship together in the Center section. Worship meetings are open to the public and last 45-60 minutes.

MAP 1: 320 Arch St., 215/627-2667, www.archstreetfriends.org; Mon.-Sat. 10am-4pm, worship meetings Wed. 7pm and Sun. 10:30am; $2 donation suggested

BETSY ROSS HOUSE

Did she or didn't she? The debate over whether or not Betsy Ross actually sewed the first American flag rages on, but the fact that she led a fascinating life is indisputable. Married and widowed three times, Betsy was shunned because her first husband was not a Quaker. She was eventually welcomed back into the Society of Friends when she married her third husband—a Quaker—John Claypoole.

Built in 1740, her bandbox-style home had one room on each floor and a winding staircase from the basement to the top. Betsy made a living as an upholsterer while she lived here in 1773-1785, but she wasn't the only one; a variety of shopkeepers and artisans lived and worked in the home over its long history, including a shoemaker, an apothecary, and a cigar maker. Period furniture, including some of Betsy's belongings, can be seen in the seven tiny rooms connected by narrow hallways and low doorways. A 25-minute audio tour provides a history of the house and Betsy's life, with an alternative audio tour complete with a scavenger hunt available for kids.

MAP 1: 239 Arch St., 215/686-1252, www.betsyrosshouse.org; Mar.-Nov. daily 10am-5pm, Dec.-Feb. Tues.-Sun. 10am-5pm; $5 adult, $4 child (12 and under), student, or senior; $7 audio tour includes admission

CHRIST CHURCH

In its heyday, Christ Church counted many of Philadelphia's elite among its members—including 15 of the signers of the Declaration of Independence. Basically, everyone who was anyone came here to pray. The first parish of the Anglican Church in Pennsylvania and the birthplace of the American Episcopal Church, it is referred to as the nation's church.

At its founding in 1695, the modest brick-and-wood structure resembled the typical Quaker meeting houses that dominated early Philadelphia. That is a far cry from what you'll see today—one of the finest and most elaborate examples of colonial Georgian architecture in the world. Rebuilt in 1727-1744, the church was designed by Dr. John Kearsley and modeled on the work of famed British architect Christopher Wren. The tower was added in 1754 with funds raised from a lottery organized by Benjamin Franklin, making the church the tallest structure in the colonies for 75 years to follow.

Inside, you'll see William Penn's baptismal font (donated in 1697 by All Hallows Church in London), a chandelier installed in 1740, and a pulpit built by Thomas Folwell in 1769. William White, church rector for 57 years, first bishop of Pennsylvania, and chaplain of the Continental Congress, is also buried here. When the parish grew too large, St. Peter's Church was established as an offshoot for Society Hill members. The church remains active to this day, and 20-minute guided tours are offered when service is not in session.

MAP 1: 20 N. American St., 215/922-1695, www.christchurchphila.org; Mon.-Sat. 9am-5pm, Sun. 1pm-5pm, closed Mon. and Tues. in Jan. and Feb.; free, suggested donation $5 adult, $2 student

CHRIST CHURCH BURIAL GROUND

In 1790, Ben Franklin's funeral was attended by more than 20,000 people. Here he rests, alongside his wife and young son and more than 5,000 other early Philadelphians. In 1719, the overcrowded grounds of Christ Church a few blocks away could no longer fit more bodies, so this plot was purchased on the "outskirts of town" to accommodate its members. The site was closed to the public for 25 years, but it reopened in 2003 after an intensive renovation. More than 1,400 markers remain, many so old and worn down that the names are no longer visible. During a tour you'll learn about the prominent figures and ordinary folks who were buried here. While 80 percent of the burials took place before 1840, the most recent was in 1994. Legend has it that it's good luck to throw a penny on Ben's grave.

MAP 1: Arch St. btwn. 4th and 5th Sts., 215/922-1695, www.christchurchphila.org; Mar.-Nov. Mon.-Sat. 10am-4pm, Sun. noon-4pm, Dec. Fri.-Sat. noon-4pm, weather permitting; closed Jan. and Feb.; $2 adult, $1 student, $10 for groups up to 25

CURTIS CENTER AND *DREAM GARDEN* MOSAIC

The building was commissioned by Curtis Publishing, one of the largest and most influential publishers of the early 20th century. Curtis was responsible for the still-popular *Ladies Home Journal,* founded in 1883, and the *Saturday Evening Post,* founded in 1728 but purchased by Curtis in 1897. Curtis Publishing operated out of this building, built in the 1890s, for many years. It's an office building today, and the only reason to visit is for a glimpse of the *Dream Garden* mosaic just inside the 6th Street entrance. Tiffany Studios and artist Maxfield Parrish combined artistic visions to brighten the Curtis Center lobby with the dazzling *Dream Garden* mosaic. The 15-by-49-foot intricately designed mosaic combines light, glass, and color in a mesmerizing landscape. Louis Comfort Tiffany was hired to work with Philadelphian Parrish to execute a design based on Parrish's painting *The Dream Garden.* The mosaic was completed in 1916 and has been on display ever since—despite casino-owner Steve Wynn's attempt to take it to Vegas. Wynn purchased the masterpiece in 1988, but public outcry inspired Pew Charitable Trust to pay $3.5 million to keep it in place.

MAP 1 DETAIL: 601-45 Walnut St., 215/627-7280; Mon.-Fri. 8am-6pm, Sat. 10am-1pm; free

ELFRETH'S ALLEY

Clichéd but true, walking through this narrow cobblestone street is like stepping back in time. Occupied since 1702, Elfreth's Alley is the oldest continuously occupied residential street in the United States. Federal and

Top: Betsy Ross House. **Bottom:** colonial-era homes in Elfreth's Alley.

Georgian homes—complete with horse posts and shoe scrapes—have been immaculately preserved, and the entire street is on the Philadelphia Register of Historic Properties. Small by today's standards, one of the homes is said to have housed up to 27 people from eight different families at one time. There's very little car traffic, and no modern appliances are visible in the windows looking out on the narrow alley, making the bustle of today's Old City feel far away.

The street was named after blacksmith Jeremiah Elfreth, who lived here and was responsible for building many of the homes. In 1755, he built the home that stands today as a museum and the only home regularly open to the public. The others are private homes. Many residents open their doors during two annual fundraisers for preservation programs. **Fete Day** is a celebration with music, a parade, and historical reenactments, usually held on the first or second Saturday in June, and **Deck the Alley** is a holiday event held in early December.

MAP 1: Btwn. Front and N. 2nd Sts. and Quarry and Arch Sts., museum and shop in Houses 124 and 126, 215/627-8680, www.elfrethsalley.org; museum: Apr.-Sep. Fri.-Sun. noon-5pm; guided tours $5 adult, $2 child (6-12), $12 family, offered on the hour and half hour; self-guided tour $3 adult, $1 child (6-12)

FIRST BANK OF THE UNITED STATES

Although it's closed to the public, the architecture of the oldest national bank in the country is worth a peek as you stroll through Old City. Designed by Samuel Blodgett and James Windrim in the Classical Revival style influenced by the ancient Greeks, the building was constructed in 1795-1797. An eagle, the relatively new national symbol at the time, sits atop the portico. The bank as an institution began in 1791 during Alexander Hamilton's term as treasury secretary. It was part of an attempt to deal with the massive debt the government accrued during the Revolutionary War and to create standard currency for all of the states. George Washington signed the first bank charter, drafted by Congress in 1791, and the bank opened in Carpenters' Hall until it moved here in 1795. The bank charter lasted 30 years but was abandoned by Congress in 1811. The building was restored for the bicentennial in 1976.

MAP 1 DETAIL: 116 S. 3rd. St.

FRANKLIN SQUARE

Franklin Square was a desolate, neglected piece of prime real estate in the heart of Old City for many years. But in 2006, a $6 million renovation project transformed it into a lovely landscaped park with kid-friendly attractions, including an 18-hole mini-golf course, two playgrounds, and an old-fashioned carousel. Four brick paths lead to an original restored 1838 marble fountain in the center. SquareBurger, a Stephen Starr-owned snack bar, offers burgers, fries, and frozen treats. One of the five squares of green space William Penn planned for Philadelphia, Franklin Square was originally named Northeast Square; it was renamed in honor of Benjamin Franklin in 1825.

MAP 1: 6th and Race Sts., 215/629-4026, www.historicphiladelphia.org; playgrounds open daily 10am-5pm, extended until 7pm in summer; other attractions vary with season; park free; carousel $3, free 2 and under; mini-golf $9 adult, $7 child (3-12)

PENN'S LANDING

Penn always dreamed of building an attractive waterfront area lined with trees, but it didn't actually happen until about 300 years after he first landed here. The area was vacant and dilapidated until the late 1960s, when the city and developers saw its potential and began to build. Penn's Landing is now home to recreational parks, an ice-skating rink, several historic attractions, modern dining and entertainment options, and expensive condominiums. It includes roughly 10 blocks along the Delaware River from Vine Street to South Street, and several footbridges connect it to Old City and Society Hill over I-95. May through September be sure to visit **Spruce Harbor Park,** a pop-up beer garden strung with hammocks and twinkling fluorescent lights that frequently hosts outdoor markets and free musical performances.

From Penn's Landing, check out the **Benjamin Franklin Bridge,** the largest suspension bridge in the world at the time it was completed in 1926. Designed by Paul Philippe Cret, who also designed the Benjamin Franklin Parkway, it was built to connect Center City with Camden, New Jersey. A lighting system added for the bicentennial celebration makes the view especially beautiful at night.

The **Great Plaza** at Chestnut Street is home to a tiered amphitheater that hosts numerous festivals, including a New Orleans-inspired festival on Memorial Day and a weekend-long blues festival in July. In summertime, concerts and events are often held here, including the fireworks display for the Sunoco Welcome America Independence Day celebration. Inscribed stones in the ground highlight Philadelphia as a "City of Firsts." A few blocks south, check out the **International Sculpture Garden,** an open-air art installation that aims to honor the impact of other cultures on the American experience. The diverse collection includes two pre-Columbian spheres (300-1525), the largest Nandi sculpture (c. 1500) ever to leave India, and two Korean Chosen Dynasty memorial figures.

MAP 1: 101 S. Columbus Blvd. near Spruce St., 215/922-2386, www. delawareriverwaterfront.com

U.S. MINT

From half-eagles of yore to George Washingtons of today, there isn't a penny, shilling, or bird you can't find in the U.S. Mint. Behind the concrete columns, enormous printing and coin presses make every variety of coin and bill in U.S. currency. Elite artisans etch microscopic details into each mold and print, and money is processed, printed, and shipped five days a week. In less than 24 hours the mint will have made $1 million, so they can easily afford the free admission for guests. The U.S. Mint is more than a workshop; it showcases the history of our nation's currency-making process. On display are the presses and tools that crafted the first gold eagle coins (each coin was nearly handmade), as well as information on the development of the National Treasury and early mint facilities. This facility opened in 1969 as Philadelphia's fourth mint.

MAP 1: 151 N. Independence Mall East (enter on 5th and Arch Sts.), 215/408-0110, www. usmint.gov; Mon.-Fri. 9am-4:30pm, closed on federal holidays; free; government-issued ID required

WELCOME PARK

In 1982, the Friends of Independence National Historical Park created Welcome Park in honor of the 300th anniversary of William Penn's founding of Pennsylvania. Named after his ship, *The Welcome*, the open-air monument was built on the spot where his home stood in 1699-1701. A dollhouse-size replica of the home, the Slate Roof House, is part of the display. Penn's original plan for Philadelphia is etched in marble on the ground, and a miniature version of the statue of Penn above City Hall occupies the center. Along two walls, a timeline of his life and of early Philadelphia history is displayed.

MAP 1: 2nd St. and Sansom Alley

Society Hill Map 1

ATHENAEUM

The Athenaeum is a must-see for architecture and design enthusiasts, or anyone looking for a glimpse into the finest in 19th-century living. Established as a research library in 1814, its first member was renowned architect William Strickland in 1820. Strickland's 1839 proposal for a building to house the library on Washington Square was the first drawing acquired by the Athenaeum. It now contains more than a million books, architectural drawings, photographs, and manuscripts representing the work of more than 1,000 American architects, and it is considered the premier landmark devoted to American architecture in 1800-1945. The 1st-floor gallery is open to the public with rotating exhibits, but you'll need to make an appointment in advance to tour other areas. Designed by architect John Notman in 1845, the building is one of Philadelphia's first brownstones. The relatively simple exterior belies the ornate reading rooms and 24-foot ceilings inside.

MAP 1 DETAIL: 219 S. 6th St., 215/925-2688, www.philaathenaeum.org; Sep.-May Mon.-Fri. 9am-5pm and Sat. 11am-3pm, June-Aug. Mon.-Fri 9am-5pm; free; valid photo ID required

One of the nation's earliest social scenes, Headhouse Square has brought the Society Hill community together since the 18th century. Most of the founders lived within walking distance of this colonial square, and since 1745, traders, artisans, and craftspeople have sold and traded goods here on weekends. The Shambles, a covered brick courtyard stretching along 2nd Street between Pine and Lombard Streets, was built in 1803 for the community's market master, the bazaar's official goods inspector. Now home to stylish restaurants, cafés, bars, and shops, the area maintains much of the energy it must have had 250 years ago. The market tradition continues today as locals and tourists stroll the charming cobblestone street during seasonal craft shows, art exhibitions, and a great farmers market, which is usually held on Sundays (May-Dec. 10am-2pm).

MAP 1: 2nd St. btwn. Pine and Lombard Sts.

MOTHER BETHEL A.M.E. CHURCH AND RICHARD ALLEN MUSEUM

Former slave and preacher Reverend Richard Allen was forced to sit in the balcony of the mixed-race church he attended, St. George's Methodist. So in 1797, along with Absalom Jones and others, he founded Mother Bethel A.M.E. Church, a place where African Americans could worship without restrictions. Mother Bethel, the first African Methodist church in America, occupies the oldest piece of land continuously owned by African Americans in the country. The original building built on this piece of land was a modest converted blacksmith shop, but the current building—the church's fourth incarnation, built in the 1890s—is a stunning example of 19th-century Romanesque Revival architecture. Light streams through the expansive stained-glass windows and creates a warm glow on the elaborate woodwork.

The church basement contains the Richard Allen Museum, home to Allen's tomb along with a small but fascinating collection of exhibits highlighting the history of the church and African American history. Allen, born in 1760, was a slave in the Germantown section of Philadelphia who bought his own freedom in 1782 and became a prominent politician and abolitionist activist. His church became an important station on the Underground Railroad and was used as a school where slaves were taught to read. It also played a significant role in the birth of the first black periodical and insurance company, and Frederick Douglass and Sojourner Truth were among the many famous leaders who spoke here. The museum's artifacts include the original pulpit constructed by Allen, his Bible, ballot boxes used to elect church officers, and a wooden pew from the original blacksmith's shop.

MAP 1: 419 S. 6th St., 215/925-0616, www.motherbethel.org; museum: Tues.-Sat. 10am-3pm, and after Sun. service noon-1pm; call ahead to request tour; free

Old Pine, as it's commonly called, was once known as the church of the patriots because so many of its parishioners, including John Adams, were strong supporters of the Revolution. It was the third Presbyterian Church in Philadelphia but is the oldest one still standing today. Established in 1768, the pale-yellow church stands on its original foundation and has its original brick walls, but it was expanded twice during the 19th century. The church was almost destroyed after the British occupied it and used it as a hospital during the Revolutionary War, burning many of the pews for warmth during the cold winter. The shaded graveyard holds more than 3,000 early Philadelphians, including at least 50 Revolutionary War soldiers, making it a site that inspires many ghost stories. Guided tours are available by appointment.

MAP 1: 412 Pine St., 215/925-8051, www.oldpine.org; Mon.-Sat. 10am-5pm; call ahead; free

OLD ST. JOSEPH'S CHURCH

This tiny chapel served as the city's first Catholic parish in 1733 for just 11 Philadelphia families. Despite the general unpopularity of Catholics in Philadelphia at the time, William Penn's 1701 Charter of Privileges called for religious tolerance and granted land to as few as 10 people wishing to start a religious congregation. This church became the only place under British rule where Catholic mass was legal. Ben Franklin advised church leaders to install an iron gate, which turned out to be a good call, considering Quakers once had to prevent a Protestant mob from interrupting services here. The church was, however, damaged during anti-Catholic riots in the 1830s. The current building is the third on this site, dating from 1839, and the parish remains active, but visitors are free to explore when no mass is in service. Notice the stained-glass windows above the altar, glass mosaics on the north and south walls, and the ceiling painting, *The Angelic Exaltation of Saint Joseph into Heaven*, by Italian artist Filippo Costaggini, whose work also appears in the Capitol in Washington, DC.

MAP 1 DETAIL: 321 Willings Alley, off 4th St. btwn. Walnut and Locust Sts., 215/923-1733, www.oldstjoseph.org; Mon.-Fri 9:30am-4:30pm when no service; call ahead; free

OLD ST. MARY'S CHURCH

While Old St. Joseph's was the first, Old St. Mary's was the second Catholic parish in Philadelphia. The two churches were run as one unit until 1830. Built in 1763 by master carpenter Charles Johnson, the church was enlarged in 1810 and has seen several renovations since. Notice the marble pieta crafted by French sculptor Boucher, the crucifix carved by William Rush, and two stories of stained-glass windows. The church contains a 1791 baptismal font, brass chandeliers from Independence Hall, and Bishop Conwell's chair.

The cemetery has been in use since 1759, when graves were transported here from crowded Old St. Joseph's and Washington Square. It is higher than street level because a top layer of graves was added after the 1793 yellow fever epidemic required much more space for bodies. Notable people buried here include Commodore John Barry (known as father to the U.S. Navy), General Moylan (aid to George Washington), Thomas Fitzsimons (a member of the Continental Congress who helped draft the Constitution), and Michel Bouvier, great-great-grandfather of Jacqueline Kennedy Onassis. The church is open to visitors when there is no service.

MAP 1: 252 S. 4th St., 215/923-7930, www.oldstmary.com; Mon.-Sat. 9am-5pm when no service; call ahead; free

PENNSYLVANIA HOSPITAL

Although Benjamin Franklin was best known as an inventor and scientist, he also dabbled in medicine. Realizing the importance of a medical care facility, he consulted esteemed doctor Thomas Bond, and together they founded the nation's first hospital in 1751. The hospital sparked a boom of medical advancements and made Philadelphia the hub of medicine and surgery in the western hemisphere.

Now part of the University of Pennsylvania healthcare system, the hospital remains an integral center of medical research and teaching and one of the city's best hospitals in many fields. Since it is a functioning hospital, only a few areas are open to the public. Guided tours can be scheduled by appointment Thursday and Friday at 10am and 1pm, or a brochure that details the hospital's history can be purchased in the gift shop for a self-tour (each for a suggested donation of $4). On a tour, you'll see Benjamin West's epic painting *Christ Healing the Sick in the Temple* and the oldest existing surgical amphitheater in the United States—constructed on the top floor in 1804 to take advantage of natural light.

MAP 1: 800 Spruce St., 215/829-3370, www.uphs.upenn.edu/paharc; Mon.-Fri. 9am-4pm; free, $4 suggested donation for tours

PHILADELPHIA CONTRIBUTIONSHIP

In 1736, Ben Franklin founded Philadelphia's first fire brigade, the Union Fire Company, and in 1752, he helped establish the first property insurance company in the country. The Philadelphia Contributionship for the Insurance of Houses from Loss by Fire laid the groundwork for modern insurance companies. Fire and fireproofing buildings were longtime interests of Ben Franklin, who once told a friend that in case of fire "you may be forced to leap out of windows and hazard your neck to avoid being overroasted." John Stow, who recast the Liberty Bell after it cracked, was responsible for casting the Contributionship's official symbol, the hand-in-hand fire mark, which can be seen on buildings around town.

Constructed in 1836, the building remains the headquarters of the Contributionship, still an active insurance company. It also contains a small ground-floor museum open to the public. Among the memorabilia are fire marks, firefighters' hats, miniature engines, lanterns, and a silver "speaking trumpet" used to convey orders at fire sites. You'll learn interesting tidbits about the history of firefighting—like how rival fire companies fought one another at the scenes of fires because whoever put out the fire received payment; some members went on to form the city's most violent gangs. The museum maintains home surveys for many old Philadelphia residences, including those of Ben Franklin and John Penn (William Penn's son). The museum and 2nd-floor rooms are open by appointment only.

MAP 1 DETAIL: 212 S. 4th St., 215/627-1752, www.contributionship.com; Mon.-Fri. 9am-4pm; call ahead; free

PHYSICK HOUSE

Named after the "father of American surgery," Dr. Philip Syng Physick, the four-story Federal-style home was built in 1768 by wine importer Henry Hill and served as the home and office of Dr. Physick in 1815-1837. Here, he designed numerous revolutionary operative instruments, invented the stomach pump, pioneered the use of autopsy for research, and advanced cataract surgery. He also offered medical advice to presidents and created America's first carbonated beverage. He even began an antismoking campaign way before its time.

The home was rehabilitated by the Annenberg family during the late 1960s and has been largely restored to its original character. French and colonial art and Neoclassical furniture decorate the 1st floor, while the 2nd floor is entirely dedicated to Physick's work, showcasing his surgical inventions. The home contains one of the largest gardens from 19th-century Philadelphia.

MAP 1: 321 S. 4th St., 215/925-7866, www.philalandmarks.org; Thurs.-Sat. 11:00am-3pm, Sun. noon-3pm, call ahead; $8 adult, $6 student and senior, $20 family, free under 6

POWEL HOUSE

Built in 1765, this stately Georgian mansion was home to Samuel and Elizabeth Powel, a prominent 18th-century couple, and is the finest surviving example of an upper-class colonial townhouse. Samuel Powel was a third-generation Philadelphian who spent years traveling in Europe like many wealthy young men of his time. He married Elizabeth Willing upon his return and became mayor of Philadelphia during the Revolution. The Powels were friendly with all the VIPs of the period, including Benjamin Franklin, John Adams, the Marquis de Lafayette, and George and Martha Washington, and political discussions and grand parties often took place here. Martha and George Washington even celebrated a wedding anniversary here, and a thank-you note written by George himself after a lovely night is on display in the home.

The British briefly took over the home during their occupation of Philadelphia during the war and kindly allowed the Powels to stay in their own servants' quarters. By the early 20th century, the home was in terrible disrepair and was almost converted into a parking lot. Frances Wister, founder of the Philadelphia Society for the Preservation of Landmarks, raised money to buy it in 1931, and over the next decade restored it to its early appearance. Among the trademarks of upper-class colonial America seen here are a decorative arts collection (including a china set given as a gift by Martha Washington), portraits of the Powels, and a formal walled garden.

MAP 1: 244 S. 3rd St., 215/627-0364, www.philalandmarks.org; Thurs.-Sat. 11am-3pm, Sun. noon-3pm, tours on the hour, last one at 3pm; $8 adult, $6 student and senior, $20 families, free child 6 and under

ST. PETER'S EPISCOPAL CHURCH

Designed by Scottish-born architect Robert Smith, this Georgian-style building opened in 1761 as an alternative to the overcrowded Christ Church, a far walk in the mud on rainy days for some members. It was run jointly with Christ Church until 1832. In stark contrast with the Quaker ideals that shun hierarchy in the nearby Friends' meeting houses, the church pews here were available for purchase, so the richest members literally bought the best seats in the house. The towering spire designed by William Strickland in 1842 was built to house a gift of eight bells given to the church by the Whitechapel Foundry in London, where the Liberty Bell was made. Among the famous members buried in the church graveyard are portraitist Charles Willson Peale; chiefs of the seven Iroquois tribes who died during the smallpox epidemic in 1793; James Polk's vice president, George Mifflin Dallas; Benjamin Chew, owner of Cliveden, the site of the 1777 Battle of Germantown; and Nicholas Biddle, president of the Second Bank of the United States. No guided tours are offered, but you can call 215/554-6161 from your cell phone for an audio tour or download it to your MP3 player from the website in advance. Feel free to knock if the door is locked.

MAP 1: 313 Pine St., 215/925-5968, www.stpetersphila.org; daily 9am-4pm; free

THADDEUS KOSCIUSZKO NATIONAL MEMORIAL

Thomas Jefferson called Polish-born Thaddeus Kosciuszko "as pure a son of liberty as I have ever known." A former Polish count, Kosciuszko developed innovative military engineering that contributed to several important victories in Revolutionary War battles. After the war, he returned to Poland but came back several years later to collect his military payment and consult with Dr. Benjamin Rush about injuries he had suffered while unsuccessfully defending his homeland against tsarist Russia. During his stay, he was treated as a hero and visited by local leaders, including Vice President Jefferson.

The small Georgian-style boarding home where he stayed, built in 1775-1776 by Joseph Few, has been converted into a memorial and museum maintained by Independence National Historical Park. The 1st floor displays his military innovations, the 2nd floor his bedroom. In addition to entertaining the leaders of the day, he is rumored to have entertained many a young lady here as well. A short video reveals additional details about his life.

MAP 1: 301 Pine St., 215/597-7130, www.nps.gov/thko; Apr.-Oct. Sat.-Sun. noon-4pm; free

Center City East   Map 2

ARCH STREET UNITED METHODIST CHURCH

North of the Masonic Temple and City Hall on Broad Street stands another architectural gem, the Arch Street United Methodist Church. The Gothic Revival structure has a white-marble exterior and impressive stained-glass windows, and it houses a multi-stop Stanbridge organ made in 1870. The church was founded in 1862 and built on a former coal yard in 1864-1870. The active congregation hosts many community and social events, including regular workshops about Native American heritage. View it from the outside any time, but for a tour of the inside, you'll have to go on a Wednesday morning.

MAP 2: 55 N. Broad St., 215/568-6250, www.archstreetumc.org; tours Wed. 10am-1pm; free

CHINATOWN FRIENDSHIP GATE

There's no question you're in Chinatown when you see the colorful Friendship Gate, which forms an arch 40 feet above 10th Street near Arch Street, with the words "Philadelphia Chinatown" appearing in Chinese characters. A collaboration between leading architect Sabrina Soong, other Chinese engineers and artisans, and members of the local community, it was built in 1984. In celebrating the traditional Qing Dynasty style, this grand gateway to Chinatown was partially constructed with tiles from Philadelphia's sister city, Tianjin. It is the first gate constructed by Chinese artisans outside of China.

MAP 2: 10th and Arch Sts.

★ CITY HALL

City Hall stands proudly on the site of the original Center Square, named as one of the five original squares William Penn planned for the city in 1682. The city was originally concentrated in Old City along the Delaware River, where its earliest residents settled, so it made sense that local government offices were located nearby in Independence Hall, originally called the State House. But Penn predicted that the city would eventually expand westward toward the Schuylkill River, and he envisioned this space at its geometric center as the perfect locale for city government. Even though Penn left the city for good in 1701, his well-laid plan came to fruition two centuries later, when construction of the current City Hall was completed for city offices in 1901.

Renowned architects John McArthur Jr. and Thomas U. Walter designed the masterpiece that stands today—one of the world's finest examples of

Sculptures near City Hall

More than 250 sculptures designed by Alexander Milne Calder adorn the magnificent City Hall. While you're in the area, be sure to check out some of the other nearby sculptures.

Clothespin

Across 15th Street on the west side of City Hall stands Claes Oldenburg's 45-foot steel *Clothespin*. Sleek and modern, it offers a stark contrast to City Hall's ornate design. Oldenburg has compared his clothespin to Constantin Brancusi's *The Kiss*, and many agree that the shape is reminiscent of lovers holding one another. The *Clothespin* has also been viewed as a symbol of holding, or clipping, the old with the new in Philadelphia.

LOVE

At the intersection of 15th Street and John F. Kennedy Boulevard is John F. Kennedy Plaza, known to locals as Love Park because of the sculpture by Robert Indiana that stands proudly at its center. It is said that the crooked "O" in the bright-red letters that spell "love" is there to remind us that nothing—including love—is perfect. Positioned at an angle so the Benjamin Franklin Parkway spreads out behind it with the Art Museum in the distance, the sculpture was installed for the city's bicentennial in 1976 and quickly became an iconic image of the City of Brotherly Love.

Government of the People

Just north of City Hall across John F. Kennedy Boulevard, you can't miss Jacques Lipchitz's large *Government of the People,* one of several art installations in the plaza of the Municipal Services Building. The abstract bronze sculpture of hands and limbs gripping each other was built in the 1970s during the era of the polarizing mayor Frank Rizzo. Nearby stands a large replica of Rizzo himself, who fittingly has his back to Lipchitz's statue. He purportedly cut off city funding for the statue that he hated and was quoted as saying, "It looks like some plasterer dropped a load of plaster." Ah, the history of Philadelphia municipal politics.

French Second Empire architecture. Construction began in 1871 and took 30 years and at least 1,000 people to complete. The design was influenced by the Palais des Tuileries and the new Louvre in Paris, evidenced in the turreted courtyard stair towers, slate mansard roof with dormer windows, and the paired columns that create the cozy illusion that the building is just three stories high instead of eight. A solid-granite ground floor is 22 feet thick in some areas—strong enough to support the brick structure faced with marble. The 548-foot center tower stands as the tallest masonry structure in the world supported without a steel frame.

Famed sculptor Alexander Milne Calder designed the more than 250 sculptures on the building's exterior. The symbolically rich sculptures include representations of seasons, continents, allegorical figures, and of course the crown jewel—the 37-foot-tall, 27-ton **William Penn Statue** at the top. There was for many years an unofficial but long-respected agreement that no building would be built taller than Penn's head, but the city's growth eventually demanded that it grow up (both literally and figuratively). In 1987, Liberty One was built, the first of a series of skyscrapers that now tower high above Billy Penn.

While City Hall looks small in today's skyline, it remains one of the most impressive and unique buildings in all of Philadelphia and perhaps the world. It is also the largest municipal building in the country, covering more than 14.5 acres of space on its eight floors. Just as Independence Hall once housed the three branches of national government when Philadelphia was the nation's capital in the early 19th century, City Hall today houses segments of all three branches of city government. It is the home base of the mayor, city council, and civil trial courtrooms.

While the vast majority of the 700 rooms are standard offices, several of the spaces are truly spectacular. City Council Chambers, the Mayor's Reception Room, Conversation Hall, the Caucus Room, and the Supreme Court Room are lavish, impressive meeting rooms. Security measures require that you visit the building as part of a building tour, offered on weekdays at 12:30pm. It covers all the impressive rooms of the building that are not in use at the time of the tour, including the tower. The full tour takes about 90 minutes, but a tower tour alone, offered throughout the day, lasts about 15 minutes. A small elevator (capacity of only four; claustrophobics beware) takes visitors to an observation deck at the base of the Penn Statue for a panoramic view of the city. The view from the top makes the site's prime location at the very center of Penn's original Philadelphia apparent. Tours depart from room 121 of the East Portal. Summer months can be busy, so plan to stop early in the morning to reserve a tour spot for later in the day.

MAP 2: Broad and Market Sts., 215/686-2840; tower tours Mon.-Fri. 9:30am-4:15pm; building tour including tower Mon.-Fri. at 12:30pm; building tour $12 adult, $8 senior and child (3-18); tower tour only $6 adult, $4 senior and child (3-18)

LIBRARY COMPANY OF PHILADELPHIA

The country's very first lending library was founded by Benjamin Franklin in 1731, when he was only 25 years old. In its original Old City location, which is today called Library Hall, it served as the Library of Congress during the time that Philadelphia was the nation's capital. The only intact colonial-era library and the oldest circulating library in the nation, it was the largest library in the nation until 1850. In its current location on Locust Street, it remains an excellent resource on 17th- to 19th-century American society and culture with more than half a million rare books, graphics, manuscripts, and an array of artwork, prints, and photographs of early Philadelphia. While you'll need an appointment to get into the print room, there are free revolving exhibits that draw from the collections and are open to the public.

MAP 2: 1314 Locust St., 215/546-3181, www.librarycompany.org; Mon.-Fri. 9am-4:45pm, print room by appt. only; free

Philadelphia's Masonic Temple is a magnificent work of art and architecture both inside and out, which is no surprise considering it was built for and by the world's top masons. While masons of today represent practically every profession, the earliest members were highly skilled stoneworkers. The Grand Lodge of England (GLE) was founded in 1717 and spread to the U.S. colonies by the 1730s, making Freemasonry the oldest continuous fraternal organization in the world.

The building, designed by James Windrim, was completed in 1873, and the interior was decorated under the supervision of artist George Herzog over a 20-year period. The library and museum contain artifacts from the early masons, including George Washington's Masonic apron, and while they can be visited alone, you would be missing out on the best part without a guided tour of the entire building. Paintings of former Masonic Grand Masters, including Ben Franklin and George Washington, line the grand staircase and hallways, and hand-painted wooden sculptures by William Rush, the "father of American sculpture," are on display. Seven spectacular meeting rooms stand as a tribute to the seven "ideal" forms of architecture. Oriental Hall replicates parts of the Alhambra; Gothic Hall is a tribute to the European Knights Templar made famous in Dan Brown's *The Da Vinci Code;* and Egyptian Hall is adorned with hieroglyphics so accurate that archaeology students from the University of Pennsylvania visit to study them. Other styles include Renaissance, Ionic, Corinthian, and Norman, and on a tour, you'll find each room more fascinating and breathtaking than the one before. There is one minor, intentional mistake in the design of each room, to acknowledge that only God is perfect and all human work is flawed.

The masons are shrouded in mystery. While the knowledgeable and friendly tour guides are willing to share information about many aspects of their history, don't bother asking them to reveal all their secrets or to explain why women are still not admitted—believe me, I tried.

MAP 2: 1 N. Broad St., 215/988-1917, www.pamasonictemple.org; tours Tues.-Fri. 10am, 11am, 1pm, 2pm, and 3pm, Sat. 10am, 11am, and noon, tours not available at times due to special events; call ahead; library and museum only $7; tour including library and museum $13 adult, $8 student, $5 child, $7 senior, $30 family, free for active Pennsylvania masons, military, and children under 5

★ READING TERMINAL MARKET

Picture the Reading Terminal Market more than a century ago amid a mass of trains bringing goods and people in and out of the city, and you'll see how far it has come in its long history. Today, it is flanked on one side by the Gallery, a massive urban mall, and on the other by the state-of-the-art Convention Center. It has survived the Great Depression, World War II, and the decline of the railroads, and it is as much a marvel today as it was at the turn of the 20th century.

Reading Terminal opened its doors in 1892 in response to a backlash against outdoor markets, which were beginning to be viewed as a health

Top: ornate detail in the Masonic Temple. Bottom: Reading Terminal Market.

hazard. The new market was laid out in a tidy grid system similar to the streets of downtown Philadelphia. Twelve aisles and four larger avenues were aligned in the spacious cavern beneath the elevated train shed of the Reading Railroad. Proximity to the railroad made it the perfect place for shipping and receiving goods and provided easy access for Pennsylvania Dutch merchants to sell their wares.

In the 1970s, the Reading Railroad filed for bankruptcy and attempted to dismantle the market to make it easier to sell the terminal. Fortunately, they changed their minds and began efforts to revitalize it in the 1980s. What remains is one of Philadelphia's most proud and well-utilized sites. Now, the railroad runs underneath the market instead of above it, and Amish merchants still have a significant presence, bringing some of the best baked goods, meat, and produce. They have been joined by vendors selling everything from cheesesteaks to Vietnamese cuisine to fresh-baked cookies, making it an excellent place to stop for lunch. It's also one of the best spots in Philadelphia to buy affordable and delicious produce, meats, seafood, and a dizzying array of prepared foods. Philadelphia chefs from many local restaurants visit the market early each morning to pick up the freshest ingredients to serve. Nonfood goods are also available, including jewelry, books, artisan candles, gourmet cookware, and crafts from around the globe.

MAP 2: 12th and Arch Sts., 215/922-2317, www.readingterminalmarket.org; Mon.-Sat. 8am-6pm, Sun. 9am-5pm

ST. STEPHEN'S EPISCOPAL CHURCH

This is the only church designed by William Strickland, Philadelphia's leading colonial architect, that remains standing in Philadelphia today. Completed in 1823, it was modeled after St. Stephen's Church in Vienna and enlarged in 1878 by architect Frank Furness, who was responsible for the ornate stencils on the walls. The church's design marked the end of the Neoclassical style and was one of the earliest examples of what became known as Gothic Revival architecture. The site also happens to be where Benjamin Franklin flew the first kite.

MAP 2: 19 S. 10th St., 215/922-3807, www.ststephensphl.org; by appt.; free

Center City West   Map 3

COMCAST CENTER

Designed by Robert A. M. Stern Architects, Pennsylvania's tallest building opened in 2007 at 975 feet and 58 stories tall. With its sustainable design based on LEED principles, it is one of the tallest green office buildings in the United States. It was built as headquarters to the largest U.S. cable company, Comcast, but it is more than just an office building. Stop inside the lobby to see **The Comcast Experience,** an LED wall measuring 83.3 feet wide and 25.4 feet high that broadcasts a variety of images throughout the day—from historic sites to nature footage to a holiday show that runs every 15 minutes between Thanksgiving and the New Year. *Witness Humanity in Motion*, an art installation of life-size figures that appear to be striding along girders high above the lobby. The building includes a half-acre landscaped public park, a grand new entrance to Philadelphia's Suburban Station, and a few high-end shops and a food court.

MAP 3: 17th St. and JFK Blvd., 215/496-1810, www.themarketandshopsatcomcastcenter. com; market and shops Mon.-Fri. 8am-7pm, Sat. 8am-5pm; free

Museum District
Map 4

BOATHOUSE ROW
The converted historic homes that serve as clubhouses to some of Philadelphia's rowing clubs also provide one of the city's most famous sights—Boathouse Row. The homes are old, and some are very interesting architecturally, but the sight is especially pretty and most famous for the way it looks at night from I-76 when the lights outlining the homes reflect onto the Schuylkill River. Designed in 1979 by architectural lighting designer Raymond Grenald, the lights helped revitalize Boathouse Row and brought them renewed status as a city attraction. The busiest stretch of the Schuylkill River Trail runs along Boathouse Row and is always crowded with walkers, runners, bikers, and others out to enjoy the scenery when the weather is pleasant.

MAP 4: Kelly Dr. along the Schuylkill River behind the Art Museum, www.boathouserow. org

CATHEDRAL BASILICA OF SAINTS PETER AND PAUL
The Cathedral Basilica of Saints Peter and Paul is Philadelphia's largest brownstone and its most architecturally impressive Italian Renaissance structure. Home to the Archdiocese of Philadelphia, it was built in 1846-1864 and modeled after the Lombard Church of St. Charles (San Carla al Corso) in Rome. Four massive Corinthian columns, a vaulted copper dome, and eight side chapels are just the beginning of the church's grandeur. Constantino Brumidi, also credited with painting the dome of the Capitol in Washington, led the design team. The ornate cathedral accommodates 2,000 people. The Crypt of the Bishops in the lower level holds the bodies of six Philadelphia bishops and archbishops.

MAP 4: 18th St. and Benjamin Franklin Pkwy., 215/561-1313, www.cathedralphila.org; Mon.-Fri. 7:30am-5pm, Sat. 9am-5:15pm, Sun. 8am-6:30pm, guided tour after Sun. 11am mass and by appt.; free

EAKINS OVAL
The large oval with a monument across the street from the Art Museum was named for Thomas Eakins (1844-1916), the famous Philadelphia realist painter best known for *The Gross Clinic* and *The Agnew Clinic*. It

was dedicated in 1897 at the Green Street entrance to Fairmount Park and moved to this spot in 1928 when construction on the parkway was completed. The centerpiece is **Washington Monument,** designed by German sculptor Rudolf Siemering in 1897. The bronze and granite replica of George Washington in uniform on a horse sits high atop a granite pedestal looking toward City Hall, and his face was made from an impression taken during his life. Surrounding him, four pairs of Native American figures and animals each guard a pool of water representing the four great waterways of America—the Mississippi, the Potomac, the Delaware, and the Hudson. The 13 steps that lead to the pedestal represent the original 13 states, and each side represents aspects of the American journey—victory in the war, warning against the dangers of slavery, westward movement, and the march of the army. Sit on this symbolic statue with the Art Museum in one direction and the parkway and City Hall in the other for a great photo op.

MAP 4: Benjamin Franklin Pkwy. in front of the Philadelphia Museum of Art

★ EASTERN STATE PENITENTIARY

A walk through Eastern State Penitentiary offers a glimpse into a world rarely seen by ordinary citizens. This eye-opening site forces visitors to imagine the lives of those behind bars and to consider the controversial history and ideals of the past and present criminal justice system.

When it opened in 1829, the penitentiary's novel design and philosophy were considered radical experiments. Benjamin Franklin and Benjamin Rush were among the members of the first prison reform group in history— the Philadelphia Society for Alleviating the Miseries of Public Prisons— who supported the prison. Famed architect John Haviland won the design competition to build the prison, and one of his competitors, William Strickland, oversaw construction. The castle-like structure occupies 11 acres in what was then considered the outskirts of town and today is the Fairmount neighborhood. It was the most expensive structure ever built in the country at the time.

An alternative to the overcrowded prisons of the time, the Quaker-inspired goal of Eastern State was to reform criminals through strict isolation. It was founded on the belief that when left to their own devices without the influence of the outside world, prisoners would become penitent, or remorseful. Prisoners ate, worked, and lived in their cells, with an hour each day in a small private outdoor courtyard. When it was necessary to move through public spaces, hoods were placed over prisoners' heads so they couldn't see one another. The concept and the architecture became a model for prisons worldwide, and approximately 300 prisons on four continents were modeled on the innovative floor plan in which a central guard post is flanked with multiple sections extending from the center.

While the intentions of the founders were presumably good, the failings of the isolation system quickly became clear, and the prison faced accusations of inhumane treatment of prisoners. The first investigation into the possibility of questionable practices took place in 1832. In 1842, Charles

Top: the Cathedral Basilica of Saints Peter and Paul. Bottom: Eastern State Penitentiary.

Dickens visited and said: "The system is rigid, strict, and hopeless solitary confinement, and I believe it, in its effects, to be cruel and wrong." It wasn't until 1913 that the confinement system was abandoned.

In 1970, the prison closed, and there was talk of tearing it down and using the space for commercial property. Fortunately, a task force set out to preserve what is now considered a National Historic Landmark. In 1994, Eastern State opened for daily tours. Visitors are required to sign a waiver stating that they are aware of the poor condition of the building before entering, but areas deemed unsafe are closed to the public.

Different tours take place throughout the day in which guides tell stories of prisoners, escapes, and more, but the well-made self-guided audio tour, "Voices of Eastern State," is a great option. Actor Steve Buscemi's voice, along with those of real prisoners and guards that served here, will guide you to more than 20 fascinating sites throughout the prison that reveal its rich history. Among the famous prisoners who did time here was Al Capone, who was apparently given royal treatment during his eight-month stay. A peek into his restored cell reveals a cushy apartment with antiques, rugs, oil paintings, and the sounds of a waltz that he frequently played on his radio.

If you happen to be in town and have a high tolerance for fear, the already-spooky site is transformed into the annual **Terror Behind the Walls**, a haunted house, every night in October.

MAP 4: N. 22nd St. and Fairmount Ave., 215/236-3300, www.easternstate.org; daily 10am-5pm, last entry 4pm; $14 adult, $12 senior, $10 student and child (7-12), not recommended for children under 7

FAIRMOUNT WATER WORKS INTERPRETIVE CENTER

Stroll above the scenic Fairmount Dam just behind the Art Museum and learn about Philadelphia's 200-year relationship with the Schuylkill River. You will be in good company; out-of-town admirers have included Mark Twain and Charles Dickens, who praised the site for its technical ingenuity and natural and architectural beauty. The nation's first municipal water-delivery system, now a National Historic Landmark, was completed in 1822. Using steam engines and later waterwheels, it pumped water uphill from the Schuylkill River into a reservoir where the Art Museum now stands. The kid-friendly exhibits in the interpretive center explain the importance of waterways to urban centers and illustrate the storied history of this once cutting-edge facility.

MAP 4: 640 Waterworks Dr., 215/685-0723, www.fairmountwaterworks.org; Tues.-Sat. 10am-5pm, Sun. 1pm-5pm; free

FREE LIBRARY OF PHILADELPHIA

The central branch of the Free Library of Philadelphia, just off the Benjamin Franklin Parkway, opened in 1927 and contains more than seven million items and special collections. While parts of it are in need of repair or updating, many signs of the Beaux Arts building's original grandeur can signs posted throughout the building describe each space and its history.

During an hour-long tour of the Rare Books Collection on the 3rd floor, you'll see a cuneiform from 2800 BC; *Book of the Dead* scrolls; Charles Dickens's mummified pet raven, Grip, believed to have inspired Edgar Allan Poe's famous poem *The Raven*; and original manuscripts and first editions of both Dickens and Poe. The collection also contains the **William McIntyre Elkins Library,** which was transported from the collector's home in Briar Hill just outside Philadelphia and recreated panel by panel. It contains an extensive Dickens collection and Dickens's own desk and lamp.

The library regularly hosts free films, lectures, and children's programs, and rotating exhibits in the 1st-floor Fleisher Gallery. A roof deck affords a great view of the city but is only open for special events—or if you can sweet-talk a staff member into taking you up for a peek. Stop at the H.O.M.E Page Café in the east wing for lunch, coffee, snacks, and wireless Internet service. A massive renovation and restoration project is in the works to add a modern state-of-the-art addition to the library, connected by bridges to the original building.

MAP 4: 1901 Vine St., 215/686-5322, www.library.phila.gov; Mon.-Thurs. 9am-9pm, Fri. 9am-6pm, Sat. 9am-5pm, Sun. 1pm-5pm, tour rare books collection Mon.-Fri. 11am or by appt.; free

LEMON HILL MANSION

Lemon Hill was built in 1800 by wealthy merchant Henry Pratt on land formerly owned by Declaration of Independence signatory Robert Morris. Of particular architectural note are the curved doors, windows, and fireplaces in the two oval rooms that look out over the lush gardens. The property was the first purchased by the city for the creation of its Fairmount Park system and holds a special place in local, mercantile, and horticultural histories. Check it out high on the hill across the street from the Schuylkill River Path near Boathouse Row—recognizable by its lemon-colored paint.

MAP 4: Sedgley Dr. and Lemon Hill Dr., 215/232-4337, www.lemonhill.org; Apr.-mid-Dec. Thurs.-Sun. 10am-4pm, Jan.-Mar. by appt.; $5 adult, $3 student and senior

★ PHILADELPHIA MUSEUM OF ART

Whether you've come to see the world-renowned art collection, take photographs outside at one of the most picturesque spots in the city, or run up the steps in the footsteps of Philly's Rocky Balboa (hopefully you'll do all of the above), just be sure to come. Easily Philadelphia's most impressive museum and the third-largest museum of art in the United States, the Philadelphia Museum of Art is a sight to behold inside and out. Rising high at the end of the Benjamin Franklin Parkway and serving as the gateway to Fairmount Park, it is known to locals simply as the Art Museum.

Founded during the nation's first centennial in 1876, originally as a museum of decorative arts housed in Fairmount Park's Memorial Hall, it relocated to its current location in 1928. Its chief designer, Julian Abele, was

Rocky's Home

Ben Franklin is certainly Philadelphia's most famous historical son, but almost equally revered is the city's most famous fictional son, Rocky Balboa. More than just a character in a movie, Rocky has come to represent Philly's scrappy, fighting, underdog spirit. In the classic 1976 movie, Rocky, played by Sylvester Stallone, is shown training (often as the sun comes up with inspirational music playing) in and around many Philadelphia landmarks, from the Italian Market to the steps of the Philadelphia Museum of Art.

In 1982, a bronze 8-foot, 6-inch, 1,500-pound statue of Rocky was constructed, and much debate ensued over where his replica belonged. For many years, it was at the top of the Art Museum steps, fists raised above his head in the classic pose from the movie, but some people deemed it uncouth to have him so prominently displayed in front of a world-class museum of art. Rocky was eventually relegated to a spot outside of the Spectrum sports arena in South Philadelphia, which some considered more fitting since he is an athlete (albeit a fictional one). But that was still not quite right, and many visitors who went looking for him at the Art Museum, which many termed the "Rocky Steps," were not happy to find him missing from his post.

A compromise was reached in 2006 and Rocky was returned to the Art Museum, but rather than standing prominently at the top of the steps, he now stands on a more modest street-level pedestal next to the East Entrance. It seems that Rocky has finally found a permanent home.

Feel free to run up the steps for a classic photo op. And don't be embarrassed—even locals have done it at least once in their lives. Just don't make the mistake that some visitors do and forget to actually go into the museum. While Rocky deserves a few snaps of the camera, the museum beyond the steps is the real draw.

the first African American graduate of the University of Pennsylvania's architecture school. Inspired by temples he saw while traveling in Greece, he designed the museum to look like three linked Greek temples. Made of Minnesota dolomite, the massive Greek Revival building is adorned with rich color in the detailed friezes. Be sure to walk around outside and take in all the elaborate details, and don't miss the intricate, brightly painted sculptures along the top. If you're looking for the 8-foot, 6-inch, 1,500-pound statue of Rocky, it is located on a street-level pedestal next to the East Entrance steps.

Inside, take in what you can of the more than 200 galleries showcasing more than 225,000 works of art. Don't miss some of the 80-plus carefully decorated period rooms, which will transport you through time and all over the world. The museum hosts some of the most famous traveling exhibits in the art world, often serving as one of, if not the only, U.S. stop, so be sure to check the website to find out what is there. Every Friday evening, you can come for **Art After 5** (5pm-8:45pm) for live music (usually international or jazz), food, and wine in the Great Stair Hall, as well as access to select galleries, all for the price of admission.

Top: Fairmount Water Works Interpretive Center. **Bottom:** the Philadelphia Zoo.

Now there is still more to see just across the street with the 2007 addition of the **Ruth and Raymond G. Perelman Building** (Fairmount and Pennsylvania Aves., included in price of ticket to Main Building; for Perelman alone $10 adult, $9 senior, $7 student and child 13-18, pay what you wish first Sun. of month and every Wednesday from 5pm-8:45pm). The preserved Art Deco building is the first major expansion in 80 years. Modern gallery spaces, state-of-the-art visitor amenities, study centers, and educational resources are just some of the features offered in the impressive new space, which can be reached on foot or by free shuttle from the Main Building every 15 minutes Tuesday-Sunday 10am-5pm.

MAP 4: 26th St. and Benjamin Franklin Pkwy., 215/763-8100, www.philamuseum.org; Tues.-Sun. 10am-5pm, Fri. open until 8:45pm; $20 adult, $18 senior, $14 student and child (13-18), free 12 and under, pay what you wish first Sun. of month and every Wed. 5pm-8:45pm, additional fee for special exhibits

★ **PHILADELPHIA ZOO**

Founded in 1874, the oldest zoo in the country is also one of the very best. The zoo is continually evolving, and each year there are new and increasingly exotic animals along with updated exhibits and attractions. The **Channel 6 Zooballoon** (Apr.-Oct. weather permitting, $12 pp, $40 family of four), takes visitors on an exhilarating 10-minute trip 400 feet above the ground for a 360-degree view of the city. In addition to being a fun ride, the balloon is a historical tribute to the first North American passenger balloon flight, taken by Philadelphia pilot Jean-Pierre Blanchard in 1785; President George Washington was among the onlookers.

The zoo occupies 42 acres in West Fairmount Park, complete with winding landscaped paths and historic architecture, including the country home of William Penn's grandson. The botanical collections include more than 500 plant species, and animal sculptures include Heinz Warneke's giant *Cow Elephant and Calf* and Henry Mitchell's popular *Impala Fountain and Hippo Mother and Baby.* The long history of the zoo includes the first orangutan and chimp births in a U.S. zoo (1928), the world's first children's zoo (1957), and the first U.S. exhibit of white lions (1993).

You could easily spend a day watching the carnivores feed in Carnivore Kingdom, walking among flying birds in the Jungle Bird Walk, and hanging out with the primates in the interactive PECO Primate Center. Kids love to feed and ride the animals in the Children's Zoo, play in the giant Treehouse, and ride the Amazon Rainforest Carousel.

MAP 4: 3400 W. Girard Ave., 215/243-1100, www.philadelphiazoo.org; Mar.-Oct. daily 9:30am-5pm, Nov.-Feb. daily 9:30am-4pm; $23 adult, $19 child (2-11)

GLORIA DEI (OLD SWEDES' EPISCOPAL CHURCH)

Swedes settled along the banks of the Schuylkill and Delaware Rivers as early as 1638, long before William Penn arrived. The earliest church still standing in Pennsylvania was built for a group of early settlers in 1698-1700. Check out the massive Swedish-style marble baptismal font, which was crafted in Philadelphia and added to the church in 1731. Miniature wooden replicas of ships that carried Swedish settlers here in the early 17th century hang from the ceilings. The church is home to a one-room museum operated by Independence National Historical Park that displays a historical map and other artifacts from the church's early days. Sea captains and Revolutionary War soldiers are among those buried in the cemetery. The church is used regularly for worship and other community activities, but the doors are open to the public.

MAP 5: S. Columbus Blvd. and Christian St., 215/389-1513, www.old-swedes.org; Tues.-Sun. 9am-4pm; call ahead; free

PHILADELPHIA'S MAGIC GARDENS

In the 1960s, a group of young artists moved into a run-down section of South Street and helped transform the neighborhood into something beautiful. At the forefront were Isaiah Zagar and his wife, Julia, who returned from the Peace Corps in 1969 and opened the Eyes Gallery at 4th and South Streets to sell the textiles, woodcarvings, and ceramics they had collected in South America. They decorated their store with anything and everything they found in the neighborhood, especially the many pieces they discovered in an abandoned glass warehouse. Isaiah Zagar began creating mosaics with a variety of materials—glass being his material of choice—and hasn't stopped since.

Zagar's trademark mosaics can be seen all over the city on homes, businesses, and in murals, but the pinnacle is his beautiful, trippy home and studio—the Magic Gardens. Every square inch has been covered with colorful tiles, bottles, mirrors, and other everyday materials to create an abstract collage. Take a self-guided or guided tour of the Magic Gardens and grab a brochure that lists the addresses of more than 60 nearby murals of Zagar's unmistakable public artworks, which you can explore on your own any time of the year. On weekends April-October, you can also take an hour-long guided walking tour of the gardens and nearby murals.

MAP 5: 1020 South St., 215/733-0390, www.philadelphiasmagicgardens.org; Wed.-Mon. 11am-6pm; self-guided tour $10 adult, $8 student, military and seniors, $5 child 6-12, free for children 5 and under; guided site tour and guided walking tour $15 adult, $12 students, seniors and military, $8 child

30TH STREET STATION

Locals probably forget to stop and appreciate the beauty of Philadelphia's 30th Street Station while they run for their trains, but it happens to be one of America's finest transportation hubs and one of the few remaining grand railroad stations in the country. The Pennsylvania Railroad needed a location between New York and Washington on what is now known as the Northeast Corridor, and Philadelphia was the obvious choice. Serving as a stop on the regional rail line within the city and suburbs, and as the main hub into and out of the city by rail, 30th Street has all the modern necessities—eateries, bookstore, and gift shops—along with magnificent architecture.

The Neoclassical structure was built in 1929-1934 by Graham, Anderson,

City of Murals

Philadelphia boasts more than 3,000 murals—more than any other city in the entire world. The colorful, larger-than-life artworks brighten schools, community centers, businesses, and homes from Center City and the Avenue of the Arts to outlying neighborhoods that most tourists and even some residents rarely see. Especially in parts of the city where urban blight is at its worst, the murals bring beauty and a sense of community pride to neighborhoods that need it most, and the Mural Tours provide visitors with an interesting and safe way to explore these areas.

The **Mural Arts Program** traces its roots to the mid-1980s, when the city was plastered with graffiti. Muralist and community activist Jane Golden was hired to redirect the energies of graffitists into mural painting. She still runs the program, which has not only alleviated much of the graffiti problem, but also empowered young artists and contributed to neighborhood revitalization in many parts of the city. Professional artists are hired to work closely with residents to create murals that tell the stories of the spaces they inhabit.

While the magnificent works of art speak for themselves, a guided tour is the best way to experience them. The Mural Arts Program (215/925-3633, www.muralarts.org) offers **trolley tours** ($32 adult, $30 senior, $28 child 12 and under) of various sections of the city on Saturdays at 10am May-November, and Fridays at 1pm June-August. Tours last 1.5-2 hours. The **Mural Mile Walk** ($22 pp), offered Saturday and Sunday April-November at 11am and 3pm, covers two miles and 15 murals in Center City. Reservations are strongly recommended. **Segway tours** ($85 pp) are offered on occasion. One new tour option is known as **Love Letter** ($22 pp) and features 50 rooftop murals designed by famous graffiti artist Stephen Powers (aka ESPO). Participants take in the artworks from SEPTA's elevated train and several platforms. The tour departs at 10:30am on Saturday and at 1pm on Sunday January-May and September-December.

Be sure to check the website for a full schedule of tours and special events, as the Mural Arts Program is always expanding to offer more murals and more ways to experience them.

Probst & White and is now listed on the National Register of Historic Places. The 90-foot-high ceilings create an old-school sophistication, making it easy to imagine an early 20th-century bustle not all that different from today. Inside, there is a sculpture by Walker Hancock created in 1950 to honor Pennsylvania Railroad employees killed during World War II; it includes archangel Michael lifting the body of a soldier from the flames of war.

The station has had its share of movie fame. It's been featured in the 1983 film *Trading Places* and M. Night Shyamalan's *Unbreakable* (2000), but its most famous screen moment is from the classic scene in *Witness* (1985), in which a young Amish boy traveling through Philadelphia with his mom witnesses a murder in the bathroom of the station. Fortunately, it was just a movie and the station is generally a safe place.

MAP 6: 2955 Market St., 800/872-7245, www.amtrak.com; daily 24 hours

UNIVERSITY OF PENNSYLVANIA

A member of the Ivy League, the University of Pennsylvania, more commonly known as Penn, is the oldest and most esteemed of Philadelphia's universities. With Ben Franklin among its founders, it was the first official university in the country when it opened in 1740. Franklin helped design an educational program that included practical applications in commerce and public service along with classics and theology, laying the groundwork for the multidisciplinary and liberal arts curriculums practiced at many modern universities today (blame Ben for all those annoying general-ed requirements). The campus moved to its current site in West Philly in the 1870s after more than a century in Center City. Accessible to Center City by several bridges that can be crossed by car, on bike, or on foot, the neighborhood is called University City for Penn (and nearby Drexel University).

The centerpiece of campus is **Locust Walk,** an idyllic ivy-covered walkway spanning several blocks through the heart of campus, lined with trees and stately architecture. If school is in session, you're likely to see students here promoting fraternity parties, clubs, and events, and no matter when you come, you'll see several monuments to Ben Franklin along the way, including the bronze sculpture on a bench near 36th and Walnut Streets (a popular photo op), and a large statue on a pedestal near 34th and Walnut Streets.

Across from that statue, you'll see a sculpture of a large broken button, courtesy of Claes Oldenberg, also responsible for the *Clothespin* sculpture near City Hall. Just beyond the button is the **Van Pelt Library,** an excellent place to study, read, use free Internet, or visit the rare books room on the 6th floor. The library is open to the public with a photo ID. There are many notable buildings worth exploring on campus, including the rotating exhibit in the Arthur Ross Gallery in the stunning **Fisher Fine Arts Library** (just across College Green from the Van Pelt Library). And all true sports fans will want to see the historic basketball arena, the **Palestra** (220 S. 32nd St.).

MAP 6: Btwn. 34th and 38th Sts. and Walnut and Spruce Sts., 215/898-5000, www. upenn.edu

WOODLANDS CEMETERY AND MANSION

A National Historic Landmark, Woodlands consists of 300 hundred sprawling acres of land along the west bank of the Schuylkill River, home to a cemetery, gardens, and a Neoclassical mansion. Famous Philadelphia lawyer Andrew Hamilton purchased the land in 1735, and the mansion was built in 1787 by his grandson William. The 16-room manor was one of Philadelphia's finest estates for many years. An active botanist, Andrew's gardens and greenhouses contained more than 10,000 different plant species, including several grown from seeds harvested during Lewis and Clark's expeditions. His was considered the largest collection of plants on the continent at the time.

After William's death in 1813, much of the property was sold, and in 1840, Woodlands Cemetery Company purchased the remaining grounds. Woodlands, along with Laurel Hill Cemetery, served as an innovative improvement to the overcrowded city-church cemeteries that dominated early Philadelphia. Both cemeteries were unique in their elaborate landscaping and architecture and in their isolated locations.

Today, winding brick paths from the original landscape are lined with headstones of many notable Philadelphians that were buried here, including Thomas Eakins, Rembrandt Peale, the Drexel and Biddle families, surgical pioneer Dr. Samuel Gross, and railroad magnates Asa Whitney and John Edgar Thompson.

If you visit when the office is open, grab a map showing where the famous people are buried. You can also tour the mansion, which is undergoing a much-needed renovation but serves as an impressive example of Neoclassical architecture.

MAP 6: 4000 Woodland Ave., 215/386-2181, www.woodlandsphila.org; cemetery open daily, mansion hours vary; call ahead; free

Northern Liberties   Map 7

EDGAR ALLAN POE NATIONAL HISTORIC SITE

One of America's most famous writers, Edgar Allan Poe (1809-1849), lived in this three-story brick home with his wife, Virginia, and his mother-in-law, Maria Clemm. He was a Philadelphia resident for only a year before moving to New York City in 1843, but this was one of the most productive years in his writing life. It was here that he wrote *The Black Cat,* which describes a basement very similar to the one in the home, as well as three of his most acclaimed masterpieces: *The Tell-Tale Heart, The Fall of the House of Usher,* and *The Gold Bug.* This is the only one of the three homes Poe lived in throughout his life that stands today. Visitors can tour the rooms, cellar, and exhibits and watch a short film about Poe, his family, and contemporaries. The site is operated by Independence National Historical Park.

MAP 7: 532 N. 7th St., 215/597-8780, www.nps.gov/edal; Fri.-Sun. 9am-5pm; free

NATIONAL SHRINE OF ST. JOHN NEUMANN

Catholics come from far and wide to pray to the shrine of St. John Neumann (1811-1860). Born in Bohemia, Neumann became an American Catholic Church bishop in Philadelphia in 1852. His credits, according to some, include founding the Catholic school system and a religious order for women. The beloved bishop died at the age of 48 and was enshrined in a crypt in the basement of Saint Peter's Church, as he had requested. Devoted followers have come to pray to him ever since, and many believe their prayers were answered. Word spread of the believed "miracles" and the saint's popularity soared. In 1977, he was canonized and declared "America's first saint" by Pope Paul VI. People continue to come from all over the world to pray to him. Scenes from his life are depicted on stained-glass windows next to the glass case that holds his preserved body. The church is an active parish and not a big tourist stop, so if you're fascinated by the shrine or you believe in miracles, call first to see if it is okay to come for a visit.

MAP 7: St. Peter's Catholic Church, 1019 N. 5th St., 215/627-3080, www.stjohnneumann. org; by appt.; free

RODEPH SHALOM SYNAGOGUE

The oldest Ashkenazic congregation in the western hemisphere, founded in 1795, has had several homes over its long history. The current synagogue, located just north of Center City and built in 1927, is a striking example of Moorish architecture. A large dome, starburst skylights, stained-glass windows, an ark supported on marble columns, and bronze-and-enamel doors are just a few of the highlights. The Broad Street Foyer houses the *Leon J. and Julia S. Obermayer Collection of Jewish Ritual Art,* containing more than 500 ceremonial objects dating to the 1700s. Call in advance to schedule a tour at this active congregation.

MAP 7: 615 N. Broad St., 215/627-6747, www.rodephshalom.org; call ahead; free

Fairmount Park   Map 9

LAUREL HILL CEMETERY

If wandering around a cemetery isn't your idea of a good time, then clearly you've never visited Laurel Hill. The centuries-old architecture and beautiful view of the Schuylkill River from the raised, sprawling grounds make it a worthwhile stop. On a tour of the ancient mausoleums and gravestones, you'll learn about the fascinating lives—and deaths—of many of Philadelphia's earliest and most notable residents, including almost 40 Civil War-era generals, six *Titanic* survivors, and members of the prominent

Rittenhouse, Elkins, Widener, and Strawbridge families. Self-guided tours are always available, and special themed tours are offered several times a month.

Until the 1830s, city cemeteries were as crowded and unsanitary as the streets they butted up against. Bodies filled small churchyards in packed residential and commercial areas, and when space ran out, additional layers of graves were often added on top of the existing graves. A picturesque rural burial ground was a revolutionary idea at the time. Laurel Hill was intended to be a dignified resting place for the departed as well as a country retreat for the living. Today, it attracts joggers and horticulturalists as much as architecture and history buffs. Its vast archives of contracts, maps, photographs, and documents are a resource for historians, genealogists, and scholars.

MAP 9: 3822 Ridge Ave., 215/228-8200, www.thelaurelhillcemetery.org; Mon.-Fri. 8am-4:30pm, Sat.-Sun. 9:30am-4:30pm, closed major holidays; free admission, $5 self-guided tour and map, $15-20 for most guided tours

SMITH CIVIL WAR MEMORIAL

Framing the street on the way to Memorial Hall (home of the Please Touch Museum) from Center City stands the large bronze Smith Civil War Memorial. Erected in 1897-1912 with funds provided by its wealthy namesake, Richard Smith, it includes a bronze statue of Smith himself, along with accomplished war heroes Generals Hancock and McClellan, and others. The memorial is made up of two separate towers on each side of the street, and the base of each tower is a curved wall with a built-in bench. They're known as the whispering benches; if you sit at one end and whisper, someone at the other end can hear you.

MAP 9: Avenue of the Republic, W. Fairmount Park

HISTORIC HOMES OF FAIRMOUNT PARK

In the 18th and early 19th centuries, many wealthy Philadelphians built retreat homes along the elevated, picturesque banks of the Schuylkill River in Fairmount Park. They offered a quick escape from the ills of urban life, including summer heat and epidemics like typhoid and yellow fever. A number of these historic houses have been preserved and are open to the public. The homes offer a glimpse into the lives of early Philadelphians, while showcasing early architectural styles and period furnishings. Cedar Grove, Sweetbriar, and Belmont are on the west side of the river, while the rest are on the east side. The houses are operated by various civic organizations and have various hours and admission costs.

BELMONT MANSION

Built in the late 18th century, Belmont Mansion is one of the finest examples of Palladian architecture in the United States standing today. The land was purchased in 1742 by William Peters, an English lawyer and land agent for William Penn's family. He designed the mansion and formal gardens, and later passed it on to his son, Richard. In the turbulent times of the Revolution, Richard served as Secretary of the Board of War for the Revolutionary Army and Pennsylvania Delegate to Congress under the Articles of Confederation. George Washington, John Adams, Thomas Jefferson, and James Madison all stayed here at various times. After the Revolution, Richard became Speaker of the Pennsylvania Assembly, Pennsylvania State Senator, Judge of the United States District Court, and an environmental scientist and prominent abolitionist. In 2007, after a long restoration project, the American Women's Heritage Society opened the house as an interpretive and educational center and **Underground Railroad Museum.** On a tour, you'll learn about the role of the home and its owners and slaves in history and in the abolitionist movement.

MAP 9: 2000 Belmont Mansion Dr., 215/878-8844, www.belmontmansion.org; Tues.-Fri. 11am-5pm, Sat.-Sun noon-5pm by appointment only; $7 adult, $5 student, senior, and child, free under 6

CEDAR GROVE

In 1746, wealthy widow Elizabeth Coates Paschall acquired land in the Frankford section of the city, where she built a large house for herself and her three children. Over subsequent generations, Cedar Grove grew with multiple additions and renovations, most notably when Elizabeth's granddaughter Sarah and her husband, Isaac Wistar Morris, doubled its size around 1800. They added a formal parlor, new kitchen, and a 3rd floor. The house was in Frankford until the 1920s, when it was moved brick by brick to Fairmount Park. Today, tourists and history buffs can stroll through the mansion and take in the fine mix of Federal, Baroque, and Rococo architectural styles, including notable features like the large kitchen with original utensils and a two-sided wall of closets on the 2nd floor.

MAP 9: 1 Cedar Grove Dr., 215/763-8100, www.philamuseum.org/historichouses; Apr.-Dec. Thurs.-Sun. tours at 11am, 1pm and 2:30pm, 11am-5pm; $8 adult, $5 senior, student and youth (13-18)

LAUREL HILL MANSION

Laurel Hill Mansion was built by Rebecca Rawle around 1767, after she lost her first husband. During the Revolutionary War, the house was seized from her and her second husband, Philadelphia mayor Samuel Shoemaker, because they were considered British sympathizers. It was later returned to the family and occupied by Rebecca's son William Rawle, who became a noted lawyer and founded the Philadelphia Bar Association. The elegant Georgian structure was augmented with wings on the southern and northern sides. Its position on a bluff overlooking the Schuylkill River makes it particularly notable.

MAP 9: 7201 N. Randolph Dr., 215/235-1776, www.laurelhillmansion.org; Apr.-mid-Dec. Thurs.-Sun. 10am-4pm; $8 adult, $3 senior, free under 12

Historic Germantown

Founded by German settlers in 1881, Germantown is home to stops on the Underground Railroad, Philadelphia's only Revolutionary War battle, and the country's first paper mill. Today, it's an urban neighborhood in the northwest section of the city that is well worth the 15-minute drive from Center City for history lovers. While you're here, stop for a hike in the Wissahickon or have lunch in Mt. Airy, Chestnut Hill, or Manayunk.

The **Germantown Historical Society** (5501 Germantown Ave., 215/844-1683, www.germantownhistory.org, Tues. 9am-1pm, Thurs. 1pm-5pm, and by appt., $3 adult, $2 seniors and student) has an extensive collection of artifacts and a small museum open to the public. It is headquarters for **Historic Germantown** (www.freedomsbackyard.com), a partnership of 16 local attractions, including all of those highlighted here. A passport for admission to all 15 ($25 pp, $45 family) can be purchased in person or online.

Upper Germantown

Historic RittenhouseTown (208 Lincoln Dr., 215/438-5711, www.rittenhousetown.org, most weekends in summer 1pm-5pm, $5 adult, $2.50 senior and child) pays homage to the area's earliest settlers—the German immigrants drawn to Pennsylvania for religious freedom. William Rittenhouse (originally Wilhelm Rittenhausen), leader and minister of a small Mennonite community, built North America's first paper mill in this wooded enclave on the edge of Wissahickon Creek in 1690. He developed a self-sufficient industrial village containing more than 40 buildings, including homesteads, workers' cottages, a church, a school, and a firehouse. Seven buildings remain and are open for tours.

During the Revolutionary War, the Battle of Germantown took place at **Cliveden** (6401 Germantown Ave., 215/848-1777, www.cliveden.org, Apr.-Dec. Thurs.-Sun. noon-3:30pm, and by appt., $10 adult, $8 student). The stately Georgian home was built in 1764-1767 for Benjamin Chew, who was banished due to his British ties. Lucky for him, he was absent during the bloody battle of October 1777. British troops on their way to Philadelphia broke into Cliveden for protection while American troops fired muskets and cannons from across the street at **Upsala**, another historic home.

The **Johnson House** (6306 Germantown Ave., 215/438-1768, www.johnsonhouse.org, Feb.-Oct. Thurs.-Fri. 10am-4pm and Sat. 1pm-4pm, year round Sat. 1pm-4pm, and by appt., $8 adult, $6 senior, $4 student), built in 1765-1768, was home to three generations of Quaker abolitionists and became an important station on the Underground Railroad in the 1850s.

Wyck (6026 Germantown Ave., 215/848-1690, www.wyck.org, Apr.-mid-Dec. Wed.-Sat. noon-4pm, $8 pp, free during farmers market June-Nov. Fri. noon-4pm) was used by British troops as a field hospital during the Battle of Germantown, but its real interest lies in the nine generations of a Quaker family that lived there, seen through 100,000-plus artifacts accumulated over 300 years.

Just off of Germantown Avenue, the **Ebenezer Maxwell Mansion** (200 W. Tulpehocken St., 215/438-1861, www.ebenezermaxwellmansion.org, Thurs.-Sat. noon-4pm, last tour 3:15pm, $7 adult, $5 student), built in 1859, is a classic example of the lavish Victorian architecture popular in the area in the mid-19th century and contains a small exhibit space.

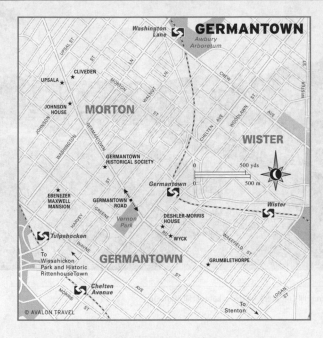

Lower Germantown

The **Deshler-Morris House** (5442 Germantown Ave., 215/965-2305, www.nps.gov, closed for tours as of printing, call ahead), also called the Germantown White House, was home to George Washington on two occasions: in 1793 when he came to escape the yellow fever epidemic and again for vacation the following summer. Ironically, his enemy, British general Howe, also stayed here after winning the Battle of Germantown.

With a name straight out of a Harry Potter book, **Grumblethorpe** (5267 Germantown Ave., 215/843-4820, www.philalandmarks.org, call ahead, $8 adult, $6 student and senior, $20 family, free under 6) was originally called John Wister's Big House because it had multiple stories. Built in 1744 for wine importer John Wister, it's a classic example of 18th-century Pennsylvania German architecture. General James Agnew stayed here after being wounded in the Battle of Germantown; he died in the front parlor, and his bloodstains remain on the floor.

Stenton (4601 N. 18th St., 215/329-7312, www.stenton.org, Apr.-Dec. Tues.-Sat. 1pm-4pm and by appt., $5 adult, $4 student and senior, free under 6) is one of the best-preserved Georgian mansions in Philadelphia. Built in 1730 for James Logan, secretary to William Penn, the mansion, grounds, and barn are open for tours. The barn contains an exhibit of agricultural tools dating from the 18th and early 19th centuries.

Top: Laurel Hill Cemetery. **Bottom:** Laurel Hill Mansion.

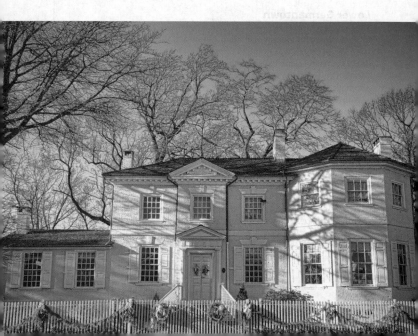

Before John Adams became president, he declared Mount Pleasant to be "the most elegant seat in Pennsylvania," validating its owners' high ambitions. Built in 1762-1765 by Scottish ship captain John Macphearson and his wife, Margaret, the house was intended to make a grand statement with its exquisite architecture high above the Schuylkill River. Architect Thomas Neville, a protégé of Independence Hall architect Edmund Woolley, designed his own interesting Scottish interpretation of the Georgian style. Among many noteworthy owners were national traitor Benedict Arnold and Jonathan Williams, a great-nephew of Benjamin Franklin and first superintendent of West Point. It is currently unfurnished, so visitors have to imagine what it would look like with all the finest furnishings. At the time of publication, Mount Pleasant was closed for maintenance. Call or check the website for updates.

MAP 9: 3800 Mount Pleasant Dr., 215/763-8100, www.philamuseum.org/historichouses

STRAWBERRY MANSION

Although Strawberry Mansion shares a name with a nearby section of the city that has been long distressed by poverty and crime, the largest of Fairmount Park's historic houses knew nothing of urban decay in its heyday in a then-rural setting. Dating to around 1790, it was built for renowned lawyer Judge William Lewis, now best remembered for drafting the United States' first law abolishing slavery. Lewis built the middle section of the house, and the Greek Revival-styled wings were added by the next owner, Judge Joseph Hemphill. With two floors of furniture and decorative arts from the Federal, Regency, and Empire styles, the home offers a glimpse into another time. The name Strawberry Mansion comes from Mrs. Grimes, a resident who sold strawberries and cream from the house in the mid-19th century.

MAP 9: 2450 Strawberry Mansion Bridge Dr., 215/228-8364, www. historicstrawberrymansion.org; Jan.-mid-Apr. Tues.-Sat. 10am-4pm, mid-Apr.-Dec. Tues.-Sun. 10am-4pm; $8 adult, $5 senior, free under 12

WOODFORD MANSION

Woodford is a classic example of early Georgian architecture built for Philadelphia's elite class. William Coleman, a local merchant and friend of Benjamin Franklin, bought this tract of land and built his home here in 1756-1758. David Franks purchased the home in 1771 and added the second story and back wing, but he only lived there until 1778, when he was sent to England and the house was confiscated because he was a British sympathizer. It was later acquired by Isaac Wharton, whose mother, Rebecca Rawle, built nearby Laurel Hill Mansion. The home stayed in that family until it was acquired by the city in 1868. Inside, you will see a large collection of 18th- and early 19th-century English, Continental, and American decorative arts.

MAP 9: 33rd and Dauphin Sts., 215/229-6115, www.woodfordmansion.org; Tues.-Sun. 10am-4pm; $8 adult, $5 senior, student and youth (13-17), free under 13

ELKINS PARK
BETH SHOLOM SYNAGOGUE

While Jewish synagogues in the Philly region are plentiful, especially in the nearby northern suburbs, only one of them was designed by legendary architect Frank Lloyd Wright. Beth Sholom Synagogue, meaning "House of Peace" in Hebrew, was built to house the congregation when it moved from North Philadelphia to Elkins Park in the 1950s. It is the only synagogue Wright ever designed, and it was the last project he completed before his death. The design is heavy with sacred imagery. A large glass pyramid calls to mind both a mountain and a tent, which Wright referred to as a "luminous Mount Sinai." The congregation is of the Conservative doctrine, with a membership of about 1,000 families. As it's an active congregation, be sure to call ahead if you wish to go inside.

MAP 10: 8231 Old York Rd. (Route 611), Elkins Park, 215/887-1342, www. bethsholomcongregation.org; call ahead; free

CAMDEN RIVERFRONT

In summertime, the best and fastest way to cross the Delaware River to reach Camden, New Jersey, is on the **RiverLink Ferry** (215/559-2399, www. delawareriverwaterfront.com/), which runs daily Memorial Day-Labor Day and on weekends for the rest of the months of May and September. It can also be reached via a short drive across the Ben Franklin Bridge or the **high-speed train** line to New Jersey (PATCO, 856/772-6900, www. ridepatco.org).

ADVENTURE AQUARIUM

During its first 10 years, the New Jersey State Aquarium at Camden played perpetual second fiddle to larger aquariums in Baltimore and Washington, DC, but after a full renovation and expansion, it reopened in 2005 as the new and much-improved Adventure Aquarium. Anchoring the steadily developing Camden waterfront, the aquarium holds over 8,000 animals in a variety of aqueous and semi-aqueous habitats. Besides the countless varieties of fish, it is also home to seals, penguins, and polar bears. Exhibits include the humongous Ocean Realm featuring native Atlantic fish, the Amazon-themed Irazu River Falls, the Touch-a-Shark interactive tank, the West African River Experience with huge Nile hippos and exotic river fish, and much more. Adventure Aquarium also features a 150-seat "4-D" theater showing nature documentaries and commercial-run movies in addition to kid-friendly interactive shows.

MAP 10: 1 Riverside Dr., Camden, NJ, 856/365-3300, www.adventureaquarium.com; daily 9:30am-5pm; $24.95 adult, $22.45 child (2-12), free under 2

Considered America's most decorated battleship, the *New Jersey* earned 19 battle and campaign stars for outstanding service throughout World War II, the Korean War, Vietnam, and the Gulf War. Built in the Philadelphia Naval Yard and launched on December 7, 1942, it is now docked in Camden and open to the public for tours, events, and even overnight visits. At 887 feet and 45,000 tons, the longest battleship ever built is the length of nearly three football fields and more than 11 stories high. On a tour you'll see exhibits detailing the ship's history. Climb up ladders and into the 16-inch gun turret and watch the 4-D flight simulator, "Seahawk," recreate a World War II-era dogfight over Iwo Jima. For a surcharge, you can take the expanded Firepower Tour, which highlights the ship's weapon systems.

MAP 10: 62 Battleship Pl., Camden, NJ, 866/877-6262, www.battleshipnewjersey.org; May-Labor Day daily 9:30am-5pm, Sept.-Oct. daily 9:30am-3pm, Nov.-Dec. Sat.-Sun. 9:30am-3pm, Dec. 26-31. daily 9:30am-3pm, closed Jan.; $21.95 adult, $17 senior, veteran, and child (5-11), free child under 4 and military

Restaurants

Old City 91

Society Hill 99

Center City East. 100

Center City West. 105

Museum District. 113

South Philadelphia 114

University City. 126

Northern Liberties. 129

Fishtown 132

Chestnut Hill 135

Manayunk. 136

Greater Philadelphia. 138

PRICE KEY

$ Entrées less than $10

$$ Entrées $10–20

$$$ Entrées more than $20

The Philly food scene has evolved into one of the best in the country, attracting increasing numbers of foodies to sample the diverse cuisine. Centuries-old mom-and-pop eateries share the streets with stylish bistros and fine-dining restaurants courtesy of world-renowned chefs and restaurateurs, including Iron Chef Jose Garces, who has opened nine critically acclaimed restaurants here.

Philly has one of the best BYOB scenes in the country due to strict limits on local liquor licenses, which is great for us because it means a generally inexpensive way to dine out and save money on jacked up drink prices. Gastropubs, bars that serve high-quality cuisine—forget the old standard fare from the deep fryer—also make an excellent option for dining in a lively, causal setting. In fact, the dining scene is generally laid-back and casual, with a few exceptions at the very high or trendy end, mostly around Rittenhouse Square and Old City. For the most part, anything goes as far as dress, including jeans and sneakers.

And while it goes without saying that the Philadelphia food scene today extends far beyond cheesesteaks, unless you're a strict vegetarian there is no excuse for not sampling at least one of the greasy delights; they're just not the same anywhere else. Philly's other longstanding culinary trademarks include hoagies (subs in other parts of the country), soft pretzels, and water ice, all of which can be found just about anywhere. No visit to Philadelphia is complete without a stop at two other historic landmarks, Reading Terminal Market and the Italian Market, for a vast variety of affordable ethnic cuisine and a totally unique atmosphere.

Previous: Tequilas Restaurant; South Philly Barbacoa.

Highlights

★ **Best BYOB:** With its savory Old World Italian dishes and mouthwatering desserts, **Mercato** never disappoints. Plus, you can bring your own bottle and save your money for all that delicious food (page 101).

★ **Best Bucket List Culinary Experience:** Okay, so you might drop almost a month's worth of rent on one meal at **Vetri**, but chances are you'll remember this six-course tasting for the rest of your life (page 103).

★ **Best Special Occasion Restaurant:** At **XIX,** or Nineteen, located on the 19th floor of the Park Hyatt at the Bellevue, you'll be treated to perfectly prepared cuisine and panoramic views in one of the city's most elegant settings (page 104).

★ **Best Neighborhood Restaurant: Bridgid's** is a shining star in the Fairmount neighborhood, offering a stellar beer selection and a small but high-quality lunch and dinner menu. Both the prices and atmosphere are friendly (page 113).

★ **Best Brunch:** Eager locals flock to **Sabrina's Café** for heaping portions of delicious omelets and stuffed French toast. Be prepared to wait for a table on weekends—it's worth it (page 115).

★ **Most Socially Conscious Restaurant:** At **White Dog Café,** a University City mainstay, the focus is on locally sourced ingredients and progressive business practices; the result is ultra-fresh, delicious food (page 129).

★ **Best Coffee:** For true strong-coffee lovers, **La Colombe** is the spot. This is the coffee served by many of the city's other great coffee shops, so why not go straight to the source (page 132)?

★ **Best Delivery:** While most places only deliver within a short range of their shop, **Tiffin** offers service to all of Center City and well beyond. It also happens to serve the best affordable Indian food in town (page 132).

★ **Best Pizza: Pizzeria Beddia** may very well be the best pizza in America, if not the world (page 134).

The number of healthy options has also increased, with many restaurants focusing on fresh, locally grown ingredients in keeping with the national trend in this direction. Considering the many nearby farms in Pennsylvania and New Jersey, this isn't hard to do. A great number of farmers markets are available across the city, especially in the warmer months, many from our Amish neighbors who come into the city to sell their goods. In 2010, the local Tourism Board launched an excellent website, Philly Homegrown (http://food.visitphilly.com), to encourage people to support the local food movement and help them find local farmers markets and other food purveyors.

Beyond the select sampling of restaurants, coffee shops, and markets I've included to help get you started, there are approximately 4,000 others for you to discover on your own. In addition, the food trucks on many corners of Center City and University City should not be overlooked, as many of them offer amazingly tasty fare for unbeatable prices; just join the longest lines and you can't go wrong. Now go out and eat.

Old City
Map 1

For as many historic sites as there are in Old City, there are at least as many restaurants. With stylish bistros, fine dining, gastropubs, pizza joints, and practically every ethnic specialty, there is something for every taste and budget. Options line Market and Chestnut Streets between Front and 5th Streets, as well as the nearby side streets.

ASIAN
BUDDAKAN ⑤⑤⑤
Perhaps the most famous member of Stephen Starr's renowned restaurant empire, Buddakan has a modern Asian-themed atmosphere complete with a massive statue of Buddha. The over-the-top, if borderline cheesy, decor contributes to an unforgettable experience in the low-lit dining room. The large menu features fusion dishes like wasabi-crusted filet mignon, raw tuna on flatbread, and hot and sour scallops with tofu and black mushrooms. There is certainly more authentic Asian cuisine in the city, but Buddakan offers a fun night-on-the-town atmosphere, delicious but pricey drinks, and undeniably tasty, creative dishes.

MAP 1 DETAIL: 325 Chestnut St., 215/574-9440, www.buddakan.com; Mon.-Thurs. 11:30am-2:30pm and 5pm-11pm, Fri. 11:30am-2:30pm and 5pm-midnight, Sat. 5pm-midnight, Sun. 4pm-10pm

MORIMOTO ⑤⑤⑤
Though the Iron Chef himself now spends most of his time in the New York location, this original eponymous restaurant is still a jewel (and also a Stephen Starr spectacle). The space will wow you before you even sit down, with its ultramodern dining room dimly lit with alternating multicolor

lights and a cutting-edge design with lots of curved edges. It only gets better from there, with amazing sushi, sashimi, seafood, steak, salads, and several eat-till-you-die *omakase* (chef's tasting) options. Though your wallet will suffer for it, Morimoto is a must for any real restaurant lover—it's an experience.

MAP 1: 723 Chestnut St., 215/413-9070, www.morimotorestaurant.com; Mon.-Thurs. 11:30am-2pm and 5pm-10pm, Fri. 11:30am-2pm and 5pm-midnight, Sat. 5pm-midnight, Sun. 5pm-10pm

CAFÉS

OLD CITY COFFEE $

Since 1984, this popular Old City coffeehouse has been roasting and brewing what many locals consider the city's best java. Sit inside the warm and cozy shop or snag a seat outside for great people watching. A small but tasty selection of bagels, scones, muffins, and cookies is served along with a few breakfast and lunch options, such as salads, soups, and breakfast sandwiches. Free wireless Internet is available, so get comfortable and stay awhile. Old City Coffee also has a booth in Reading Terminal Market, offering take-away and very limited seating.

MAP 1: 221 Church St., 215/629-9292, www.oldcitycoffee.com; Mon.-Fri. 6:30am-7pm, Sat. 7am-7pm, Sun. 7am-6pm

WEDGE AND FIG $

The adorable Wedge and Fig in the heart of Old City is a cheese lover's paradise. Formerly a cheese shop, it is now a full-service bistro serving "build-your-own grilled cheese sandwiches," inventive paninis, fresh salads, and house-baked pastries. Everything is thoughtfully prepared with quality ingredients, including some of the "world's best cheeses." Bring your own bottle of wine and hide out in the back patio, complete with enchanted secret garden vibe.

MAP 1: 160 N. 3rd St., 267/603-3090, www.wedgeandfig.com; Tues.-Thurs. 11am-8pm, Fri. 11am-9pm, Sat. 10:30am-9pm, Sun. 10:30am-3:30pm

COLONIAL AMERICAN

CITY TAVERN RESTAURANT $$$

The previous regulars at this historic tavern and restaurant include some guys you may have heard of, including George Washington, Benjamin Franklin, John Adams, and Thomas Jefferson. The original tavern, completed in 1773, was much the same as the current restored replica completed in 1976. In its early incarnation, the tavern was more than just a bar and eatery as we know it today. Without modern office buildings, this was where people met to discuss important business. The colonial-garbed waiters and period furnishings are true to the era, as is the menu inspired by foods popular in colonial times. Chef Staib turns out West Indies pepper pot soup, Martha Washington-style colonial turkey pot pie, braised rabbit, and pan-seared brook trout. A place like this is in real danger of being kitschy, but with the food and atmosphere as good as they are, no one seems to mind. Don't miss the sweet-potato-and-pecan biscuits, supposedly a favorite of Thomas Jefferson.

MAP 1 DETAIL: 138 S. 2nd St., 215/413-1443, www.citytavern.com; Mon.-Thurs. 11:30am-9pm, Fri.-Sat. 11:30am-10pm, Sun 11:30am-8pm

FOOD COURT
THE BOURSE ⑤

If you're looking for a quick bite in the middle of sightseeing or need to feed a big, choosy family, the Bourse is a cheap, convenient option. Just across the street from the Liberty Bell, Independence Hall, and the Constitution Center, you'll find a mall-like food court offering the standards: fast food, pizza, cheesesteaks, Chinese food, and a candy shop. Several touristy knick-knack and memento shops can also be found inside the grand old building. Built in 1895, the Bourse (meaning "place of exchange" in Middle French) was the brainchild of George E. Bartol. During a visit to Hamburg, he decided that Philadelphia needed a *bourse* of its own. It once housed Philadelphia's stock, grain, and maritime exchanges and was renovated into its current form in the 1980s.

MAP 1 DETAIL: 111 S. Independence Mall East (N. 5th St. btwn Ludlow and Ranstead Sts.), 215/625-0300; year-round Mon.-Sat. 10am-6pm, Mar.-Nov. additional hours Sun. 11am-5pm

ITALIAN
GIANFRANCO PIZZA RUSTICA ⑤

Serving up the best pizza in Old City, this is a great place to grab a quick slice in the middle of sightseeing or bar hopping. The thin crust, fresh tomato sauce, and a vast variety of standard and interesting toppings (including pesto, artichokes, broccoli rabe, and prosciutto) keep customers coming back. Calzones, stromboli, and sandwiches round out the tasty offerings. You may have to wait a bit for your order at lunchtime on weekdays, but it's well worth it. Two additional outposts can be found in Center City East (248 S. 11th St., 215/923-9134) and in South Philly (2124 S. Broad St., 215/551-2300).

MAP 1 DETAIL: 6 N. 3rd St., 215/592-0048, www.gianfrancopizzaphilly.com; Mon.-Thurs. 10am-10pm, Fri. 10am-11pm, Sat. 10am-10pm, Sun. 10am-9pm

LA FAMIGLIA RISTORANTE ⑤⑤⑤

Luxurious and elegant, La Famiglia pampers guests with old-school Italian charm, classic decor, and tuxedoed waitstaff. The Sena family serves an authentic taste of traditional Naples, with perfectly prepared antipasti, pasta, seafood, veal, and steak dishes. Choose a glass or bottle of wine from the expansive cellar dating from the 1940s. Save room to sample the dessert cart, or enjoy a cheese course, sorbet, ice cream, or traditional biscotti.

Top: Morimoto. **Bottom:** Fork.

Considering the steep price, this is a place best reserved for special occasions, but this Italian indulgence makes for an unforgettable evening. **MAP 1:** 8 S. Front St., 215/922-2803, www.lafamiglia.com; Mon. 5:30pm-9:30pm, Tues.-Thurs. noon-2:30pm and 5:30pm-9:30pm, Fri. noon-2:30pm and 5:30pm-10pm, Sat. 5:30pm-10pm

POSITANO COAST BY ALDO LAMBERTI $$

Near the center of Old City's club scene, Positano Coast by Aldo Lamberti offers a refined take on contemporary southern Italian cuisine, with dishes including grilled lamb, pan-seared branzino, eggplant Napoleon, and homemade gorgonzola gnocchi. Choose between large plates and small plates for sharing. An ample outdoor covered seating area on the 2nd floor allows patrons to feel the breeze and observe the passersby, or snag one of the comfy couches or a table in the back lounge. Extensive selections of fine wines and organic cocktails are available, and Positano Coast also offers diners a BYOB option on Sunday and Monday. Happy hour Monday-Friday 5pm-7pm includes $5 glasses of wine, along with food and cocktail specials. **MAP 1 DETAIL:** 212 Walnut St., 215/238-0499, www.positanocoast.net; Mon. 5pm-10:30pm, Tues.-Thurs. 11:30am-10:30pm, Fri. 11:30am-11pm, Sat. noon-11pm, Sun. 11am-9:30pm

MIDDLE EASTERN
ZAHAV $$$

Meaning "gold" in Hebrew, Zahav opened in 2008 and immediately began to receive the restaurant equivalent of gold medals. Among its many accolades, it was named the city's best restaurant in 2009 by *Philadelphia* magazine, awarded the highest rating from Philadelphia's premier food critic Craig Laban in 2012, and won the James Beard award for International Cooking in 2016. It's tucked away on an Old City side street in a beautiful space with ultrahigh ceilings and ultralow lighting. Israeli-born chef Solomonov offers a modern take on his authentic native cuisine. Start with the amazing hummus and house-baked *laffa*, and the *salatim*, a daily selection of eight small salads. Next, choose several small plates and skewers or go for the ultimate tasting experience—*mesibah* (meaning "party time"). You'll be treated to an array of the restaurant's best small plates along with the signature dish, a mouthwatering whole-roasted lamb shoulder—yum. **MAP 1 DETAIL:** 237 St. James Pl., 215/625-8800, www.zahavrestaurant.com; Sun.-Thurs. 5pm-10pm, Fri.-Sat. 5pm-11pm

NEW AMERICAN
THE CONTINENTAL $$

Stephen Starr's restaurant empire began with the Continental, and two decades later it's still one of his best. Chic yet casual, the martini bar/upscale diner occupies a prime Old City corner, making it a convenient stop while sightseeing or shopping. The restored classic 1950s diner has a funky mod decor with intimate leather booths illuminated by giant martini-olive-shaped lamps, as well as outdoor street-side seating. It's both a popular stop for drinks and appetizers before a night of clubbing nearby and an inviting brunch/lunch destination with classics like eggs Benedict, buttermilk flapjacks, and plenty of hearty sandwiches. The dinner menu, consisting of tapas and larger plates, is more experimental with dishes like teriyaki filet mignon with wasabi mashed potatoes or seared tuna over creamy mushroom risotto, infusing American comfort food with international flavors.

MAP 1: 138 Market St., 215/923-6069, www.continentalmartinibar.com; Mon.-Thurs. 11:30am-10pm, Fri. 11:30am-11pm, Sat. 10am-11pm, Sun. 11am-10pm

FARMICIA ⑤⑤

Farmicia is one of the least typical "Old City" spots in Old City; the simple, fresh flavors of the food and drinks and the friendly, casual atmosphere are a refreshing change from the sometimes over-prepared, trendy offerings at some nearby establishments. The focus of the food is organic, locally grown, and made with artisan ingredients, and, of course, only the best breads from Metropolitan Bakery are used. Best of all, at no additional charge you can BYOB anytime.

MAP 1 DETAIL: 15 S. 3rd St., 215/627-6274, www.farmiciarestaurant.com; Tues.-Thurs. 11:30am-3pm and 5:30pm-10pm, Fri. 11:30am-3pm and 5:30pm-11pm, Sat. 8:30am-3pm and 5:30pm-11pm, Sun. 8:30am-3pm and 5pm-9pm

FORK ⑤⑤⑤

Hip, sophisticated bistros come and go like the breeze in trendy Old City, but Fork has remained fantastic since the mid-'90s, reinventing itself multiple times over the years. High ceilings, velvet curtains, wrought-iron chandeliers, and soft lighting create an elegant yet cozy atmosphere. Owner Ellen Yin and Chef Eli Kulp offer a seasonal menu that changes daily and focuses on locally sourced ingredients. Don't miss the extensive and generous fruit-and-cheese platter or the strong specialty cocktails.

MAP 1 DETAIL: 306 Market St., 215/625-9425, www.forkrestaurant.com; Mon.-Thurs. 5:30pm-10pm, Fri. 5:30pm-10:30pm, Sat. 5pm-10:30pm, Sun. 11am-3pm and 5pm-9:30pm

HIGH STREET ON MARKET ⑤⑤

While it's less expensive than its sister restaurant Fork, High Street on Market is equally if not more impressive, which is no small feat. The open kitchen churns out inventive rustic American cuisine all day long with an emphasis on their artisanal breads, baked in-house. Though I would happily eat three meals a day here, brunch may be the best time to visit, thanks in large part to the irresistible bread and the locally roasted Rival Bros.' coffee they serve. High Street on Market has been drawing large crowds, especially since being named one of America's best restaurants by *Bon Appétit* magazine in 2014, so call ahead or be prepared to wait.

MAP 1 DETAIL: 308 Market St., 215/625-0988, www.highstreetonmarket.com; Mon. 7am-3:30pm, Tues-Thurs. 7:30am-3:30pm and 5:30pm-10pm, Fri. 7:30am-3:30pm and 5:30pm-10:30pm, Sat. 8am-3:30pm and 5:30pm-10pm, Sun. 8am-3:30pm and 5:30pm-9:30pm

JONES $$

With its Brady Bunch-inspired decor, Jones is the homiest outpost in local restaurateur Stephen Starr's vast and trendy gastronomic empire. Shag carpeting and stone fireplaces set the tone; but while the interior takes its cues from 1970s suburbia, the reasonably priced comfort food includes some decidedly contemporary twists. Alongside mashed potatoes, meatloaf, and fried chicken and waffles, you can find pistachio-crusted tilapia and seared tuna tacos. There's also a good selection of tasty if overpriced drinks, including the Pink Mustache, the Derby, and the Morning Glory.

MAP 1: 700 Chestnut St., 215/223-5663, www.jones-restaurant.com; Mon.-Thurs. 11:30am-11pm, Fri. 11:30am-midnight, Sat. 9:30am-midnight, Sun. 9:30am-11pm

SNACKS AND SWEETS

FRANKLIN FOUNTAIN $

The perfect addition to historic Old City, Franklin Fountain has the feel of an authentic old-school ice cream and soda shop, even though it's only been around for a few years. Sit at the marble countertop and enjoy a banana split or sundae made with creamy homemade ice cream. Or try a classic egg cream, made with milk, flavored syrup, and club soda. Servers dressed in traditional soda jerk gear and the building's early details, including tin walls and ceiling and a mosaic tile floor, help set the mood. If you haven't satisfied your sweet tooth with the ice cream, candy, or homemade fudge, stop into **Shane Candies** (110 Market St., 215/922-1048) a few doors down; the oldest candy shop in Philadelphia has been owned and operated by the same family for nearly 100 years.

MAP 1: 116 Market St., 215/627-1899, www.franklinfountain.com; Sun.-Thurs. 11am-midnight, Fri.-Sat. 11am-1am

SPANISH

AMADA $$$

At Amada, the vibe is always stylish, fun, and energetic, but the main reason it's so hard to get a table here is the food—delectable, authentic Spanish tapas created by internationally acclaimed chef Jose Garces, arguably Philly's hottest chef. Watch through the open kitchen as chefs prepare cured meats, artisan cheeses, and traditional and creative inventions in beautiful preparations. Whether you want savory, salty, or sweet, the robust flavors

Philly's Iron Chef

Tinto

The Philly restaurant scene has been blessed with quite a few nationally renowned chefs over the years, but perhaps none are more impressive than our very own Jose Garces. Born to Ecuadorian parents and raised in Chicago, chef Garces began his culinary training in his grandmother's kitchen and has come a long way since then. In 2009, Garces was named "Best Chef Mid-Atlantic" by the James Beard Foundation and (drumroll, please) he went on to defeat Bobby Flay in the final round and win Food Network's *The Next Iron Chef* competition—all by his mid-30s. Lucky for us, 9 of his 14 restaurant ventures are located right here in Philly.

Garces's first venture, **Amada,** an enormously successful Andalusian tapas bar and restaurant in Old City, opened in 2005. Much to everyone's delight, by 2010, he had opened six more restaurants, each with its own style and cuisine, all bringing a burst of life to the local dining scene. In Center City West, **Tinto,** a wine bar and restaurant inspired by the Basque region of Spain and France, sits just next door to **Village Whiskey,** a bar serving over 80 whiskies, upscale bar snacks, and arguably the best burgers in the city. For modern Mexican at its best, Garces offers **Distrito** in University City. **JG Domestic,** on the ground floor of the Cira Center just across the bridge in University City, offers the best food and spirits from local (get it, domestic?) growers.

It's easy to run up a high tab at any of these spots with the excellent beer, wine, and cocktail selections offered, so if you'd rather spend money on food and save a bit in the booze department, visit **Garces Trading Company** in Center City East. A gourmet market and café featuring artisanal cheese, charcuterie, and deep-dish pizza, to name a few highlights, it also offers an attached market with a wine store inside—the only restaurant of its kind in the entire city. Just grab a bottle and enjoy it with your meal.

on the menu are sure to please. A full bar offers an extensive wine list, as well as red and white sangria, the perfect accompaniment to any dish.

MAP 1 DETAIL: 217-219 Chestnut St., 215/625-2450, www.amadarestaurant.com; Mon.-Thurs. 11:30am-2:30pm and 5pm-10pm, Fri. 11:30am-2:30pm and 5pm-11pm, Sat. 11am-2:30pm and 5pm-11pm, Sun. 11am-2:30pm and 5pm-10pm

Society Hill   Map 1

Society Hill is primarily residential except for the areas that border Old City, Washington Square, and South Street. Headhouse Square, encompassing several blocks of 2nd Street just north of South Street, is packed with bars and restaurants, and Penn's Landing, the waterfront strip along the Delaware, has a few worthwhile offerings just a short walk across a footbridge from Society Hill.

MEXICAN
XOCHITL $$$

This Headhouse Square restaurant (pronounced SO-cheet) offers upscale, creative twists on authentic Mexican cuisine in a cozy setting. Start with the delicious guacamole made tableside or fresh ceviche. An extensive tequila list can be served by the shot or flight or made into a variety of margaritas or specialty drinks. Save room for dessert; the apple cider *churros* are just divine. The tequila bar downstairs is a good alternative for tequila lovers who would rather drink and hear a DJ spin than eat a full dinner. Go for happy hour during the week, 5pm-7pm, for great drink specials at the upstairs bar.

MAP 1: 408 S. 2nd St., 215/238-7280, www.xochitlphilly.com; Mon.-Thurs. 5pm-10pm, Fri.-Sat. 5pm-11pm, Sun. 4pm-9pm

NEW AMERICAN
MOSHULU $$$

Dining on a docked ship offers the romantic experience of being surrounded by water without the seasickness that comes with a typical dinner cruise. Built in 1904, the *Moshulu* had been used for shipping goods; it served as a warehouse on water and was confiscated twice during wars over the course of its long life. But interesting as its history is, the real reason to come is for quality food in the heart of Penn's Landing. What could have easily become a cheesy tourist trap is instead an elegant restaurant offering classics like filet mignon, crab cakes, and salmon in updated, tasteful variations. On Sunday, an upscale buffet brunch is offered for $40 per person, and while prices are a bit steep, the experience is memorable. To experience the boat for less money, visit the Bongo Bar on the upper deck for drinks and a lower-priced, tasty bar menu. It sometimes features live music.

MAP 1: 401 S. Columbus Blvd., 215/923-2500, www.moshulu.com; Mon.-Thurs. 5pm-10pm, Fri.-Sat. 5pm-11pm, Sun. 10am-2:30pm and 5pm-9pm

This expansive area is packed with restaurants, with the majority concentrated in Chinatown, Washington Square West, and along the Avenue of the Arts. In addition to Chinese restaurants, Chinatown has Cambodian, Vietnamese, Burmese, and other offerings. Washington Square West, also known as the Gayborhood, offers plenty of restaurants, BYOBs, and bars serving great food, especially along Pine Street, Spruce Street, and 13th Street south of Market. Avenue of the Arts offers mostly large, upscale, and often overpriced chains catering to the thick wallets of the theater crowd.

ASIAN

SAMPAN ⑤⑤⑤

Renowned chef Michael Schulson served as chef at many other acclaimed restaurants and opened the stunningly successful Izakaya in Atlantic City before returning to Philly (which he calls home) to open Sampan in the heart of Midtown Village in 2009. The upscale modern Asian menu specializes in "Asian street flavors." The menu changes seasonally, but you may find tasty small plates like crab wonton tacos or beef or lobster carpaccio, along with entrées like soy glazed sea bass and Peking duck. Lunch is also popular with *bahn mi*, the Vietnamese-style hoagie, a favorite. An outdoor "graffiti bar," with walls covered in graffiti by local artists, is a great place to kick back and have a drink while waiting for your table.

MAP 2: 124 S. 13th St., 215/732-3501, http://sampanphilly.com; Sun.-Tues. 4pm-10pm, Wed.-Thurs. 4pm-11pm, Fri.-Sat. 5pm-midnight

1225 RAW SUSHI AND SAKE LOUNGE ⑤⑤⑤

The sleek, modern lounge-like decor comes complete with red walls, a bamboo ceiling, and high-backed booths, as well as a welcoming outdoor courtyard with additional seating. Creative salads, meat dishes, and cooked plates do not disappoint, but the highlight of the menu is definitely the sushi. The chef turns out generous and beautiful portions of fresh sashimi, maki, and nigiri in inventive combinations. The full bar serves beer, wine, and specialty drinks, many made with sake from the extensive selection. Try a flight of four different types of sake ($15 standard, $20 premium).

MAP 2: 1225 Sansom St., 215/238-1903, http://1225raw.com; Mon.-Fri. noon-3pm and 5pm-11pm, Sat. noon-11pm

VIETNAM RESTAURANT ⑤⑤

One of the city's most popular Vietnamese restaurants occupies a warm, inviting space in the heart of Chinatown. It's hard to go wrong with anything on the reasonably priced menu. Crispy spring rolls and tender summer rolls are top-notch, as is the grilled barbecue platter that lets you sample a range of appetizers. For entrées, catfish cooked in a clay pot and a variety of vermicelli and pho dishes do not disappoint. You may have to wait for a table on weekends, but you can order a strong specialty drink from the full bar to pass the time. Vietnam's main competitor is **Vietnam Palace** (222 N. 11th St., 215/592-9596), just across the street. It's also a local favorite, and each has staunch supporters, so try both if you have time. And if you happen to be in University City when your Vietnamese food craving hits, you can now try **Vietnam Café** (816 S. 47th St., 215/729-0260), a stylish bar and restaurant by the owners of Vietnam Restaurant that became an instant success upon its opening in 2009.

MAP 2: 221 N. 11th St., 215/592-1163, www.eatatvietnam.com; Sun.-Thurs. 11am-9:30pm, Fri.-Sat. 11am-10:30pm

CAFÉS
RAY'S CAFÉ AND TEA HOUSE ●

Ray's serves the best, and most expensive, coffee in Chinatown, along with a wide selection of teas, bubble teas, and a small Thai food menu. Coffee is made to order from exotic ground beans using the siphon method and brewed with spring water. Some brews are rather pricey, but true coffee connoisseurs will find it worth it. Coffee and tea drinks are all served in an elegant display with a fruit tart or homemade cookie.

MAP 2: 141 N. 9th St., 215/922-5122, www.rayscafe.com; Mon.-Thurs. 8:30am-6:30pm, Fri. 8am-8:30pm, Sat. 11:30am-8:30pm

EUROPEAN BISTRO
GARCES TRADING COMPANY ●●●

Jose Garces outdoes himself with his gourmet market and upscale café with an attached wine store—the only restaurant of its kind in the entire city. The restaurant functions as a BYOB, but you can choose from a great selection of beer or wine on the premises and pay retail prices rather than marked-up restaurant prices. The delicious menu features artisanal cheese and charcuterie from France, Spain, Italy, and the United States, as well as antipasti, deep-dish pizzas, pastas, and grilled entrées. Try the tasting menu for a little bit of some of the best items on the menu. In addition to lunch and dinner, brunch (weekends 11am-3pm) is a popular way to experience this excellent European-style bistro.

MAP 2: 1111 Locust St., 215/574-1099, www.garcestradingcompany.com; Mon.-Thurs. 5pm-9pm, Fri. 5pm-10pm, Sat. 10:00am-3pm and 5pm-10pm, Sun 11am-3pm and 5pm-9pm

ITALIAN
★ MERCATO ●●●

This tiny cash-only BYOB is always noisy and crowded due to close tables, an open kitchen, and its immense popularity. Start with a plate of bread and artisan cheese paired with an olive oil tasting. Then choose from an array of pasta, fish, and meat dishes that combine old-world Italian slow cooking with updated flavors and preparations. While you can't go wrong with anything on the menu, favorites include the whole grilled artichoke appetizer and the pan-seared diver scallops over wild mushroom and pea risotto. A

Bring Your Own Bottle

While it's easy to spend a few hundred bucks on dinner for two at Philadelphia's top restaurants, it's just as easy to keep it under $50 by bringing your own bottle to one of the city's many BYOBs, which often rival and at times surpass their liquor-serving counterparts in quality of cuisine. While locals have long complained about Pennsylvania's strict liquor licensing laws and high taxes on liquor sales, the fringe benefits are out of this world. The law makes it difficult and expensive for a new business to serve liquor, with a set number of liquor licenses available that must be bought from another business that is going out of business. As a result, Philly has arguably the largest and best BYOB scene in the entire country, with something for every taste and budget. With so many BYOBs, restaurants have to maintain very high food standards to compete. Most BYOBs, or BYOs, maintain a casual, comfortable neighborhood vibe, even though many are centrally located in the major neighborhoods, and very few of them have corkage fees, an annoying charge of around $10 for opening your wine. This charge is more likely at a place that has a bar of its own but also allows the BYO option, and the fee should always be clearly noted on the menu.

There are BYOBs in every Philly neighborhood, and a few not to miss include **Mercato, Audrey Claire,** and **Dmitri's** (South Philly location). Some restaurants, like **Farmicia,** offer a full bar but also let you bring your own bottle if you prefer. While wine is the drink of choice for most BYOB-ers, there are also places where other drinks are brought to the table. It is common to bring beer to casual spots like **Jamaican Jerk Hut, Tacconelli's Pizzeria,** and **Pizzeria Beddia**.

Purchasing alcohol in Pennsylvania is not always simple. There are beer distributors and state-run Wine & Spirits shops, but beer cannot be sold at the same store as wine and booze. Hours are limited, with most of the spirits shops closing between 7pm and 9pm. Very few beer or wine stores are open on Sunday, so plan ahead. Many bars sell six-packs to go, but you can expect to pay higher premiums for the convenience. Visit www.pawineandspirits.com for the state store locations, or ask a local to point you in the right direction.

And be sure to check out the most convenient addition to the BYOB scene in Philly in the form of **Garces Trading Company.** A novel concept and the only one of its kind in the city, the restaurant has a wine boutique attached to the restaurant, offering an excellent selection minus the steep restaurant markups, so you have the best of both worlds. You can BYO without having to plan in advance. Just grab a bottle and take it to your table, where your waiter will open it for you; you pay about the same as you would at any wine store.

bittersweet molten chocolate lava cake and a mascarpone cheesecake are just two of the excellent desserts. Reservations are not taken, so you'll often have to wait for a table—especially on weekends—but it's well worth it.
MAP 2: 1216 Spruce St., 215/985-2962, www.mercatobyob.com; Mon.-Thurs. 5pm-10:30pm, Fri.-Sat. 5pm-11pm, Sun. 5pm-10pm

★ **VETRI** $$$

A dinner at Vetri is the kind of once in a lifetime experience that will stay with you long after you've finished the dessert course. Operating out of a Colonial-style townhouse on Spruce Street, the intimate 32-seat restaurant is one of the most influential Italian restaurants in the country. A native Philadelphian trained in Bergamo, Italy, Chef Marc Vetri offers the tasting menu only at his namesake restaurant. After a conversation with the waitstaff, the kitchen will create a personalized six-course tasting paired with complementary wine. Reservations are required, however there is no formal dress code.

MAP 2: 1312 Spruce St., 215/732-3478, www.vetriristorante.com; Mon.-Thurs. 6pm-close, Fri.-Sat. 5:45pm-close, Sun. 5pm-close

MEDITERRANEAN

BARBUZZO $$$

Barbuzzo is owned by Marcie Turney and Valerie Safran—the juggernaut restaurateurs responsible for Lolita (Mexican), Jamonera (Spanish), Little Nonna's (Italian) and Bud and Marilyn's (American) all located on or near 13th Street in the Gayborhood. All of their restaurants are highly recommended, but Barbuzzo has been called the best restaurant in Philly by several local critics. The cozy farmhouse motif with weathered wood walls and an open kitchen is instantly inviting. Tables are narrow and set close together, but the din is loud enough—even on a Monday night—to converse without the people at the next table hearing every word. The small plates are meant to be shared, which is good because you'll want to taste every single savory dish that arrives at the table, from the well-balanced meat, cheese, and vegetable boards to creative pizzas and perfectly prepared pasta, fish, and meat dishes. Save room for the *budino* (pudding); the pot of creamy, salty, crunchy deliciousness is a taste you'll remember long after the meal is over. From 10:30pm to midnight Sunday-Thursday, you'll find reduced prices on drinks and rotating menu items.

MAP 2: 110 S. 13th St., 215/546-9300, www.barbuzzo.com; Mon.-Sat. noon-3pm and 5pm-midnight, Sun. 5pm-midnight

VALANNI $$

With one wall of exposed brick, dim pendant lighting, and plenty of candlelight, the mood is romantic yet fun at this stylish Mediterranean-Latin restaurant and bar. The bar is often filled with regulars who come for the strong, delicious specialty cocktails. Small plates, which can be eaten as appetizers or alone as a tapas-style meal, include lobster-and-crab macaroni and cheese, spicy pulled chicken empanadas, and grilled beef kabobs, and large plates include several varieties of paella. Desserts are enormous and delicious, especially the deep-fried oreo beignets and the caramelized

RESTAURANTS
CENTER CITY EAST

rum bananas. Happy hour, Monday-Friday 5pm-7pm, offers half-priced tapas and $5 drinks.

MAP 2: 1229 Spruce St., 215/790-9494, www.valanni.com; Mon.-Thurs. 4:30pm-10:30pm, Fri. 4pm-11pm, Sat. 11am-3pm and 4pm-11pm, Sun. 11am-3pm and 4pm-10pm

MEXICAN
LOLITA ⊖⊖

The first restaurant from restaurateurs Valerie Safran and Chef Marcie Turney, Lolita remains a favorite. High-quality ingredients and savory flavors make the contemporary Mexican dishes—like grilled spice-rubbed pork chops or shiitake and lancaster jack cheese enchiladas—stand out. The *fundido con queso y chorizo*—homemade tortillas served with a generous portion of melted oaxaca and chihuahua cheeses, roasted poblano, smoked brandied chorizo, and Mexican oregano for dipping—is a delicious but filling appetizer meant to be shared. Their extensive cocktail selection features six mouth-watering margaritas made with exotic flavor combinations like jicama and cilantro.

MAP 2: 106 S. 13th St., 215/546-7100, www.lolitaphilly.com; Sun.-Tues. 5pm-10pm, Wed.-Thurs. 5pm-10:30pm, Fri.-Sat. 5pm-11pm

NEW AMERICAN
★ XIX ⊖⊖⊖

The 19th floor of the Park Hyatt at the Bellevue is dripping with elegance befitting a restaurant occupying one of the city's finest and oldest hotels. Perfect for a celebration or romantic dinner, XIX (pronounced "nineteen") offers outstanding modern American cuisine, and the knowledgeable sommelier makes excellent pairing recommendations from the extensive wine list. The innovative menu takes full advantage of seasonal and local ingredients, and his creative flavor combinations always seem to hit the mark. A raw bar occupies the center of the main dining room under the high domed ceiling. But the most alluring aspect of the room is the spectacular view of the city through the expansive windows. If you don't have a few hundred dollars to drop on dinner for two, you can still enjoy the elegant atmosphere with breakfast, lunch, or brunch or a visit to the bar, which offers an ample, delicious menu at much lower prices. A classic afternoon tea is served by reservation only.

MAP 2: Broad and Walnut Sts. (19th fl. in the Park Hyatt Philadelphia at the Bellevue), 215/790-1919, www.hyatt.com/corporate/restaurants/nineteen-restaurant/en/home.html; daily 6:30am-10pm, afternoon tea 2pm-4pm

SNACKS AND SWEETS
CAPOGIRO ⊖

Capogiro Gelato Artisans provides customers with deliciously dense, creamy traditional Italian ice creams in countless fruity and savory flavors that change with the seasons. In addition to traditional flavors like hazelnut and strawberry, there are innovative offerings like rosemary/

honey/goat's milk and mascarpone fig. Not your grandmother's ice cream cone, a very small cup will cost you around $5, but it is worth every cent. Ideal for a sweet ending to a date or a break in the middle of a day of shopping, Capogiro has three additional locations for your pleasure (Center City West: 117 S. 20th St., 215/636-9250; University City Philly: 3925 Walnut St., 215/222-0252; and South Philly: 1625 E. Passyunk Ave., 215/462-3790).

MAP 2: 119 S. 13th St., 215/351-0900, www.capogirogelato.com; Mon.-Thurs. 7:30am-10:30pm, Fri. 7:30am-1am, Sat. 9am-1am, Sun. 10am-11:30pm

VEGETARIAN

VEDGE ⑤⑤⑤

This 100 percent vegan restaurant is so good that it could convince a die-hard carnivore to give up meat—at least for the night. Housed in the historic Tiger Building, a restored Frank Furness-designed townhouse in midtown, Vedge has an elegant yet homey atmosphere. Award-winning chef and owner Rich Landau has been credited with revolutionizing the way chefs work with vegetables. Using locally sourced, seasonal ingredients, his inventive creations expand the possibilities of a vegan diet. Their natural wine list earned Vedge a spot on Wine Enthusiast's list of best restaurants in 2016.

MAP 2: 1221 Locust St., 215/320-7500, www.vedgerestaurant; Mon.-Thurs. 5pm-10pm, Fri.-Sat.5pm-11pm

Center City West   Map 3

This part of town is chock-full of good restaurants. In addition to the city's most elegant eating establishments, you will find trendy bistros, casual coffee shops where you can grab a tasty lunch, and plenty of bars serving food. Walnut Street and the surrounding side streets are lined with restaurants between Broad and 18th Streets, including several directly on Rittenhouse Square, with some of the best on 20th Street just off the square.

ASIAN

FUJI MOUNTAIN ⑤⑤⑤

This sushi bar and restaurant is one more attraction signaling the rebirth of this section of Chestnut Street west of Broad, which used to shut down once the happy hour crowds left for the day. Besides serving up some of the city's best sushi and sashimi, the four-floor restaurant boasts a kara-oke room available for private rental for up to 30 people, where you can belt out the best Japanese and American pop favorites while enjoying a full bar and food menu. Other rooms in the complex offer traditional Japanese dining, with delicious entrées, appetizers, bottle service, and cocktails. Fuji Mountain takes online orders and delivers to nearby addresses.

MAP 3: 2030 Chestnut St., 215/751-0939; Mon.-Fri. 11:30am-2:15pm and 5pm-1:30am, Sat.-Sun. 3pm-1:30am

VIC SUSHI BAR 💲💲

Vic serves no-frills, quick, affordable, consistently good sushi. The friendly staff welcomes you to sit at one of the six bar seats, and BYOB if you like, but with delivery and take-out options, it doesn't matter that the seats are often filled. Don't miss the sashimi appetizer with two perfect pieces each of everyone's favorites—yellowtail, tuna, and salmon—for $8.95. Continue with the unbeatable deal of three basic eight-piece rolls of your choice for $10.95 (yes, that's all three rolls for a total of $10.95). Or have fun with creative specialty rolls (like the Lover Roll—spicy tuna, avocado, and cucumber roll topped with salmon, eel, and avocado), which are unique, delicious, and filling and range in price $9-14.

MAP 3: 2035 Sansom St., 215/564-4339, www.vic-sushi.com; Mon.-Thurs. 11:30am-9:30pm, Fri. 11:30am-10pm, Sat. 12:30pm-10pm

CAFÉS

ANTS PANTS 💲

As the website of this seemingly oddly named café explains, "ants pants" is an Australian colloquial term meaning "the best" or "height of fashion." Well, if I were Australian, I would say that the coffee, food, and atmosphere at this small local haunt are the ants' pants. They serve breakfast, lunch, and brunch, and while snagging a seat on the weekend is often challenging, at most other times this is a place where you can sit for hours over your coffee, book, or laptop (free wireless Internet is provided). Don't miss the crème brûlée-battered French toast, the dill scrambled eggs with feta, or the delicious spinach salads. When the weather is nice, sit outside in the small back patio area.

MAP 3: 2212 South St., 215/875-8002, www.antspantscafe.com; Mon.-Fri. 7am-4pm, Sat.-Sun. 8am-4pm

CARIBBEAN

JAMAICAN JERK HUT 💲💲

When the weather is nice, continue past the somewhat cramped interior to the choice seating area—the large backyard patio filled with tables for dining alfresco. You might wait awhile for your food, but if you've got sunshine or a pleasant breezy night, good friends, and a few Red Stripes to pass the time at this unique BYOB, time will fly. Flaky patties stuffed with beef, chicken, or vegetables are a great starter, and the menu features something for meat lovers and vegetarians alike. Spice-sensitive diners should avoid the jerked dishes—they pack a punch. Curried dishes, while still flavorful, are more manageable, and all the homemade juices are worth sampling. While the place is a bit run-down and the outdoor space is surrounded by a chain fence and the sides of houses, the place has got character—so much in fact that this is where the wedding was held in the last scene of *In Her Shoes*. Remember that movie?

MAP 3: 1436 South St., 215/545-8644; Mon.-Thurs. 11am-11pm, Fri.-Sat. 11am-midnight, Sun. 3pm-10pm

FRENCH
PARC $$$

This Parisian-style brasserie is a Francophile's dream come true, from the delicious escargot to the black tie service. Like a true bustling brasserie, Parc is elegant yet relaxed. The sprawling 300-seat restaurant is the perfect place to dine before a big night on the town or to relax with a cappuccino after shopping on Walnut Street. With ample outdoor seating overlooking Rittenhouse Square, Parc could not be lovelier on a warm spring night. The menu features French classics like crab galette, steak frites, and a charcuterie plate, all executed perfectly. The drink menu includes the potent and delicious Sazerac, made with absinthe, and the iconic champagne cocktail, the Kir Royal.

MAP 3: 227 S. 18th St., 215/545-2262, www.parc-restaurant.com; Mon.-Thurs. 7:30am-11pm, Fri. 7:30am-midnight, Sat. 10am-midnight, Sun. 10am-10pm

IRISH
THE BLACK SHEEP $

A block from always-jumping Rittenhouse Square, The Black Sheep is a multidimensional Irish pub. It has three levels where you can drink, watch a game, play darts, or sample traditional Irish dishes like shepherd's pie, Guinness stew, and bangers and mash. Sunday brunch offers staples like traditional Irish breakfast and eggs Benedict, but the menu is not strictly limited to traditional Irish fare, with lamb tacos and grilled filet mignon sliders also pleasing options. Wednesday nights feature Quizzo, a group trivia game that goes well with a perfect pint of Guinness.

MAP 3: 247 S. 17th St., 215/545-9473; daily 11am-2am

MARKET
DI BRUNO BROS. $

Philadelphia's answer to Dean & Deluca began as a small family-run cheese shop in the Italian Market in 1939. The original shop (930 S. 9th St., 888/322-4337) still exists in the heart of the market and offers a modest sampling of the massive array of cheeses, stuffed olives, flavored oils, spreads, charcuterie, produce, and prepared foods offered in this two-floor mega-store on Chestnut Street that opened in 2004 to immediate success. While the Italian Market location cannot be beat for character, the Chestnut Street store sells everything the original store offers along with a separate fish and meat market, a coffee, baked goods, and gelato bar, and an upstairs café with full salad bar, deli, cooked entrées, and sushi bar. Whether you're looking for a quick bite, a fully prepared meal to eat in Rittenhouse Square, all the ingredients you need to throw a big party, or a perfect gift basket for your food-loving friend, Di Bruno Bros. has it all. It's a bit pricey, but both stores are stocked with enough free samples of breads, oils, and cheeses that you may find you're no longer hungry for lunch by the time you make it to the cash register.

MAP 3: 1730 Chestnut St., 215/665-9220, www.dibruno.com; Mon.-Fri. 9am-8:30pm, Sat. 9am-8pm, Sun. 9am-7pm

MEDITERRANEAN
AUDREY CLAIRE ⑤⑤

Audrey Claire was at the forefront of Philadelphia's popular BYOB on-slaught when she opened her eponymous cash-only restaurant in 1996. She continues to pack guests into the small but airy corner location near Rittenhouse Square, with guests vying for outside tables when the weather is nice. The seasonal menu is divided into small and large plates, and each section offers standouts. You may find seared brussels sprouts unlike any-thing you were fed at home, or a pear-and-gorgonzola flatbread blending sweet and tart flavors to perfection. Among the large dishes, grilled rack of lamb and a hearty pork chop are both stellar, and the nightly specials often utilize the season's freshest ingredients. **Twenty Manning Grill** (261 S. 20th St., 215/731-0900), also owned by Audrey, is just a block north across 20th Street. A stylish bistro, also with an open, airy feel, Twenty Manning has a full bar and modern dishes heavy on seafood, including a small raw bar. **MAP 3:** 276 S. 20th St., 215/731-1222, www.audreyclaire.com; Sun.-Thurs. 5pm-10pm, Fri.-Sat. 5pm-11pm

MEXICAN
TEQUILAS RESTAURANT ⑤⑤⑤

Upscale authentic Mexican cuisine is served in an eclectic yet elegant setting in a converted old brownstone. High ceilings and dim lighting welcome you into the grand, mirrored bar area offering more than 100 different tequilas. Partitioned into three separate additional dining areas, the large restaurant maintains a cozy feel. But the reason locals and visi-tors keep coming back is the food. Choose from excellent meat and seafood entrées, and do not miss the fresh, limey ceviche or the divine guacamole to start. Order sangria and margaritas by the glass, pitcher, or carafe. Oh, and be sure to mention it if it happens to be your birthday. The staff will sing to you in Spanish and bring out a free shot of tasty, sweet tequila mixed with cinnamon and other tasty, secret ingredients.
MAP 3: 1602 Locust St., 215/546-0181, www.tequilasphilly.com; Mon.-Thurs. 11:30am-2pm and 5pm-10pm, Fri. 11:30am-2pm and 5pm-11pm, Sat. 5pm-11pm, Sun. 11:30am-8pm

NEW AMERICAN
MONK'S CAFÉ ⑤⑤

You'll often have to wait while crammed into the front entrance like sar-dines at this extremely popular spot, but it's worth it. If you're lucky, you'll nab a bar seat and drink from the extensive Belgian beer collection until your table is ready (or eat at the bar). Avoid weekends or go at an off time unless you can stand crowds and the smells of delicious food wafting past your empty stomach for up to an hour. Don't miss the famous farm-raised mussels available in a variety of delicious sauces made with different kinds of beer, garlic, and other exciting ingredients; they are served with the also-famous *pommes frites* with bourbon mayonnaise dipping sauce. But it's hard to go wrong with anything on the reasonably priced menu. The salads, burgers with a variety of toppings, and sandwiches are as delicious as the entrées.

MAP 3: 264 S. 16th St., 215/545-7005, www.monkscafe.com; daily 11:30am-2am, food served until 1am

ROUGE $$$

Occupying prime real estate directly on Rittenhouse Square, Rouge is always packed. Snagging a table from happy hour onward can be difficult, especially on weekends. Enjoy a drink at the elegant bar while you wait for a table, or go for lunch when prices are lower and it's not usually quite as busy. The scene is dominated by beautiful, wealthy yuppies letting their highlighted hair down after work, but the view of the square from the bar—or, better yet, a sidewalk table—is excellent, and may just make you forget about the steep prices. You'll pay the premium for the location, but the American cuisine with a French flair is quite good, and far superior to its nearby neighbors. The generous tuna tartare appetizer is reason enough to stop in.

MAP 3: 205 S. 18th St., 215/732-6622, www.rouge98.com; Mon.-Fri. 11:30am-2am, Sat.-Sun. 10am-2am

VERNICK $$$

Vernick has been a mainstay on every Best of Philly list since its inception and has received more than its fair share of national recognition. It's notable, then, that this elegant, award-winning, food forward fine-dining establishment somehow manages to feel casual. Perhaps it's the well-deserved confidence of the staff that keeps pretension at bay. The food is perfection, the drinks are perfection, and service is perfection. Be sure to sample liberally from Vernick's selection of small plates, particularly the crudo. Then fill up with their "toast," pillowy soft sourdough bread with just the right amount of chewiness and char, topped with anything from peekytoe crab to steak tartare. You cannot go wrong.

MAP 3: 2031 Walnut St., 267/639-6644, www.vernickphilly.com; Tues.-Sun. 5am-11pm

SEAFOOD
OYSTER HOUSE $$$

The Mink family has been serving fresh oysters in Philadelphia since 1947. Sam Mink originally purchased a seafood restaurant in South Philly called Kelly's; his son David moved the restaurant and renamed it Sansom Street Oyster House in 1976. The restaurant was sold in 2000, but it came back to the Mink family in 2009 when David's son Sam (named after his grandfather) bought it back and opened it as Oyster House. Today's Oyster House offers fresh, traditional comfort seafood with modern embellishments along with a clean, bright, modern look. David brings his own vision and

Top: Parc. Bottom: Vernick.

youth to the spot while still maintaining the focus on high-quality seafood passed down through his family. An extensive raw bar is offered alongside old-school staples like snapper turtle soup and a lobster roll. The restaurant draws a big "Oyster Hour" crowd for $1 oysters of the day, $3 draft beers, and $3 oyster shooters Monday-Friday 5pm-7pm and Saturday 9pm-11pm.

MAP 3: 1516 Sansom St., 215/567-7683, www.oysterhousephilly.com; Mon.-Thurs. 11:30am-10pm, Fri.-Sat. 11:30am-11pm

SEAFOOD UNLIMITED ⑤⑤

This casual, friendly Rittenhouse Square seafood restaurant serves perfectly fresh fish with a menu that changes daily. Each dish is done just right, and with prices that are relatively low—especially for this area—it is a long-time local favorite. The New England and Manhattan clam chowders are excellent; fresh oysters on the half shell never disappoint; and the steamed lobster stuffed with crab imperial is a classic. But the best way to go is to check out the fish case up front and see for yourself what looks best on any given day. Then choose to have it grilled, fried, pan-seared, or broiled with herb butter. You will not be disappointed.

MAP 3: 270 S. 20th St., 215/732-3663, www.seafoodunlimited.com; Mon.-Thurs. 5pm-10pm, Fri.-Sat. 5pm-11pm, Sun. 5pm-9pm

SNACKS, SWEETS, AND BREAD
LEBUS ⑤

A classic grassroots independent-business success story, LeBus started serving food to University of Pennsylvania students out of a school bus more than 25 years ago. Today, in addition to several retail locations, it supplies wholesome artisan breads to more than 500 clients, including the Four Seasons and Saladworks. Using ancient European recipes and natural ingredients, LeBus breads are known for their full flavors, from the signature French baguette and raisin walnut bread to croissants, muffins, and bagels. The Rittenhouse store is a popular morning stop for coffee, baked goods, and sweet treats, and lunch is popular for its homemade soups, quiches, and sandwiches. Be warned: snagging croissants or bagels after noon can be difficult. The food is take-out only, no inside seating. If you're in Manayunk, stop at **Winnie's LeBus** (4266 Main St., 215/487-2663, www.lebusmanayunk.com) for breakfast, lunch, dinner, or weekend brunch, and you'll be treated to LeBus breads served in or with many of the dishes.

MAP 3: 129 S. 18th St., 215/569-8299, www.lebusbakery.com; Mon.-Fri. 8am-6pm, Sat.-Sun. 9am-5pm

METROPOLITAN BAKERY ⑤

With five locations throughout the city, you're never far from the delicious breads, bagels, pastries, and coffee of Metropolitan Bakery. More than 30 varieties of bread are sold at the shops and also served and sold at many other local restaurants and markets. Well known for their signature

French berry rolls, homemade granola, and croissants, Metropolitan offers an array of single rolls as well as whole loaves along with other gourmet treats like olive oils, coffees, teas, jams, cheeses, and spreads. Each shop is a little different, but all offer amazing gourmet treats. The additional locations are Home Page Café in the Free Library of Philadelphia (1901 Vine St., Mon.-Fri. 8am-5pm), University City (4013 Walnut St., Mon.-Fri. 7:30am-7pm, Sat.-Sun. 8am-7pm), Reading Terminal Market (12th and Arch Sts., Mon.-Sat. 8am-6pm, Sun. 9am-5pm), and Chestnut Hill (8607 Germantown Ave., 215/753-9001, Mon.-Fri. 7:30am-7pm, Sat. 8am-6pm, Sun. 8am-5pm).

MAP 3: 262 S. 19th St., 215/545-6655, www.metropolitanbakery.com; Mon.-Fri. 7:30am-7pm, Sat. 8am-6pm, Sun. 8am-5pm

TAPAS

TINTO ⑤⑤⑤

Spanish for red wine, Tinto—one of Philadelphia's hottest restaurants and wine bars—lives up to its name. More than 100 varieties of Spanish and French wines fill the handcrafted wooden grids that completely surround the intimate space. Reminiscent of an elegant yet rustic wine cellar, the dining area is complete with high tasting tables and a 22-foot bar covered in black-and-white Spanish tiles. The second venture after Amada of acclaimed chef-owner Jose Garces, the inventive Basque menu featuring *pinxtos* (the Basque equivalent of tapas), charcuterie, cheeses, *mariscos* (shellfish), brochettes, and *bocadillos* (sandwiches) remains one of the most popular restaurants in the city.

MAP 3: 114 S. 20th St., 215/665-9150, www.tintorestaurant.com; Mon.-Thurs. 5pm-10pm, Fri.-Sat. 5pm-11pm, Sun. 10:30am-2pm and 5pm-10pm

VEGETARIAN

MAMA'S VEGETARIAN ⑤

If you find yourself in need of a quick bite in Center City, you could do a lot worse than Mama's, whether you're a vegetarian or not. This no-frills kosher eatery stars hefty portions of falafel on freshly baked pita. The sandwich is filling; the platter, which comes with hummus and vegetables, is almost enough for two. The menu is limited, but standouts include the eggplant and the crisp french fries. The small, packed eatery is not the best place to linger, especially during the lunch rush, but it is a cheap, tasty place to refuel.

MAP 3: 18 S. 20th St., 215/751-0477, www.mamasvegetarian.com; Mon.-Thurs. 11am-9pm, Fri. 11am-3pm, Sun. noon-6pm, closed on Jewish holidays

Museum hopping makes you hungry. While most of the museums have at least a café, and the Art Museum has several decent dining options, there are many more options nearby, lining Fairmount Avenue and the surrounding streets.

CAFÉS

MUGSHOTS COFFEEHOUSE & CAFÉ $

Mugshots is a classic neighborhood coffeehouse that happens to sit just down the street from the Eastern State Penitentiary, making it a convenient stop for visitors to this major historic site. Stop in for coffee, lunch, or a snack from the tasty menu of salads, sandwiches, wraps, and baked goods. Take a break to read, study, chat, or go online (there is free wireless Internet as well as one computer available to the public with a 15-minute suggested time limit). In addition, the environmentally and socially conscious business serves only fair-trade, organic coffees, supports local farms, and recycles absolutely everything.

MAP 4: 1925 Fairmount Ave., 267/514-7145, www.mugshotscoffeehouse.com; Mon.-Fri. 6:30am-8pm, Sat.-Sun. 7am-7pm

NEW AMERICAN

★ BRIDGID'S $$

This neighborhood restaurant and bar has all the right ingredients: affordable, delicious food, an impressive beer list, and a cozy, friendly atmosphere complete with fireplace. It's no wonder it's such a popular local favorite. The first but not the last Philadelphia establishment to specialize in Belgian beers, Bridgid's offers an excellent selection of brews from around the world. The menu changes frequently, but you can expect to find classic Italian dishes along with cozy comfort food like honey-fried chicken and filet Roquefort. Stop in for the unique and delicious brunch menu, served daily.

MAP 4: 726 N. 24th St., 215/232-3232, www.bridgids.com; Mon.-Sat. 4pm-11pm, Sun. 11am-3pm and 4pm-10pm

JACK'S FIREHOUSE $$

Occupying a 19th-century firehouse that still features the original mahogany interior and brass fire pole, Jack's Firehouse is a unique dining experience in Philadelphia, inside and out. The spacious outdoor dining area offers views of historic Eastern State Penitentiary across the street. Renowned chef Jack McDavid offers generous portions of American food with a southern flair using local, farm-fresh ingredients. North Carolina-style crab cakes, Cajun grilled shrimp, and the ever popular ribs are highlights. Lunch and weekend brunch menus are big hits with locals as well as with visitors to the Eastern State Penitentiary.

MAP 4: 2130 Fairmount Ave., 215/232-9000, www.jacksfirehouse.com; Mon.-Fri. 11:30am-4pm and 5pm-10:30pm, Sat. 11am-3pm and 5pm-10pm, Sun. 11am-3pm and 4pm-9pm

LONDON GRILL $$

Since 1991, London Grill has been a Fairmount staple. One of the first of an onslaught of bars and restaurants on this stretch of Fairmount Avenue, it remains one of the best. The restaurant has evolved since its early days, with Asian, Latin American, and Mediterranean twists on the modern American menu. There are several different cozy dining areas to choose from; the back dining room, surrounded by glass and resembling a greenhouse, is my favorite for a quiet meal, and the sidewalk tables are popular when the weather is nice. The restaurant is open for dinner daily, lunch Tuesday-Friday, and brunch on weekends. The bar/café area offers a lively atmosphere, sometimes with live music, a solid beer list, and an all-day menu until 11pm on weeknights and midnight on weekends. Don't miss happy hour with $3 drinks 5pm-7pm and $3 small plates 4pm-7pm on weekdays.

MAP 4: 2301 Fairmount Ave., 215/978-4545, www.londongrill.com; Mon. 4pm-2am, Tues.-Fri. 11am-2am, Sat.-Sun. 10am-2am

South Philadelphia Map 5

South Philly is many locals' favorite place to eat. There is an abundance of traditional and contemporary Italian restaurants in and around the Italian Market on 9th Street, with a concentration of affordable Asian and Mexican eateries on nearby Washington Avenue. South Street and East Passyunk Avenue are also chock-full of restaurants, gastropubs, and BYOBs. South Philly is also, of course, home to an abundance of cheesesteak joints, including the dueling Pat's and Geno's on opposing corners at 9th Street and Passyunk Avenue.

ASIAN

BING BING DIM SUM $$

This lively dim sum joint on Passyunk Avenue serves Cantonese-style Chinese food with South Philly flair. The proudly inauthentic Bing Bing Dim Sum has brightly painted walls with bold graphics, communal tables, and a noisy, fun atmosphere. Though the menu is constantly changing, you can expect to see eclectic dishes like South Philly Italian-inspired roast pork bao buns and lamb dumplings spiked with African spices.

MAP 5: 1648 E Passyunk Ave., 215/279-7702, www.bingbingdimsum.com; Mon.-Thurs. 5pm-10pm, Fri. 5pm-11pm, Sat. noon-11pm, Sun. noon-10pm

FEDERAL DONUTS $

Federal Donuts serves nothing but fried chicken, donuts, and coffee. The chain is owned by James Beard award-winning chef Mike Solomonov, of Zahav fame, whose motto here is: "we only serve three things and they have to be perfect." The Korean-style fried chicken bursts with flavor thanks to a liberal coating of dry spices like sour and cream and onion or coconut curry. The "fancy style" donuts feature inventive flavor combinations in every color of the rainbow. The original location, which opened in South Philly in 2001, was such a smash success that they now have three other locations, Center City (1632 Sansom St., 215/665-1101), Northern Liberties (701 N. 7th St., 267/928-3893), and West Philly (3428 Sansom St., 267/275-8489) and an outpost at Citizens Bank Park (1 Citizens Bank Way, 866/800-1275).

MAP 5: 1219 S 2nd St., 267/687-8258, www.federaldonuts.com; daily 7am-3pm

★ SABRINA'S CAFÉ $

Oh, Sabrina's…just the thought of your delicious food and ridiculously oversized portions is enough to lift many a hungover local from bed to come and wait an hour or more to be seated for brunch. Considered by many to be the best brunch spot in Philadelphia (with Honey's Sit 'n Eat a close competitor), Sabrina's offers every configuration of standard breakfast fare, as well as proprietary specialties like its famous challah French toast stuffed with cream cheese, chocolate, and caramelized apples and covered with berry-orange syrup—yum. Best known for its exquisite all-day brunch menu, Sabrina's also offers quite a good lunch and dinner, with a nice variety of soups, sandwiches, wraps, and entrées. The cozy eatery stretches by twists and turns across several former row houses and offers outdoor seating that's great for people-watching on nice days. It has been such a success that in 2007 the owners opened **Sabrina's Café and Spencer's Too** (215/636-9061) at 18th and Callowhill in the Fairmount neighborhood, which offers many of the same delicious menu items along with a few different options.

MAP 5: 910 Christian St., 215/574-1599, www.sabrinascafe.com; daily 8am-5pm

SAM'S MORNING GLORY DINER $

There is something indescribably cozy about drinking coffee from a metal mug, camping-style. The home-cooked meals have a flair that makes them more upscale than your average greasy-spoon diner but still a little grittier than Sabrina's, around the corner. Brunch is the house specialty here, and it's made with plenty of fresh, local ingredients. Check your diet at the door and sink your teeth into the gigantic breakfast burrito, one of several frittatas, or the pecan waffle with whipped peach butter. The wait for

Top: Federal Donuts. Bottom: Sabrina's Café.

weekend brunch can be brutal, so go early and wait with everyone else, or, better yet, go on a weekday.

MAP 5: 10th and Fitzwater Sts., 215/413-3999, www.themorningglorydiner.com; Mon.-Fri. 7am-3pm, Sat.-Sun. 8am-3pm

CAFÉS

ANTHONY'S ITALIAN COFFEE HOUSE ⑤

Enjoy a perfectly brewed espresso, cappuccino or regular cup of joe in an authentic old-school Italian Market coffeehouse. Dark-wood paneling and pictures of the Italian Market's early days set the mood, while delicious panini, cannoli, cookies, and perfect coffee are the real draw. If you need more to satisfy your sweet tooth, visit **Anthony's Chocolate House** (915 South St.) a few doors down for a wide array of delicious homemade chocolates and sweets.

MAP 5: 903 S. 9th St., 800/833-5030, www.italiancoffeehouse.com; Mon.-Fri. 7am-7pm, Sat. 7am-8pm, Sun. 7:30am-5pm

CHAPTERHOUSE CAFÉ ⑤

One of the city's best coffee shops, Chapterhouse Café is barely a block from the bustling concrete jungle of South Street, but it might as well be on a different planet. The minimalist white walls, dark-wood floors, and spare but comfortable black-and-silver seats are brightened by rotating installations of paintings and mobiles by local artists hanging on the walls. You're likely to see multiple people with square-framed glasses sipping lattes and being creative, or at least looking like they are. Besides great coffee, you'll find cocoa, Italian sodas, teas, and a small selection of sandwiches. And though you'll have to show up early before they run out of bagels, there's always a good selection of pastries and muffins available.

MAP 5: 620 S. 9th St., 215/238-2626, www.chapterhousecafe.wordpress.com; daily 7am-10pm

HAWTHORNES CAFÉ ⑤⑤

Foodies and beer lovers alike will find a little slice of heaven at this self-proclaimed beer boutique and gourmet eatery, which opened in 2009 on a quiet corner near South Street. Owners Chris and Heather Hawthorne converted an empty warehouse space into a cozy little café, complete with hardwood floors, fireplace, and cute personal touches. A unique concept in Philadelphia, it functions as both a six-pack shop and a restaurant. In addition to a small selection of draft beers, you can choose from the expansive beer refrigerator stocked with over 1,000 domestic and exotic brews. Grab some to go or pick one out to drink here over breakfast, brunch, lunch, or dinner. Brunch on weekends is extremely popular, but there is not a bad time to visit. The tasty modern American menu changes seasonally, with a focus on fresh, local ingredients, and the prices are very reasonable for the high-quality cuisine.

MAP 5: 738 S. 11th St., 215/627-3012, http://hawthornecafe.com; Tues.-Fri. 9am-10pm, Sat. 9am-10:30pm, Sun. 9am-9pm

CHEESESTEAKS AND SANDWICHES

FAMOUS 4TH ST. DELICATESSEN $

Simple, bright, and cheery, this corner sandwich shop may not look like much, but it has a long list of notable clientele. City politicians, prominent business folk, and regular-old people have found their way to this classic Jewish deli since it opened in 1923. Owned by the same family for more than 80 years, it changed hands in 2005, but the food is still top-notch. Sandwiches are stacked high, and while the prices are a little steep for corned beef or pastrami on rye (over $18), they're large enough to split and still have leftovers.

MAP 5: 700 S. 4th St., 215/922-3274, www.famous4thstreetdelicatessen.com; daily 8am-9pm

JIM'S STEAKS $

Although there are three additional outposts in Northeast Philadelphia, Springfield, and West Philadelphia (the original, 431 N. 62nd St., 215/747-6617), it's the South Street location that is famous. With a line that wraps around the corner on weekend nights, Jim's Steaks is a Philadelphia landmark that is rarely left out of any "great cheesesteak" debate. Signed photographs of famous people who have dined here line the walls on two floors. The menu offers more options than Jim's famous competitors Pat's and Geno's a few blocks to the south, with more fixin's, along with hoagies, soups, Italian sausage, and vegetarian steaks, but the classic cheesesteak with fried onions and Cheez Whiz is hard to beat. Bright fluorescent lights can be tough on the eyes during late-night visits, but if you're passing by after a night out on the town, you will find it hard to resist the smell wafting out onto the street.

MAP 5: 400 South St., 215/928-1911, www.jimssouthstreet.com; Mon.-Thurs. 10am-1am, Fri.-Sat. 10am-3am, Sun. 11am-1 am

PAT'S KING OF STEAKS $

Pat's occupies the most famous cheesesteak corner in Philly, and hence the world, along with its rival Geno's Steaks (1219 S. 9th St., 215/389-4166, www.genosteaks.com, daily 24 hours) across the street. As the story goes, in 1930, Pat Olivieri owned a South Philly hot dog stand. One day he wanted something different for lunch and put chopped meat in a bun instead of his usual hot dog, and the cheesesteak was born. While the cheesesteaks on this corner are not necessarily the best in Philly, they are pretty darn good, and there is always a crowd. Everyone has their fave between the two; I prefer Pat's for the simple old-school decor (compared with the neon headache

Cheesesteaks 101

As much as I'd love to give you a definitive answer to the question of where to get the best cheesesteak in Philly, there just isn't one. The argument will never be settled because it's truly a matter of personal preference. Some like the rolls toasted and crispy, while others prefer them soft and chewy. Some like it dripping with grease, while others complain that too much grease makes the roll soggy. Some like the meat diced as thinly as possible, while others prefer slightly larger slices or even small chunks. Some love fake, yellow Cheez Whiz, but most opt for American or provolone cheese. Regardless, the one indisputable fact is that cheesesteaks are just not the same anywhere else. The closest I've come to a perfect cheesesteak outside of Philly is at the New Jersey Shore, and not surprisingly, it turned out the chef hailed from Philly. While it's a fact that locals eat cheesesteaks regularly, we try to keep our consumption in check. Let's be honest; they're not exactly health food.

What Makes a Great Cheesesteak

All good cheesesteaks start with a roll that is chewy—not airy or tough—and many of the best spots in town use Amoroso's brand, a local company that's been around since 1904. The meat should generously fill the roll—leaving an inch of meatless roll is a definite no-no. Fried onions and either hot or sweet peppers are common additions, but beyond that, you're getting into fancy-schmancy territory. Some like to add pizza sauce, making it a pizza steak, or tomato, lettuce, onion, and mayo, making it a cheesesteak hoagie. Others opt for the only slightly healthier chicken cheesesteak, in which chicken is substituted for the beef. (It's technically a misnomer to call it a chicken cheesesteak since there is no steak involved, but cheesechicken just doesn't have the same ring to it.) While each of these varieties is delicious in its own right, cheesesteak virgins are advised to keep it simple and stick with the classic beef cheesesteak (with fried onions and hot or sweet peppers if you like) and American cheese.

How to Order

While not everyone is hard-core about ordering correctly, in South Philly or anywhere there is a long line, it's best to know what you're doing. First, don't *ever* order a Philly cheesesteak—you're in Philly, so that part goes without saying. The basic rule of thumb is to minimize the words you need to convey what you want, so don't bother saying the word "cheesesteak" if that is the main thing the establishment serves. Cheesesteak is implied, so you can just give the specs: "Whiz wit," means Cheez Whiz with fried onions, and "prov without" means—yes, you guessed it—provolone cheese without fried onions. These rules are most strictly observed at Pat's and Geno's, the famous dueling spots that share the intersection of 9th Street and Passyunk Avenue in South Philly. Of the two, I prefer Pat's to the neon-bedazzled Geno's, in part because the meat at Pat's is chopped more finely and in part because of the questionable sign at Geno's that reads "This is America, when ordering please speak English." While there are certainly better cheesesteaks out there, this corner offers a worthwhile cultural experience. Perhaps best of all, it is the only place where you can find cheesesteaks (and cheese fries if you really want to go all out) 24 hours a day. While you wait in line, be sure to check out the autographed photos of celebs on the walls of both—everyone from Justin Timberlake to Oprah has been here.

Top: Pat's King of Steaks. **Bottom:** Geno's Steaks.

that is Geno's, especially after a few beers) and for the slightly superior sandwiches. Whichever you choose, visiting this corner is a worthwhile cultural experience for all newcomers to Philly.

MAP 5: 1237 E. Passyunk Ave., 215/468-1546, www.patskingofsteaks.com; daily 24 hours

FRENCH
BEAU MONDE ⑤

At this French crêperie, the elegant interior—with its foil prints and bright windows—perfectly complements its delicious food. Though the menu does include other items (including a cheese plate and chicken satay), it is primarily a place to enjoy perfect thin crepes in a variety of sweet and savory combinations. Fillings include cheeses, flavored butter, chicken, nutella, grilled vegetables, and fruits, and any combination your heart desires can be yours, for dinner, lunch, brunch, or just dessert. And, to top it all off, if you have to wait for a table, you can have a drink upstairs at L'Etage, a kickin' little bar and lounge.

MAP 5: 624 S. 6th St., 215/592-0656, www.creperie-beaumonde.com; Mon. noon-10pm, Tues.-Fri. noon-11pm, Sat. 10am-11pm, Sun. 10am-10pm

ITALIAN
RALPH'S ⑤⑤

Ralph's opened in 1900, laying its claim as the oldest family-owned Italian restaurant in the United States. While the food might no longer be the very best Southern Italian fare in the city, it is still reliably good, hearty, and authentic. Best of all, this traditional two-floor eatery has unbeatable old-school ambience. It will transport you to a Mafioso-inspired time, which, minus the killing and espionage, makes for a fun, classy atmosphere and offers a glimpse into a piece of local history. Your first bite of the stellar eggplant parm or spaghetti and meatballs makes the debate over whether you're eating sauce or gravy immediately irrelevant; it's delicious either way. And don't forget to order mussels in garlicky red sauce and sop it up with bread. The service can be patchy and credit cards are not accepted, so bring your easy-going attitude and some cash and you'll be in for a good night.

MAP 5: 760 S. 9th St., 215/627-6011, www.ralphsrestaurant.com; Sun.-Thurs. 11:45am-9:45pm, Fri.-Sat. 11:45am-10:45pm

MEXICAN
SOUTH PHILLY BARBACOA ⑤

Once a beloved taco cart, the brightly painted, mosaic-covered brick-and-mortar outpost is now a cult restaurant-industry favorite. Their signature taco is made with Barbacoa lamb, slow roasted over an open flame. The tender roasted lamb is carved to order and piled onto soft, fluffy blue corn tortillas. Dress them liberally with pickled cactus, cilantro, fresh lime, and house-made hot sauce. Barbacoa keeps early and slightly unusual hours

Italian Market

the Italian Market

One of the oldest and largest outdoor markets in the United States, Philly's **Italian Market** (9th St. btwn Wharton and Fitzwater Sts., Tues.-Sat. 9am-5pm, Sun. 9am-2pm, www.phillyitalianmarket.com) dates back more than a century. An influx of Italian immigrants arrived in Philadelphia in the early 20th century, and the market developed to cater to the new community. It has been bustling ever since, and many of the vendors and shops have remained the same. A living, breathing historic site, the market offers a glimpse into a time before supermarkets, when eating was a community effort. It spans about nine blocks, with the bulk of the action centering on 9th Street between Christian Street and Washington Avenue. The numerous stalls and shops include fish, meat, and cheese shops, cafés, and a few selling books or household goods. Though parts of it are dilapidated and the street is often in dire need of a good scrub, the market holds all the delicacies of Italy: paper-thin slices of prosciutto, juicy mounds of mozzarella, succulent olives, and some of the freshest bread, pasta, and produce in Philadelphia.

Locals, tourists, and gourmands alike can explore and discover the myriad goodies and shops in the Italian Market while soaking in the atmosphere. Notice the giant mural of Frank Rizzo, the controversial, polarizing 1970s Philadelphia mayor whose likeness occupies a full wall at 9th and Montrose Streets, and recall Rocky Balboa's famous jog down the street. If you visit in winter, you may even see old men warming their hands over giant barrels of fire. The area continues to attract immigrants of many origins, and a significant number of Vietnamese, Korean, Chinese, and Mexican business owners have set up shop alongside the Italian shops—enriching the culinary and cultural experience for everyone.

(they open at 5am on the weekends), so it's perfect for a speedy yet sumptuous lunch.

MAP 5: 1703 S 11th. St., 215/694-379; Tues.-Thurs. 10am-3pm, Fri. 9am-5pm, Sat.-Sun. 5am-5pm

MOROCCAN
MARRAKESH RESTAURANT ⑤⑤⑤

Tucked away in a small alley just off South Street, accessible by a nearly unmarked door that you may have to knock on to enter, Marrakesh is a hidden gem for those who can actually find it. Belly dancers make their way through the dimly lit mazelike interior. Comfortable seating strewn with cushions makes for a cozy, romantic atmosphere. Waiters in traditional Moroccan garb serve a lovely, lengthy seven-course meal (around $30 per person) that you eat with your hands. Go hungry, allow at least two hours, and pace yourself. Each course is delicious, from the stuffed phyllo pastry to the moist chicken to the tender lamb, to the baklava and mint tea at the end. Drown in the waves of delicious food, but don't try to finish everything or you'll never make it to the seventh course. You can BYOB or order from the small wine list.

MAP 5: 517 S. Leithgow St., 215/925-5929, www.marrakesheastcoast.com; daily 5:30pm-9:30pm

NEW AMERICAN
HUNGRY PIGEON ⑤⑤

In the heart of historic Fabric Row is the Hungry Pigeon, a breath of fresh air amid the shabby-chic shops. The airy, light-filled corner restaurant has a casual, cool vibe. The menu features an ever-changing selection of locally sourced organic dishes. Some feature classic comfort food, while others feature more adventurous fare, like the crab gnocchi with uni butter. They even occasionally feature pigeon, which is surprisingly delicious, on the dinner menu. However, the meal that really shines here is breakfast/brunch, thanks to their world-class pastries and coffee.

MAP 5: 743 S 4th St., 215/278-2736, www.hungrypigeon.com; Mon.-Fri. 7am-11pm, Sat.-Sun. 9am-midnight

PIZZA
MARRA'S PIZZA ⑤

On the recently hip stretch of Passyunk Avenue that now is home to many new, often upscale, trendy restaurants, Marra's is a taste of the old South Philly neighborhood. In 1920, Salvatore and Ciarina Marra came to America from Naples, Italy and opened the restaurant. They even built their own brick oven with bricks from Mt. Vesuvius. Generations of the Marra family have run the joint ever since. Join the ranks of locals, visitors, and even celebs—including Frank Sinatra and John Travolta—who have come to sit in the red vinyl booths to eat huge portions of homemade pasta, mussels, calamari, and antipasti. While the hearty Italian dishes are very good, the best reason to come is for the delicious thin-crust pizza.

MAP 5: 1734 E. Passyunk Ave., 215/463-9249, www.marrasone.com; Tues.-Thurs. 11:30am-10pm, Fri. 11:30am-11pm, Sat. noon-11pm, Sun. 1pm-9pm

SEAFOOD

DMITRI'S $$

It's not easy to get a table at this tiny cash-only BYOB that doesn't accept reservations, but it's well worth the wait. Be sure to come at least an hour before you're hungry, and don't even bother trying on weekends during prime dinner hours. Once seated, you will be treated to an affordable menu of fresh, grilled Mediterranean-inspired seafood like shrimp, scallops, bluefish, and octopus. Most dishes are sautéed and marinated with fresh, simple flavors like olive oil, garlic, lemon, and red wine vinegar. Don't miss the perfect hummus and baba ghanoush served with grilled pita wedges or the avocado citrus salad for starters. There is an additional location in Northern Liberties (944 N. 2nd St., 215/592-4550, Mon.-Thurs. 5:30pm-10pm, Fri.-Sat. 5:30pm-11pm, Sun. 5pm-10pm) that *does* accept reservations.

MAP 5: 795 S. 3rd St., 215/625-0556, www.dmitrisrestaurant.com; Mon.-Thurs. 5:30pm-10pm, Fri.-Sat. 5:30pm-11pm, Sun. 5pm-10pm

SNACKS AND SWEETS

ISGRO PATICCERIA $

Opened in 1904 by Mario Isgro, who studied culinary arts in Vienna and Messina before coming to Philadelphia, this popular old-school South Philly bakery has been owned and operated by members of the same family for over a century. Recipes for the award-winning cannoli (my personal fave), cookies, and cakes have been passed down through generations and have garnered a loyal following in generations of Philadelphians. Sweet aromas fill the street outside the row house storefront, and traditional Italian ricotta *baba au rhum, fogliatella,* jelly-filled croissants, hazelnut genoise, and chocolate cake with layers of ganache and raspberry jam fill the glass cases inside. Be warned: The line often wraps well around the block during the holidays.

MAP 5: 1009 Christian St., 215/923-3092, www.bestcannoli.com; Mon.-Sat. 8:30am-6pm, Sun. 8am-4pm

JOHN'S WATER ICE $

Who needs a tiny $5 cup of Capogiro gelato when you can have a John's water ice for $1.50? Well, both are wonderful, but just make sure you get to John's at least once if you're in Philly in the summer. On a hot day or night, there is nothing better than a cool, light water ice, and there is no place better to get one than John's. The corner storefront serves perfectly smooth water ice with no ice chunks and just the right amount of sweetness. There are only four regular flavors—cherry, lemon, chocolate, and

With many of its top restaurants receiving national acclaim, Philly has become a real foodie town. But when you're in need of a quick bite, it's hard to beat the longtime culinary classics that are as iconic to Philly as the Liberty Bell. Be sure to try all of the following at least once while you're here.

Hoagies

Most locals would argue that hoagies, loosely translated as Philly's version of the hero or sub, are in a league of their own in the sandwich family. Exactly why hoagies are better than other sandwiches is debatable, but the bread certainly plays a large part. Many use Amoroso's rolls (a Philly institution since 1904) or their own gourmet bread, but never airy, tasteless rolls. A few spots to try are: **Sarcone's** (734 S. 9th St., 215/922-1717, www.sarconesdeli. com), **Paesano's** (1017 S 9th St., 215/440-0371, www.paesanosphillystyle. com), and **Koch's Deli** (4309 Locust St., 215/222-8662, www.kochsdeli.com).

Soft Pretzels

With a history dating to early German settlers of the area, the soft pretzel remains a strong local tradition. Indulge in a perfectly browned soft pretzel topped with rock salt and smothered with yellow mustard. It should be chewy—not hard or soggy—and is always best fresh out of the oven. Try **Center City Pretzel Co.** (816 Washington Ave., 215/463-5949, www. centercitypretzel.com) or the **Philly Pretzel Factory** (1532 Sansom St., 215/569-3988, www.phillysoftpretzelfactory.com), a mostly local chain with multiple locations.

Water Ice

Pronounced locally as "wooder ice," water ice is an essential part of summer in the city. Vastly superior to the supermarket variety of Italian ice or snow cones (syrup drizzled over ice), a proper water ice has a perfectly smooth, creamy consistency—often blended with real bits of fruit. Try **John's Water Ice** (701 Christian St., 215/925-6955, www.johnswaterice.com) or **Rita's** (239 South St., 215/629-3910, www.ritaswaterice.com), a Philly-born chain that's spreading real water ice throughout the country. Most places are open from late spring through early fall, which is fine because no one wants to eat anything with the word "ice" in it in winter.

pineapple—and sometimes a few special flavors on weekends. Vanilla, chocolate, or butter pecan ice cream can be mixed with any water ice flavor for a gelati, which is also delicious, but if you're a water-ice virgin, stick with the basics.

MAP 5: 701 Christian St., 215/925-6955, www.johnswaterice.com; open in summertime, hours vary

VIETNAMESE
NAM PHUONG $

A great location for hungry groups on a budget, Nam Phuong is renowned for its extensive menu, heaping portions, and economical prices. The fact that the food is actually stellar is an additional bonus. With over 200 dishes to choose from, it's easy for a diner to become a little overwhelmed. Fortunately, the attentive waitstaff will guide you in the right direction. Pho (soup) and *bun* (a rice-noodle dish offered with a variety of meats) are common crowd favorites, and the papaya salad and summer rolls with a thick, perfect peanut sauce are not to be missed.

MAP 5: 1110-1120 Washington Ave., 215/468-0410, www.namphuongphilly.com; daily 10am-10pm

University City

Map 6

People rarely venture across the bridge to U City just for dinner even though it's a hop away; there is something about the area being separated from Center City by a body of water that creates a mental block. But when they do, they wonder why they don't do it more often. With so many affordable restaurants serving a variety of ethnic cuisine, it is well worth "the trip." There are great options on Sansom Street off 34th just off Penn's campus, on the Baltimore Avenue corridor, and in the area around 40th and Walnut Streets.

ASIAN
VIENTIANE CAFÉ $

This tiny West Philly eatery serves excellent Laotian, Vietnamese, and Thai dishes at equally excellent prices. With most entrées under $15, it is a favorite for both students and neighbors and makes a great date spot for Penn students on a budget. Plus, it's a BYOB, making it even more affordable. Meat-lovers and vegetarians will find plenty of choices on the menu, from perfect pad thai, soups, satay, spring rolls, and well-spiced curry dishes.

MAP 6: 4728 Baltimore Ave., 215/726-1095, www.vientiane-café.com; Mon.-Sat. 11am-3pm and 5pm-10pm

CAFÉS
GREEN LINE CAFE $

Named for the #34 trolley that runs by on Baltimore Avenue, this comfortable coffee shop is a gathering place for the University City community. It serves Penn and Drexel students, professors, families, punk anarchists, kids, and just about everyone else in the neighborhood. Don't come here looking for free wireless, there is none. Standard coffee shop pastries and lunch fare are offered, and the café hosts a variety of events and artist exhibits. The concept proved so successful that other locations opened: **Green Line on Locust** (4426 Locust St., 215/222-0799, Mon.-Sat. 7am-9pm, Sun. 8am-8pm) and **Green Line-Powelton Village** (3649 Lancaster Ave., 215/382-2143, Mon.-Fri. 7am-6pm, Sat. 8am-4pm, Sun. 8am-5pm).

MAP 6: 4239 Baltimore Ave., 215/222-3431, www.greenlinecafe.com; Mon.-Thurs. 6:30am-9:30pm, Fri. 6:30am-9:30pm, Sat. 7am-9pm, Sun. 8am-9pm

Top Five Philly Food Trucks

Those small, sparkling-metal mini kitchens on wheels throughout the city often serve surprisingly good food at prices that cannot be beat. Frequented by everyone from students to the white-collar elite, food trucks can be found in the downtown business district near City Hall and Love Park, near the universities, and in areas with lots of nightlife, like Fishtown. With seasoned professionals and impossibly hot grills, food trucks churn out meals in a jiffy, so even the longest lines usually move fast. Choose from bagels, egg-and-cheese sandwiches, cheesesteaks, pizza, and hoagies to practically every ethnic food under the sun—even sushi. A good rule of thumb when choosing a food truck is to join the longest lines; they not only serve the best-tasting fare, but you can also rest assured that the hygiene levels are satisfactory if locals keep coming back.

- The **Magic Carpet** (34th and Walnut Sts., 36th and Spruce Sts., www.magiccarpetfoods.com) is a University City favorite with two locations that serve up delicious vegetarian and vegan cuisine.

- If you don't have the time or money to sit down at Fishtown's impeccable Wm. Mulherin's Sons you can track down **Pitruco** (www.pitrucopizza.com) for a taste of their delicious wood-fired pizza at one of their many regularly scheduled stops.

- Very few things in life are more satisfying than mac and cheese. **Mac Mart** (www.macmartcart.com) takes this classic comfort food to a whole new level with its decadent toppings.

- **Foolish Waffles** (www.foolishwaffles.com) has got to be one of the hardest-working food trucks in Philadelphia. In addition to their regularly scheduled stops throughout the city, you are all but guaranteed to find them at any event where food trucks gather (which is practically every Philly event). They combine sweet and savory flavors for a fantastic meal any time of day.

- **Hub Bub Coffee** (38th and Spruce Sts., www.hubbubcoffee.com) serves high-end coffee and espresso drinks alongside freshly baked breakfast pastries. You will find them at their steady West Philly location bright and early seven days a week (7am during the week and 8am on the weekend) because a good cup of coffee is not something you want to leave to chance.

ETHIOPIAN

DAHLAK ✪

Dahlak is a local gem a bit beyond the environs of the universities, offering delicious and authentic Ethiopian and Eritrean fare, which is scarce in Philly. For those who don't know, East African food usually comes in the form of flavorful stews eaten by hand with moist, spongy *injera* bread rather than utensils. Dahlak offers a good selection of meat and meat-free dishes, which can be anywhere from mild to pretty darn hot, so be clear on the level of spice you want. The bar, which is popular with students and local hipsters, serves food every night till close.

MAP 6: 4708 Baltimore Ave., 215/726-6464, www.dahlakrestaurant.com; daily 4pm-2am

FRENCH
MARIGOLD KITCHEN $$$

The oldest continually operating BYOB in the city (which says a lot in a city as old as Philadelphia), Marigold Kitchen is a local favorite. The tiny kitchen of the converted University City row home sits on a tree-lined residential street. While the style of cuisine has seen many incarnations and been under many different chefs throughout the restaurant's long history, the cozy atmosphere remains a constant. The menu changes almost daily, with only the freshest ingredients used in the inventive French cuisine. Sunday brunch is not to be missed.

MAP 6: 501 S. 45th St., 215/222-3699, www.marigoldkitchenbyob.com; Tues.-Sat. 5:30pm-11:30pm

MEXICAN
DISTRITO $$$

Iron Chef Jose Garces's establishment is a perfect fit for the university-dominated community. The two-story restaurant exudes a fun, high-energy vibe with fluorescent green and pink decor complete with a bustling open kitchen and a variety of seating from traditional tables to cozy circular booths to a car revamped as a booth. It's kitschy but fun for a night out on the town; Distrito's modern Mexican tapas are really tasty. Distrito continues Garces's trademark tapas style, so order lots of small plates and share. Two tasting menus offer a chance to sample smaller portions of many dishes. Don't miss the fresh ceviches, tuna tostadas, or the *huaraches los hongos*. The margaritas and the spicy, strong, and delicious Hemingway cocktail are highlights of the creative cocktail menu.

MAP 6: 3945 Chestnut St., 215/222-1657, www.distritorestaurant.com; Sun.-Thurs. 11:30am-9pm, Fri.-Sat. 11:30am-10pm

NEW AMERICAN
JG DOMESTIC $$$

In a bright, open setting on the ground floor of the Cira Center, just across the bridge from Center City in University City, JG Domestic proves that American food can be just as flavorful and creative as any food. With JG Domestic, Iron Chef Jose Garces has another success, just across the street from 30th Street Station, by serving the very best food and spirits from domestic purveyors. The delicious menu changes daily and includes snacks, small and large plates, and a cheese cart. Even the drinks are American-made beer, wine, and spirits. An array of plants and wood set the tone, adding to the feel that you're eating only the freshest food available, close to the source.

MAP 6: 2929 Arch St., 215/222-2363, www.jgdomestic.com; Mon.-Fri. 11:30am-7pm

★ WHITE DOG CAFÉ $$$

The success of this one-of-a-kind Philly gem tucked into three adjacent Victorian brownstones can be credited to longtime community activist Judy Wicks, who opened the restaurant in 1983 and went on to prove that progressive and socially conscious business models can work. Her goal was not based purely on profit maximizing, but also on maintaining a positive relationship with the environment and the community—which unfortunately remains a novel concept in the business world today. Each week, local farmers deliver meat from humanely treated animals and organic, hormone- and pesticide-free ingredients, so the menu changes regularly with the seasons. An advanced composting system in the backyard helps reduce and efficiently dispose of the restaurant's waste. Wicks sold the restaurant in 2009, but she remains involved with the new management, which is committed to upholding the original mission. Best of all, the modern American dishes are made with fresh, organic, local ingredients and you can taste the difference. Visit for lunch, dinner, or weekend brunch, or have drinks and some of the best burgers in town at the bar. Check the website to find out more about the many events at the restaurant.

MAP 6: 3420 Sansom St., 215/386-9224, www.whitedog.com; Mon.-Thurs. 11:30am-9:30pm, Fri. 11:30am-10pm, Sat. 10am-10pm, Sun. 10am-9pm

Northern Liberties   Map 7

Northern Liberties has plenty of restaurants, gastropubs, and BYOBs. In general, the prices are lower, the vibe more laid-back, and the scene more bohemian than in Old City or Center City.

JEWISH AND SOUTHERN

HONEY'S SIT 'N EAT $

This bustling café blends hearty down-home flavors of Southern/Jewish comfort food. Brunch is served all day, drawing the big crowds for the challah French toast, Frisbee-size pancakes, and homemade biscuits and gravy. But while it was breakfast that made Honey's famous, lunch and dinner are also delicious. Don't overlook the long list of specials, which may include fried green tomatoes, lobster macaroni and cheese, and an assortment of vegetarian and vegan options. Dine alfresco if you can snag a table, and save room for dessert if at all possible—it won't be. There is a new second location in Center City West that stays open for dinner (2101 South St., 215/732-5130; Mon.-Sat. 7am-10pm, Sun 7am-5pm).

MAP 7: 800 N. 4th St., 215/925-1150, http://honeyssitneat.com; Mon.-Fri. 7am-4pm, Sat.-Sun. 7am-5pm

NEW AMERICAN
NORTH THIRD $$

At one of the best gastropubs in town, every square inch of the dimly lit bar and restaurant is covered with conversation pieces, from tribal masks and oil paintings by local artists to artifacts. Classic, perfectly prepared bar fare like burgers, wings, and fish and chips shares space on the menu with salmon, baby back ribs, and a perfect pulled pork sandwich. With good cocktails and a solid beer list, you can't go wrong whether stopping in for a drink or a meal.

MAP 7: 801 N. 3rd St., 215/413-3666, www.norththird.com; Mon.-Wed. 5pm-midnight, Thurs.-Fri. 5pm-1am, Sat. 10am-3:30pm and 5pm-1am, Sun. 10am-3:30pm and 5pm-midnight; bar open daily until 2am

STANDARD TAP $$

One of the most popular bar/restaurants not just in Northern Liberties, Standard Tap is where many a night out in No-Libs begins and ends. Both floors of the large converted corner house are filled with tables and booths in various rooms and cozy nooks. Regulars and newcomers come to enjoy the great beer selection (including many local brews), upscale but affordable bar food, and the cool but unpretentious vibe. The burgers and fries are some of the city's best. Check out the chalkboard wall menus to see what other sandwiches, salads, and entrées are offered on any given night, and visit the website to find out about the many goings-on at this neighborhood gathering place.

MAP 7: 2nd and Poplar Sts., 215/238-0630, www.standardtap.com; Mon.-Fri. 4pm-1am, Sat.-Sun. 11am-3pm and 4pm-1am

SPANISH
BAR FERDINAND $$

Liberties Walk is a pedestrian path that is home to a sprinkling of appealing eateries and shops, including this authentic tapas bar. Choose the quieter, more romantic dining areas with tables and booths, or the fun, sociable bar—especially happening on weekends. Owner and longtime No-Libs local Owen Kamihira emphasizes the importance of the authentic tapas experience, so feel free to come for dinner or just have a few bites while you drink, as is customary in Spain. Hot and cold tapas range from tiny bites to larger portions and cost $4-16; they include olives, oysters, cured meats and cheeses, and interesting configurations of empanadas and skewers. An excellent selection of Spanish wine is available by glass or bottle, along with sangria, beers, and specialty cocktails.

MAP 7: 1030 N. 2nd St., 215/923-1313, www.barferdinand.com; Mon.-Thurs. 5pm-midnight, Fri. 5pm-1am, Sat. 11am-3pm and 5pm-1am, Sun. 11am-3pm and 5pm-midnight

Philly's Gastropubs

In a town as food obsessed as Philadelphia, you don't have to go to an up-scale restaurant for an amazing meal. Gastropubs have become a mainstay in the Philly dining scene. At gastropubs the food is at least as big a draw as the drinks—as opposed to places where chicken fingers and wings are par for the course and jalapeño poppers are gourmet cuisine. Serving everything from lobster spring rolls to seared tuna to colorful salads, gastropubs are generally affordable, casual places to eat and drink, and they are many locals' choice for dinner on an average night. Many of these spots do still serve the classic bar food like burgers—but those burgers are likely to be stuffed with Roquefort cheese or topped with truffles and served on a gourmet roll. And you will usually be able to choose a salad to accompany it in lieu of fries, but if you do opt for fries, they may be sweet potato fries with a bourbon-mayo dipping sauce. These places serve great food and are a worthwhile stop whether for a meal or just a few drinks. Most of them also feature a nice variety of beers to match the meal.

Old City

- **Eulogy Belgian Tavern** (page 143)

- **The Plough and the Stars** (page 144)

Center City

- **Monk's Café** (page 108)

- **Good Dog** (page 151)

- **Sidecar Bar & Grille** (page 152)

South Philly

- **Devil's Den** (page 154)

- **Royal Tavern** (page 156)

Northern Liberties

- **Johnny Brenda's** (page 163)

- **Standard Tap** (page 130)

- **North Third** (page 130)

Fishtown has become an exciting hub for dining and going out. If you plan to follow dinner with drinks, dancing, or a concert, then you've come to the right place. There are plenty of casual restaurants here as well as a new crop of upscale eateries.

CAFÉS
★ LA COLOMBE $

La Colombe, a Philadelphia company gone global, opened its stunning flagship store in the heart of Fishtown in 2014. The 11,000-square-foot warehouse hosts their roasting facilities as well as a coffee-filtered rum distillery, open kitchen, bakery, and bar. The creamy draft latte, a cold espresso concentrate mixed with whole milk and served over ice is a must. The food is simple but satisfying, featuring an extensive assortment of breads and pastries baked on site, as well as sandwiches and salads. Exposed brick walls feature a huge mural by legendary graffiti-writer-turned studio artist, Stephen Powers aka ESPO. There is plenty of seating so stretch out and stay awhile, but bring a friend, or a book, because Wi-Fi is not on the menu.
MAP 7: 1335 Frankford Ave., 267/479-1600, www.lacolombe.com; Sun.-Thurs. 7am-7pm, Fri.-Sat. 7am-9pm

INDIAN
★ TIFFIN $

What started as a take-out and delivery service expanded into a small sit-down restaurant due to popular demand for delicious, affordable Indian food. The menu is filled with classic dishes along with a few more creative specials offered daily. The flavors hit right on the mark each time. Delivery service is available in most areas of the city, including Center City, Old City, Northern Liberties, Washington Square, University City, Fishtown, Queen Village, Bella Vista, Temple University campus, and Fairmount, and the service area is always expanding. Three different meal packages are offered for delivery every weekday, and at least one package is vegetarian. Best of all, the packages, called tiffins, cost only $8.50 (vegetarian) or $9.50 (meat) each. Options change daily and are always reliably good, but you have to place an order by 10am for lunch delivery and by 2pm for dinner. Place an order online or by phone, or just go to eat in or take out from the full menu anytime. Thanks to another location in Mt. Airy (7105 Emlen St., 215/242-3656), most of Northwest Philadelphia can now enjoy Tiffin as well.
MAP 7: 710 W. Girard Ave., 215/922-1297, www.tiffin.com; Sun.-Thurs. 11am-10pm, Fri.-Sat. 11am-11pm

ITALIAN
WM. MULHERIN'S SONS $$

Fishtown's most sophisticated restaurant, Wm. Mulherin's Sons, was once a 19th century, family-owned whiskey-blending and bottling facility of

Top: La Colombe. Bottom: Wm. Mulherin's Sons.

the same name. The long-shuttered doors opened in 2016 to instant and widespread acclaim, serving rustic Italian cuisine and wood-fired pizzas. The impeccably restored interior exudes an effortlessly hip atmosphere, lauded as a "perfect place to post up for a late night dinner date," by *Vogue* magazine. Upstairs is an equally chic four-room boutique hotel.

MAP 7: 1355 N Front St., 267/753-9478, www.wmmulherinssons.com; Sun.-Thurs. 5pm-11pm, Fri.-Sat. 5pm-midnight

PIZZA

PIZZA BRAIN $

There are many great pizza places in this section of the city, but none quite like Pizza Brain. Philadelphia artist and extreme pizza enthusiast Brian Dwyer spent a year traveling around the world collecting pizza memorabilia before opening Pizza Brain on Frankford Avenue in 2012. He is now the Guinness record holder for his collection, so Pizza Brain is not just a top-notch pizzeria; it is also a mini museum. The walls and floors are lined with pizza-themed quirky collectables; think Teenage Mutant Ninja Turtles ephemera, album artwork, and all manner of pop culture artifacts. The artisan pizza is made with fresh, locally sourced ingredients and comes in over a dozen varieties, from the traditional Plain Jane pie, to the exotic, like a Vietnamese Banh Mi slice. For dessert, go next door to **Little Babies Ice Cream,** connected to Pizza Brain through an open doorway. Little Babies serves small-batch, superpremium regular and vegan ice cream in traditional or insane flavors, such as, well, pizza of course.

MAP 7: 2313 Frankford Ave., 215/291-2965, www.pizzabrain.org; Mon.-Thurs. 11am-9pm, Fri.-Sat. 11am-11pm, Sun. noon-10pm

★ PIZZERIA BEDDIA $

This small, unassuming pizza shop in Fishtown is kind of a big deal. Ever since Pizzeria Beddia was named best pizza in America by *Bon Appétit* magazine in 2015, people have been lining up around the block for it. *Bon Appétit* described eating here as a "hauntingly beautiful experience," and it's not an exaggeration. The shop has no seating and no phone. Owner Joe Beddia makes just 40 pies a day, each one by hand using simple fresh ingredients. They sell out nightly, and when they're out, they're out, which means lining up before opening is the only way to guarantee you'll get a pie. But the transcendent pie with its crispy, thin, blackened crust is worth the inconvenience. Hang out next door at Johnny Brenda's and sample their extensive local beer selection while you wait. Pizzeria Beddia accepts cash only and is a BYOB.

MAP 7: 115 E Girard Ave., www.pizzeriabeddia.wordpress.com; Wed.-Sat. 5:30pm-close, Fri.-Sat. 5:30pm-10:30pm

The majority of restaurants in Northwest Philadelphia are located on or near Germantown Avenue in Chestnut Hill or on Main Street in Manayunk, both bustling business strips in otherwise residential neighborhoods. Both areas also have excellent cafés and gourmet markets, including the Chestnut Hill Farmers' Market just behind the Chestnut Hill Hotel. The nearby neighborhoods of Mt. Airy, East Falls, and Roxborough also have a few neighborhood gems.

ASIAN

OSAKA JAPANESE RESTAURANT ⑤⑤⑤

A contemporary Japanese restaurant with a full sushi bar, Osaka is a Chestnut Hill favorite for a night on the town. Don't let the traditional decor complete with tatami room fool you; the kitchen turns out modern Asian fusion dishes and inventive specialty rolls using only the freshest ingredients. Cocktails, including those made with sake, are strong and delicious.

MAP 8: 8605 Germantown Ave., 215/242-5900, www.osakapa.com; Mon.-Thurs. 11:30am-2:30pm and 5pm-10pm, Fri.-Sat. 11:30am-2:30pm and 5pm-11pm, Sun. 5pm-10pm

CHEESESTEAKS AND SANDWICHES

MCNALLY'S TAVERN ⑤

Just when you thought you couldn't get any more artery clogging than the cheesesteak, along comes the Schmitter. In addition to beef, onions, and extra cheese, the Schmitter comes with tomatoes, salami, and a special secret mayonnaise-y sauce. The sandwich has become a widely known Philly phenomenon that is now also sold at Citizens Bank Park during Phillies' games, but this is where it all began. McNally's also offers plenty of less intimidating house specialties, soups, salads, and good-old regular cheesesteaks and hoagies, which suddenly seem healthy next to the Schmitter. A casual spot in the refined Chestnut Hill neighborhood, McNally's has a long history. An early incarnation of the restaurant was established in 1921 by Rose McNally to provide lunch for the trolley operators, including her husband, who drove outside on Germantown Avenue. Her great-granddaughters operate the business today out of the same house the family bought to accommodate the growing business in 1927.

MAP 8: 8634 Germantown Ave., 215/247-9736, www.mcnallystavern.com; Mon.-Sat. 11am-11pm, Sun. noon-8pm

FRENCH

PARIS BISTRO AND JAZZ CAFE ⑤⑤⑤

A great addition to the many old staples of the Chestnut Hill dining scene, this upscale French menu offers excellent classic French cuisine and drinks in a lovely 1930s-inspired space with rich furnishings and a tin ceiling. Go downstairs to hear a live jazz band Thursday-Sunday. Check the website for details and snag a reservation, especially in the jazz room. Paris also serves up an excellent brunch on weekends.

MAP 8: 8201 Germantown Ave., 267/766-5372, www.elpoquito.com; Mon. 5pm-9pm, Tues.-Thurs. 11:30am-10pm, Fri.-Sat. 11:30am-11pm, Sun. 11:30am-9pm

MEXICAN
EL POQUITO ⓢⓢ

Perfect margaritas, excellent Mexican food "served with a whimsical approach," and a lively bar atmosphere with just the right lighting make this a favorite date night or happy hour destination in Chestnut Hill. Start off with guacamole or one of the ceviches (tuna is my favorite) and move on to tacos, enchiladas, or fajitas, with a nice selection of seafood, meat, and vegetarian options. Save some room for the churros y chocolate. You will thank me for that. There is a large bar and plenty of booths inside, or dine alfresco when the weather is nice. Lunch is served Thurs.-Sun. and brunch on weekends.

MAP 8: 8229 Germantown Ave., 215/2424-6200, www.parisbistro.net; Mon.-Thurs. 11:30am-2:30pm and 5pm-10pm, Fri. 11:30am-2:30pm and 5pm-11pm, Sat. 5pm-11pm, Sun. 10:30am-2:30pm and 5pm-10pm

Manayunk   Map 8

CAJUN
BAYOU BAR & GRILL ⓢ

With most items under $10, the Bayou is an affordable place to eat among some of its more pricey neighbors on Main Street. Cajun and Creole classics like gumbo, jambalaya, and Creole chili are served along with standard pub fare like burgers, appetizers, and award-winning buffalo wings. The hard-shell crabs are a big hit. In existence since 1993, it's a local favorite that draws a regular crowd for dining and an even more regular crowd for the bar scene. A friendly and lively atmosphere, nightly drink and happy hour specials, football games, and a covered outdoor deck when the weather is nice are just some of the highlights. In search of more upscale Cajun-inspired cuisine? Check out **Bourbon Blue** (215/508-3660, www.bourbon-blue.com) at Main and Rector Streets.

MAP 8: 4245 Main St., 215/482-2560, www.thebayoubar.com; daily 11am-midnight

NEW AMERICAN
JAKE'S AND COOPER'S WINE BAR ⓢⓢⓢ

One of the few true fine-dining restaurants in Manayunk is Jake's. In existence since 1987, Jake's serves upscale modern American cuisine in an elegant setting. It has earned the coveted four stars from *Mobil Travel Guide* and high praise from *Zagat, Gourmet, Wine Spectator,* and the *Philadelphia Inquirer,* among others, over its long history. The adjoining Cooper's Brick Oven Wine Bar offers a more casual and affordable alternative to Jake's, Cooper's serves gourmet pizza with seasonal toppings, small plates, and a few traditional favorites from Jake's in a modern space with an open kitchen.

MAP 8: 4365 Main St., 215/483-0444; Jake's: Mon.-Thurs. 5:30pm-9:30pm, Fri. 5:30pm-10:30pm, Sat. 5pm-10:30pm, Sun. 10:30am-3pm and 5pm-9pm; Cooper's: Sun.-Thurs. 11:30am-10pm, Fri.-Sat. 11:30am-11pm

MANAYUNK BREWERY AND RESTAURANT ❂❂

A former textile factory, the restaurant and brewery is now a staple of Manayunk's Main Street. In addition to their classic menu offerings, there is also a sushi bar, stone pizza oven, and a rotisserie. From burgers to crab cakes to raw tuna, there is something for every taste and budget on the extensive menu. Several different bars offer a large selection of beer, wine, and drinks, including the popular in-house brews. It has one of the nicest and largest alfresco dining areas in the city, so be sure to sit on the back deck overlooking the Schuylkill River if you visit when the weather is nice. There are often events and live entertainment, including a live jazz brunch on Sundays, 10:30am-2:30pm. The brewery even offers kayak tours in the warmer months. Explore the Schulykill on kayak, stopping for a lunch break and enjoy a pint upon return. Book ahead.

MAP 8: 4120 Main St., 215/482-8220, www.manayunkbrewery.com; Mon.-Thurs. 11am-midnight, Fri.-Sat. 11am-2am, Sun. 10:30am-midnight

PIZZA

THE COUCH TOMATO CAFÉ ❂

University of Delaware graduates promise quick service of "Manayunk cuisine without the Manayunk prices" at their cozy, laid-back café. In addition to the extravagantly topped 20-inch gourmet pizzas cooked to perfection over pizza stones, they offer salads, soups, wraps, calzones, and desserts. Indoor and outdoor seating are available, but convenient curbside pickup and a wide delivery make takeout a popular option.

MAP 8: 102 Rector St., 215/483-2233, www.couchtomato.com; Sun.-Thurs. 11am-10pm, Fri.-Sat. 11am-11pm

The following are a select number of restaurants that fall outside the major neighborhoods outlined in this book. Within the Philadelphia city limits but not in the central neighborhoods, they are included because they are well worth the short trip.

CHEESESTEAKS AND SANDWICHES

CHUBBY'S STEAKS ❸

This seemingly unimpressive sandwich stop is regarded as one of the best in the city, making the trip to Roxborough in Northwest Philadelphia well worth it. With steaks this filling, side dishes won't be necessary, but fries (mmm, cheese fries) or onion rings are a good addition if you've got a big appetite. Have a beer with your cheesesteak at the bar or in the back booths, or grab a six-pack to go. Just across the street, you'll see **Dalessandro's** (600 Wendover St. at Henry Ave., 215/428-5407), another local favorite. Like the Pat's and Geno's rivalry in South Philly, locals have their favorite on this Roxborough corner. I prefer Chubby's.

MAP 10: 5826 Henry Ave., 215/487-2575; Mon.-Thurs. 11am-1am, Fri.-Sat. 11am-2am, Sun. 11am-11pm

JOHN'S ROAST PORK ❸

Pat's and Geno's get all the publicity, followed by Jim's, but ask a real Philly eater who serves the best sandwich in town, and your answer very well may be John's. On the same South Philadelphia corner since 1930, John's is a no-frills joint with little more than a counter and an outdoor table for accommodations. The cheesesteaks—greasy, oozing cheese on perfect rolls—are simply delicious. The roast pork sandwiches, it should go without saying, are also exceptional.

MAP 10: 14 E. Snyder Ave., 215/463-1951, www.johnsroastpork.com; Mon.-Fri. 7am-7pm, Sat. 9am-7pm

NEW AMERICAN

VALLEY GREEN INN ❸❸❸

While Fairmount Park is most popular for hiking, biking, or visiting historic homes, there is one more reason to go—a totally elegant dining experience in the middle of Wissahickon Park. The Valley Green Inn draws crowds as a destination in itself. Built in 1850, the building once served as the Valley Green Hotel but has since been converted into a restaurant. The menu changes seasonally with classic offerings like New Zealand rack of lamb alongside modern dishes like crab and shrimp spring rolls. Sunday brunch is popular and the perfect time to take in the idyllic setting along the creek surrounded by towering trees. With no other houses in sight, you'll feel like you're visiting a remote colonial-era farmhouse. The interior matches the feel with its period furnishings and unfinished hardwood floors. Additional seating on the wooden front porch provides some of the best alfresco dining around when the weather is nice.

MAP 10: Valley Green Rd. at Wissahickon, 215/247-1730, www.valleygreeninn.com; Mon.-Thurs. noon-4pm and 5pm-9pm, Fri. noon-4pm and 5pm-10pm, Sat. 11am-4pm and 5pm-10pm, Sun. 10am-3pm and 5pm-9pm

PIZZA

TACCONELLI'S PIZZERIA ⑤

Giovanni Tacconelli came to Philly in 1918 and with the help of some friends built a massive 20-square-foot brick oven. For many years he used it just for baking bread, until the 1940s when he started using it to make pizza. Now, five generations later, Tacconelli's ultrathin-crust pies—still baked in that same handcrafted oven—remain a Philly tradition. People travel from all over the city and beyond to the Port Richmond neighborhood, which is not by any stretch a typical stop on the tourist or even local dining circuit. The cash-only BYOB offers a variety of toppings, and in addition to the excellent tomato sauce, white pizza is a popular choice. You have to call a day ahead to reserve your dough; if you show up unannounced, you could wait over an hour, and they may run out. Grab a seat near the oven and watch the expert pizza makers whip out pizzas almost as quickly as you can eat them.

MAP 10: 2604 E. Somerset St., 215/425-4983, www.tacconellispizzeria.com; Wed.-Thurs. 4:30pm-9:30pm, Fri.-Sat. 4pm-10pm, Sun. 4pm-9pm

Nightlife

Old City 143
Center City East 145
Center City West 149
South Philadelphia 154
University City 157
Northern Liberties 158
Fishtown 163

Nightlife in Philly spans the cheesy, swank, hip, and dive-y, along with everything in between. And while there is no shortage of upscale martini spots and velvet-lined lounges, Philly is by and large a casual city, where many locals can be found hanging out at the corner bar on an average night.

Neighborhood bars can reveal much about local culture without breaking the bank. A Yuengling lager or a beer from Philadelphia Brewing Co., the local brews of choice, usually won't cost you more than $3. Philadelphia is a paradise for beer lovers, with beer gardens popping up in unexpected locations all over town during the warmer months. Gamers can find heated karaoke competitions, team trivia games (known locally as Quizzo), or pool tournaments throughout the city. And there is plenty of high-quality bar food, so when deciding where to eat dinner, bars should be considered.

Though there are countless exceptions, the busiest nightlife scenes can loosely be classified by area. Old City bars and clubs tend to cater to a young, decked-out, bar-hopping crowd, including many youngsters from New Jersey looking for a night on the town. The somewhat more sophisticated lounges and bars around Rittenhouse are hopping for happy hour, since this is also where most of the skyscrapers are located, but the area gets a bit quieter late at night. South Street has a mixed but generally grungier feel, with pool tables and pitchers of beer. Northern Liberties and Fishtown have been known as the hip, artsy parts of town, but they have become the destination of choice for youngsters of all types for the great concentration of bars, clubs, and concert venues. East Passyunk Avenue in South

---

Previous: the Trocadero Theatre; Johnny Brenda's.

Look for ★ to find
recommended nightlife

Highlights

★ **Best Quizzo Game:** In a city where competitive bar sports are all the rage, there is no shortage of intense Quizzo (team trivia) games. **Fergie's**—with big prizes and fierce competition—offers the best of the best (page 145).

★ **Best Karaoke:** A Chinatown gem, **Yakitori Boy** has public and private karaoke rooms, where you can croon the night away while sipping Sapporo and snacking on sushi (page 145).

★ **Best Gay Nightlife: Woody's** has been the center of gay nightlife in Philly for nearly 40 years. Check out their themed nights (page 148).

★ **Best Dive Bar:** More than just a dive bar, **Bob & Barbara's** is a local institution. The $3 special—a shot of whiskey and a can of PBR—can't be beat, and unique weekly events attract a diverse crowd (page 149).

★ **Best Place to Drink Like a Mobster:** The delicious, strong drinks at **Franklin Mortgage & Investment Co.** don't come cheap, but you'll feel like Al Capone at this hidden speakeasy that pays homage to the Prohibition era (page 149).

★ **Best Bar Burger:** Philly's own Iron Chef, Jose Garces, serves up perfect juicy Angus burgers along with more than 80 varieties of whiskey at **Village Whiskey** (page 152).

★ **Best Wine Bar:** The food, microbrews, and, of course, the wine are spectacular at **Tria.** With three Center City locations, you're never far from delicious cheese and a perfect Cab (page 154).

★ **Best Dance Club and Diner in One:** One of the best dance clubs in Northern Liberties, **Silk City** is also home to an adjoining upscale diner and an outdoor beer garden (page 160).

★ **Best Music Venue:** A beautiful space with superb sound quality, **Union Transfer** is heaven on earth for music lovers (page 161).

★ **Best Beer Garden:** Fire pits, heat lamps, and massive beer steins make it possible to enjoy **Frankford Hall**'s spacious courtyard all year round (page 163).

Philly is also increasingly popular as a nightlife destination for locals and anyone else in the know.

Fans of live music will be happy to know that every major and minor act comes through Philly, and on any given night—especially on weekends—you can find national headliners, up-and-comers, and open-mic stages in diverse venues across the city. In addition to the live music venues listed, many of the bars in this chapter offer live music on select nights of the week. From intimate clubs to hipster bars to acoustically superb venues, Philly has the perfect stage for every act.

Most bars and clubs in Philly close at 2am sharp, and most don't have a dress code. That said, there is always a major concert, DJ, or late-night party happening somewhere around town; just ask a friendly local or check out the weekly paper, *PW*, or www.uwishunu.com, the official tourism blog of Philadelphia, for extensive listings of nightlife events. Happy hour specials abound across the city, usually 5pm-7pm on weekdays. Some bars offer late-night or early afternoon specials as well.

Old City

Map 1

BARS

EULOGY BELGIAN TAVERN

Just three blocks from Independence Hall, this two-story row house bar immediately feels like home. But with over 300 international and domestic craft-brewed bottled beers and over 20 on draft, it's just that much better than your fridge full of Bud. Try a pint of Eulogy's Busty Blonde, brewed in Belgium exclusively for Eulogy, and don't miss the highlight of the stellar pub fare, the Belgian *frietjes* (fries) served with a delicious dipping sauce. In typical Old City form, it's packed on weekend nights, and getting a seat can be very difficult.

MAP 1: 136 Chestnut St., 215/413-1918, www.eulogybar.com; Mon.-Wed. 5pm-2am, Thurs.-Sun. 11am-2am; no cover

KHYBER PASS PUB

This cozy, casual bar is a welcome respite in a sea of Old City's upscale establishments. The dimly lit well-worn dining room services standard bar food with a Southern Creole flair that happens to be fantastic. Hickory smoked meats, like brisket or pulled pork come with your choice of classic sides like mac and cheese or collard greens. The draft list is extensive and exotic. The Khyber Pass promises good food and a solid beer menu in a chill setting.

MAP 1 DETAIL: 56 S. 2nd St., 215/238-5888, www.khyberpasspub.com; daily 11am-2am; no cover

Order a Lager

Yuengling lager, that is. In Philly—in most of Pennsylvania, in fact—lager is synonymous with the Yuengling brand. The first Yuengling beer was brewed in 1829 in Pottsville, Pennsylvania, making the brewery America's oldest. While the brewery makes other beers, including a porter, the traditional golden lager is the most popular. Considered better than other domestic brews at about the same price, it is many locals' drink of choice. So if you want to fit in, sidle up to the bar and order a lager. The minute you say "Yuengling lager," it's obvious you're not from around here.

LAS VEGAS LOUNGE

Despite its fancy name and worn-out red pleather booths, the Las Vegas Lounge is definitely more of a cheap neighborhood bar than a chic lounge. Those wanting to get away from the trendier Old City spots can venture a few blocks west to this local hangout. Nightly drink specials offer reduced prices on the already cheap drinks. The large space has plenty of seating, pool tables, and a Ms. Pac-Man game. Food consists mostly of typical greasy bar apps and sandwiches, which goes down nicely with that 20-ounce draft beer that is the norm for most patrons at LVL, as it's affectionately termed.

MAP 1: 704 Chestnut St., 215/592-9533, www.lasvegaslounge.com; Mon.-Sat. 11am-2am, Sun. 5pm-2am; no cover

THE PLOUGH AND THE STARS

This high-ceilinged restaurant/bar has an elegant appearance with a casual vibe. By day it's a respectable place to grab a nice sit-down lunch on the main floor or on the balcony of the high-ceilinged space. By night it lives up to its prime Old City location and hosts some of the loudest partying and excessive drinking in town. Though ostensibly Irish, The Plough's menu has a decidedly contemporary flair, with a seasonal menu and a fairly extensive wine and drinks list alongside the traditional shepherd's pie and fish-and-chips. Serving lunch, dinner, and weekend brunch, it also has a good bar menu available until midnight except on Saturdays. It is home to what many claim to be the best pint of Guinness in the city. The traditional Irish music session on Sundays 5pm-9pm welcomes all to bring an instrument and join in the fun.

MAP 1: 123 Chestnut St. (enter on 2nd. St.), 215/733-0300, www.ploughstars.com; Mon.-Fri. 11:30am-2am, Sat.-Sun. 10:30am-2am; no cover

BARS

DIRTY FRANK'S

Dirty Frank's is a total and complete dive, not one of those pseudo-dives that is hip and dive-y in an intentional way, but a real, true dive. The bartenders are aloof, the beer is cheap, and the crowd is very, very down-to-earth. The booths are torn, the walls are covered in graffiti, and the bathrooms, well, just avoid them if you can. But if you're looking for a place to sit in a booth and kick a few back without going broke, this is a perfectly good place to do so. The only touch of class is the mural, courtesy of the Mural Arts Program, on the outside of the building, consisting of famous Franks, including Frankie Avalon, Aretha Franklin, Franklin Delano Roosevelt, Frank Zappa, Frankenstein, St. Francis of Assisi, and Frank Sinatra.

MAP 2: 347 S. 13th St., 215/732-5010; daily 11am-2am; no cover

★ FERGIE'S

Fergie's Irish bar has the attitude of a neighborhood dive bar with zero pretentiousness, even though it's in the heart of Center City and offers a much nicer setting and far better food and beer. You'll find entertainment and events on most nights, including live music and the popular Open Mike Night (Mon. at 9pm), which draws a regular, talented crowd. But the busiest nights of all are often Tuesday and Thursday, when you can go upstairs to play or watch the most competitive Quizzo game in the city. Regulars come early to reserve their favorite tables; come at least by 8pm for the 9pm game and bring your smartest friends. It's free to play, and the first-place winner gets a $50 credit off the bill, and second place gets $25 off the tab.

MAP 2: 1214 Sansom St., 215/928-8118, www.fergies.com; Mon.-Sat. 11:30am-2am, Sun. 4pm-2am; no cover

★ YAKITORI BOY

In the scattered abyss of karaoke nights around the city, you can count on Yakitori Boy as a place to work out those pipes publicly seven days a week. In the heart of Chinatown, the sleek Japanese restaurant and sushi bar is popular for dinner, a snack, or drinks, but karaoke is the major draw. For the exhibitionist, there is a large communal room where you'll have to wait your turn, and for the shyer singer or perhaps the microphone hog, there are private rooms of varying sizes that can be rented by the hour. Channel your favorite rock star as you belt out tunes in the soundproof booth while efficient servers appear at the push of a button serving up Sapporo, sushi, champagne, or whatever your heart desires. It's almost too good to be true, at least until the bill comes; you'll be having so much fun crooning, it'll be easy to rack up a high tab here.

MAP 2: 211 N. 11th St., 215/923-8088, www.yakitoriboy.com; daily 5pm-2am; no cover

Top: Dirty Frank's. **Bottom:** a.bar.

Many claim that the gay scene in Philly is third only to New York and San Francisco and perhaps ties with Chicago in its offerings. Best of all, the bars and clubs are all within a few blocks of each other in Washington Square West (the "Gayborhood") in the heart of Center City, so head out that way, and you will quickly find more in addition to those listed here.

THE BIKE STOP

Philly's leather bar for nearly three decades is a chill neighborhood watering hole, where you can gather with friends and enjoy cheap pitchers—and the occasional spanking. Depending on the night, patrons might see sitcom re-runs on the flat-panel TVs or watch a leather-clad man getting whipped on stage; it's the luck of the draw. The little-used 3rd floor offers a small dance floor, but it's the downstairs Pit Stop room (Wed., Fri., and Sat. 10pm-2am) that draws a crowd for its underwear-only Wednesdays and cruise-y weekend nights. Beer and alcohol specials abound throughout the week.

MAP 2: 206 S. Quince St., 215/627-1662, www.thebikestop.com; Mon.-Fri. 4pm-2am, Sat.-Sun. 2pm-2am; no cover

TAVERN ON CAMAC

Tavern on Camac is an "only in Philly" type of place. The popular historic tavern is an old-fashioned piano bar with nightly live entertainment. Meanwhile, head upstairs to **Ascend** for one of the city's best dance floors on weekends along with nightly entertainment during the week, including karaoke and game shows (daily 9pm-2am). Patrons of all ages switch between high-energy house music and melodic show tunes several times throughout the night, all in one historic building on Camac Street.

MAP 2: 243 S. Camac St., 215/545-0900, www.tavernoncamac.com; daily 4pm-2am; no cover

U BAR

U Bar was formerly Uncles, a legendary gay dive bar. The place has been cleaned up and remodeled but not much else has changed. The friendly neighborhood bar has a decent jukebox and welcoming bartenders, and the crowd typically includes businessmen, old friends, and the occasional college student. On warmer days, the large picture windows are open to the street for great people watching. And if you happen to be a young, cute guy, there are often a few "uncles" willing to buy you a few drinks.

MAP 2: 1220 Locust St., 215/546-6660; daily 11am-2am; no cover

VOYEUR

This is the only club in the Gayborhood that stays open after hours, so while the main floor is often sparsely populated for most of the night, it picks up around 2am for another hour and a half of dancing and debauchery. It has a large mezzanine that offers amazing wraparound views of the main floor below.

MAP 2: 1221 St. James St., 215/735-5772, www.voyeurnightclub.com; Fri.-Sat. 9pm-3:20am, weeknight hours vary, call or check website; cover varies

★ WOODY'S

Woody's is the epicenter of gay nightlife in Philadelphia. The huge venue has half a dozen bars spread out over two floors, an upstairs dance floor, and a restaurant on the street level. The decor is nothing to write home about—think early '80s dive with flourishes of ski lodge—but the bartenders are friendly and they have a heavy hand with the booze and the crowd is diverse and welcoming.

MAP 2: 202 S. 13th St., 215/545-1893, www.woodysbar.com; Tues.-Sun. 4pm-2am; $10 Thurs.-Sat.

LIVE MUSIC
TROCADERO THEATRE

A landmark on the outskirts of Chinatown, this former burlesque theater is one of the city's most versatile venues. The main roster most frequently consists of up-and-coming punk rockers, metal enthusiasts, and the occasional indie rock stalwart courtesy of R5 Productions, and on Monday nights, the venue even doubles as a movie theater, showing both newish releases and cult classics. The Balcony is a smaller venue located on the 2nd floor, providing the pregaming and after parties with DJs and a smaller yet just as mighty stage.

MAP 2: 1003 Arch St., 215/922-6888, www.thetroc.com

WINE BARS
VINTAGE

The wine menu changes regularly, but an excellent selection of at least 60 wines by the glass and around 20 by the bottle are available at this French bistro and wine bar. With most glasses $6-10 and some bottles in the $30 range, it's cheaper than you'd pay for a glass of lesser wine at most bars. An appealing atmosphere, large windows, and high ceilings attract wine and food lovers who come for a mix of classic and creative French dishes.

MAP 2: 129 S. 13th St., 215/922-3095, www.vintage-philadelphia.com; Mon.-Fri. 4pm-2am, Sat.-Sun. 2pm-2am; no cover

BARS

A.BAR

The intimate 42-seat a.bar, situated at the base of the hotel AKA Rittenhouse Square, offers some of the best people watching in one of the most scenic corners of the city. The space itself is polished and minimal, featuring an impressive raw bar as its focal point. In addition to oysters, a.bar serves a selection of seasonal small plates to snack on. Their award-winning wine selection is the perfect complement to the light fare.

MAP 3: 135 S 18th St., 215/825-7030, www.akitchenandbar.com; Mon.-Fri. 11:30am-10pm, Sat. 10am-2:30pm and 3pm-2am, Sun. 10am-2:30pm and 5pm-10pm; no cover

THE BARDS

In a sea of Irish pub imposters, The Bards is the real thing. Any Guinness aficionado (except for the ones who swear by The Plough and the Stars in Old City) will tell you that this is the best place in Philly to grab a pint of the dark stuff. Outfitted in an Irish literary theme, The Bards is a good place to read or write while you sip a pint and feast on fish-and-chips on a quiet weekday afternoon. Weekend nights and Quizzo nights (Thurs. 9pm) are a bit rowdier.

MAP 3: 2013 Walnut St., 215/569-9585, www.bardsirishbar.com; daily noon-2am; no cover

★ BOB & BARBARA'S

Bob & Barbara's is simply cool without having to try. It opened in 1969 and very little has changed. B & B is the originator of the "Citywide Special," a shot of whiskey and a can of Pabst Blue Ribbon for the irresistible price of $3; even if you think you don't like PBR, you'll find yourself craving one after being surrounded by wall-to-wall vintage posters advertising it. An organ combo plays "liquor-drinking music" on weekends, so despite the dirt cheap prices and dirty floors, the place has an air of class. On any given night you'll find a diverse crowd here for various events, including Ping-Pong and bingo tournaments, a drag show, and even a competitive drunken spelling bee. (I once came in second to a guy who had "Born to Spell" tattooed on the inside of his lip.) Bob & Barbara's accepts cash only.

MAP 3: 1509 South St., 215/545-4511, www.bobandbarbaras.com; daily 3pm-2am; no cover

★ FRANKLIN MORTGAGE & INVESTMENT CO.

Blink and you'll miss this clandestine but classy speakeasy. The doors to the basement barroom are pitch-black, and the subtle signage doesn't exactly scream saloon, but once inside and finally seated you'll feel like a mobster. According to the bar's website, in the 1920s the Franklin Mortgage & Investment Co. served as the front for the largest alcohol ring in the country, an operation dwarfing even that of Al Capone. This swank, sexy

Top: Village Whiskey. **Bottom:** Garage.

space pays authentic homage to pre-Prohibition era barrooms with artful, delicious, and strong cocktails. That delicious drink made with only the freshest ingredients will cost you about $14. But you're not just paying for the drink; you're paying for the ambience. Only as many patrons as there are seats may enter at a time, so the bad news is there is often a long wait, especially on weekends, but the good news is you'll also never wait in line for the restroom, fight for the bartender's attention, or feel a sweaty guy breathing down your neck while you're pressed up against the bar.

MAP 3: 112 S. 18th St., 267/467-3277, www.thefranklinbar.com; Mon.-Sat. 5pm-2am, Sun. 5pm-2am; no cover

GOOD DOG

This unassuming bar in the heart of Center City has the feel of a casual neighborhood spot. Featuring canine-themed decor, it's popular with locals for its great food, great location, and great vibe, and is sometimes short on seating. If you can't score a booth downstairs or a table upstairs during high-traffic times, pull up a seat at the bar and order one of the many regionally brewed beers on draft, or head up to the 3rd floor for standing room only. Many people come for the Good Dog signature burger stuffed with Roquefort cheese (voted one of the best burgers in Philly by the premier local food critic) and a side of mixed traditional and sweet potato fries. Food is served until 1am.

MAP 3: 224 S. 15th St., 215/985-9600, www.gooddogbar.com; daily 11:30am-2am; no cover

GRACE TAVERN

This small, unassuming bar on the edge of Center City South was one of the neighborhood's best-kept secrets until one of the major weekly papers, *PW*, named it the number one bar in Philadelphia. Soon, bar-goers from across the city were coming out to enjoy what neighbors have known all along. Pressed tin ceiling and walls and an elegant old-fashioned mirrored bar bring a touch of class to this chill neighborhood spot. The menu is small but mighty, offering a variety of burgers that come with your choice of delicious fries or (almost) equally delicious spicy green beans, along with a few salads, sandwiches, and jambalaya.

MAP 3: 2229 Grays Ferry Ave., 215/893-9580, www.gracetavern.com; daily 11:30am-2am; no cover

McGLINCHEY'S

Somewhat of an urban enigma, this quintessential dive bar is in the heart of the Center City action. Waitresses are charmingly informal and prices are dirt cheap, especially for pitchers of domestic draft classics like Yuengling, Yards, and Rolling Rock, with Guinness not much more. The bar is dark, dingy, and lined with booths. You can order a hot dog with all the fixin's, listen to the rock 'n' roll-packed jukebox, or play Ms. Pac-Man at an old-school sit-down-style game. It's one of the very few places in town where you can still smoke, so be prepared to leave smelling like you did even if you don't. Cash only.

MAP 3: 259 S. 15th St., 215/735-1259, www.mcglincheys.com; Mon.-Sat. 10:30am-2am, Sun. 10:30am-2am; no cover

PUB AND KITCHEN

Just a few blocks from Rittenhouse Square sits one of the best gastropubs in town. Be careful not to miss the cream-colored brick building on the corner of 20th and Lombard with a black pabbit (half pig/half rabbit) painted on the front; there is no sign outside, adding to the allure. While it's most definitely a bar, with its lively scene and a good showing for watching sporting events on the big-screen TVs behind the bar, to come and not try the food would be a real shame. The menu is small, but nothing on it disappoints, from staples like the P&K Cheeseburger and the roasted pork sandwich to more expensive but always delicious entrées that change seasonally and use only the freshest, usually local, ingredients. Save room for dessert; you won't regret it.

MAP 3: 1946 Lombard St., 215/545-0350, http://thepubandkitchen.com; Mon.-Fri. 4pm-2am, Sat.-Sun. 11am-2am; no cover

SIDECAR BAR & GRILLE

Sidecar is a mecca of good food, drink, and fun in an otherwise mostly residential neighborhood. Partly for that reason, but also because it is a really great bar with good vibes, excellent food, and a well-chosen beer list, it is always busy. When the weather is nice, the outdoor tables on two sides nearly double the available seating. Specials throughout the week include an extended weekday happy hour (4pm-7pm) with excellent prices on some of the appetizers and discounts on beer and drinks. The kitchen is open until 1am every night, which is unusual in a town where it can be hard to come by anything other than cheesesteaks past 11pm.

MAP 3: 2201 Christian St., 215/732-3429, www.thesidecarbar.com; Mon.-Fri. 4pm-2am, Sat.-Sun. 9am-2am; no cover

TEN STONE

Just on the edge of Center City, in this rapidly growing stretch of South Street, Ten Stone is a popular spot with both neighbors and students from University City just across the South Street Bridge. A cozy hangout with a pool table, fireplace, dart board, and sports broadcasting on multiple flat screens, the bar serves craft beers and solid pub grub.

MAP 3: 2063 South St., 215/735-9939, www.tenstone.com; Mon.-Sat. 11:30am-2am, Sun. 10am-2am; no cover

★ VILLAGE WHISKEY

Take Philly's own Iron Chef Jose Garces, a tiny space, no reservations accepted, and what many consider the best burgers in the city, and you'll understand why there is always a wait at Village Whiskey. The only Garces

Philly's Music Roots

Philly-born chart-toppers like Pink, Eve, and Will Smith are familiar names to anyone breathing, but Philadelphia's diverse musical history goes well beyond that. Classical composers like Alexander Reinagle, Rayner Taylor, and Susannah Haswell Rowson made their names in the 18th century, while the 19th century was given over to English opera, religious orchestrals, and gospel. In the 20th century, Philly was at the center of the national musical consciousness with vibrant jazz musicians like John Coltrane, Dizzy Gillespie, Eddie Lang, and Joe Venuti.

In the 1950s, Dick Clark took center stage with *American Bandstand,* drawing attention to local acts like Bobby Rydell and Frankie Avalon, as well as the nascent phenomenon known as rock 'n' roll. The '60s and '70s were most notably marked by contributions of African American musicians, including girl groups like Brenda & the Tabulations, Barbara Mason, Claudine Clarke, and the (Patti) LaBelle Sisters. As they fired up the charts, the production team of Gamble and Huff created "The Sound of Philadelphia." TSOP, for short, is a rich, funk-driven sound created with large ensembles of string and horn instruments—a break from the blues-oriented sound of earlier rhythm and blues. The TSOP studio, Philadelphia International Records, still stands at Broad and Spruce Streets.

More recent Philly musicians include Boyz II Men, Lisa Lopes (TLC's "Left Eye"), Eve, Beanie Sigal, the Roots, Jill Scott, Jedi Mind Tricks, Kurt Vile, The War on Drugs, and Meek Mill. Mega DJ and producer Diplo cut his teeth throwing warehouse parties in Philly. The music scene today is as alive as it has ever been; there is a stage and an audience for everyone here in Philly.

spot that is more bar than restaurant and that does not specialize in Latin cuisine, this venue is based around one of his other loves—whiskey. When you finally get a table, choose from more than 80 different whiskeys, served neat or on the rocks, or one of the delicious cocktails. Reminiscent of a classic American speakeasy, the food menu is small, but there's no reason to consider anything other than a perfect, juicy Angus burger with your choice of toppings, like Roquefort cheese, caramelized onions, a fried egg, or truffled mushrooms, all extra—meaning that a $13 burger may cost $20 when you're done with it. The ultimate is the Whiskey King burger ($26), served with blue cheese, applewood-smoked bacon, and a heaping portion of foie gras. And if you're going that far, don't forget to order the duck fat fries. Yum.

MAP 3: 118 S. 20th St., 215/665-1088, www.philadelphia.villagewhiskey.com; Mon. 11:30am-11pm, Tues.-Thurs. 11:30am-midnight, Fri. 11:30am-1am, Sat 10:30am-1am, Sun 10:30am-11pm; no cover

LIVE MUSIC
FIRST UNITARIAN CHURCH
The original venue for R5 Productions, the independent show promotions agency, this Unitarian church has become a renowned house of a different kind of worship for the local punk rock scene. Many of independent rock

music's best up-and-coming acts make their Philly debuts in the church's basement. A small stage offers an intimate perspective that larger venues don't allow, while the loud acts and hyped attendees create an atmosphere worthy of a much larger arena. No alcohol is served, so this is always an all-ages venue.

MAP 3: 2125 Chestnut St., 215/821-7575, www.r5productions.com; hours and entry fee vary depending on event

WINE BARS

★ TRIA

The three stars at Tria are wine, cheese, and beer. Whether you prefer a bold Cabernet or a full-bodied Riesling, the long wine list leaves nothing to be desired. But if you prefer, a selection of microbrewed beers from around the world offers an alternative. Artisan cheeses, cured meats, bruschetta, salads, and sandwiches are offered, and while it's possible to order a relatively simple chicken sandwich, only food virgins should leave without sampling the numerous other sensuous delights. A cheese tasting paired with exotic accompaniments is an essential part of the experience. There is a second location in Center City East (1137 Spruce St., 215/629-9200), and a third Tria outpost, **Tria Taproom** (2005 Walnut St., 215/557-8277), in Center City West, offering an amazing selection of beer and wine on draft, small and large plates, and gourmet brick-oven pizzas.

MAP 3: 123 S. 18th St., 215/972-8742, www.triacafe.com; daily noon-1am; no cover

South Philadelphia   Map 5

BARS

DEVIL'S DEN

This cozy gastropub has an insanely long list of draft and bottle beers to choose from—I mean, like, insane. You'll find pretty much any domestic or imported beer your heart desires; try a generously portioned flight of four if you can't choose just one. You'll find offerings like oysters and mussels in a variety of sauces alongside standard bar fare like burgers and pulled pork sandwiches. Lots of wood, low lighting, and a fireplace make for a pleasant atmosphere. While weekends get busy, this is still a place where you can enjoy conversation without shouting across the table. Stop for beers, brunch, snacks, or a full dinner. Happy hour (Mon.-Fri. 5pm-7pm) offers half-priced drafts and tapas.

MAP 5: 1148 S. 11th St., 215/339-0855, www.devilsdenphilly.com; daily 11am-2am; no cover

GARAGE

Until recently Garage was just another greasy auto garage on Passyunk Avenue. Now it's a lively bar specializing in canned beer and Pickle Backs (a shot of whiskey followed by a pickle juice chaser—try before you judge). Bathed in the neon glow from neighboring Geno's and Pat's Steaks, you are welcome to BYO cheesesteak, but they also host a variety of impressive local chefs in the food cart parked permanently inside the bar. The beer selection is vast, and the food cart offerings are usually very tasty. Garage caters to your inner child with arcade games like pinball and Skee-Ball as well as a pool table. All things considered, the atmosphere is less testosterone fueled then you might expect. There is a second location in Fishtown on Frankford Avenue (100 E Girard Ave.).

MAP 5: 1231 E Passyunk Ave., 215/278-2429, www.garagephilly.com; Mon.-Fri. 5pm-2am, Sat.-Sun. 11am-2am; no cover

THE GOOD KING TAVERN

Bella Vista's cozy French tavern is low-key but on point. Friendly, knowledgeable bartenders serve classic hard-hitting libations with a side of good conversation. Dimly lit with a vintage cherry wood bar, intimate booths, and a pressed-tin ceiling, the decor invokes 1920s Paris. Try the delicious-but-dangerous Sazerac, made with absinthe and rye, or the Vesper (equal parts gin and vodka served up with a dash of the citrusy French aperitif, Lillet). They also serve good, reasonably priced wines and classic French food with daily chalkboard specials.

MAP 5: 614 S 7th St., 215/625-3700, www.thegoodkingtavern.com; daily 5pm-2am; no cover

FOUNTAIN PORTER

Fountain Porter has the bones of a traditional South Philly tavern with a host of hipster-approved upgrades. This cozy little watering hole has a vast and diverse rotating draft beer selection. Bartenders spin classic records on vinyl at conversation-friendly volumes. They also serve a no-frills $5 burger that just so happens to be one of the best in the city. There's really nothing not to love about this gem of a bar.

MAP 5: 1601 S 10th St., 267/324-3910, www.fountainporter.com; Mon.-Fri. 5pm-2am, Sat.-Sun. 11am-2am; no cover

PUB ON PASSYUNK EAST (POPE)

Located in the heart of charming Passyunk Square, the Pub on Passyunk East (POPE for those in the know) is the quintessential corner bar, with dark lighting, stained glass, and an old-fashioned juke box. The crowd is an eclectic mix of old and young South Philadelphians and youngsters from all over the city who come for the great atmosphere. The food menu is basic (stick with simple items like chicken wings or pierogi), but the beer menu is extraordinary. Beer geeks will have a field day here, as fancy beers like Hitachino Nest from Japan are often priced below the norm.

MAP 5: 1501 East Passyunk Ave., 215/755-5125, www.pubonpassyunkeast.com; daily 11am-2am; no cover

ROYAL TAVERN

A gorgeous antique wooden bar is the centerpiece of this great neighborhood bar in Bella Vista, just a few blocks from the Italian Market. The converted row home is usually filled with regulars chatting and drinking at the bar or dining at small tables. There is a solid beer selection as well as tasty, reasonably priced salads, sandwiches, and entrées. While some people come just to drink, the majority come to eat as well.

MAP 5: 937 East Passyunk Ave., 215/389-6694, www.royaltavern.com; Mon.-Fri. 11:30am-2am, Sat.-Sun. 10am-2am; no cover

TATTOOED MOM

This South Street gem's cheap prices and casual, grungy atmosphere make it a popular hangout. The first floor is painted an odd shade of green and has strange sculptures perched just outside its windows, but it could be considered upscale compared to what you'll see when you venture up the stairs. The funky second floor walls are covered in graffiti from floor to ceiling, and two pool tables occupy the entire front room. Farther back is a bar and still farther is a room with a variety of seating, including a few bumper cars. Standard pub fare—poppers and mozzarella sticks—is available on both floors.

MAP 5: 530 South St., 215/238-9880, www.tattooedmomphilly.com; daily noon-2am; no cover

DANCE CLUBS

THE DOLPHIN TAVERN

The Dolphin Tavern was a beloved go-go and billiard bar that closed its doors in 2012. It was dive-y yet comfortable, with the look and feel of a South Philly grandparents' den. This was the place that opened at 6am on the day of the World Series parade and served $1 double shots of whiskey to anyone wearing the Phillies logo. The Dolphin was brought back to life in 2013 by the same team that opened the top-notch concert venue Union Transfer and the Delaware Avenue dance spot, Morgan's Pier. They cleaned it up a bit and replaced the pool tables with a disco dance floor and a DJ booth where some of Philadelphia's best DJs hold court, and burlesque dancers in outrageous costumes keep inhibitions to a minimum.

MAP 5: 1539 South Broad St., 215/278-7950, www.dolphinphilly.com; Wed.-Sat. 8pm-2am; cover varies

L'ETAGE

Just off South Street above the delicious crêperie Beau Monde lies a decadent little dance club that regularly packs the house. The French-themed lounge has a beautiful dark-wood bar, comfy leather banquettes, and a cozy dance floor that gets packed on weekends. Nightly entertainment includes everything from DJs to cabarets and story slams to movies. Check the website to see the calendar. On weekend nights, you can rely on dance-able tunes and a full house; come before 10pm to avoid the $5 cover.

MAP 5: 624 S. 6th St., 215/592-0656, www.creperie-beaumonde.com; Tues.-Thurs. and Sun. 7:30pm-1am, Fri.-Sat. 7pm-2am; cover varies by event, Fri.-Sat. $5 after 10pm

LIVE MUSIC
THEATRE OF LIVING ARTS

Lovingly referred to as the TLA, this South Street staple provides an inti-mate setting for performances by bands ranging from the independent to the infamous. Often an alternative-rock showcase, the venue has hosted many of today's most beloved indie darlings. Patrons can enjoy a great view from anywhere inside with two floors of space and plenty of room to dance.

MAP 5: 334 South St., 215/922-1011, http://venue.tlaphilly.com; cost varies by event

University City

Map 6

BARS
CAVANAUGH'S

Cavanaugh's is University City's premier sports bar. Hosting a rowdy crowd for professional and college games—especially when the Eagles or one of the Big 5 local college basketball games are on—it is a good place to be part of the action if you're into that scene. Food and drink specials abound, ca-tering to the light-walleted college crowd. The local favorite, College Night, draws coeds by the masses for dirt cheap drinks and free pizza. Although at Cavanaugh's, every night is really college night.

MAP 6: 119 S. 39th St., 215/386-4889, www.cavanaughsrestaurant.com; Mon.-Sat. 11am-2am, Sun. noon-2am; no cover

NEW DECK TAVERN

Always bustling, New Deck Tavern is a worthwhile stop on the University City circuit even if you're not a college student. The Irish ivy-covered pub has been delighting not just students but the entire U City community for over two decades. Large portions of tasty bar food and a good selection of beer are served inside or outside on the patio. Quizzo, live acoustic music sessions, and karaoke are regular events.

MAP 6: 3408 Sansom St., 215/386-4800, www.newdecktavern.com; daily 11am-2am; no cover

LIVE MUSIC
ROTUNDA

Straddling the fuzzy line where University City becomes the grittier part of West Philly, the Rotunda offers an excellent reason to cross over. An old church transformed into a community and artistic space now hosts live music and events, including rock, jazz, hip-hop, theater, spoken word, film, DJs, panels, art installations, flea markets, and much more. The alcohol- and smoke-free venue welcomes all ages, and, best of all, most events are free. Audiences are diverse but tend toward the eager undergrad and ac- tivist types. Many attendees enjoy drinks at one of the nearby bars before stumbling in for a free show.

MAP 6: 4014 Walnut St., 215/573-3234, www.therotunda.org; cost varies, but most events are free

WORLD CAFÉ LIVE

World Café Live represents another big step in making University City worth the trip across the river from Center City. Two truly lovely perfor- mance spaces, Upstairs Live and Downstairs Live, have been carved out of an old 40,000-square-foot Art Deco factory building, hosting indepen- dent, contemporary, and folk artists several nights a week. The venue's diverse performance lineup isn't the only draw; it also serves delicious food and drinks. Also housed in the building are the studios for WXPN, the noncommercial radio station whose nationally syndicated *World Café* program gave the venue its name. Come for a show, a meal, or happy hour for discounted drinks and food, weeknights 5pm-6pm and 10pm-11pm.

MAP 6: 3025 Walnut St., 215/222-1400, www.worldcafelive.com; Mon.-Fri. 11am-2am, Sat.-Sun. 5pm-2am; cost varies by event

Northern Liberties   Map 7

BARS
MORGAN'S PIER

Just beneath the Ben Franklin Bridge is Morgan's Pier, a relatively new bar/ restaurant with a cool waterfront vibe. The outdoor bar is named for George C. Morgan, one of the construction workers who helped erect the bridge in the 1920s. Still unfinished, he decided to traverse the width of the river by tightrope, walking along a thin beam. He reached Camden and was fired on the spot. Morgan's Pier recalls that era with Boardwalk Empire-inspired decor. During the day and early evening, the breezy Pier is a restaurant, serving upscale picnic fare and craft beer. At night, it's a raucous club fea- turing local and international DJs and live music.

MAP 7: 221 N. Columbus Blvd., 215/279-7134, www.morganspier.com; May-Sept. Mon.-Fri. 4pm-2am, Sat.-Sun. 11am-2am; cover varies

700 CLUB

On other days, the 700 Club is just a neighborhood hangout, but on Thursday-Saturday nights after 10pm, the 2nd floor becomes a sweaty free- for-all as the DJ spins hip-hop, indie rock, and '80s music for the mostly

Philadelphia Craft Beer

Yards Brewing Co.

Beer has always been a big part of Philadelphia's culture. According to a letter written by William Penn, early Philadelphians home brewed their beer from scratch using molasses infused with sassafras or pine. During the 19th century, the neighborhood known as Brewerytown, on the banks of the Schuylkill River, became a hub of commercial beer production. At its peak, more than 90 breweries operated within the city proper, many within a concentrated ten-block area in Brewerytown. Sadly, the beer boom came to an end in 1917, when Congress passed the 18th Amendment prohibiting the sale and transportation of alcohol. All breweries were ordered to cease production.

Today, Philadelphia is once again one of the nation's best beer towns, chock-full of award-winning gastropubs and breweries. Local beer production is alive and well. There are the well-known and widely distributed **craft breweries** like Flying Fish, Victory, Yards, Sly Fox, and local favorite Philadelphia Brewing Company; **big brewpubs** like Dock Street and Iron Hill; and newer **microbreweries** like Crime and Punishment and Earth Bread and Brewery that continue to spring up, winning accolades and broadening the scope of local production. Rare brews from near and far are commonplace on the menus of fine dining establishments and dive bars alike.

Most breweries offer tours and tastings at their facilities, but if you're interested in a different kind of beer experience, try one of the following:

- **Philly Beer Week** (www.phillybeerweek.org), held each June, brings countless beer events—but in reality, every week is beer week here.

- The **Philadelphia Horticultural Society** (215/988-8800, www.phsonline.org) has created pop-up beer gardens—temporary outdoor gastropubs that hold court in all types of unusual places, from the Philadelphia Zoo to the rooftops of abandoned buildings.

- A number of organizations such as **Philly Brew Tours** (215/866-2337, www.phillybrewtours.com), **Urban Adventures** (215/280-3746, www.urbanadventures.com) and **Liberty Brew Tours** (267/606-7403, www.libertybrewtours.com), organize brewery-hopping tours imbued with the storied local history.

The Best in Indie Music: R5 Productions

Born in 1996, R5 is a local promotion company named for the SEPTA regional rail that connects the Main Line to Center City. Founded by Ardmore native Sean Agnew with the express purpose of bringing back quality indie rock to a city that was often skipped over by touring bands due to lack of suitable venues, the idea was to give audiences big shows in small spaces for a more intimate live-music experience. With no alcohol served and generally low prices, the shows cater to all ages, but especially to the younger set. R5 has hosted many of today's best names in indie music at a variety of small-but-mighty venues, including the staple **First Unitarian Church;** bars, like **The Barbary** and **Johnny Brenda's;** and dance halls, like **Starlight Ballroom.** In 2011 Agnew opened his own place, **Union Transfer,** a beautiful midsize music venue.

R5 Productions has become synonymous with Philadelphia's independent music scene. Punk and indie crowds no longer need to travel to New York or DC to see their favorite acts play, nor do they have to pay double admission price to see old favorites play larger, overcrowded clubs and arenas. Likewise, bands can come to Philly and play to the whole audience and not just to the people in the front row. And the fact that many of them come at all, as opposed to a decade ago, can be gratefully attributed to R5. Agnew's philosophy is "for the kids, by the kids," and no self-respecting music lover in Philly would have it any other way. Check out www.r5productions.com for lineup and venue information.

twentysomething crowd. It looks and feels like Grandma's house—complete with old, musty furniture and a pseudo-kitchenette as a bar—but the lights are low enough to hide the stains on the upholstery and to encourage you to dance like no one is watching. The 700 Club takes you back to the days of high school parties, when your parents were out of town, and drinking was an exhilarating, illicit event. Best of all, there is never a cover, and drinks are reasonably priced. This is also a great place to catch local and international soccer games on the telly.

MAP 7: 700 N. 2nd St., 215/413-3181, www.the700.org; Mon.-Sat. 4pm-2am, Sun. 2pm-2am; no cover

★ **SILK CITY**

Part diner and part dance club, Silk City is your one-stop shop for Saturday night. Formerly a truck stop called DeeDee's Diner, a hole-in-the-wall serving cheap booze and beer out of questionable taps, Silk City is now one of the most popular party spots in the city. One side is a snazzy diner and bar serving gussied-up food that goes beyond standard diner fare. The adjoining club/lounge hosts popular DJs and live acts, and a Saturday night dance party is always packed. The outdoor beer garden is a lovely place to knock a few back on a nice summer night.

MAP 7: 435 Spring Garden St., 215/592-8838, www.silkcityphilly.com; bar and diner daily 10am-2am, lounge usually 10pm-2am; cover usually $5-10 for club, no cover for diner

W/N W/N

Pronounced "win win," this cooperatively owned combination coffee shop and cocktail bar is the kind of progressive, original concept that one might only expect to find in Philadelphia. Located directly across the street from Union Transfer, W/N W/N is a great place to meet for a drink pre or post show. The crowd is usually young, diverse, and artistic, and their dance parties tend to be unforgettably raucous. Check their calendar before you go because depending on the night you'll either find patrons reading quietly or swinging from the rafters.

MAP 7: 931 Spring Garden St., www.winwincoffeebar.com; Tues.-Thurs. 5pm-midnight, Sat. 11am-2am, Sun. 11am-midnight; no cover

LIVE MUSIC
ELECTRIC FACTORY

Founded in 1968 and housed in a converted electric factory, this archetypal Philly venue has two floors, each equipped with a full bar and seating area, ensuring ample visibility and elbow room from every section. With a performance roster ranging from mainstream radio's premier rock bands to the newest hip-hop crazes, the Factory has become a rite of passage for bands graduating from the smaller local venues and the fans willing to follow them.

MAP 7: 421 N. 7th St., 215/627-1332, www.electricfactory.info; cost varies by event

★ UNION TRANSFER

Union Transfer is arguably Philly's best live music venue. Part owner, R5 Productions creator Sean Agnew, spent more than a decade independently promoting shows at DIY venues throughout the city before opening Union Transfer in 2011. The 1,000-person-capacity venue is large enough to host some of the biggest names in indie rock and hip-hop without feeling soulless like some other comparably sized corporate venues. The cavernous space was built in the early 1900s as a farmers market and luggage depot and still has many of its original features, like wood-paneled walls, sweeping cathedral ceilings, stained-glass windows, and antique chandeliers. It was redesigned with the concertgoers' interests at heart, and sight lines and sound quality at a premium. There is not a bad seat in the house, and the sound is impeccable.

MAP 7: 1026 Spring Garden St., 215/232-2100, www.utphilly.com; cost varies by event

NIGHTLIFE NORTHERN LIBERTIES

Top: Barcade. **Bottom:** Frankford Hall.

BARS

BARCADE

Located on Frankford Avenue, the warehouse-lined industrial zone turned nightlife hotspot. This Brooklyn transplant is a combination bar and arcade, featuring classic video games and craft beer. The spacious converted garage holds more than 40 antique arcade games and a lengthy, ever-rotating list of premium ales. Nostalgia and beer is a heady combination for the generation that grew up on games like Donkey Kong and Ms. Pac-Man.

MAP 7: 1114 Frankford Ave., 215/634-4400, www.barcadephiladelphia.com; Mon.-Thurs. 3pm-2am, Fri.-Sun. noon-2am; no cover

LOCO PEZ

Tucked into a mostly residential fold of Fishtown, Loco Pez ("crazy fish" in Spanish) was a neighborhood dive bar reanimated as a hipster taco joint. With its wallpaper and wood paneling, dim yellow lighting, drop ceiling, and Formica countertops, the bar looks like a 70s time capsule. Once a week Loco Pez features a dollar taco night, which is announced the day-of on the restaurant's Facebook page. Their margaritas are perfect, made with fresh ingredients and not too sweet, and they have an excellent selection of tequila to choose from.

MAP 7: 2401 E Norris St., 267/886-8061, www.locopez.com; Mon.-Fri. 5pm-2am, daily 11am-2am; no cover

★ FRANKFORD HALL

Frankford Hall is Philadelphia's most popular German-style beer garden. The spacious open-air courtyard has communal picnic-table seating and the bar serves up seasonal drafts in massive steins. Outdoor heat lamps make the garden usable even in the chillier months, while indoor seating is also available. With his trademark showmanship, Stephen Starr transformed this old warehouse into one of the most popular bars in Fishtown. On weekends there are often lines around the block, especially on warm nights. The concession-style kitchen keeps with the German theme, serving cheese spaetzle, pork schnitzel, and half a dozen styles of sausage. Ping-Pong tables and board games give the place a playful, festive vibe.

MAP 7: 1210 Frankford Ave., 215/634-3338, www.frankfordhall.com; Mon.-Fri. 4pm-2am, Sat. noon-2am, Sun. 11:30am-2am; no cover

JOHNNY BRENDA'S

Johnny Brenda's is the embodiment of Fishtown's alternative, effortlessly cool vibe. The charmingly rustic music venue and bar serves surprisingly excellent seafood, including oysters on the half shell and exclusively local craft beer. The intimate 2nd-floor concert venue that was handcrafted from a converted flophouse was a backdrop for the latest *Rocky* installment,

Creed. The performance space boasts spectacular sound quality and a bar and balcony worthy of a much larger arena. The venue hosts local and international bands and even the occasional private party, which—thanks to its size and setting—is essentially what every concert at Johnny Brenda's feels like.

MAP 7: 1201 N. Frankford Ave., 215/739-9684, www.johnnybrendas.com; daily 11am-2am; bar and restaurant no cover; stage and dance areas cover varies by event

COMEDY CLUBS
PUNCH LINE PHILLY

Punch Line Philly, a comedy club on Frankford Avenue, has filled a niche in Fishtown's nightlife scene. The club is owned and operated by Live Nation, the national entertainment corporation that also owns the 2,500-capacity music venue next door, The Fillmore. Punch Line, which is tiny by comparison, has an intimate, "anything goes" atmosphere. Legendary comedian Dave Chappelle was the first performer to christen the stage at Punch Line Philly's grand opening in 2016. You can expect more big names to light up the little stage.

MAP 7: 33 E Laurel St., 215/309-0150, www.punchlinephilly.com, cost varies by event

DANCE CLUBS
THE BARBARY

The Barbary is one of the wildest dance clubs in Philadelphia. Catering to a mostly early 20s hipster crowd, this dive-y night club is either your idea of heaven or hell. The two-story bar is regularly filled to capacity with a sweaty, gyrating mob. Owned by a prominent Philly DJ, the club hosts varied weekly and monthly dance parties. There are indie rock, hip-hop, and retro nights, karaoke parties on Sundays, and the occasional live act. A visit to The Barbary usually results in a hazy yet memorable evening; be sure to document it in their awesome photo booth.

MAP 7: 951 Frankford Ave., 215/634-7400; daily 10pm-2am; cover varies by event

Arts and Culture

Old City 168

Center City East................ 173

Center City West.............. 177

Museum District............... 178

South Philadelphia 181

University City................. 182

Northern Liberties............. 183

Fairmount Park 184

Greater Philadelphia........... 186

Look for ★ to find
recommended arts venues

Highlights

★ **Best Art House Cinema:** Between the three Ritz movie houses run by **Landmark Theatres** in Old City, you can always find that foreign, indie, or artsy movie you've been dying to see (page 168).

★ **Best Concert Halls:** The **Academy of Music** (page 173), built in 1857, and the **Kimmel Center** (page 174), built in 2001, are Philly's most esteemed world-class venues. The two superstars of the Avenue of the Arts also represent the best of historic and modern architecture in Philly.

★ **Most Contentious Museum:** The **Barnes Foundation,** home to one of the world's finest collections of postimpressionist art, settled into a spectacular space on the Benjamin Franklin Parkway after a court battle decided its location (page 178).

★ **Most Interactive Museum: The Franklin Institute** showcases the best scientific advancements in history. The interactive museum is a giant playground for adults and children alike (page 179).

★ **Best Kids' Museum:** The hands-on exhibits at the sprawling **Please Touch Museum** are so much fun that kids won't realize they're learning (page 184).

The Franklin Institute

P hiladelphia is brimming with world-class museums, theaters, and galleries. There are museums devoted to practically every slice of Philadelphia's rich history and diverse culture, from renowned art, science, and history museums to museums honoring different ethnic groups. Top national acts and shows pass through Philly every day. And the contemporary art scene is expansive, ranging from the up-and-comers to the nationally known.

The Benjamin Franklin Parkway, dubbed the Museum District, is home to some of the biggest and best, including the Philadelphia Museum of Art, the Rodin Museum, Academy of Natural Sciences, The Franklin Institute, and the Barnes Foundation, which relocated from its suburban home to Center City in 2012.

The Avenue of the Arts, the section of Broad Street that extends south from City Hall, is home to most of the city's first-run theater and classical concert venues, from the grand old Academy of Music to the stunningly modern Kimmel Center. Additional concert venues are spread throughout the city, ranging from the huge Wells Fargo Center, hosting the top national acts, to casual, open-air stadiums like the Mann Center for the Performing Arts in Fairmount Park.

The multitude of art galleries, large and small, range from traditional to "outsider," and ongoing events and open houses like First Fridays make them accessible to everyone. Galleries can be found all over the city, selling and showcasing items that range from reasonably priced to limited-edition, nationally known pieces. The galleries around Rittenhouse tend to be at the high end, while Northern Liberties and Chinatown are home

Previous: the Academy of Natural Sciences; the Barnes Foundation.

to more independent artists and co-ops, and Old City has the greatest concentration of galleries of all kinds. Listings here are a small sampling of what is available, but there are way too many to even begin to scratch the surface. Visit www.visitphilly.com/music-art/art-museums-galleries/ for many more listings.

Check *PW*, the free weekly paper for listings of special events at the numerous museums, theaters, galleries, and concert venues. Also, note that the Philadelphia Museum of Art is listed in the *Sights* chapter rather than here because it is an iconic sight to behold both inside and out.

Old City

Map 1

CINEMA
★ LANDMARK THEATRES

When Philadelphians want to see movies that don't feature loud explosions, foolish gags, or flashy nudity, they usually head to one of the Ritz movie houses in Old City. A total of 12 screens are spread out over the three different Ritz theaters: **Ritz at the Bourse, Ritz Five,** and **Ritz East.** Concessions include the standards—Jujubes and Raisinets—along with more upscale offerings that vary by theater but may include Toblerone and Lindt chocolates, yogurt-covered pretzels, coffee, and tea. The art house chain was acquired by Landmark Theatres, but the theaters maintain the Ritz name along with its mix of independent, international, and all-around good artsy-fartsy programming. There is a parking lot at the Bourse and Ritz East; have your ticket validated at any of the theaters for a reduced rate.

MAP 1 DETAIL: Ritz 5 (214 Walnut St.), 215/440-1184; Ritz at the Bourse (400 Ranstead St.), 215/440-1181; and Ritz East (125 S. 2nd St.), 215/925-7900, www.landmarktheatres.com

GALLERIES
CLAY STUDIO

For more than 40 years, the Clay Studio has been a veritable fixture in Philadelphia's urban art community. As you walk down the hallway leading to the gallery, which features funky mosaic tile work by local artist-celeb Isaiah Zagar (of the Magic Gardens), you'll know you're in for a treat. The gallery displays juried solo exhibits, work from local emerging ceramists, and artists from its highly competitive studio-run residency and fellowship programs. The Clay Studio offers a little something for every taste, ranging from functional vessels like coffee mugs and vases to more conceptual work like sculptures and installations.

MAP 1: 139 N. 2nd St., 215/925-3453, www.theclaystudio.org; Tues.-Sat. 11am-6pm, Sun. noon-6pm; free

Art for All: First Fridays

First Friday has become the most popular ongoing event in the city since its start in 1991. On the first Friday evening of each month, art galleries throughout the city open their doors to the public for free, some with the added allure of free wine, beer, snacks, and even music, creating a festive atmosphere. The galleries feature practically every form of art, including painting, drawing, photographs, designer furniture, crafts, glass, and more, which range from traditional to truly offbeat. While some of it is relatively affordable for purchase, many people go out just to look. Most galleries are open 5pm-9pm.

While the nexus of the action is in Old City between Market and Vine and Front and 3rd Streets (visit www.oldcityarts.org for more information), additional events are springing up with increasing frequency in other areas of the city, especially in the artist enclaves of Northern Liberties and Fishtown. In addition, some of those galleries hold open houses on **Second Thursdays,** distinguishing themselves from the more mainstream First Friday. **Crane Arts** (1400 N. American St., 215/232-3203, www.cranearts. com), home to artist studios and a gallery space, holds ongoing Second Thursday events.

SNYDERMAN-WORKS GALLERIES

In an expansive 6,000-square-foot space in Old City, this popular gallery is considered by some to be a must-see on the national art circuit. Formerly two different complementary galleries, the Snyderman Gallery and the Works Gallery, they are now commingled. Among other things, the gallery showcases the continually evolving areas of studio furniture and sculptural glass, and hosted one of the first exhibits of Dale Chihuly's renowned botanical glass work and architect Robert Venturi's furniture designs for Knoll. It is also dedicated to ceramics, jewelry, textiles, and fiber. Stark white walls, two-story rooms, and delicate work atop a series of pillars offer a lovely setting for intricate handiwork in a variety of materials.

MAP 1: 303 Cherry St., 215/238-9576, www.snyderman-works.com; Tues.-Sat. 10am-6pm; free

MUSEUMS

AFRICAN AMERICAN MUSEUM IN PHILADELPHIA

Founded in 1976 in honor of the bicentennial celebration, the African American Museum in Philadelphia was the first museum in a major U.S. city dedicated to celebrating African American culture and history. The museum holds over 750,000 objects, including arts, artifacts, clothing, furniture, weapons, documents, photographs, records, and diaries highlighting the African diaspora, African American history in Philadelphia, and the contemporary achievements of African Americans. With frequent additions of permanent and rotating exhibits, the museum also hosts a variety of lectures and educational programming.

MAP 1: 701 Arch St., 215/574-0380, www.aampmuseum.org; Thurs.-Sat. 10am-5pm, Sun. noon-5pm; $14 adult, $10 senior, student, and child (4-12)

FIREMAN'S HALL MUSEUM

Benjamin Franklin had the unprecedented idea of starting a fire insurance company in Philadelphia in the 1730s; he is just one of many people and advancements honored at the Fireman's Hall Museum, which is operated by the Philadelphia Fire Department. Housed in a restored 1902 firehouse, the museum pays tribute to the brave men and women who fight fires and risk their lives for public safety. The collection of firefighting history and memorabilia includes an array of axes, hoses, tools, fire trucks, and parade badges dating as far back as the 1800s.

MAP 1: 147 N. 2nd St., 215/923-1438, www.firemanshall.org; Tues.-Sat. 10am-4:30pm, 10am-9pm first Fri. of month; free, donations accepted

INDEPENDENCE SEAPORT MUSEUM

Independence Seaport Museum explores the city's rich maritime history in a fitting location on Penn's Landing, overlooking the Delaware River. The exhibits *Bound for Philadelphia* and *Coming to America* highlight the city's immigration history and its importance in the growth of the nation's population, while exploring the hardships and hazards often faced by immigrants who crossed the Atlantic in search of a new life. Enjoy the excellent views of the Delaware River throughout many of the exhibit spaces, making it easy to imagine the people landing on that very shore in centuries past. Exhibits about small crafts, industrial shipping, and deep-diving technology add a modern aspect to the museum. While you're here, you can explore the USS *Olympia,* which served as a flagship in the Spanish-American War, and the USS *Becuna,* a World War II submarine. Both National Historic Landmarks are open during museum hours, and on the first Saturday of each month (noon-4pm) get a behind-the-scenes guided tour of the ship, including areas normally closed to the public.

MAP 1: Penn's Landing, 211 S. Columbus Blvd., 215/413-8655, www.phillyseaport.org; daily 10am-5pm; $16 adult, $12 senior, child (3-12), student, and military

NATIONAL LIBERTY MUSEUM

Just two blocks from the Liberty Bell and Independence Hall, the National Liberty Museum celebrates the profound accomplishment of creating a free society. The museum's varied galleries explore topics of heroism, freedom, diversity, faith, and more, and pay homage to people who have contributed to the creation of a free country. The fine art gallery features an array of sculptures, paintings, and an impressive collection of delicate glass works that explore the idea of the beauty and fragility of freedom. Galleries

Top: Ritz at the Bourse. Bottom: Independence Seaport Museum.

include *Coming to America, Heroes from Around the World,* and *Heroes of 9/11 Memorial.*
MAP 1 DETAIL: 321 Chestnut St., 215/925-2800, www.libertymuseum.org; daily 10am-5pm; $7 adult, $6 senior, $5 student, $2 child (5-17), $15 family

NATIONAL MUSEUM OF AMERICAN JEWISH HISTORY

The only museum in the world that tells the story of more than 360 years of Jewish life in America is in the heart of Philadelphia's Independence Mall. The museum is a strikingly modern five-story, 100,000-square-foot building with an all-glass facade symbolizing accessibility, the open nature of America, and the fragility of democracy. The museum celebrates this history through more than 30,000 artifacts, permanent and rotating exhibits, and interactive displays. While the focus of several other museums, most notably the United States Holocaust Memorial Museum in Washington, DC, is on the Jewish experience before coming to America and the oppression and genocide of Jews, this museum is about the accomplishments, struggles, and experiences of Jews here in America. Beginning with the first permanent Jewish settlement in 1654 and continuing through to the present day, the museum tells diverse stories of Jews in America.
MAP 1 DETAIL: 101 S. Independence Mall East (N. 5th St. btwn Market and Ludlow Sts.), 215/923-3811, www.nmajh.org; Tues.-Fri. 10am-5pm, Sat.-Sun. 10am-5:30pm, closed on major U.S. and Jewish holidays; $12 adult, $11 senior and youth (13-21), free 12 and under and active military

PHILADELPHIA HISTORY MUSEUM

This Greek Revival building on the edge of Old City originally housed The Franklin Institute until it was relocated to its current large space on the Benjamin Franklin Parkway. The long neglected Philadelphia History Museum (formerly the Atwater Kent) reopened in 2012 after a three-year, multimillion dollar renovation. Dedicated to all things Philly history related, the museum has an extensive if disparate collection of Philadelphia artifacts. Anything from George Washington's presidential desk to Joe Frazier's boxing gloves can be found at the museum. Since their high-tech renovation, visitors can further explore any topic that piques their interest on electronic tablets.
MAP 1: 15 S. 7th St., 215/685-4830, www.philadelphiahistory.org; Tues.-Sat. 10:30am-4:30pm; $10 adult, $8 senior, $6 student, free 12 and under

POLISH AMERICAN CULTURAL CENTER AND MUSEUM

This small museum in the heart of Old City honors Polish culture and heritage and celebrates the contributions of its citizens to the United States and the world. The center was founded in February 1981 and offers a small display of memorabilia and biographical materials about famous Poles, including religious leader John Cardinal Krol, Revolutionary War heroes Thaddeus Kosciuszko and Casimir Pulaski, composers Fryderyk Chopin and Ignacy Jan Paderewski, and scientists Marie Curie and Nicholas

Copernicus. There is a prominent display on Pope John Paul II. Exhibits highlight Polish traditions that immigrants brought to the United States, including *pisanki* (painted Easter eggs) and decorative wooden plates.

MAP 1 DETAIL: 308 Walnut St., 215/922-1700, www.polishamericancenter.org; Jan.-Apr. Mon.-Fri. 10am-4pm, May-Dec. Mon.-Sat. 10am-4pm; free

THEATER
ARDEN THEATRE COMPANY
When it moved from Center City to Old City in 1995, the Arden Theatre helped reinvigorate what was then still an old industrial neighborhood on the verge of transformation. Since 1988, Arden has been producing top-quality productions of plays, musicals, and children's shows. On its 360-seat main stage and 175-seat blackbox, shows range from reinterpretations of Shakespeare and Shaw to works by emerging playwrights.

MAP 1: 40 N. 2nd St., 215/922-1122, www.ardentheatre.org

PAINTED BRIDE ART CENTER
The Painted Bride Art Center was founded in 1969, and it moved from South Street to Old City in 1982—long before the former warehouse neighborhood was the hot spot it is today. Stepping past the colorful mirror-and-tile mosaic exterior, you'll enter a large gallery space showcasing the works of daring young artists. The theater features dance, world music, performance, jazz, and more, plus many socially conscious or political works with a focus on advocacy for excluded communities. The Bride features local faves and international stars and is responsible for Philadelphia's longest-running jazz series.

MAP 1: 230 Vine St., 215/925-9914, www.paintedbride.org

Center City East
Map 2

CONCERT VENUES
★ ACADEMY OF MUSIC
Nobly dubbed the Grand Old Lady of Broad Street, the Academy of Music has been a proud institution since 1857. It is the oldest grand opera house in the United States still functioning as an opera house today. The regal Renaissance theater is adorned with wood carvings, ceiling murals, and a massive crystal chandelier hanging elegantly overhead. Home to the Opera Company of Philadelphia and the Pennsylvania Ballet, the Academy of Music is no stranger to the most gifted musicians that come through the city. Over the years it has hosted Igor Stravinsky, Richard Strauss, Pyotr Tchaikovsky, Joan Sutherland, and a myriad of other world-renowned artists and composers.

MAP 2: Broad and Locust Sts., 215/893-1999, www.academyofmusic.org

The Kimmel Center opened its doors in 2001 and provided the city with a venue that easily deserves the bold label of world-class. Architect Rafael Viñoly and acoustics company Artec Consultants combined efforts in creating this magnificent crown jewel of the Avenue of the Arts. With two posh theaters, imported exotic wood finishes, and a soaring vaulted glass ceiling rising 150 feet above the lobby, the Kimmel is breathtaking. Its resident companies include the renowned Philadelphia Orchestra, the Chamber Orchestra of Philadelphia, and the Philadelphia Chamber Music Society, but it's much more than just a venue for "ladies who lunch." The Kimmel is also home to local dance company PhilaDanco and a pop orchestra, Peter Nero and the Philly Pops. It also is the venue for many of the biggest name concerts that come through Philadelphia, with shows spanning every musical genre, along with many free concerts. Performances are held in the innovative music halls, offering incredible acoustics and aesthetics. The expansive Verizon Hall seats over 2,500 on its red velvet chairs, and the more intimate Perelman Theater holds 650. Before or after a performance, you can stroll through the Dorrance H. Hamilton Roof Garden to enjoy the great views. If you can't come for a show, come and take the free hour-long tour of the venue, offered daily at the information desk at 1pm.

MAP 2: 260 S. Broad St., 215/790-5800, www.kimmelcenter.org

GALLERIES

FABRIC WORKSHOP AND MUSEUM

The only nonprofit arts organization of its kind in the United States, the Fabric Workshop and Museum is devoted to creating new work in new materials. The museum and shop is a successful collaboration between emerging and famous artists experimenting with a multitude of unfamiliar media—often, but not solely, fabric. Founded in 1977, the museum displays permanent and rotating exhibits. Located in a former industrial building near the Convention Center, it contains three exhibition galleries, a video lounge, a shop, and artist studios. Just down the street, the **New Temporary Contemporary** (1222 Arch St.) offers additional exhibition space.

MAP 2: 1214 Arch St., 215/561-8888, www.fabricworkshopandmuseum.org; Mon.-Fri. 10am-6pm, Sat.-Sun. noon-5pm; free

SPACE 1026

This well-known collaborative art space/gallery hosts quirky events and sometimes also doubles as a venue for indie bands, performances, and film screenings. Occupying two floors of space used by a community of local artists and art enthusiasts, it often displays work that has roots in pop surrealism and comic books, and specializes in screen printing. Unique shows such as a flipbook festival are not uncommon. There are no official hours, but you can stop by anytime and ring the bell or call ahead to make sure someone is there to let you in.

MAP 2: 1026 Arch St., 2nd Fl., 215/574-7630, www.space1026.com; no official hours; free

Top: the Academy of Music. Bottom: the Kimmel Center.

MUSEUMS

PENNSYLVANIA ACADEMY OF THE FINE ARTS

Having recently celebrated its 200th anniversary—take that, Guggenheim!—the Pennsylvania Academy of the Fine Arts is the oldest art school and museum in the country. Inside the National Historic Landmark building, holdings include paintings and other artworks by many of the masters, including Cecilia Beaux, William Merritt Chase, Frank Duveneck, Thomas Eakins, Winslow Homer, Childe Hassam, and Edmund Tarbell. Eakins was also a controversial and paradigm-shifting director of PAFA. Now, the academy he led is one of the most prestigious art schools in America—a must-see for any art lover. The **Morris Gallery** exhibitions on the ground floor are free.

MAP 2: 118 N. Broad St., 215/972-7600, www.pafa.org; Tues., Thurs., Fri. 10am-5pm, Wed. 10am-9pm, Sat-Sun. 11am-5pm; $15 adult, $12 senior, student, and youth (13-18), free child 12 and under

THEATER

FORREST THEATRE

Built in the late 1920s by the Shubert organization and named for legendary 19th-century actor Edwin Forrest, the Forrest Theatre hosts traveling musicals, comedies, and dramas. With most first-run Broadway fare setting up shop at the nearby Academy of Music, it is frequently empty, which is unfortunate since the building is lovely. If you get a chance to see a show in this historic theater, you will not be disappointed.

MAP 2: 1114 Walnut St., 800/447-7400, www.forrest-theatre.com

PHILADELPHIA THEATRE COMPANY AND SUZANNE ROBERTS THEATRE

The first of several eager young theater companies to take 1970s Philly by storm, the Philadelphia Theatre Company has evolved into one of the most respected arts organizations in the region. Not content to merely rehash classics or safely import successful traveling shows, it has held over 100 world and Philadelphia premieres by playwrights including Terrance McNally, Christopher Durang, and Naomi Wallace. But the plays aren't the only new and exciting thing for the company; after a long residency at the small Plays & Players Theater in the Rittenhouse neighborhood, in 2007 the company moved into its stunning new home, named the Suzanne Roberts Theatre for its benefactor. The 370-seat theater is among the city's top theaters on the Avenue of the Arts.

MAP 2: 480 S. Broad St., 215/985-0420, www.phillytheatreco.org

WALNUT STREET THEATRE

The official state theater of Pennsylvania is the Walnut Street Theatre, the oldest continually operating theater in the English-speaking world. It opened in 1809 as a circus house but is now known for more high-minded productions. Luminaries who have graced its stage include Edwin Booth,

Marlon Brando, Henry and Jane Fonda, Audrey Hepburn, and Sidney **177**

Poitier. Besides the 1,000-plus-seat main theater, it also holds Studios 3
and 5, smaller houses for second-stage productions and rentals to outside
theater companies.

MAP 2: 825 Walnut St., 215/574-3550, www.walnutstreettheatre.org

WILMA THEATER

We may never get to see David Mamet in drag, but the Wilma Theater is
named after Shakespeare's fictional female alter ego. Since the early 1970s,
the company has been staging daring, tradition-defying productions of new
plays and classics, including works by Tom Stoppard, Sophocles, Arthur
Miller, Tennessee Williams, Bertolt Brecht, and, yes, Mamet. Even in its
beautiful and spacious home on the Avenue of the Arts, it hasn't lost the
intimate feeling that makes small theaters so appealing.

MAP 2: 265 S. Broad St., 215/546-7824, www.wilmatheater.org

Center City West Map 3

CONCERT VENUES
CURTIS INSTITUTE OF MUSIC

One of the most prestigious music conservatories in the world occupies
an equally prestigious spot in the heart of Rittenhouse Square. While its
foremost goal is teaching gifted students classical music, it was founded on
the philosophy of learning by doing. Performances include operas; orchestra, solo, and chamber music recitals; and a family concert series. While
some performances are held at other nearby theaters, many are held on-
site at Field Concert Hall. Prices vary greatly, but more than 100 student
concerts are free and open to the public. They are generally held Monday,
Wednesday, and Friday at 8pm; call the student hotline (215/893-7902) to
confirm.

MAP 3: 1726 Locust St., 215/893-7902, www.curtis.edu

MUSEUMS
MUTTER MUSEUM

Gross or cool? The Mutter Museum, a fascinating showcase of medical
oddities founded in 1858 by the College of Physicians of Philadelphia, is a
little bit of both. Exhibits include a wall of real eyeballs, President Grover
Cleveland's tumor, the tallest skeleton in the country, and the world's largest colon. Impressive portraits and other artworks by famous Philadelphia
artists Thomas Eakins and John Singer Sargent are on display alongside
body parts in jars. With such a weird array of science and medicine, you
are bound to learn something—if you can stomach it.

MAP 3: 19 S. 22nd St., 215/560-8564, http://muttermuseum.org; daily 10am-5pm; $16
adult, $14 senior, $11 student and youth (6-17), $13 military, free 5 and under

THEATER
ADRIENNE THEATRE

Just a quick walk from Rittenhouse Square but worlds away from the big theater houses on the Avenue of the Arts, the Adrienne Theatre offers an intimate space for small theater companies. Actually, it offers three different spaces of varying sizes. Named for theater professional Adrienne Neye, the theater hosts resident companies, including ComedySportz, an interactive improv comedy show. The largest resident company is the socially minded InterAct Theatre, whose mission is to produce plays that explore the cultural, social, and political issues of the day. The intention is admirable, so we'll look the other way if InterAct's sometimes heavy-handed productions are a touch didactic. Still, when good, these shows hit a real nerve, whether they're examining America's appetite for war, complex racial questions, or the role of the outsider in society. One thing's certain: You'll find works here that broach topics no other company will touch, and the mission is admirable and necessary.

MAP 3: 2030 Sansom St., 215/568-8077, www.adriennelive.org

Museum District
Map 4

MUSEUMS
ACADEMY OF NATURAL SCIENCES

A skeleton replica of a 42-foot-long, 7.5-ton *Tyrannosaurus rex* smiling with razor-sharp teeth greets guests upon entering the Academy of Natural Sciences. From dinosaurs to apes to tigers, the exhibits take visitors through evolutionary history from the Mesozoic era to the present day, capturing animal life across the planet in glass-enclosed, realistic-looking habitat displays. Children love to take part in archaeological digs and to see the live animal exhibits.

MAP 4: 1900 Benjamin Franklin Pkwy., 215/299-1000, www.ansp.org; Mon.-Fri. 10am-4:30pm, Sat.-Sun. 10am-5pm; $17.95 adult (over 13), $13.95 child (3-12), $14.95 senior, and military, free under 3, additional fee for special exhibits

★ BARNES FOUNDATION

Eccentric art collector Albert C. Barnes probably never could have imagined his little art collection would cause such trouble. His legacy, the Barnes Foundation, is an awesome multibillion-dollar collection of Impressionist and Expressionist works by Cézanne, Gauguin, El Greco, Goya, Manet, Matisse, Modigliani, Monet, Picasso, Renoir, and Van Gogh, along with impressive African sculptures and much, much more. Cosseted away at Barnes's former estate in the Philadelphia suburbs of Merion since the 1920s, the collection was embroiled in a lengthy battle over whether to move to a more accessible Center City location. Some of the same suburban neighbors who complained about visitor traffic fought for it to stay once they realized they might lose it, while Philadelphia city officials have longed to acquire it for the city for the revenue and tourism it attracts.

After much debate, it was finally decided in court that the museum would move to the Benjamin Franklin Parkway. In 2012, the Barnes Foundation reopened on the Museum District corridor that is home to many of Philadelphia's other top museums, including the Philadelphia Museum of Art, The Franklin Institute, Academy of Natural Sciences, and the Rodin Museum. The design team meticulously rebuilt the museum to reflect Barnes's original curation, from the paint colors to the placement of every work of art.

This world-class collection is a must-see, not just for the art, but also for the unique vision the Barnes Foundation imparts. Anyone interested in learning more about the battle over the Barnes can watch *Art of the Steal*, an interesting documentary about the collection and Albert Barnes himself, a fascinating man who made a fortune on a medical invention and spent most of it creating one of the world's best collections of art.

MAP 4: 2025 Benjamin Franklin Pkwy., 215/278-7000, www.barnesfoundation.org; Wed.-Mon. 10am-5pm; $25 adult, $23 senior, $10 student and youth (6-18), free child 5 and under

★ THE FRANKLIN INSTITUTE

Scientist and inventor Benjamin Franklin would be proud of the impressive museum named for him and dedicated to one of the major focuses of his life work—expanding knowledge of the universe through science. A larger-than-life statue of Ben welcomes guests into the grand high-ceilinged lobby. The large museum showcases many of Franklin's own inventions along with countless technological and scientific advances through history with interactive exhibits that are often as interesting and educational for adults as they are for children. Visitors can explore the engine room of a real 19th-century locomotive, take in the vast expanse of the cosmos in *Space Command,* and learn how the human body and the laws of physics work together in the *Sport Zone.* The institute hosts the world's best traveling science exhibits in addition to ever-expanding permanent displays. A planetarium show is included with the price of admission. One of the best surround-style IMAX theaters in the country and a 3-D theater (the Franklin Theater) round out the museum's diverse offerings, and admission can be added to a museum ticket or purchased for a separate fee if visited individually.

MAP 4: 222 N. 20th St., 215/448-1200, www2.fi.edu; daily 9:30am-5pm; $19.95 adult, $15.95 child (3-11), free under 3, additional fee for IMAX or Franklin Theater and other special exhibits

RODIN MUSEUM

Many will recognize Auguste Rodin's famous sculpture *The Thinker,* which welcomes visitors into the museum dedicated entirely to the French artist's work. Walk past the garden and fountain to see many of his other

Top: The Franklin Institute. Bottom: the Rodin Museum.

masterpieces, including *The Gates of Hell,* framing the main entrance of the impressive building. Wander through the high-ceilinged, marble-floored rooms and you'll be amazed by Rodin's endless true-to-life sculptures of the human body—he was especially skilled at and obsessed with creating human hands. Exhibiting one of the largest Rodin collections in the world, the small but lovely museum provides an in-depth look at not only his work, but also his thought processes and his life. Some of his original tools, early sketches, and journals are on display.

MAP 4: 22nd St. and Benjamin Franklin Pkwy., 215/568-6026, www.rodinmuseum.org; Wed.-Mon. 10am-5pm; $10 donation suggested

South Philadelphia Map 5

CINEMA
UNITED ARTISTS RIVERVIEW STADIUM 17
You can count on the Riverview to run all the top blockbusters in this large, adequate, but unremarkable and sometimes not entirely well-kept megaplex. You certainly won't be getting the Ritz experience, but if you need to catch the latest natural disaster summer blockbuster, this is your place.

MAP 5: 1400 S. Columbus Blvd., 844/462-7342

GALLERIES
FLEISHER ART MEMORIAL
This Bella Vista neighborhood gem is home to a small rotating gallery of drawings, paintings, sculptures, and photographs by mostly local artists, but perhaps the coolest thing about Fleisher are the low-priced or free classes offered on an ongoing basis. You heard that right—free! This is a great opportunity for everyone from beginners to advanced artists to hone their skills in a supportive and affordable environment. Advanced workshops and classes, including photographs, sculpture, art history, and drawing and painting, are offered for very reasonable fees.

MAP 5: 719 Catharine St., 215/922-3456, www.fleisher.org; Mon.-Wed. 10:30am-6pm, Thurs.-Fri. 10:30am-5pm; free

MUSEUMS
MUMMERS MUSEUM
"What is a mummer?" you may ask. A mummer is a lavishly costumed, dancing, marching, instrument-playing, feather-and-sequin-covered Philadelphian who brings the city's unique brand of celebration to fever pitch. The purest example of Philadelphia's spirit, the mummers celebrate every occasion but none more so than the New Year, which they usher in with a parade on Broad Street. If you haven't seen a mummers parade before, it is a sight not to be missed. While the earliest mummers date back to ancient Egypt, the tradition of mummers in Philadelphia began in the

late 17th century and has held strong ever since. Mummers are joyous, passionate, and proud, and their traditions have become an important part of Philadelphia's history. The Mummers Museum in South Philadelphia pays homage to their remarkable history.

MAP 5: 1100 S. 2nd St., 215/336-3050, www.mummersmuseum.com; Wed.-Sat. 9:30am-4pm; free

University City

Map 6

CINEMA

INTERNATIONAL HOUSE

Possibly the strangest and coolest dorm ever, International House is home to over 400 international students studying at area colleges and universities. It's also a nexus of cultural and artistic programming for University City and Philly as a whole. I-House offers an extensive and jaw-droppingly diverse series of film screenings, art shows, installations, live music, food festivals, dance performances, speakers, and more. The auditorium has a large projection screen, and while not quite up to par with a typical movie theater as far as quality, this place is much cooler than anything typical, and you'll see movies here that you won't see anywhere else.

MAP 6: 3701 Chestnut St., 215/387-5125, www.ihousephilly.org

RAVE MOTION PICTURES UNIVERSITY CITY 6

This theater (formerly the Bridge: Cinema de Lux until 2010) opened its doors in University City in 2002, making many local moviegoers very happy. No longer did we have to brave sticky floors and the stinky bathrooms of Riverview or drive to a megamall in the suburbs or Cherry Hill, New Jersey, to see a first-run blockbuster. The clean, spacious theater offers plush stadium seating, a specialty coffee bar, and a bar and lounge. Located near plenty of dining options, it's a convenient spot for a dinner-and-a-movie date.

MAP 6: 4012 Walnut St., 215/386-9800, www.ravemotionpictures.com

MUSEUMS

INSTITUTE OF CONTEMPORARY ART

One day, the lay public will understand the difference between modern, postmodern, and contemporary art, but until then, the Institute of Contemporary Art is keeping its name direct and to the point. The ICA, nestled away on Penn's campus in University City, hosts exhibitions, commissions works, produces publications, and holds educational programs. Hopefully, those classes will be able to explain why a gallery showing Rothko would never put up a piece by Duchamp.

MAP 6: 118 S. 36th St., 215/898-7108, www.icaphila.org; Wed. 11am-8pm, Thurs.-Fri. 11am-6pm, Sat.-Sun. 11am-5pm; free

A paradise for the Indiana Jones at heart, the University of Pennsylvania's museum houses a magnificent chest of archaeological treasures. It opened in 1899 and today contains more than 100 unique displays and one million artifacts representing practically every corner of history and prehistory. Trace the earliest *Homo sapiens'* routes as you walk the long artifact-lined corridors and wander through rooms that offer glimpses into centuries and civilizations past. Decipher North America's earliest hieroglyphics in the Mesoamerica exhibit; walk before the enormous sphinx at the Palace of the Pharaoh Merenptah; and advance through the technology, art, politics, and religion of the Etruscans, Greeks, Canaanites, and Romans.

MAP 6: 3260 South St., 215/898-4000, www.penn.museum; Tues.-Sun. 10am-5pm, first Wed. 10am-8pm; $15 adult, $13 senior, $10 student and child (6-17), free child under 6 and Penn staff and students

Northern Liberties   Map 7

GALLERIES
VOX POPULI AND KHMER GALLERY

These two distinct galleries are not related other than by nature of being housed in the same large warehouse just north of Chinatown. Vox Populi hosts contemporary exhibitions, including experimental film, cutting-edge installations, and a wide range of work mostly by Philadelphia-based artists. It also hosts numerous indie and experimental musical performances and has a sophisticated feel while remaining a true DIY artist collective.

Khmer, in the basement level, features original and reproduction Cambodian sculpture, artwork, jewelry, and photographs. Many of the pieces are massive and way out of the price range of mere civilians—try upward of $50,000 for a marble garden statue—but some of the jewelry and small artwork is more affordable, and the space is fun to wander through even if you're not looking to furnish a massive Asian-themed restaurant or estate.

MAP 7: 319 N. 11th St.; Vox, 3rd Fl., 215/238-1236, www.voxpopuligallery.org; Khmer, basement, 215/922-5600, www.khmerartgallery.com; Vox, Wed.-Sun. noon-6pm; Khmer, Wed. and Fri.-Sat. 11am-4pm; free

THEATER
NEW FREEDOM THEATRE

Most of the action on the Avenue of the Arts goes on below Market Street, while Freedom Theatre struggles to keep North Broad Street hopping. The oldest African American theater in Pennsylvania, Freedom has in the past showcased fine plays based on African American stories, like Toni Morrison's *The Bluest Eye*. Its operations today consist primarily of

conducting theater and dance classes for kids and adults, with some performances conducted through the Performing Arts Training Program.
MAP 7: 1346 N. Broad St., 888/802-8998, www.freedomtheatre.org

Fairmount Park

Map 9

CONCERT VENUES
MANN CENTER FOR THE PERFORMING ARTS

Located in leafy Fairmount Park, the Mann provides a large open-air venue for a diverse range of performances. Originally a summer home for the Philadelphia Orchestra, today the Mann hosts instrumental music, jazz, opera, pop, dance, drumming, and ballet. It has also hosted many big-name pop and rock musicians, although most of the very biggest names now perform at the larger Susquehanna Bank Center in Camden instead. It holds up to 4,000 under the pavilion and up to 10,000 on the lawn and terrace. On nice summer nights, bring a picnic and come for an orchestra performance.
MAP 9: 5201 Parkside Ave., 215/878-0400, www.manncenter.org

MUSEUMS
★ PLEASE TOUCH MUSEUM

This 38,000-square-foot playground is a kid's dream come true, and with an emphasis on learning, development, and encouraging imagination through play, it's a place parents can feel great about taking their kids. With a name like Please Touch, it's obvious the museum is meant to be enjoyed hands-on; children can dress up in costumes, operate flying machines, drive a SEPTA bus, and much, much more. There is so much to do that some locals take their kids on a near-weekly basis. The museum has been a favorite for families since it opened in Center City in 1976, but since it moved to its much larger and impressive current space in 2008, it is truly a world-class kids' museum. While kids won't care, parents should note that the building, Memorial Hall, is a National Historic Landmark that was built for the World's Fair in 1876 but was left abandoned for many years in between; it is wonderful to see this fantastic space put to such great use.
MAP 9: 4231 Avenue of the Republic, 215/581-3181, www.pleasetouchmuseum.org; Mon.-Sat. 9am-5pm, Sun. 11am-5pm; $17 adult and child, free child under 1

Top: the Please Touch Museum. Bottom: the Wells Fargo Center.

CONCERT VENUES
WELLS FARGO CENTER

Philly provides venues aplenty for all kinds of spectator activities, but for major music acts and professional basketball and hockey, only the Wells Fargo Center will do. The state-of-the-art indoor arena has changed owners and names several times since it opened, but in 2010, it became the Wells Fargo Center, owned by Comcast-Spectacor. It hosts at least 250 events a year with room for more than 20,000, and there are very few if any bad seats in the house. It is home to the Philadelphia Flyers, the 76ers, the Soul (indoor football), and the Wings (lacrosse), and Billy Joel, Madonna, Ray Charles, KISS, and just about everyone else you can think of has performed here. Any huge names that are not performing here are probably playing at the Susquehanna Bank Center in Camden, New Jersey.

MAP 10: 3601 S. Broad St., 215/336-3600, www.wellsfargocenterphilly.com

MUSEUMS
AMERICAN SWEDISH HISTORY MUSEUM

Swedish colonists settled in the Delaware Valley in the mid-1600s—long before William Penn arrived—and this museum aims to preserve their history. The nation's oldest Swedish museum, it was founded in 1926 on the 150th anniversary of the drafting of the Declaration of Independence. Built on land given to colonist Sven Skute by Sweden's Queen Christina in 1653, the building was modeled after a 17th-century Swedish manor. Numerous artifacts fill the galleries showcasing the history of the colonists, including collections of early Swedish furniture and handmade peasant dolls. Other exhibits honor famous Swedes such as author Carl Sandberg, inventor/seaman John Ericsson, and Alfred Nobel, who invented dynamite and established the Nobel Prize. Located a bit out of the way in deep South Philly, it's worth a trip for history buffs or anyone interested in Swedish culture.

MAP 10: 1900 Pattison Ave., 215/389-1776, www.americanswedish.org; Tues.-Fri. 10am-4pm, Sat.-Sun. noon-4pm; $8 adult, $6 senior and student, $5 child (5-11), free child under 5

Sports and Activities

Old City 190
Society Hill 190
Center City East............... 191
Center City West.............. 193
Museum District 195
University City................ 197
Northern Liberties............. 201
Chestnut Hill 203
Manayunk 204
Fairmount Park 204
Greater Philadelphia........... 207

Look for ★ to find
recommended recreational activities

Highlights

★ **Best Place to Take a Nap:** From May to October, **Spruce Street Harbor Park** becomes an all-ages playground strewn with hammocks, food trucks, and family-friendly games (page 191).

★ **Best Hiking and Biking Trail:** The **Schuylkill River Trail** winds around both sides of the river. The easily accessible and popular 8.4-mile paved stretch known as "the loop" extends out behind the Art Museum. Those wanting a longer ride can continue all the way to Valley Forge and beyond (page 193).

★ **Best City Park: Rittenhouse Square** is the crown jewel of the ritzy Rittenhouse neighborhood in Center City West. The beautifully landscaped park occupies a prime piece of real estate amid many of the best restaurants and shops in the city, making it a favorite resting place for locals and visitors alike (page 193).

★ **Best Skate Park: Paine's Park** was completed in 2013 and instantly became the favorite hangout of local skateboarders (page 196).

★ **Best Bowling Alley:** If you've never thought of bowling as particularly hip, then you've never been to **North Bowl.** This popular Northern Liberties spot offers a late-night lounge along with two levels of lanes (page 201).

★ **Best Place to Get Away from it All:** In the northwest section of the city, **Wissahickon Park** offers 1,800 acres of towering trees and scenic trails (page 203).

Spruce Street Harbor Park

Philadelphia is home to Fairmount Park, the largest urban municipal park system in the world. Fairmount Park encompasses East and West Fairmount Parks—large areas that straddle the Schuylkill River—in addition to 63 distinct neighbor-

hood parks and gardens and hundreds of miles of hiking and biking trails, including the popular Schuylkill River Trail. Those in search of less-trafficked areas head to the Wissahickon in the northwest section of the city or to one of the many nearby suburban parks and nature reserves.

Beyond the endless recreational opportunities on land, Philadelphia's two major rivers—the Delaware and Schuylkill—offer water enthusiasts a place to enjoy kayaking, rowing, boating, and water tours. Gardens, arboretums, dog parks, playgrounds, and sports fields are abundant throughout the city, and they often double as venues for events, markets, and festivals in spring and summer. Visit Philadelphia Parks & Recreation (www.phila.gov/recreation) for more information about all things outdoors.

Sports fans should try to catch at least one professional game while in town. In addition to the four major long-standing professional teams—the Eagles (football), Phillies (baseball), Flyers (hockey), and 76ers (basketball)—the city gained a professional soccer team, the Union, in 2010, which quickly earned a strong fan base. Win or lose, there is simply no city more impassioned and committed to its teams than Philadelphia. An example of just how seriously this city takes its sports is that former Philadelphia mayor, then Pennsylvania governor, Ed Rendell, hosts the Eagles postgame show every Sunday, which he did even while he was in office. Rooting for—and talking trash about—our teams brings the city together, perhaps more than anything else.

Old City

Map 1

ICE-SKATING
BLUE CROSS RIVER RINK AT PENN'S LANDING

When the temperature drops, the city and the Ben Franklin Bridge become a scenic backdrop for skaters gliding on the outdoor Blue Cross River Rink. Straddling the Delaware River at Penn's Landing, the River Rink is a nice way to spend a winter day with kids or on a date. Most skating sessions run for two hours, which is enough time to skate, but plan ahead so you don't arrive in the middle of a session. Holiday parties, New Year's Eve countdowns, and St. Valentine's soirees are just a few of the special events that take place throughout the season.

MAP 1: Market St. and S. Columbus Blvd., 215/925-7465, www.delawareriverwaterfront. com; Nov.-Feb. Mon.-Thurs. 6pm-9pm, Fri. 6pm-1am, Sat. 12:30pm-1am, Sun. 12:30pm-9pm, extended hours btwn Christmas and New Year's Eve; $3 admission, $10 rental, $17-$20 parking

Society Hill

Map 1

PARKS AND GARDENS
ROSE GARDEN AND MAGNOLIA GARDEN

While touring the sights of Old City and Society Hill, take a minute to stop and smell the roses. A cobblestone path leads through the Rose Garden, a tribute to the signers of the Declaration of Independence and the Constitution planted by the Daughters of the American Revolution, a volunteer women's service organization dedicated to promoting patriotism and preserving American history. The buds peak in June. Just across the street, the smaller Magnolia Garden was built in honor of George Washington, who apparently loved the magnolia tree. The 13 magnolia trees bordering the garden represent the 13 original colonies.

MAP 1 DETAIL: Locust St. btwn 4th and 5th Sts.

WASHINGTON SQUARE PARK

A quieter counterpart to Rittenhouse Square, Washington Square serves a similar purpose for the Old City and Society Hill neighborhoods it straddles. The leafy respite is a place to sit and eat, read, or just take a break from it all amid a bustling urban area. Originally called Southeast Square when it was founded in 1682, it was renamed in 1825 as a tribute to George Washington. Used as a burial ground for troops during the Revolutionary War and for victims of the yellow fever epidemics that followed, it wasn't until the surrounding neighborhoods developed that the square transformed into its current shape. In 1952, a major renovation included the creation of a monument to the soldiers and sailors of the Revolutionary War. Designed by architect G. Edwin Brumbaugh, the *Tomb of the Unknown Soldier* occupies an area near the center, serving as a memorial for the soldiers buried below. A constant flame burns to honor them.

MAP 1: Btwn Walnut and Locust Sts. and 6th and 7th Sts.

★ SPRUCE STREET HARBOR PARK

There is no place on earth quite like Spruce Street Harbor, the nautical urban oasis on the Delaware River. The dynamic landscape is embellished with floating gardens and landscaped barges. Kick your feet up in one of the many hammocks hanging from the dense tree canopy strewn with Technicolor twinkling lights. A variety of tasty food and alcoholic beverages are served from trucks owned and operated by acclaimed local chefs like Jose Garces and Michael Solomonov. Play free family-friendly games like boccie, ping pong, shuffleboard, or corn hole. On the weekends there are often free events from concerts to craft markets.

MAP 1: 301 S. Columbus Blvd., 215/922 2386, www.delawareriverwaterfront.com; May-Oct., Sun.-Thurs. 11am-11pm, Fri.-Sat. 11am-1am

Center City East   Map 2

BOWLING
LUCKY STRIKE LANES

Lucky Strike Lanes is the Beverly Hills of bowling, bringing a slice of Los Angeles—where the swank chain originated—to Philadelphia. You'll pay a high price for the surprisingly good cuisine, modern technology, and posh clubby scene. The concept is based on the circa-1960 Hollywood Star Lanes, so there is a faux-vintage element to the decor. A strictly enforced dress code forbids sweats, jerseys, headgear, construction boots, and sleeveless or "excessively baggy T-shirts," making Lucky Strike the most exclusive—okay, only exclusive—alley in town. The 24 lanes can get crowded on Friday and Saturday nights, but many come in just for the scene or to play pool on one of the six tables. Reservations are accepted to rent lanes by the hour but not to pay per game. You must be 21 to enter after 9pm, and food and drink specials are available during happy hour (Mon.-Fri. 4pm-7pm).

MAP 2: 1336 Chestnut St., 215/545-2471, www.bowlluckystrike.com; Sun. noon-midnight, Mon.-Thurs. 11:30am-midnight, Fri. 11:30am-2am, Sat. noon-2am

FITNESS CENTERS
12TH STREET GYM

Located in the heart of the Gayborhood, the facility is one the largest in the city, with a 22-station strength-training circuit, cardio machines galore, a roof deck, pool, sauna, juice bar, and full-size basketball and racquetball courts. More than 60 weekly group fitness classes include old standbys like cardio, abs, yoga, and Pilates, along with tae-bo, mixed martial arts, and fun dance classes like hip-hop and zumba. A membership is one of the better deals among the first-rate gyms, but a one-day pass costs $20. Many members also frequent the **Soleil Tanning Center** next door; it's owned by the gym but you don't have to be a gym member to use it.

MAP 2: 204 S. 12th St., 215/985-4092, www.12streetgym.com; Mon.-Thurs. 5:30am-11pm, Fri. 5:30am-10pm, Sat. 8am-8pm, Sun. 8am-7pm; $359/year with $99 initial fee

PARKS AND GARDENS
DILWORTH PARK

In 2014, the underused plaza on the west side of City Hall underwent a $55 million renovation that transformed it into the perfect welcome mat for commuters and visitors. This multi-season, interactive park is exemplary of the way Philadelphia seamlessly blends its historic infrastructure with modern innovation. Dilworth Park includes a landscaped lawn, an outdoor café operated by Chef Jose Garces, a choreographed spray ground that children adore, a performance space, and free WiFi. During the colder months, the fountain converts into an ice-skating rink that is open seven days a week. Admission to the Rothman Ice Rink is $5 for adults and $3 for children ages 10 and under. Skate rentals are available for $9 a pair.

MAP 2: 1 S 15th St., www.ccdparks.org/dilworth-park; daily 6am-1am

YOGA
MAMA'S WELLNESS JOINT

Local yoga teacher and doula Paige Chapman opened Mama's Wellness Joint in 2013. Mama's provides a range of wellness workshops and yoga classes, including women's and men's, prenatal, family, and children's yoga, as well as Reiki, birth and breastfeeding education, and infant care classes, among other offerings and specialty workshops. There is also an in-house massage therapist offering traditional and prenatal massage and a retail space with holistic health, beauty, and edible products.

MAP 2: 1100 Pine St., 267/519-9037, www.mamaswellnessjoint.com

HIKING AND BIKING TRAILS
★ SCHUYLKILL RIVER TRAIL

The city's most popular trail continues well beyond the city and into surrounding counties. When all the paving is complete, it is projected to be about 130 miles long. It follows the Schuylkill River from Center City and connects with Valley Forge National Park, which offers many additional trails. Whether you want a short ride or an all-day outing, there is a section of this trail to suit most needs. It is mostly flat and paved. It consists of several Fairmount Park trails and the Manayunk Canal Tow Path, so terrain varies somewhat along the way. The trail can be accessed in Center City via stairs or ramps on Market, Chestnut, or Walnut Streets; on the street level on Locust Street; or just behind the Art Museum. The busiest portion is the River Drive Recreational Loop, commonly referred to as the loop. This 8.4-mile paved stretch begins and ends near the Art Museum, winds around both sides of the river, and crosses the East Falls Bridge. Exercise caution when walking or riding here, especially with children or on weekends, as it gets very crowded on nice days. **Lloyd Hall** (1 Boathouse Row), the first boathouse behind the Art Museum, has a café, restrooms, and bicycles and inline skates available to rent by the hour on weekends April-October.

MAP 3: Many access points along the Schuylkill River throughout Philadelphia and beyond, 215/683-0200, www.schuylkillrivertrail.com

OBSERVATORY
ONE LIBERTY OBSERVATION DECK

Warning: this attraction should be avoided by those with a fear of heights! One Liberty Observation Deck features dizzying panoramic views of Philadelphia and beyond from the 57th floor of One Liberty Place, a Center City skyscraper with a shopping center and food court on the lower floors. The newly opened observation deck is the tallest of its kind in the city. The attraction also features interactive installations, including touch screen monitors that allow visitors to zoom in on the live action hundreds of feet below. Guided tours of One Liberty are offered free with the price of admission.

MAP 3: 1650 Market St. Suite #5700, 215/561-3325, www.phillyfromthetop.com; daily 10am-10pm, $19 adult, $14 youth (ages 3-11), free under 3

PARKS AND GARDENS
★ RITTENHOUSE SQUARE

When the weather is nice, it can be difficult to find a bench in Rittenhouse Square, especially during lunchtime. In fact, the pretty tree-lined park in the swankiest part of town is pretty hoppin' throughout the year, yet it

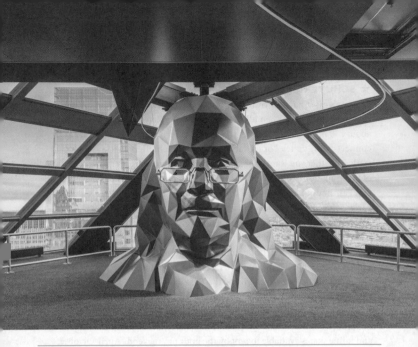

Top: One Liberty Observation Deck. Bottom: Rittenhouse Square.

somehow remains a peaceful respite from the Center City bustle—right in the middle of it all. A convenient break from skyscrapers and upscale shops just beyond its perimeter, the square is filled with suits on lunch break, families, dogs, artists, musicians, and a few homeless people as well. Rittenhouse was called Southwest Square until 1825, when it was renamed for famous Philadelphia astronomer and clockmaker David Rittenhouse (1732-1796), descendant of William Rittenhouse of paper-mill fame. Architect Paul Cret, also responsible for the Benjamin Franklin Parkway and many of its buildings, designed the entrances, the central plaza, the stone railings, the pool, and the fountain in 1913. If you can't snag a bench, there is usually space to sit along the walls surrounding the center fountain—great for people watching—and many people bring a blanket and set up on the grass with a picnic lunch.

MAP 3: Btwn 18th and 19th Sts. and Walnut and Locust Sts.

YOGA
DHYANA YOGA

What started as a lovely little studio founded by an inspiring yoga instructor, Dhyana has expanded to include locations in Northern Liberties, Fairmount, and Haddonfield, New Jersey. Classes are offered in a wide variety of styles, including Vinyasa, Kundalini, and Anusara, and include beginner and advanced options. If the additional studios are anything like the original, you can count on top-notch classes taught by inspiring instructors. Check the website for the frequent workshop offerings. A single class costs $15 with packages offered for repeat yogis. Additional studios are located in Northern Liberties (1030 Liberties Walk, Suite 601) and Fairmount (2000 Spring Garden St.).

MAP 3: 1611 Walnut St., 215/496-0770, www.dhyana-yoga.com

Museum District
Map 4

BIKE RENTALS AND REPAIRS
FAIRMOUNT BICYCLES

A full-service bike shop not too far from the Schuylkill River Trail and very close to Eastern State Penitentiary, Fairmount Bicycles offers hybrid bikes with racks for rent at reasonable prices. They also sell new and refurbished bikes.

MAP 4: 2015 Fairmount Ave., 267/507-9370, www.fairmountbicycles.com; Tues.-Sun. 11am-7pm; $7/hour, $35/full day

WHEEL FUN RENTALS

Located near Lloyd Hall, the first boathouse just behind the Art Museum, the Wheel Fun Rentals kiosk provides a convenient way to rent bikes to ride

Bike-Friendly Philly

an Indego Bike Share kiosk

Bicycling is an excellent way to see the city, eliminating the problems of parking, traffic, and waiting for and spending money on public transportation. And since Center City is mostly flat, it's an easy ride. There is an increasing network of bike-friendly streets with wide bike-only lanes; for your safety and comfort, use these routes whenever possible because Philly drivers can be a bit stingy about sharing the road. A map of routes can be found at the **Independence Visitor Center** or http://phillymap.com. **The Bicycle Club of Philadelphia** (www.phillybikeclub.org) is also a great resource for bike enthusiasts. Founded in 1979, the club sponsors recreational cycling activities open to the public for a small fee and promotes bicyclists' rights and safe biking practices.

You can take a variety of guided bike tours with **Philly Bike Tour Co.** (2015 Fairmount Ave., 215/521-2150, http://phillybiketours.com/, prices vary). The Classic City Tour is a slow-paced four-hour ride that covers about 12 miles and hits the most famous city sites, like the Rocky Steps and the Liberty Bell. The Art is All Around Tour tells the story of Philadelphia's wealth of public art from murals to sculpture.

If you'd rather explore on your own (and on the cheap) **Indego Bike Share** (www.rideindego.com) is the way to go. There are more than 50 Indego stations scattered around the city, each with a stable of roughly 20 bikes. Use your credit card to rent a bike by the hour and return it to any Indego station when you're done.

along the Schuylkill River Trail. Road bikes, tandem bikes, and assorted surreys are available for rent.

MAP 4: 1 Boathouse Row, 215/232-7778, www.wheelfunrentals.com; Memorial Day-Nov. 13th daily, Nov. 14th-Mar. 6th Wed.-Sun 9am-4pm, Mar. 7th-May 27th daily 10am-sunset; road bike $15/hour, $50/day

PARKS AND GARDENS

★ **PAINE'S PARK**

Skateboarding advocates spent over a decade fighting and fundraising to make this world-class skateboard park a reality. The $5 million,

75,000-square-foot skatepark finally opened in May of 2013 to the great delight of area skateboarders. Paine's Park is a multi-use urban plaza designed with nonskateboarders and spectators in mind as well. Some of the benches and ledges were specifically made to be unskateable, and, unlike many skateparks, aesthetic beauty was a high priority to the designers. The park is a triumph of urban design that sits on a hill south of the Benjamin Franklin Parkway and has views of the Schuylkill River and the Philadelphia Art Museum.

MAP 4: Martin Luther King, Jr. Dr. and Benjamin Franklin Pkwy.

SISTER CITIES PARK

Sister Cities is a beautiful little plot of green in the heart of the Museum District, next to Logan Square and the Cathedral Basilica of Saints Peter and Paul. The pristine park features a children's garden with a waterfall and pond, a café, and a satellite office of the Independence Visitor Center, where you can find tourist information and event listings and purchase museum tickets. During the spring and summer you'll see children (and some adults) climbing the mini hiking path, floating toy sailboats in the brook, or running through sprinklers.

MAP 4: N. 18th St. btwn Race and Vine Sts.

YOGA
WAKE UP YOGA

Wake Up's original Vinyasa studio is in Fairmount; they also have a South Philly location (1839 E. Passyunk Ave.). Each studio offers several 90-minute classes a day varying in level of difficulty, but people at all levels are welcome to any class. Wake Up emphasizes the physical, spiritual, and philosophical aspects of yoga as much if not more than the physical workout and seeks to provide a nurturing, supportive atmosphere for students. Most single classes cost $15, but they offer discounts for students, single parents, and the recently unemployed.

MAP 4: 2329 Parrish St., 215/235-1228, www.wakeupyoga.com

University City · Map 6

BIKE RENTALS AND REPAIRS
NEIGHBORHOOD BIKE WORKS

Neighborhood Bike Works is a very cool nonprofit whose mission is "to create educational, recreational, and career-building opportunities for youth through bicycling in the Philadelphia area, and to promote cycling as an environment-friendly, healthy form of transportation." Among many youth and adult programs, the University City location offers free repairs and classes. It's known as the bike church because it is located in the basement of St. Mary's Church, and visiting is literally and figuratively an underground experience. The warehouse offers used and salvaged bike parts at a minimal price—normally ranging just $1-10—and there is no service charge since you do the work yourself. The veteran volunteer bike mechanics that facilitate the repairs are sometimes understaffed. Stick it out and have patience; they are always willing to help. They can even assist you in building a custom bike from scratch. The nonprofit has expanded in recent years and now has locations in North and South Philly, although the bike church in University City remains one of a kind.

MAP 6: 3916 Locust Walk (Penn's campus btwn Walnut and Locust Sts. near 40th St.), 215/386-0316, www.neighborhoodbikeworks.org, Tues.-Fri. 2pm-6pm, Sat. 10am-2pm

ICE-SKATING
UNIVERSITY OF PENNSYLVANIA ARENA

An impressive donation by the University of Pennsylvania's Class of 1923 funded this facility. Built in 1972, it is located in University City just across the Walnut Street Bridge from Center City. Frequented by Penn students and home to collegiate events for more than 30 years, this rink hosts ice hockey, figure skating, and speed games. The arena boasts 18,000 square feet of skating surface, six locker rooms, and 2,900 seats and is open to the public for skating when other events are not taking place. It is also home to the Philly Roller Girls, a women's roller derby club.

MAP 6: 3130 Walnut St., 215/898-1923, www.business-services.upenn.edu/icerink; Sept.-Mar. Mon., Wed., and Fri. noon-1:30pm, Sat. 5:45pm-7:15pm, Sun. 1:30pm-3pm; $6 weekday, $7 weekend, $3 rental

PARKS AND GARDENS
CLARK PARK

Established in 1895, this nine-acre park in West Philadelphia is a treasured community asset, offering lots of green space for picnics and sports and serving as a venue for many community gatherings. There are plenty of pleasant places to sit and relax on any given day, and a host of events and concerts bring people in hordes. They come for fresh, affordable produce at the **farmers market** (May Sat. 10am-2pm, June-Thanksgiving Thurs. 3pm-7pm and Sat. 10am-2pm, rest of the year Sat. 10am-1pm). The Uhuru Solidarity Movement runs a seasonal monthly **Flea Market** (Apr.-Oct. Sat., call 215/387-0919 for times) offering food, antiques, crafts, and more. Check out the Gettysburg Stone (a large Civil War battlefield monolith) and a life-size bronze statue of Charles Dickens and Little Nell from his novel *The Old Curiosity Shop*—a literary celebration is held in the park each February to honor Dickens's birthday.

MAP 6: 4400 Baltimore Ave., www.friendsofclarkpark.org

CIRA GREEN

Cira Centre South, the modern skyscraper at the base of University City, did a remarkable thing when it converted its garage roof into a landscaped 1.25-acre park that floats 95-feet above street level. The park is free, and the

Top: Paine's Park. **Bottom:** Sister Cities Park.

Philly Skate Culture

skateboarding at Paine's Park

Philly has long been a hot spot for skateboarding. For many years, skaters from New York, Boston, Los Angeles, and even overseas made the journey to Philadelphia's landmark **Love Park** (officially JFK Plaza). They came to thrash on its ramps, granite ledges, and stairs in a prime setting smack in the center of urban Philadelphia. Featured in practically every skate magazine there is and frequented by many pro and semipro skaters, Love Park was internationally recognized, and Philly was even chosen to host the 2001-2002 ESPN X Games as a result.

And then the city government stepped in and ruined everything. In response to damage complaints and other alleged nuisances, one of Philadelphia's major recreational assets and one of the things that made it so popular with youth came to an end. Despite many protests, the city closed Love Park to skaters in 2002 so that the suits on lunch breaks could eat in peace. Skaters were relegated to the only remaining large-scale skateboarding area in the city, **FDR Park.** Located on Pattison Avenue and Tuscany Drive at the park's south end, it's within walking (or rolling) distance to the Broad Street Subway Line. Philly's skate culture lived on in the shade of the raised highway, I-95, above. Fishbowls, ramps, innovative skate structures, and a 30-foot half pipe make this skate park pretty impressive, but the location leaves something to be desired. It's completely separate from the rest of the city, unlike prominent Love Park.

After the closing of Love in 2002, the city donated a beautiful 2.5-acre plot of land along the Schuylkill River near the Art Museum to use for **Paine's Park,** a new state-of-the art urban skate plaza. However, it was up to a small group of dedicated individuals to raise the $5 million needed to build the park. After over a decade in the works, skaters were starting to lose hope that the park would ever open. In 2013, Paine's Park finally broke ground. The multi-use plaza was designed to incorporate interesting skate-friendly surfaces with art and green spaces so that the general public can enjoy it as well. The park is a huge success and has revitalized skateboarding in Philadelphia. It represents a shift in the city's perception of skateboarders from public nuisances to valued members of the community. The momentum of Paine's Park has also helped further the progress of a number of smaller parks being erected in neighborhoods throughout the city.

general public can access it from 30th Street between Chestnut and Walnut Streets. Simply take the elevator to the 11th floor. Offering incredible views of the city skyline and Schulykill River, Cira Green is a great place for a picnic or a quiet moment of reflection.

MAP 6: 30th St. btwn Chestnut St. and Walnut St., www.ciragreen.com, daily 7am-8pm with extended hours in the summer

Northern Liberties Map 7

BOWLING
★ NORTH BOWL

In a former mechanic's garage, North Bowl has 21,000 square feet of space spread over two floors. It's a popular pre- or post-bar-hopping hangout in Northern Liberties. People come as much to hang out in the stylish yet comfortable setting as they do for the lanes. The restaurant serves much better food than you'd expect at a bowling alley, and pool tables and other games offer additional entertainment. Happy hour specials (Mon.-Fri. 5pm-7pm) promise discounts on bowling, food, and drinks and a lively after-work scene. There is often a wait for lanes on weekends, so call ahead to reserve, or snag a seat on one of the leather benches while you wait. You have to be over 21 to enter after 9pm.

MAP 7: 909 N. 2nd St., 215/238-2695, www.northbowlphilly.com; Mon.-Fri. 5pm-2am, Sat.-Sun. noon-2am; $4.95-5.95 depending on day and time, $4.40 shoe rental

SPECTATOR SPORTS
Boxing
THE LEGENDARY BLUE HORIZON

The nation's oldest boxing ring operating today, the Legendary Blue Horizon is well known in the boxing world as one of the last remaining old-school boxing venues in the country. The building dates to 1865, but it wasn't until 1961 that it became a boxing venue. It has earned the "legendary" in its title by housing some of the greatest fights in history. It has become a landmark center for training, education, and community participation, and the best boxers and teachers from the city and beyond train, fight, and teach here throughout the year. Come out for fight night to see the purest showcase of boxing available today. The Blue Horizon has been voted the "#1 Boxing Venue in the World" by *Ring* magazine and the "last boxing venue in the country" by *Sports Illustrated*.

MAP 7: 1314 N. Broad St., 215/763-0500, www.legendarybluehorizon.com

Top: North Bowl. **Bottom:** Wissahickon Park.

HIKING AND BIKING TRAILS
★ WISSAHICKON PARK

Those seeking an escape will be thrilled to learn that dense forests, lush greens, and a gentle creek exist within the city limits. The part of Fairmount Park that occupies the northwest section of Philadelphia is known as the Wissahickon. It surrounds Wissahickon Creek, which runs through the park for 7 miles. There are around 57 miles of trails snaking through the park and the Wissahickon Gorge—crossing bridges, climbing high ridges, and offering ample views. Some are rugged and hilly and others are flat with gravel. The Friends of the Wissahickon organization publishes a detailed map, available at its office in Chestnut Hill (8708 Germantown Ave., 215/247-0417, www.fow.org) and online. It includes roads, trails, buildings, bridges, dams, and statues, and it is well worth it for anyone looking for an in-depth exploration of the park. Easy access and parking can be found near Forbidden Drive, the 11-mile well-traversed gravel stretch. There are no restrooms along the trails, so use the public restrooms at the entrance near the Valley Green Inn restaurant and parking area. There are multiple entry points throughout the neighborhoods of Mt. Airy, Roxborough, and Chestnut Hill.

MAP 8: Multiple access points, main entrance Valley Green Rd. near Wissahickon

ICE-SKATING
WISSAHICKON ICE SKATING RINK

Chestnut Hill's indoor year-round ice rink is popular with families and preteens looking for a fun night out on a weekend. It's also home to youth and adult hockey leagues, skating lessons, figure skating, and a pro-skating club. Many people on the ice are members, but the general public is also welcome. Session times vary by season, but the rink is open to the public Friday evenings year-round.

MAP 8: 550 W. Willow Grove Ave., 215/247-1759, www.wissskating.com; public skate Fri. 8:30pm-10:30pm, classes, teams, and leagues other times; $9 admission, $3 rental, $1 guest card for nonmembers

PARKS AND GARDENS
MORRIS ARBORETUM

Morris Arboretum is a lovely 92-acre beautifully landscaped Victorian garden, complete with streams and sculptures featuring more than 2,500 types of plants. In the late 1800s, Compton was the summer estate of wealthy Quakers John and Lydia Morris, brother and sister. They built a lovely plant and sculpture collection on the grounds and hoped to one day add a school and laboratory of horticulture and botany. This dream was ultimately realized after their time, when in 1932 the University of Pennsylvania transformed the site into the Morris Arboretum. An interdisciplinary resource center, it is the official arboretum of the Commonwealth of Pennsylvania, listed on the National Register of Historic Places. There is an on-site café as well as frequent special exhibits and events.

MAP 8: 100 E. Northwestern Ave., 215/247-5777, www.upenn.edu/arboretum; Apr.-Oct. Mon.-Fri. 10am-4pm, Sat.-Sun. 10am-5pm, Thurs. in summer until 8:30pm; Nov.-Mar. daily 10am-4pm; $16 adult, $14 senior, $7 student, active military, and child (3-17), free child under 3 and PennCard holders

Manayunk   Map 8

BIKE RENTALS AND REPAIRS
HUMAN ZOOM

A seller of top-quality bikes, Human Zoom also has rentals and is the only place in the city that offers road bikes in addition to hybrids. It's close to the Schuylkill River Trail in Manayunk, making it convenient for anyone staying in Manayunk and wanting to spend a day on the path or ride into Center City. No reservations are accepted for hybrids—it's first-come, first served.

MAP 8: 4159 Main St., Manayunk, 215/487-7433, www.humanzoom.com; Mon.-Wed. 11am-8pm, Sat. 10am-6pm, Sun. 11am-4pm; hybrids $8/hour, $30/day (24 hours), $50/weekend (48 hours), $100/week; road bikes $40 up to 24 hours

Fairmount Park   Map 9

With more than 215 miles of scenic trails winding through Fairmount Park, there is a place for everyone to jog, hike, blade, bike, or ride horses. Paths range from paved to rocky terrain, flat to steep, and crowded to desolate. Some trails are only open to hikers or bikers, so be aware of the markers. You can grab a map of Fairmount Park at the visitor center or visit www.fairmountpark.org/trailsintro.asp for more information.

FRISBEE GOLF
SEDGLEY WOODS DISC GOLF COURSE

Established in 1977, the second-oldest disc golf course in the country occupies a lovely setting in East Fairmount Park. As its name implies, the sport is a combination of Frisbee (the only equipment used) and golf (the object is to hit specific targets in the fewest number of attempts). Considered a great course by disc golf aficionados, the Woods provides many natural obstacles. The course and parking are free and open to the public, but it's BYOD—bring your own discs.

MAP 9: East Fairmount Park, 33rd and Oxford Sts., www.sedgleywoods.com; free

PARKS AND GARDENS

FAIRMOUNT PARK

One of the best things about Philadelphia, Fairmount Park is considered the largest urban municipal park in the world, covering more than 9,200 acres. Not to brag, but for a little perspective, New York's Central Park is only 843 acres. The largest continuous sections of the park are East and West Fairmount Parks, which straddle the Schuylkill River. In addition, the Wissahickon in the northwest section of the city and Pennypack Park in the northeast section of the city are huge areas that are technically part of Fairmount Park but usually referred to by their own individual names. The entire park system encompasses 63 distinct neighborhood parks and gardens and hundreds of miles of hiking, biking, and jogging trails, including the popular Schuylkill River Trail, as well as the Center City squares Franklin Square, Logan Square, Rittenhouse Square, and Washington Square. Pretty much every patch of green in the city is technically part of Fairmount Park, but when people refer to it, they are usually referring to one of the large swaths on either side of the Schuylkill River that extend out behind the Art Museum into Northwest Philadelphia. Most recreational opportunities in the city take place in Fairmount Park, and the city's website is a great resource for all that it has to offer.

MAP 9: Multiple entrances, 215/683-0200, www.phila.gov/parksandrecreation

PHILADELPHIA HORTICULTURE CENTER

Fairmount Park's Horticulture Center includes an arboretum that dates to 1876, an expansive greenhouse built for the bicentennial celebration in 1976, and more than 20 acres of lush landscape. Paths wind through gardens, also home to a butterfly garden, a large reflecting pool, and various sculptures of poets, musicians, and animals. The inside display area contains colorful tropical plants, flowers, perennials, herbs, everlastings, and rare trees. Picnic areas are available on the grounds.

MAP 9: 100 N. Horticultural Dr. (and Montgomery Ave.), 215/685-0096; display house daily 9am-3pm; grounds Nov.-Mar. daily 8am-5pm, Apr.-Oct. daily 8am-6pm; free

SHOFUSO JAPANESE HOUSE AND GARDENS

In 1876, the Japanese Bazaar and Garden came to this area for the Centennial Exposition. While the site has changed shape several times, there has been some form of Japanese landscaping on this spot, now part of the Horticultural Center, ever since. Shofuso was designed by Junzo Yoshimura in 1954 for the Museum of Modern Art in New York to introduce Americans to Japanese design. It was relocated and reassembled here in Fairmount Park in 1958 as a gift from Japan. The authentic replica offers a glimpse into the life of a 17th-century wealthy Japanese scholar, high-ranking priest, or member of the upper class. Enjoy the tranquil setting, observe the symmetrical architecture, take part in a traditional tea

Top: Fairmount Park. Bottom: Shofuso Japanese House and Gardens.

ceremony, and learn about the history and culture of an authentic Japanese house. Tours of 30-45 minutes are offered based on staff availability.
MAP 9: Landsdowne Dr. and Horticultural Dr., 215/878-5097, www.shofuso.com; May-Sept. Wed.-Fri. 10am-4pm, Sat.-Sun. 11am-5pm; $6 adult, $4 student, child, and senior, free under 3

SMITH MEMORIAL PLAYGROUND AND PLAYHOUSE

Wealthy Philadelphians Richard and Sarah Smith wanted to create a safe, free place for children to play, so they opened one in Fairmount Park in 1899. While it has gone through several renovations since its opening, their original vision is still alive and well more than a century later. The 6.5-acre park and 24,000-square-foot playhouse offer a unique, fun, and educational play space for children 10 and under. The highlight is the giant enclosed wooden slide; built in 1905, it is large enough to accommodate about 10 kids across at a time. There is plenty for kids to play with inside the unique toy-filled mansion, and the most recent renovations and additions have made this historic play space better than ever before.
MAP 9: 33rd and Oxford Sts., East Fairmount Park, 215/765-4325, http://smithkidsplayplace.org; playground (children 10 and under) Apr.-Oct. Tues.-Sun. 10am-6pm; playhouse (children 5 and under) year-round Tues.-Sun. 10am-4pm; free

Greater Philadelphia   Map 10

HIKING AND BIKING TRAILS
PENNYPACK PARK

This 1,395-acre portion of Fairmount Park in Northeast Philadelphia is underutilized, but restoration projects over the past decade are finally bringing it to the attention of residents and visitors. Pennypack, named after the Lenni Lenape Indian word for slow-moving water, follows Pennypack Creek southeast for nine miles from Montgomery County to the Delaware River. Miles of paved and unpaved trails offer hikers, bikers, and horseback riders a variety of paths for recreation. Visit the website for a schedule of the free summer concert series held on select Wednesday evenings, featuring mostly tributes to big-name entertainers like the Beatles and Elvis. The on-site Pennypack Environmental Center offers programs at nearby Fox Chase Farm, a city-owned 112-acre working livestock farm.
MAP 10: 8500 Pine Rd., 215/574-2100, www.pennypackpark.com

PARKS AND GARDENS
BARTRAM'S GARDEN

The nation's first botanical garden is alive and well in Southwest Philadelphia. Founded in 1728 by John Bartram, a devout Quaker, the gardens and adjacent Bartram family home are both National Historic Landmarks. The 44 acres straddling the Schuylkill River feature native plants and flower gardens, ancient trees, a water garden, and a river trail. The oldest gingko tree in the country and the *Franklinia alatamaha,* a tree named for John Bartram's friend Benjamin Franklin, are just two of the notable flora you can find here. Explore the garden on your own or take a 45-minute guided tour of both the home and garden. History, science, and nature programs are also often offered. On summer weekends, you can get here via the **Schuylkill Banks River Tour** (800/979-3370, www. schuylkillbanks.org, $30 adult, $17 child 12 and under). The scenic guided boat tours depart from the Schuylkill River Trail and include a guided tour of Bartram's Gardens—a lovely three-hour trip.

MAP 10: 54th St. and Lindbergh Blvd., 215/729-5281, www.bartramsgarden.org; garden daily 10am-5pm; tours of house and garden May-Oct. Thurs.-Sun. 10am-4pm; gardens free; tours $12 adult, $10 senior and student

SPECTATOR SPORTS

In addition to the four major long-standing professional teams—the Eagles, Phillies, Flyers, and 76ers—the city gained a professional soccer team, the Union, in 2010, which quickly gained its own strong (a.k.a. maniacal) fan base. Philly has several minor league teams that play entertaining if somewhat less emotionally charged games at lower prices. It is also home to an unparalleled five college basketball teams in the Big 5: Temple, University of Pennsylvania, St. Joe's, Villanova, and LaSalle. Penn's arena, the Palestra, has a storied history, and while somewhat run-down, it remains a favorite place for b-ball enthusiasts to watch a game.

Baseball
PHILLIES

The Phillies turned Philadelphia sports culture on its head with their World Series win in 2008. The championship-clinching strikeout unleashed a wild celebration throughout the region, which culminated in a euphoric parade down Broad Street, a shared moment of joy for multiple generations of Philadelphians, sports fans and non-sports fans alike. It was the first championship of any major Philadelphia team in 25 years, forcing locals to reassess our perennial loser mentality.

The World Series victory of 2008 was followed by several successful seasons, including another World Series appearance in 2009. These winning seasons created big expectations, an ever-growing team payroll, and an aging core of talent, but the team must figure out how to transition into a new era of Phillies baseball, one separate from the memories created between 2007 and 2011.

Prior to their World Series title in 2008, a much different reality existed. No team had lost more games for more years and in more torturous ways and circumstances than the Philadelphia Phillies. The oldest pro team in the city, the Phillies had been instilling cynicism into the hearts of baseball fans since 1883 and had won a grand total of one championship—the

Philly Phanatics

The stereotype of Philadelphia sports fans is that they are a boorish, negative collection of boobirds who revel in their collective misery when their teams aren't winning titles. And while I can't completely dispute this stereotype, it isn't the full picture. The passion for sports in Philadelphia means that all of our major sports have a fan base that is ravenous, persistent, and incredibly loyal. Being a Philadelphia sports fan means expecting to lose but watching anyway—year after year. It means getting pumped every season and saying to each other "this is the year," and at the end of the season when the team loses, shaking our heads and saying "that's Philly for you."

The signature call of the Philly fan is the much used, oft-discussed, and never ambiguous "boo." Booing is done in nearly every city in America, but in Philly, booing is an act of protest, a fight for inclusion into the happenings on the field or court—our own way of participating. People boo for good reasons, like when a referee makes a bad call, and for poor ones, like a fan answering a question wrong during a time-out game. In the equal opportunity nature of booing, kids get booed when they drop a foul ball, cheerleaders get booed if they don't dance well, officials get booed, coaches get booed, and players, obviously, get booed.

But the boos are merely a small chapter in a complex relationship between the fans and the teams. As tough as the city is on its teams, a good team will always be supported by big crowds in Philadelphia—especially a good team that plays hard and has character. For all these reasons, Philadelphia is one of the few true sports towns in the country. And just remember, the relationship between the teams and the fans is like a family: You can insult your own family all you want, but if somebody else does, watch out. So if you're not from around here, be careful, especially if you're here to cheer for someone else in our arenas. Check out a game and see for yourself what a Philly crowd is all about.

World Series of 1980. In 2007, they lost their 10,000th game, setting a record for most losses of any professional team in any sport in American history.

While hardly a storied franchise for most of its history, many superb ballplayers have worn the Phillies uniform, even before 2008. The Whiz Kids of 1950 and the ragamuffin squad of 1993 gave the city thrilling rides to the World Series before losing—both remain etched in the memories of fans. The 1964 team was 6.5 games in front with just 12 games to play when they lost 10 in a row and missed the playoffs, becoming forever one of the gold standards for choking in baseball.

Citizens Bank Park opened in 2004, replacing the cavernous relic of Veterans Stadium. While many die-hard fans were resistant to the change, the bright, clean, modern stadium has been a big hit with fans and a major marketing tool for the franchise. Always a great spectator sport with its unique rhythm and laidback atmosphere, baseball in Philadelphia is, now more than ever, a fun day or night out. Crowds are a mix of families, couples, college kids, and rowdy fanatics, all united in cheering the Phillies toward victory.

It should also be noted that the Phillies Fanatic is hands-down the greatest mascot in all of sports. He alone is worth the price of admission. Tickets, relative to other professional sports, are affordable at around $20-65, but they are harder to come by than they used to be, so you'll have to plan ahead. And, although it's illegal, it's also not uncommon to encounter scalpers selling tickets outside on game day.

MAP 10: Citizens Bank Park, 1 Citizens Bank Way, 215/463-1000, www.phillies.com

Basketball
76ERS

Providing the city with countless highlights, lowlights, and players of legendary and infamous status, the 76ers, or the Sixers, has been Philadelphia's pro basketball team since 1963. Despite the team's rich history and pedigree of the franchise, their struggles have led to small crowds and diminished expectations. Following the NBA Finals appearance in 2001, the team has gone through numerous players, coaches, and rebuilding plans, all with the same result: mediocrity.

It wasn't always this way. Beginning in the 1960s with Wilt Chamberlain, the Sixers boasted star power if not always a stellar record. The fortunes of the franchise have coincided with the comings and goings of some of the greatest superstars in NBA history, including Julius "Dr. J" Erving, Moses Malone, Charles Barkley, and Allen Iverson. Unfortunately for Sixers fans, most of these stars were ultimately traded away in bad deals for the team.

Among the enduring legacies of the Sixers are the championship titles, the fierce and often personal battles waged against division rival Boston in the 1960s-1990s, the fast-breaking teams of Dr. J. and George McGinnis in the mid to late 1970s, the sustained excellence of the team from the late 1970s to mid 1980s, the explosiveness and candor of Charles Barkley, and the singular talent and heart of Allen Iverson—who in 2001 led the team to its first finals appearance since 1983. The all-time low was the 9-73 record in 1972-1973, which to this day remains the record for fewest wins in a season by a professional basketball team.

Games are played at the Wells Fargo Center, and on a good night, it is an electrifying experience. The crowd at a Sixers game is the most diverse in age and ethnicity of any of the pro teams. Tickets are generally not difficult to get and range from as low as $10 to well over $100, available online or at the stadium.

MAP 10: Wells Fargo Center, 3601 S. Broad St., 800/298-4200, www.nba.com/sixers

Football
EAGLES

In a crowded and passionate sports town, no team draws more attention than the Eagles. The combination of being a perennial contender, the national obsession with football, and Philly's general obsession with the game, has positioned the Eagles as the number one sports draw in the city and surrounding area—a standing that shows no sign of changing soon. There is a uniquely feverish connection between the town and the football team,

The Eagles are still looking for their first Super Bowl championship (before the Super Bowl existed, they won the championship in 1960), a quest that riles the fan base into a fever every autumn and so far has left them heartbroken every January. When Andy Reid became head coach in 1998, the team was following a depressing 3-13 season. Reid was at the helm during the franchise's most consistently competitive streak in 50 years, built around the polarizing talents of Donovan McNabb and the leadership of fan favorites such as Brian Dawkins and Brian Westbrook.

Reid's 14-year run ended in 2013, when he was replaced by college coach, Chip Kelly. Kelly's hiring signaled a new era of Eagles football, and one the Eagles nation hopes will result in that elusive Lombardi Trophy.

Despite competitive and exciting teams, frequent trips to the playoffs, and a roster stocked with high-profile names, the lack of a Super Bowl trophy looms large over the team and the city. Nothing short of a championship will satisfy the embattled Eagles fans, who with each passing year become more vociferous and cranky, turning Lincoln Financial Field into a notorious cauldron of noise, emotion, and the occasional drunken brawl. The party inside the stadium is an extension of the tailgate scene that begins early on Sundays and continues until kickoff. And beyond the stadium scene, football and Sunday go hand in hand in Philadelphia, as the Eagles' faithful use the entire day to drink and yell away the previous week of work and responsibility.

Possessing a bad reputation that is not entirely unwarranted, Eagles' fans don't often waste a chance to yell at opposing teams and their fans, and sometimes even at each other, in and outside of the stadium. Be warned: If you show up at a game wearing a jersey of the other team, you *will* catch heat and may be putting yourself at real risk.

Eagles tickets have become the most expensive and elusive in the city, with a long and implacable waiting list. Individual tickets go on sale before the season's start and get snapped up in a matter of minutes. The best bet for tickets is at the team website (www.philadelphiaeagles.com), or on eBay or Craigslist (www.craigslist.org), but either way you will pay hundreds of dollars to see a game. Scalpers sell tickets at the stadium in exchange for a high price and the risk of arrest for the illegal purchase.

MAP 10: Lincoln Financial Field, 1 Lincoln Financial Field Way, 267/570-4000, www.philadelphiaeagles.com

SOUL

Named for the distinct sounds of soul music that originated in Philly, the Philadelphia Soul is the city's team in the Arena Football League. Under the direction of New Jersey-born rock star Jon Bon Jovi, who founded the team in 2004, Soul games are family-friendly events at the Wells Fargo Center. With alcohol-free seating zones and games and activities for children, fans can get close to the action. The season begins in March, and ticket packages

Legendary Sports Figures

Philadelphia has been home to some of the most legendary sports figures of all time, but teams have generally seen less than their share of success considering how many superstars have played in Philly. (Perhaps that is why the most famous Philadelphia sports figure of all is a fictional character—gritty Rocky Balboa, who never fell short against all odds.) But any true sports fan should read on to understand the impact that some of the most colorful athletes of all time had on the game—and the city.

Basketball

Wilt Chamberlain was the towering center who grew up in West Philly and played for the Philadelphia Warriors and the 76ers. Combining size, strength, and agility, Wilt destroyed opponents and records. His impressive credits include 100 points in a game, 55 rebounds in a single contest, and averaging 50 points a game for an entire season. His off-court records include his famous claim of going to bed with 20,000 women.

Julius "Dr. J" Erving, a showman who joined the 76ers in 1976 and rejuvenated the sport, had a massive afro, a debonair goatee, and an in-your-face elegance that brought style and flair to the NBA. His ability to float in the air created the standard by which all high-flyers—from Michael Jordan to Vince Carter—are judged today. One of the most popular players in franchise history, he led the 1983 team to a world championship.

Charles Barkley was considered short (at six feet, six inches) and fat (sometimes topping 300 lb.) when he entered the NBA in 1984. With explosive strength and intensity, he became the face of the franchise when Dr. J retired in 1986. Arguably the greatest pure rebounder of his era, he became the shortest player to lead the league in rebounds in 1987. His relationship with fans and media was tumultuous, but he is remembered for his honesty and self-deprecating humor, remaining hugely popular in Philly.

A six-foot shooting guard who threw his body around like a football player, **Allen Iverson** was the number one overall pick in the 1996 draft when he came to Philly. His astonishing scoring ability was matched by his passion and willingness to play through injury. This, along with his frenetic style, endeared him to fans and carried him through numerous off-court distractions and tabloid headlines. There was never a dull moment with A. I., and while many bristled at his contempt for authority, the city was mesmerized by his toughness and electric abilities. He played every game like it was his last—a favorite line of his. His hopeful return to Philly for part of the 2009-2010 season ended abruptly due to injury and personal struggles, but Iverson, the Sixers' most recent superstar, still holds a place in fans' hearts.

Football

Chuck Bednarik, known as Concrete Charlie, was a linebacker and center for the Eagles in the 1950s and '60s. One of the last "two-way" players, Bednarik had mangled hands and a nasty attitude that fans loved. He is fondly remembered as the face of the only championship team in Eagles history, the 1960 NFL Champions (pre-Super Bowl, which came into existence in 1966).

Dick Vermeil coached the 1980 Eagles team that went to the Super Bowl—the team's first title game since 1960. The team played above expectations for a coach known for his intensity and 20-hour days. A victory over the Dallas Cowboys, hated rivals who had otherwise had their way with the Eagles throughout the 1970s, was a high point for the team. Unfortunately, the Eagles were routed by an Oakland Raiders team that spent nights out on Bourbon Street while the Eagles studied plays in their hotel rooms.

Reggie White, who played for the Eagles in 1985-1992, is arguably the best defensive lineman in team history. With legendary strength, he routinely tossed huge offensive linemen out of the way en route to the quarterback. A devout Christian and ordained minister, the Minister of Defense was a rare combination of athlete and leader who headed one of the best defenses in NFL history.

Hockey

Ask anyone about the Flyers and they're sure to mention **Bobby Clarke.** Captain of the Stanley Cup-winning teams of 1973-1974 and 1974-1975, Clarkie embodied the blood-and-guts effort of the hockey team and the town. A diabetic, he was never even supposed to play hockey, but his work ethic and talent were an unstoppable combination.

Bernie Parent was the goalie of those Stanley Cup-winning teams, and many astute fans agree he was the biggest part of those championships. Arguably the best goalie of his era, his record for most games won in a single season was not broken by any goalie until 2007.

Eric Lindros came to the NHL as highly touted as any player in history, and the Flyers landed him after a bitter legal proceeding with the New York Rangers. Despite his talent, his time with the team was marked by injury, bitter disputes, and, disappointingly, no Stanley Cup. He was tagged the next Wayne Gretzky or Mario Lemieux, perhaps unfairly, and he never delivered.

Baseball

Richie Ashburn, one of the few men around town who could pull off the nickname Whitey, was beloved in Philadelphia first as the center fielder for the Phillies in the 1950s and later as a radio commentator. His understated style and easy humor connected with fans, and he was adopted as a native son. His signature line, "Hard to believe, Harry" (directed to his radio partner, Harry Kalas, also a local hero), often followed a goofy blooper or awkward moment for the Phillies.

Perhaps the greatest third baseman of all time, **Mike Schmidt** played his entire career with the Phils. The cornerstone of the team that won the only world championship in franchise history in 1980, he made it look easy with great power at the plate and superior glove work at the hot corner. Despite his talent, he had a perplexingly embattled relationship with the home crowd and often heard boos. He has since become more appreciated, and a statue of him is featured outside Citizens Bank Park.

Hall of Fame pitcher **Steve Carlton** was responsible as much as anyone for leading the Phils to the 1980 World Series championship. Called Lefty for obvious reasons, he was virtually unhittable during his prime in the mid-1970s and early 1980s. Known for his surly nature, he refused to speak to reporters and was not subtle in discouraging the team manager or catcher from "disturbing" him on the mound. He also was known for his large wine collection.

The **2008 Phillies' World Series championship team** deserves a spot for their 4-1 series victory over the Tampa Bay Rays. The win rocked the city and forced Philly fans to redefine themselves as winners and find something new to complain about besides their decades-long losing streak. The team was overflowing with talent and personality (sure, all the winning didn't hurt either in making us love them), but I'd be remiss not to mention Jimmy Rollins (J-Roll), Chase Utley, Ryan Howard, Shane Victorino, Jason Werth, Cole Hamels, or General Manager Charlie Manuel—the sweet, bumbling old man who clearly kicks butt when it comes to leading a team to a championship win.

are available. This version of Philly football is a far cry from the Eagles, but with low-end tickets available for as little as $13, it offers an affordable alternative to satisfy a football fix.

MAP 10: Wells Fargo Center, 3601 S. Broad St., 888/789-7685, www.philadelphiasoul.com

Hockey
FLYERS

The Orange and Black. The Broad Street Bullies. The Philadelphia Flyers, the youngest of the professional teams in Philly, lack for nothing when it comes to owning a secure place in the mythology of the sports scene. With some of the most loyal and fervent fans in the city, Flyers hockey has always meant big hits, wild punches, and sold-out stadiums.

Created in 1967 as part of hockey's expansion, the Flyers have been a perennial contender year in and year out, coming close many times but still looking for their first championship since winning back-to-back Stanley Cups in 1973-1974 and 1974-1975. They came heartbreakingly close in 2010 with a Stanley Cup run that ended in overtime of Game 6.

The bruising style and reputation they developed in the early 1970s, which earned them the Bullies nickname, made the Flyers local heroes in Philly and one of the most hated teams in the league. The championship teams and their players forged a strong connection to the city that remains strong and partially accounts for their intense and loyal following. Fans still clamor for the style of play that was successful in the 1970s, and often a crunching check or violent confrontation between two enforcers gets the Philly crowd more juiced than a nice pass or a pretty goal. Hockey tends to take a back seat to the other three major sports in terms of its overall impact on the city, but when the Flyers are doing well, additional fans come out in droves.

Tickets can be purchased online at the team website and at the stadium. Even during down years the Flyers remain a tough ticket to nab—and an expensive one, with tickets starting around $70 and reaching upward of $150 for the best seats.

MAP 10: Wells Fargo Center, 3601 S. Broad St., http://flyers.nhl.com

Horse Racing
PARX RACING

Live thoroughbred racing and a casino draw visitors to Bensalem, about a 10-minute ride from Center City just outside of Northeast Philadelphia. Watch and bet from inside the Pennsylvania Derby Room or take a picnic lunch and enjoy the grounds when the weather is nice. Gates usually open at 11am on Friday-Tuesday year-round, although the schedule changes from time to time so call or check the website. First race of the day starts around 12:30pm.

MAP 10: 2999 Street Rd., Bensalem, 215/639-9000, www.parxracing.com

Lacrosse
WINGS

Lacrosse fans will find a rowdy crowd in the Wells Fargo Center when the Philadelphia Wings take to the turf. With constant chants, inescapable heckling, and the team's unofficial anthem, Guns & Roses' "Welcome to the Jungle," playing at every game, it's difficult to leave without a hoarse throat. The season begins in January, with NLS playoffs following in the spring.

MAP 10: Wells Fargo Center, 3601 S. Broad St., 215/389-9464, www.wingslax.com

Soccer
UNION

In 2010, Philadelphia welcomed professional men's soccer to its already fully stocked sports scene when the Philadelphia Union became the 16th team in the MLS. The Union immediately attracted a dedicated fan base of soccer enthusiasts that seems to be growing. The most loyal of all of those fans call themselves the Sons of Ben (Franklin, that is), who petitioned the MLS in 2007 to bring a team to Philly in the first place. As obsessed with their team as the guys who paint their faces green for Eagles games, the Sons of Ben make themselves known at every game. Whether or not soccer grows into an impact professional sport in the region is yet to be seen, but the high-energy games are certainly worth checking out. The attractive stadium, PPL Park in Chester, was built just for the Union as part of an effort to revitalize the waterfront in an otherwise rundown area. Just outside of Philadelphia, it is an easy drive, or it can be accessed via SEPTA's Wilmington/Newark regional rail line and a free shuttle from the station to the stadium.

MAP 10: PPL Park, 1 Stadium Dr., Chester, PA, 877/218-6466, www.philadelphiaunion. com

Shops

Old City 219

Center City East. 221

Center City West. 228

South Philadelphia 235

Northern Liberties. 239

Fishtown 240

Chestnut Hill 242

Manayunk. 242

There was a time when the most fashionable Philadelphians regularly made the two-hour trip to New York for their serious shopping needs. Today, as with most things in Philadelphia, the shopping scene has come into its own. The major shopping districts have expanded while cool independent shops have sprung up in neighborhoods throughout the city. With no shortage of boutiques, vintage shops, specialty stores, and all the chain stores you'd hope to find in a major metropolitan area, Philadelphia has everything your consumer heart desires.

Center City is the nexus of the shopping world, with the bulk of stores concentrated on or near Walnut and Chestnut Streets west of Broad, also called Rittenhouse Row. Old City, South Street, Washington Square West, and Northern Liberties are also home to large concentrations of shops, and the three shopping rows—Jewelers Row', Fabric Row, and Antique Row—offer unparalleled selections of their respective specialties. Several indoor urban shopping malls—the Gallery, Liberty One, the Shops at the Bellevue, and the Comcast Center—offer a range of standard and high-end chain stores. In addition to these malls and shopping centers, several additional standard suburban malls are located just outside the city. Plymouth Meeting Mall, Willow Grove Mall, and the Cherry Hill Mall (in nearby New Jersey) offer department stores, chain stores, food courts, and movie theaters. Chinatown sells all things Asian, and Reading Terminal Market and the Italian Market are tops for kitchenware, gourmet treats, and other specialty items. Chestnut Hill and Manayunk offer a small-town shopping

Previous: Sugarcube; Anthropologie.

Look for ★ to find
recommended shops

Highlights

★ **Best Place to Take a Break: Terme Di Aroma** offers a calm, soothing haven in the heart of bustling Old City. Take a break from sightseeing and get pampered with an aromatherapy massage or facial (page 221).

★ **Best Sports Gear:** For more than a century, **Mitchell & Ness** has been providing quality sporting gear to Philadelphia teams and locals. Today, it draws huge crowds from far beyond the city for its classic throwback jerseys (page 223).

★ **Best Gift Shop: Verde** offers a wide array of accessories and home and gift items, including gourmet chocolates, T-shirts, bags, mugs, and baby clothes, all bearing iconic yet hip Philly images (page 226).

★ **Best Bath and Body Shop:** Made using natural ingredients crafted on location, the soaps, lotions, and potions at **Duross & Langel** smell heavenly and are priced lower than at most of the upscale cosmetic chains (page 227).

★ **Best Independent Bookstore:** The small, inconspicuous **Joseph Fox Bookshop** offers an excellent selection of titles, with a friendly, helpful staff that can help you find your next favorite (page 228).

★ **Best Shoe Store: Benjamin Lovell Shoes** proves that you don't have to sacrifice comfort for style. Offering men's and women's shoes in three different locations, the store carries the top brands in the world of high-comfort shoes (page 231).

★ **Best Vintage Clothing: Retrospect Vintage** has a finely curated selection of vintage threads at thrift store prices (page 238).

★ **Best Place to Get a Handmade Messenger Bag: R.E. Load Baggage, Inc.** is the place to go for durable custom-designed bags. This grassroots company is 100 percent Philly (page 239).

★ **Best Outdoor Shopping: The Schmidt's Commons** is Northern Liberties' very own European-style plaza. It's lined with boutiques, galleries, and exquisite shops; the best time to visit is on weekends for the market, when vendors set up their wares outside (page 240).

★ **Best Vinyl Selection:** The **Philadelphia Record Exchange** is a must for all record lovers. Three full floors in a row house just off South Street are stocked with rock, jazz, soul, punk, R&B, and more (page 240).

atmosphere just a short drive from Center City, while the big-box stores on Delaware Avenue and several nearby malls round out the options.

Weekends are bustling in the major shopping areas, and the heart of Center City is pretty much always bustling. Most Center City shops are open seven days a week, but in some neighborhoods, many shops are closed on Monday. Some stores in Center City stay open a few hours later on Wednesday evening. And remember, there is no sales tax on clothing in Pennsylvania, so take full advantage if you're looking for any big-ticket items like that hot leather jacket you've had your eye on for so long.

Old City   Map 1

BOOKS
BOOK TRADER
This one-of-a-kind Old City bookstore has a laid-back staff and an even more laid-back vibe. While the store is cluttered, it is cluttered with great used books at reasonable used-book prices, so we can't complain. The perfect place to relax and hunt for great reading material, it's the antithesis of the overpriced, squeaky-clean chains taking over the world; enjoy it while it lasts. In addition to used books galore, you can find used DVDs, VHS tapes, and vinyl records, and there is a comfy couch on the 2nd-floor reading area with a view of historic Christ Church across the street, so you can feel free to stay awhile.
MAP 1: 7 N. 2nd St., 215/925-0511; daily 10am-10pm

CLOTHING AND ACCESSORIES
SUGARCUBE
Sugarcube has a great mix of precious vintage clothing and of-the-moment designs from local and national designers. It's stocked with feminine and fashionable dresses and tops and a small but excellent selection of jeans; the prices are often high but worth it for the exceptional, quality styles. The shoe selection has won a Best of Philly award, and the handbags and accessories, like everything else, are carefully chosen. Best of all, the changing room at Sugarcube is housed in an old bank vault, making you feel very secure and a little spooked while trying on your cool new clothes.
MAP 1: 124 N. 3rd St., 215/238-0825, www.sugarcube.us; Mon.-Sat. noon-7pm, Sun. noon-5pm

THIRD STREET HABIT
Most habits are easy to acquire and tough to break; Third Street Habit is no exception to this rule. The hip clothing and accessories boutique has received much praise since it opened in 2004, including being named one of the top 10 boutiques in the United States by *Lucky* magazine. Denim, retooled vintage, and distinctive accessories are among the fantastic items

lining the walls, and the knowledgeable, friendly staff is happy to help you pick out items that complement your style. Sorry wallets, there's a new habit in town, and it isn't cheap.

MAP 1: 153 N. 3rd St., 215/925-5455, www.thirdstreethabit.com; Mon.-Sat. 11am-7pm, Sun. noon-6pm

VAGABOND

A clothing boutique and yarn shop boutique that has remained popular since it opened in 2001, Vagabond's large, minimalist space houses the perfect combination of fabulous vintage frocks and ultra-stylish, sleek, and contemporary designs—many from local designers. Check out the back room for yarn, children's clothing, accessories, housewares, and monthly art exhibits. And don't be fooled by the name—while your pants certainly won't be threadbare, your pockets may be after shopping here. Clothes are definitely chic, but certainly not cheap.

MAP 1: 37 N. 3rd St., 215/671-0737, www.vagabondboutique.com; Mon.-Sat. 11am-7pm, Sun. 11am-5pm

GIFT AND SPECIALTY

SCARLETT ALLEY

Founded by mother and daughter Mary Kay and Liz Scarlett, this is the place to go for beauty and spa products, home accents, jewelry, housewares, and gifts, with a wide selection for babies and kids. Wander to the back to unearth a sweet collection of lingerie, pajamas, and slippers cozy enough to make you never want to leave the house again. Many of its products have been featured in magazines, including *Oprah* and *Lucky*. An annex called Scarlett Bride offers everything for brides-to-be outside of the dress.

MAP 1: 241 Race St., 215/592-7898, www.scarlettalley.com; Tues.-Fri. 11am-7pm, Sat. 10am-6pm, Sun. noon-5pm

SHOPPING CENTERS AND DISTRICTS

OLD CITY

Old City is not only home to the city's largest concentration of historic attractions, it is also a shopper's paradise, where tourists and locals alike flock for cool clothing boutiques and art galleries, with the largest concentration of boutiques on 3rd Street north of Market Street. Whether you're looking for books and music, vintage jeans, or furniture that doubles as artwork, Old City has it all. With great restaurants, bars, coffee shops, and an attractive, manageable several square blocks to navigate, it is also one of the most pleasant shopping areas. The best time to shop for art is during the first Friday of each month, when galleries open their doors to the public to display and sell their wares.

MAP 1: 3rd St. btwn Chestnut St. and Race St.

SPA, BATH, AND BEAUTY

★ **TERME DI AROMA**

This delightful Old City spa specializes in aromatherapy massage, wraps, and facials in an atmosphere that is sweet-smelling bliss. Soothing sounds, scents, and relaxing lighting surround you from the moment you enter the lobby. Have a cup of tea or juice and read a magazine in the cozy lounge before or in between treatments. Essential oils are chosen based on your preferences and what you hope to gain from your treatment—be it renewal and relaxation or headache and tension release. The facials are mostly gentle and relaxing, designed so you'll enjoy the process as much as the outcome, and the massages are simply divine. Prenatal, shiatsu, Reiki, reflexology, and Thai yoga massage are offered in addition to aromatherapy and deep tissue, and prices are reasonable, considering the high quality of services and atmosphere and the prime Old City location.

MAP 1: 32 N. 3rd St., 215/829-9769, www.termediaroma.com; Tues.-Fri. 11am-8:30pm, Sat. 10am-7pm, Sun. 10am-4pm

VINTAGE AND THRIFT

LOST & FOUND

Thrifters and fashion-forward females rejoice! There is a holy ground where reasonably priced, girly vintage duds and modern ultra-femme dresses, funky shoes, and colorful accessories exist together in peaceful harmony. Fun men's and women's tees and hip shoes line the walls in this small, unassuming Old City treasure with a perfect name and a super-friendly staff.

MAP 1: 133 N. 3rd St., 215/928-1311; Mon.-Thurs. 11:30am-7pm, Fri.-Sat. 11am-7pm, Sun. noon-6pm

Center City East

Map 2

BOOKS

GIOVANNI'S ROOM

Founded in 1973 and originally located on South Street, Giovanni's Room has become a mainstay on its prime corner location in the heart of the Gayborhood. One of the largest bookstores in the world that specializes in gay, lesbian, bisexual, and transgender literature, the store contains enough rainbow paraphernalia to stock a *Queer as Folk* reunion tour, in addition to shelves stocked with queer-oriented novels, magazines, videos, calendars, self-help books, travel guides, and art books. It hosts speakers and readings, and serves as a de facto community resource center. The enthusiastic staff can help you find what you need and will track down hard-to-find titles if they're not in stock.

MAP 2: 345 S. 12th St., 215/923-2960, www.giovannisroom.com; Mon.-Thurs. 11am-8pm, Fri.-Sat. 11am-9pm, Sun. 11am-7pm

Top: Lapstone & Hammer. Bottom: Mitchell & Ness.

LAPSTONE & HAMMER

Lapstone & Hammer is a sophisticated shop for the grownup "sneaker-head." Specializing in premium sportswear and menswear, Lapstone carries an exceptional collection of highly coveted sneakers as well as small-batch, locally crafted clothing brands like Fishtown-made Norman Porter bespoke Selvage denim. The beautifully restored Art Deco-era storefront is also home to a gallery space that occasionally hosts art openings and other public events.

MAP 2: 1106 Chestnut St., 215/592-9166, www.lapstoneandhammer.com; Mon.-Sat. 10am-7pm, Sun. noon-5pm

MODERN EYE

Modern Eye is an upscale eyeglass boutique that is as funky as it is elegant. The store supplies a varied international selection of cult favorite eyeglass brands and a merry band of misfits to guide you through the sometimes bewildering process of selecting face-flattering frames. The glasses are mostly prescription but there is a fine selection of shades as well. There is also an optometrist office above if your prescription is in need of updating. There is a second location in West Philadelphia (3419 Walnut Street, 215/386-5953).

MAP 2: 145 South 13th St., 215/922-3300, www.modern-eye.com; Mon.-Fri. 10am-6pm, Sat. 10am-5pm, Sun

★ MITCHELL & NESS

If sportswear makers are allowed to have a storied history, then Mitchell & Ness is the stuff of legends. Starting out in a modest downtown storefront in 1904, the two-person outfitter started crafting and retailing tennis racquets, golf clubs, and other items before moving on to specialize in team uniforms. The Phillies, Athletics (pre-Oakland, of course), and Eagles all wore their clothes. Flash forward to the present, when the team jersey has become a high-priced fashion item, and Mitchell & Ness is the supplier of choice for urban and suburban high schoolers, middle-aged men recapturing their youth, hip-hop heads, and ballers. A destination shop, it is a must for anyone interested in classic sports gear. It moved down Chestnut Street to a larger, more modern space that is more appropriate for its status. It's so popular with a national and even international crowd that a branch opened in Japan in 2007. Items can also be ordered by phone or through the website.

MAP 2: 1201 Chestnut St. (enter on 12th St.), 268/273-7622, www.mitchellandness.com; Mon.-Sat. 10am-7pm, Sun. 11am-5pm

GIFT AND SPECIALTY

AIA BOOKSTORE AND DESIGN CENTER

What began in 1976 as a resource and information center for the American Institute of Architects (AIA) attending a convention in Philadelphia has grown into much more. Architecture and design buffs will continue to find endless items of interest throughout the varied selection, while there is also

Rows and Rows

In addition to the varied neighborhood and downtown shopping districts, Philadelphia is home to Antique Row, Fabric Row, and Jewelers' Row, each offering unparalleled selections of their respective specialties and a one-of-a-kind shopping experience. Like most things in Philly, each of these "rows" has a unique history.

Antique Row

The tree-lined stretch of Pine Street concentrated between 9th and Broad Streets is a treasure trove of antiques stores and boutiques known as Antique Row. But the oldest, continuously operating antiques district in the entire country has continually evolved. So while at least 15 antiques stores remain today, the area represents a diverse mix of the old and the new. It is now also home to a wide variety of furniture, home accessories, jewelry, stained glass, clothing, and collectibles stores just steps from one another on Pine Street. Shops range from **Kohn and Kohn** (1112 Pine St., 215/923-0432, www.kohnandkohnantiques.com), established in 1932, specializing in antique furniture, glass, and collectibles, to fully modern shops to those offering a mix of antique and modern items, like **Halloween** (1329 Pine St., 215/732-7711), an impressive jewelry shop packed tight with a mix of vintage and estate pieces and unusual modern and handcrafted gems. Antique Row is also part of the Washington Square West neighborhood, straddling the Midtown Village shopping district; so there are plenty of additional stores of all kinds along the nearby streets to the north, especially along 13th Street—home to everything from books, records, and cosmetics to gay-themed specialty stores.

Fabric Row

At the turn of the 20th century, scores of Jewish immigrants settled in the southern outskirts of Center City—now South Philadelphia. The many skilled tailors and seamstresses among them were often forced to take jobs in sweatshops, creating fine clothes for the upper class. Many sold goods in pushcarts on several blocks of South 4th Street below South Street; some eventually opened their own shops, and the area became known as Fabric

plenty for the layperson to enjoy as well. The books (many ideal for a coffee table) cover a wide range of home and design topics along with collecting, tasting, urban studies, politics, and more. Plenty of quirky gifts and housewares are also available, including lighting, jewelry, puzzles, and cute baby clothes and toys. This is the store where you can find a gift for that person that already has everything—particularly if that person has a penchant for art or design. A novel collection of greeting cards and screen-printed note cards is available for anti-Hallmark types.

MAP 2: 1218 Arch St., 215/569-3188, www.aiabookstore.com; Mon.-Sat. 10am-6pm, Sun. noon-5pm

GROCERY

Half café and half specialty upscale food market, Grocery has something for everyone, whether you need an on-the-go lunch, snack, or sweet, or to

Row. What remains is a vibrant and eclectic (if a bit run-down on the outside) community of fabric shops, along with a sprinkling of clothing and shoe boutiques, a gourmet market, and cafés. While the fabric stores appear mostly the same on the outside and it is hard to know where to start, many locals have their favorites. For creating clothing or home wares, **B Wilk Fabrics** (618 S. 4th St., 215/627-1146) has a vast selection of cotton, spandex, Lycra, rayon, silk, draperies, and faux fur; and the basement of **Maxie's Daughter** (724 S. 4th St., 215/829-2226) offers a veritable fabric history of Philadelphia, with vintage textiles that haven't seen the light of day for the better half of a century. If you don't work with fabric already, the fabulous finds just may inspire you to sew your own curtains or reupholster that old, comfy chair.

Jewelers' Row

Get your bling on, on Jewelers' Row—the oldest and second-largest (after New York) diamond district in the country. Concentrated on a brick-paved stretch of Sansom Street between 7th and 8th Streets and continuing along 8th Street between Chestnut and Walnut Streets, Jewelers' Row is home to more than 300 jewelry specialists, retailers, wholesalers, craftspeople, and traders, offering a staggering variety of diamonds, precious and semiprecious stones, platinum, pearls, watches, and more. The sky is the limit on prices, but with so much competition in such a small area, good deals can often be found. Retailers include large stores like **Steven Singer Jewelers** (739 Walnut St., 215/627-3242, www.ihatestevensinger.com) and smaller ones like **Maryanne S Ritter** (704 Sansom St., 215/922-4923), with many more that can be found at www.jewelersrowusa.com.

The row was established as a center for jewelers in the years 1860-1880, but its historical significance dates back even further. Originally named Carstairs Row for builder and architect Thomas Carstairs, the row was home to 22 look-alike dwellings built in 1799-1820 and considered the first row homes in the country. They provided affordable housing and initiated a widespread housing trend that remains prevalent throughout downtown Philadelphia and much of the country today.

find a gift for a foodie friend. Owners Marcie Turney and Valerie Safran sell several of the restaurant's specialties in the store. Flavored oils, spreads, and tea are offered along with a small but excellent supply of kitchenware. **MAP 2:** 101 S. 13th St., 215/922-5252, www.grocery13.com; Mon.-Fri. 8am-8pm, Sat. 11am-7pm

TEN THOUSAND VILLAGES

It takes a village, or in this case, ten thousand, to raise a handicrafts store totally dedicated to the support of fair trade and child labor laws in the developing world. This unique chain has outposts scattered throughout the United States, offering items ranging from textiles, baskets, and jewelry to musical instruments, ceramics, and handmade soaps—crafted by artists from every corner of the globe. With a portion of the proceeds benefiting the economic vitality of these artisan communities, you and your newly purchased Bangladeshi recycled tote can shop guilt-free. You can also check out the outpost in Chestnut Hill (8331 Germantown Ave., 215/242-3040, Mon.-Thurs. 10am-6pm, Fri.-Sat. 10am-7pm, Sun. 11am-5pm), carrying many of the same as well as some other remarkable items.

MAP 2: 1122 Walnut St., 215/574-2008, www.tenthousandvillages.com; Mon.-Sat. 10am-7pm, Sun. noon-5pm

★ VERDE

Verde was named Best of Philly in 2010 for Hostess Gifts and as a One-Stop Shop by *Philadelphia* magazine, and it offers delicious chocolates that have been featured in the *New York Times Magazine;* it seems there is no one that does not love Verde. A perfect addition to the Marcie Turney and Valerie Safran empire along 13th Street, Verde does it all, from flower arrangements to sparkly jewelry to special Philly gifts and souvenirs that are tasteful, not tacky. Among the many perfect gifts you will find here are the nine-piece handcrafted chocolates, each stamped with iconic Philly images, or any of the T-shirts or adorable baby onesies from the *We Heart Philly* line.

MAP 2: 108 S. 13th St., 215/546-8700, www.verdephiladelphia.com; Mon.-Sat. 11am-8pm, Sun. noon-6pm

HOME FURNISHINGS AND ACCENTS

OPEN HOUSE

How to furnish the contemporary urban living space? Open House has found simple and functional answers that come in the shape of sleek end tables and colorful home accessories. City dwellers can rejoice at the selection of space-conserving items, including stools, side tables, hanging light fixtures, and glass storage jars of all sizes. Soft bedding, decorative rugs, minimalist kitchenware, bath and body items, and adorable baby clothes and toys round out the eclectic mix.

MAP 2: 107 S. 13th St., 215/922-1415, www.openhouseliving.com; Mon.-Sat. 11am-8pm, Sun. noon-6pm

WEST ELM

Minimalist designs and colorful palettes are what you'll find at West Elm, the nationwide home furnishings store with furniture so well made and unusual that you'll forget it's a chain store. Prices are comparable to the Crate & Barrels of the world, but with an emphasis on more modern, youthful, and spare decor. Many of the textiles appeal to a simple, breezy "Far East meets beach house" sensibility, while the lighting and wall fixtures echo a sleeker *Metropolitan Home* aesthetic. The large warehouse-like showroom space displays wares in color-coded sections.

MAP 2: 1330 Chestnut St., 215/731-0184, www.westelm.com; Mon.-Sat. 10am-8pm, Sun. 11am-7pm

MACY'S

If you've seen one Macy's, you've seen 'em all, right? Wrong! This Macy's is housed in a building that was formerly home to Wanamaker's, considered North America's first full-fledged department store. Lord & Taylor followed in this historic location and was replaced by Macy's in August of 2006. Designed to resemble Paris's Les Halles, the grand building comes complete with marble floors, elegant columns, and gold details around a grand central atrium. It also boasts one of the world's largest playable pipe organs and a 2,500-pound bronze eagle statue from the 1904 St. Louis World's Fair. A light-and-music show of the *Nutcracker* plays hourly in the central atrium during the holiday season; this old Philadelphia tradition has survived the changing of the store's ownership, drawing crowds each year. Be sure to peek inside even if you don't need to buy anything.

MAP 2: 1300 Market St., 215/241-9000, www.macys.com; Mon.-Wed. 10am-8pm, Thurs.-Sat. 10am-9pm, Sun. 11am-9pm

MIDTOWN VILLAGE

While Center City west of Broad Street, or the Rittenhouse area, is usually considered the center of downtown shopping because it is home to the major chain stores, the area east of Broad is also a shopper's paradise. While the name Midtown Village has not fully caught on yet with locals, there is no disputing that this area, roughly bordered by Market and Spruce Streets from Broad to 11th, is a bustling shopping district, and it keeps getting better. Shops, mostly unique boutiques and specialty stores, are concentrated on 13th Street, which is also home to plenty of restaurants and bars. Nearby or overlapping with Antique Row, Washington Square West, and the Gayborhood, the area offers diverse shopping opportunities.

MAP 2: 13th St. btwn Market St. and Spruce St.

SPA, BATH, AND BEAUTY

★ DUROSS & LANGEL

If smelling deliciously fragrant were your job, you could expect a promotion after a visit to this bath-and-body-product sanctuary. The big hunks of natural, organic handmade soaps in mouthwateringly sweet scents along with more subtle fragrances look good enough to eat. Candles made from natural soy wax and essential oils in scents of tangerine, Moroccan cedar, and lemon sugar are equally refreshing, and the emollient face and body washes are gentle enough for the most sensitive skin types. Hair products are also top-notch, and the ultra-moisturizing lip balm is simply divine. The local company is committed to using natural products, fair-trade policies for its raw materials, and gift packages of 100 percent recycled paper. Sign up for one of their workshops, offered on the third Sunday of most months, to learn how to whip up your own lotions, scrubs, and soaps.

MAP 2: 117 S. 13th St., 215/592-7627, www.durossandlangel.com; Mon.-Tues. 11am-7pm, Wed.-Thurs. 10am-8pm, Fri.-Sat. 10am-7pm, Sun. noon-5pm

SHOPS

CENTER CITY EAST

BOOKS

★ **JOSEPH FOX BOOKSHOP**

It's cramped. It's overcrowded with books. It's in the basement. There's no Internet and no coffee. And those are just some of the reasons we love it. Established in 1951, Joseph Fox Bookshop has always been independently owned and operated by passionate lovers of the written word. Committed to supporting and showcasing talented local authors, it may not have every book, but it has a carefully chosen selection of what the owners consider to be the best, and additional items can be special ordered. Take a step back in time to when having quality at your fingertips mattered more than having everything at your fingertips.

MAP 3: 1724 Sansom St., 215/563-4184, www.foxbookshop.com; Mon.-Sat. 9:30am-6pm, Wed. until 7pm

CHILDREN'S STORES

BORN YESTERDAY

If adults ask for Walnut Street designer shops for the latest fashions, then why wouldn't babies cry for the same? High-fashion European-style cloth-ing lines the aisles at this Rittenhouse destination in sizes up to 8 for boys and 10 for girls. Born Yesterday carries the newest designs and latest trends in infant clothing as well, so your newborn can be posh before crawling. Modern and vintage toys are available for babies up to about two years.

MAP 3: 1901 Walnut St., 215/568-6556, www.bornyesterdaykids.com; Mon.-Sat. 10am-6pm, Sun. 11am-5pm

CHILDREN'S BOUTIQUE

In business since 1966, the family-owned store carries all the big brand names, including Lacoste, Polo Ralph Lauren, Amiana, and Joan Calabrese, as well as special designs available only here. Domestic and European de-signs for children of all ages are on hand, along with shoes, toys, gifts, and select items for infants. Located at the Shops at Liberty Place, the Children's Boutique offers plenty of formal clothing for children, and orders can be placed online. Warning: It's expensive.

MAP 3: 1625 Chestnut St., 215/732-2661; Mon.-Sat. 9:30am-7pm, Sun. noon-6pm

CLOTHING AND ACCESSORIES

ANTHROPOLOGIE

This wildly successful international chain began right here in Philly. Founded by the same clothiers behind the even more wildly successful chain Urban Outfitters, this is its more sophisticated, higher-quality, pricier big sister. The three-story historic Rittenhouse Square mansion is filled with pretty, feminine, well-made clothes and accessories. Be prepared to shell out big bucks for embellished cotton sundresses in the summer and cozy, intricately detailed woolens in the frostier months. Home goods and an ample sale rack fill the lower level.

MAP 3: 1801 Walnut St., 215/568-2114, www.anthropologie.com; Mon.-Sat. 10am-8pm, Sun. 11am-6pm

BOYD'S

Finely tailored men's slacks, dress shirts, jackets, and suits are the specialty of this world-class retailer. The climate is set by extravagant marble and mahogany fixtures, while a bountiful array of doting salespeople help you navigate through the fine European import fabrics. Browse the ready-to-wear sportswear and formal attire by luxury-lifestyle purveyors like Hugo Boss, Burberry, Ferragamo, Gucci, and Zegna. A smaller selection of women's wear can also be found, with highlights including coveted designers Badgley Mischka, Narciso Rodriguez, Piazza Sempione, and Zac Posen. Stop at the in-store café for a shot of espresso or, even better, a martini in between fittings, or if you're not fully loaded, just stroll through the store to see how the other half lives.

MAP 3: 1818 Chestnut St., 215/564-9000, www.boydsphila.com; Mon.-Sat. 9:30am-6pm, Wed. until 8pm

JOAN SHEPP

Joan Shepp keeps the ladies of Rittenhouse in the business of high fashion, and the wealthiest, most fashionable ladies of Rittenhouse repay the debt by keeping Joan Shepp in business. This lofty, high-ceilinged store boasts classic wardrobe staples and trendy accents from design houses like Marni, Dries Van Noten, and Yohji Yamamoto. And no silhouette would be complete without a pair of Louboutin or Miu Miu pumps from their drop-dead-gorgeous shoe selection. If you've got cash to burn and appreciate high fashion, go now.

MAP 3: 1616 Walnut St., 215/735-2666, www.joanshepp.com; Mon.-Sat. 10am-6pm, Wed. until 8pm, Sun. noon-5pm

KNIT WIT

Chic formal dresses and basic separates line the racks of this upscale retailer. Find the latest pieces from the collections of famous designers like Alexis Bittar, Helmut Lang, or Chan Luu, to name just a few. Pick up a supple leather handbag by Romy Gold or a beaded clutch by Moyna, or snag a hot new pair of Elizabeth and James pumps or Diane von Furstenberg boots for a night on the town.

MAP 3: 1729 Chestnut St., 215/564-4760, www.knitwitonline.com; Mon.-Tues. and Sat. 10am-6pm, Wed.-Fri. 10am-7pm, Sun. noon-5pm

THEORY

This sophisticated national chain is a relatively new addition to Walnut Street. Theory supplies a collection of tasteful basics in relaxed fits and neutral palettes for the fashion-forward yet understated professional.

MAP 3: 1616 Walnut St., 215/735-1034, www.theory.com; Mon.-Sat. 10am-7pm, Sun. noon-6pm

URBAN OUTFITTERS

Back in 1970, the first of numerous Urban Outfitters to follow opened its doors in a small house on the University of Pennsylvania's campus. With the free-love climate of the 1960s not far behind, and whiffs of the disco days of the 1970s breezing in, the urban artsy bohemian set embraced the avant-garde retailer with open suede-fringed arms. Today, the funky fashion housed in this multimillion dollar international chain retailer still draws some of its clientele from its original roots, and much of its inspiration from the urban hipster crowd. The beautiful Center City warehouse-like store pays homage to the original dream with retro frocks, vintage-flavored housewares, and ironic T-shirts on four floors. By nature of its large scale, it is no longer quite as cool as it was at the outset, yet the stylish and comfy clothes at this Philadelphia original still attract youngsters in hordes. There is another store in the heart of University City (110 S. 36th St.), which is fitting, as this is the neighborhood where it all began.

MAP 3: 1627 Walnut St., 215/569-3131, www.urbanoutfitters.com; Mon.-Sat. 10am-9:30pm, Sun. 11am-8pm

GIFT AND SPECIALTY

APPLE STORE

Your basic big, bright, bustling Apple Store. It is never not packed, but the geniuses do their best to keep things moving.

MAP 3: 1607 Walnut St., 215/861-6400, www.apple.com/retail/walnutstreet; Mon.- Sat. 10am-8pm, Sun. 11am-6pm

OMOI ZAKKA SHOP

Omoi Zakka Shop is a lifestyle and gift shop for people who sweat the small stuff. The shop sells thoughtfully designed everyday goods. Most of the merchandise is imported from Asia, and the name is Japanese. *Omoi* loosely translates as "thoughts and ideas," and *zakka* is a kind of ordinary object that's been "imbued tremendous personal appeal." The young owner, Liz Sieber, believes that everyday objects can have the power to bring joy to the user. A pencil case, a trinket, a piece of jewelry, a lunch box, a key chain. None of these items would be out of place at the Zakka Shop. They recently opened a second location in Old City (41 S 3rd Street, 215/454-6910).

MAP 3: 1608 Pine St., 215/545-0963, www.omoionline.com; Mon. noon-7pm, Tues.-Sat. 11am-7pm, Sun. noon-6pm

SHOES

★ BENJAMIN LOVELL SHOES

"Style never felt so good" is the motto at Benjamin Lovell, a small, mostly local chain that stocks its shelves with a diverse range of casual and dressier footwear for men and women. The well-established brands sold include Mephisto, Ecco, Naot, and Dansko—the unifying theme for inclusion at Benjamin Lovell being comfort. Prices are somewhat high but worth every penny for the quality and durability you are buying. The Rittenhouse location has a large regular and a small discount selection, while the South Street branch (318 South St., 215/238-1969, Mon.-Thurs. 11am-8pm, Fri.-Sat. 11am-9pm, Sun. 11am-6pm) is much smaller overall but has a larger bargain section in the back, where prices are dramatically slashed at the end of each season.

MAP 3: 119 S. 18th St., 215/564-4655, www.blshoes.com; Mon.-Sat. 10am-7pm, Sun. noon-5pm

HEAD START SHOES

The shoes at Head Start are the stuff of folklore and fantasy. If it buckles, snaps, zips, clips, or is covered in studs, you'll find it here. Owner George Patti travels to Italy twice a year to select the exclusive women's styles, including gravity-defying heels and kinky cowboy boots. Find balance on a pair of Dries Van Noten platform wedges, or walk a straight line with a pair of Via Spiga Mary Janes. All the while you'll be getting a head start on the season's most distinctive styles.

MAP 3: 126 S. 17th St., 215/567-3247, www.headstartshoes.com; Mon.-Sat. 10am-7pm, Sun. 11am-6pm

UBIQ

A Philadelphia flagship of this selective chain, Ubiq positions itself as sneaker and clothing purveyor, art gallery, and all around urban-youth lifestyle destination. Walk (or skate) up the ramp on the 1st floor and you'll find yourself in sneaker and designer-T heaven. Upstairs, you'll discover a gallery to the left and a sneaker boutique to the right. Popular brands include Jordan's, Vans, Palladium, Converse, The Hundreds, and Original Fake. There is another outpost in the Gallery at 10th and Market Streets.

MAP 3: 1509 Walnut St., 215/988-0194, www.ubiqlife.com; Mon.-Sat. 11am-8pm, Sun. noon-6pm

SHOPPING CENTERS AND DISTRICTS

RITTENHOUSE ROW

If you have a deep wallet and a love of shopping, you'll find paradise in the sophisticated Rittenhouse Square area. The abundance of retail opportunities is unparalleled, with unique boutiques and high-end luxury chain stores concentrated on Walnut and Chestnut Streets west of Broad Street and the surrounding blocks. Several indoor urban malls—the Shops at Liberty Place, the Shops at the Bellevue, and the Shops at the Comcast

The King of Consumerism

The largest shopping mall in the entire country based on retail space, second only to Minnesota's Mall of America based on total size, the King of Prussia Mall (Rte. 202 at Mall Blvd., 317/636-1600, www.simon.com/mall/king-of-prussia, Mon.-Sat. 10am-9pm, Sun. 11am-6pm) is a shining beacon of materialism less than a half-hour's drive from Center City Philadelphia. Just a few miles from Valley Forge National Historical Park, the world-famous destination mall easily attracts far more visitors than the historic site. Known to locals simply as K.O.P., the mall boasts more than 400 stores and 2.8 million square feet of retail space. It has two distinct sections; the Plaza opened in 1963 as an open-air shopping mall, which has since been enclosed, and the Court was added in 1981.

In addition to all the standard stores you can imagine, there are dozens of high-end national and international upscale boutique shops and department stores, including Bloomingdale's, Nordstrom, Neiman Marcus, Versace, Hugo Boss, Donna Karan, Hermes, and Thomas Pink. It's almost too much to tackle, but with three food courts and over 40 restaurants, there are plenty of places to stop for a break and to refuel. If you're not scared away yet, check it out for yourself; just be sure to leave the Jimmy Choos at home and wear your walking shoes on any trip to K.O.P.

Center—are packed with additional mainstream and high-end retailers. In fact, all the chain staples can be found in this area, including Apple, Gap, J. Crew, Victoria's Secret, Ann Taylor, Barnes & Noble, Zara, H&M, Anthropology, and American Apparel, along with the somewhat harder-to-find chains like Theory, Lucky Jeans, Kiehl's, Barney's Co-Op, and Sephora, and high-end chains like Kenneth Cole, Brooks Brothers, BCBG, Tiffany, Madewell, and Williams-Sonoma.

MAP 3: Walnut St. btwn Broad St. and 18th St.

THE SHOPS AT LIBERTY PLACE

The Shops at Liberty Place offer an indoor urban mall experience. The central atrium is covered by a domed-glass ceiling, offering a bright and open shopping space. Shops surround the center and extend out along several hallways on two floors. Above it, the skyscraper has endless floors of offices, making the food court a popular stop for the downtown business set at lunchtime. You'll find chain clothing stores, including Express, J. Crew, and Victoria's Secret; health and beauty brands Aveda, Kiehls, and Bath & Body Works, as well as a Bloomingdale's outlet.

MAP 3: 1625 Chestnut St., 215/851-9055, www.shopsatliberty.com; Mon.-Sat. 9:30am-7pm, Sun. noon-6pm

THE SHOPS AT THE BELLEVUE

Luxury seeps through the gold-and-marble atrium of this small shopping center in the heart of Center City's Avenue of the Arts. The high-end stores make sense, considering the mall is part of the Bellevue, one of the city's finest hotels, housed in a 1904 Beaux Arts building. If your wallet is fat, stop at Nicole Miller for that last-minute cocktail dress and Tiffany & Co. for new jewels to go with it. Visit the third-largest Polo Ralph Lauren store in the world, Williams-Sonoma for delectable treats and kitchenware, and Teuscher Chocolates of Switzerland to satisfy your most decadent chocolate craving. There is a lower-level food court and a Starbucks on the main level.

MAP 3: 200 S. Broad St., 215/875-8350, www.bellevuephiladelphia.com; Mon.-Sat. 10am-6pm, Wed. until 8pm, Sun. varies by store

SPA, BATH, AND BEAUTY
BALANCE HEALTH CENTER

A true health center, as its name reveals, rather than your typical spa, this isn't a place to go to look better, but a place you go to *feel* better. Rooted in holistic health principles, the spa works with each client to develop personalized feel-better strategies. Offering an array of services to soothe or heal the mind, body, and spirit, Balance offers massage, acupuncture, chiropractic care, hypnotherapy, nutrition counseling, and yoga classes. Traditional Chinese medicine and Ayurveda, a treatment approach rooted in India, are also offered.

MAP 3: 112 S. 20th St., 215/751-0344, www.balancehealthcenter.com; daily 9am-7pm

BLUEMERCURY APOTHECARY AND SPA

Many of the women you'll see walking around Rittenhouse Square require a certain beauty quotient that can't be unearthed at the local drugstore. Enter Bluemercury. As a purveyor of luxury makeup, lotions, and potions, this upscale apothecary stocks all of the top brands, including Bobbi Brown, Bliss, NARS, and more. Picture slipping into a luscious Fresh Sugar bath, your senses soothed by the scent of the Tocca candles burning all around, followed by a dollop of skin-quenching Laura Mercier Tarte au Citron body lotion. With expert staff and pricey but decadent spa and beauty treatments, including facials, wraps, massage, and waxing, Bluemercury goes the extra mile to give the Rittenhouse elite the full pampering experience.

MAP 3: 1707 Walnut St., 215/569-3100, www.bluemercury.com; Mon.-Sat. 10am-7pm, Sun. 11am-5pm

KIEHL'S

From its 1851 start as an apothecary specializing in homeopathic remedies in New York's Lower East Side, Kiehl's has spread its old-fashioned corrugated-tin ceilings and highly organized shelves all over the world, including to this prime Rittenhouse Square location. Soothing natural and classically fragrant formulas paired with an unending dedication to customer satisfaction (check out all of the free samples) are what set this hair-and-skin-product haven apart. The unadorned packaging (and maybe also the steep prices) create what could just be a well-marketed illusion that

the products provide real medicinal value, or perhaps they actually do. In either case, most products do work remarkably well, and they smell terrific.
MAP 3: 1625 Chestnut St., 215/636-9936, www.kiehls.com; Mon.-Sat. 10am-7pm, Sun. noon-6pm

RESCUE RITTENHOUSE SPA

"Beautiful skin is a matter of choice, not chance," says Danuta Mieloch, owner and founder of Rescue Rittenhouse Spa. When you step off the elevator onto the 3rd floor of this Center City office building, you'll enter a tranquil 4,000-square-foot lounge with minimalist, soothing decor that will put you in the mood for relaxation. Mieloch and her talented staff have won numerous awards for their treatments, most notably their famous transformative facials, including peels, micro-current, and microdermabrasion. They also offer excellent massage, nail services, waxing, makeup application, and an array of high-end products.
MAP 3: 1601 Walnut St., 215/772-2766, www.rescuespa.net; Mon.-Fri. 9am-8pm, Sat. 9am-7pm

TOPPERS SPA AND SALON

In the heart of Rittenhouse Square, you'll find a spa and salon offering a diversity of spaces and services spread over its five floors. The 1st and 2nd floors offer an upscale hair and nail salon that belies the more soothing atmosphere waiting on the uppermost levels. A cozy Victorian-style sitting area and changing room, along with private massage treatment rooms, make up the 3rd floor, while the 5th-floor atrium offers the most unusual setting of all with its greenhouse-like ceiling. In addition to treatment areas, the lounge area is filled with umbrellas, chaises, and cabanas, offering an island-y vibe that will make you forget you're in the middle of the city. In addition to the Rittenhouse Square location, this semi-local chain has outlets in Devon and Bucks County, Pennsylvania, as well as Marlton, New Jersey, and Dover, Delaware.
MAP 3: 117 S. 19th St., 215/496-9966, www.toppersspa.com; Tues. and Thurs. 10am-7:30pm, Wed. 10am-8:30pm, Fri. 10am-6:30pm, Sat. 9am-6:30pm, Sun. 10am-5:30pm

VINTAGE AND THRIFT

BUFFALO EXCHANGE

This nationwide consignment thrift store aims to reuse and recycle one-of-a-kind fashions. Supply and demand dictates the ever-changing stock, which usually consists of higher-end vintage designer basics, evening wear, shoes, and accessories. With most items in excellent condition, you won't look like you just rolled out of the thrift store after shopping here, but your wallet will feel a bit like you did. You can bring in your former-favorite clothing and accessories to sell, although the buyers are discriminating,

so don't bother unless your old duds are in great shape and still likely to be
stylish in someone's mind.

MAP 3: 1713 Chestnut St., 215/557-9850, www.buffaloexchange.com; Mon.-Sat.
10am-8pm, Sun. noon-7pm

South Philadelphia Map 5

BOOKS
BRICKBAT BOOKS
A new and used bookstore on Fabric Row in South Philly, Brickbat is cozy
and homey with its soft music and pleasant lighting. With a substantive
collection of literary fiction, mysteries, children's books, attractive art and
photography tomes, and limited edition collectibles, there is something for
everyone to buy or just peruse. They also buy used books and host readings and events.

MAP 5: 709 S. 4th St., 215/592-1207, http://brickbatbooks.blogspot.com; Tues.-Sat.
11am-7pm, Sun. 11am-6pm

CLOTHING AND ACCESSORIES
MOON AND ARROW
Moon and Arrow is an artfully curated Queen Village boutique that feels
more southern Californian than South Philadelphian. It's a lifestyle store
with everything you need to embellish your home and wardrobe, and the
perfect place to find a gorgeous gift for the modern bohemian in your life.
The expansive showroom is stacked with treasures up to its soaring ceilings
and has an unusual L-shaped layout. Reach the back of the store and take
a right turn. There you'll find RareCo Vintage (410 Fitzwater St., 267/281-
4229, www.rarecovintage.com), a high-end antique art and furniture store.

MAP 5: 754 S. 4th St., 215/469-1448, www.moonandarrow.com; Tues.-Sat. 11am-7pm,
Sun. 11am-5pm

GIFT AND SPECIALTY
GARLAND OF LETTERS
When Mother Earth and Father Sky get busy, they rely on incense from the
Garland of Letters to set the mood. Philly's leading purveyor of books on
mysticism, philosophy, Eastern religion, nature worship, holistic healing,
self-improvement, massage, and more offers a soothing escape from the
bustle of South Street. With an assortment of lotions, oils, music, art, home
accessories, crystals, and, of course, incense, the atmosphere is somewhat
New Age-y, but in the best possible way. If you need to pick up a book on
the meanings of various henna tattoos, recordings of Vedic chanting, or a
Tantric sex guide, this is the place.

MAP 5: 527 South St., 215/923-5946; daily noon-9pm

Top: Head Start Shoes. **Bottom:** Via Bicycle.

The self-proclaimed "most interesting bike shop in the world," Via Bicycle is an excellent resource for buying and selling used and vintage bikes and for low-cost repairs. The shop itself is a sight to be seen with its authentic vintage decor filled with bikes and accessories. Road bikes, beach cruisers, classics, basics, and rare one-of-a-kind bikes are available for sale. You can also stop by to fill up your tires outside next to the signature yellow benches, where locals do a little fine-tuning. The mechanics are knowledgeable and friendly, prices are average, and if you have a special vintage bike that needs a repair, this is the place.

MAP 5: 606 S. 9th St., 215/627-3370, www.bikeville.com; Tues. and Thurs.-Sat. 10am-5pm, Wed. 1pm-9pm

HOME FURNISHING AND ACCENTS

ANASTACIA'S ANTIQUES

Victorian and Early American collectibles and practical pieces fill this antique furniture and accessory store. Get lost in the maze of ornate mirrors and period pieces and be sure to save time to get lost in the fantastic Bakelite bangles and Lucite-adorned clutches in the vintage jewelry cases. The staff's open and friendly vibe will make you feel right at home while they help you find the next piece to fit your personal collection—and your personal budget. Prices are reasonable, and if you live nearby, large items can be delivered to your home.

MAP 5: 617 Bainbridge St., 215/928-9111, http://anastaciasantiques.com; Thurs.-Sat. noon-6:30pm, Sun. noon-5pm

REPO RECORDS

Specializing in punk/hard-core and dance/electronic, this South Street record store has a wealth of new and used records and CDs, boxed sets, imports, hard-to-find indie singles, and B-sides. Out-of-print finds from the United Kingdom and beyond can also be found here. The downstairs is home to plenty of seven-inch vinyl, used CDs, and bargain bins with dirt-cheap offerings.

MAP 5: 538 South St., 215/627-3775, www.reporecords.com; Mon.-Fri. 11am-9pm, Sat. 11am-10pm, Sun. 11:30am-7:30pm

SHOPPING CENTERS AND DISTRICTS

EAST PASSYUNK AVENUE

This stretch of East Passyunk Avenue in South Philly has gone through a major renaissance in the past decade. Home to several centuries-old mom-and-pop shops that help it maintain its old-world character, the area has exploded with gourmet markets and coffee shops, boutique and vintage clothing and jewelry shops, garden supplies, and much more. A vibrant, young community has moved in, joining many of the families that have been rooted here for generations, and businesses keep springing up to meet their needs.

MAP 5: East Passyunk Ave. btwn Federal St. and Tasker St.

SOUTH STREET

Concentrated primarily on the blocks and side streets between Front and 8th Streets, South Street offers an eclectic mix of several hundred shops. Most are independently owned and cater to a diverse mix of people. Head shops, tattoo parlors, independent record stores, whimsical home and gift shops, and kinky lingerie and sex shops coexist on the street. From the ridiculously comfortable options at Benjamin Lovell Shoes to the cheap and trendy fashions at Bare Feet to athletic wear at Reebok and City Blue, South Street is also the place for shoes of all kinds. Venture deeper into South Philadelphia to visit the Italian Market on 9th Street between Christian Street and Washington Avenue for gourmet specialty stores and treats. Still deeper south, the ever-growing East Passyunk Avenue business district, extending south from Dickinson Street, offers an eclectic mix of boutiques, gourmet groceries, old-school South Philly clothing shops, and much more.

MAP 5: South St. btwn Front St. and 8th St.

VINTAGE AND THRIFT

PHILADELPHIA AIDS THRIFT

Philadelphia AIDS Thrift (aka PAT) follows the "one man's trash is another's treasure" model. Bring in the wares you no longer need and AIDS Thrift will sell them for you, with a significant portion of the proceeds going to local AIDS/HIV organizations. This eclectic and eccentric spot has everything from used toasters to movie posters, instructional workout videos, children's toys, lamp shades, and winter coats. You might have to dig around a bit to uncover the true gems in this massive two-story building, but rest assured you'll find them if you have the patience.

MAP 5: 710 S. 5th St., 215/922-3186, www.phillyaidsthrift.com; Mon.-Thurs. 11am-8pm, Fri.-Sat. 11am-9pm, Sun. 11am-7pm

★ RETROSPECT VINTAGE

No vintage clothing lover should leave town without making a stop at Retrospect Vintage. Owned by thrift store giant Goodwill Industries, Retrospect's buyers get first dibs on Goodwill's abundant bounty, handpick the coolest merchandise available, then carefully inspect and organize it. The result is that the shop is expertly curated to supply only the best clothing and furniture without the steep upcharge typically incurred at boutique vintage shops.

MAP 5: 508 South St., 215/925-3761, www. retrospectvintage215.com; Sun.-Tues. noon-8pm, Wed.-Sat. noon-9pm

GIFT AND SPECIALTY

ART STAR

This quirky little Northern Liberties boutique/gallery is committed to providing local budding artists an opportunity to be seen and hopefully make a buck. One-of-a-kind and limited edition ceramics, prints, clothing, dolls, and jewelry are sold on consignment. Exhibitions rotate every six weeks and range from cartoon paintings to unusual stuffed animals and other household items. Named the city's first cutting-edge craft shop by *Philadelphia* magazine, Art Star offers an eclectic mix that reflects the diverse Northern Liberties arts community.

MAP 7: 623 N. 2nd St., 215/238-1557, www.artstarphilly.com; Tues.-Sat. 11am-7pm, Sun. noon-6pm

★ R.E. LOAD BAGGAGE, INC.

Former bike messengers Roland and Ellie (the R. and E. in the company name) founded this one-of-a-kind local company in 1998 on their quest to create the perfect messenger bag. Using only the highest-quality materials, R.E. Load Baggage carefully constructs messenger and courier bags, backpacks, and just about any other type of bag that holds stuff. The best part is that each bag is custom designed and made by hand to reflect the needs and desires of the lucky owner-to-be. Specialized orders can be placed in the store, online, or over the phone, or you can choose from a small ready-made selection. The bags are pricey (upward of $250), but they are made to last a lifetime, or close anyway. Each has its own special flair chosen by you, so you're not just paying for a bag—you're paying for an extension of your personality to wear over your shoulder. R.E. Load bags are also sold at select retail stores throughout the country, mostly in bike shops.

MAP 7: 608 N. 2nd St., 215/625-2987, www.reloadbags.com; Mon.-Fri. 11am-6pm

HOME FURNISHING AND ACCENTS

JINXED

Jinxed started out as a boutique on South Street selling mostly street art and clothes, but since it moved to the Piazza at Schmidt's it has evolved into one of the best yet most affordable places to buy vintage furniture in a boutique setting. They bring in gorgeous items daily from a mysterious source they refuse to identify, often priced shockingly low. They also carry knickknacks, T-shirts, toys, and art. Their Northern Liberties store was such a success that they quickly expanded to include four other locations: **Fishtown** (1331 Frankford Ave., 215/800-1369), **Passyunk** (1835 E Passyunk Ave., 215/551-2345), **609** (609 S. 4th St., 215/928-3377) and **West Philly** (4521 Baltimore Ave., 215/921-3755) all open daily 11am-8pm.

MAP 7: 1050 N. Hancock St., 215/987-5469, www.jinxedphiladelphia.com; daily 11am-8pm

SHOPS
NORTHERN LIBERTIES

SHOPPING CENTERS AND DISTRICTS

★ THE SCHMIDT'S COMMONS

The crown jewel of Northern Liberties, The Schmidt's Commons is an open-air landscaped plaza the size of a large city block. Lined with boutiques, galleries, restaurants, bars, offices, apartments, and artist studios, it was built to mimic European city squares. The square holds a 40-by-20-foot high-definition screen that draws friendly crowds for sporting events and movie screenings, and it hosts frequent free events, including trunk shows, farmers markets, and musical festivals. Saturdays and Sundays (noon-7pm) are great days to visit, when the Market at the Piazza brings vendors selling arts, crafts, clothing, antiques, vintage goods, and more, in addition to all the permanent shops.

MAP 7: N. 2nd St. and Germantown Ave., www.theschmidtscommons.com; hours vary by store

Fishtown
Map 7

CLOTHING AND ACCESSORIES

NORMAN PORTER COMPANY

Norman Porter is a handmade denim company created by two bearded young brothers from rural Pennsylvania that are reviving the lost art of hand tailoring. Their jeans are custom made for the wearer using Japanese and American selvage denim, hammered rivets, hand stitching, and custom embossed leather patches. The shop is open to customers by appointment only. Obviously this kind of custom denim does not come cheap, but these jeans are worth every penny and will only wear better with age.

MAP 7: 150 Cecil B. Moore Ave., 215/908-4694, www.normanporter.com; by appointment only

MUSIC

★ PHILADELPHIA RECORD EXCHANGE

The Philadelphia Record Exchange is a vinyl lover's dream, with the largest selection in the city. Unless you're being watched over by a higher power, you're not likely to find a sought-after hidden classic amid the stacks, since music diehards and DJs regularly troll the shelves. But if your taste is eclectic and you have the time to browse, you'll probably get lucky and find a few gems. Record Exchange also buys music, but they are choosy and at times a bit snobby, so go in with a thick skin if you're looking to sell your childhood memories.

MAP 7: 1524 Frankford Ave., 215/925-7892, www.philarecx.com; daily 11am-8pm

Top: Jinxed. **Bottom:** Philadelphia Record Exchange.

MUSIC
HIDEAWAY MUSIC

Chestnut Hill's independent music store is a popular local stop for its excellent selection of DVDs, LPs, vintage concert posters, rock 'n' roll memorabilia, and new and used CDs. The CD selection offers contemporary and classic selections, and the vinyl collection is dominated by good old rock 'n' roll. The friendly staff in the small shop will be glad to help you find that Stones album you somehow lost track of over the years.

MAP 8: 8612 Germantown Ave., 215/248-4434, http://hideawaymusic.org; Mon.-Sat. 10am-5pm, Sun. 11am-5pm

SHOPPING CENTERS AND DISTRICTS
GERMANTOWN AVENUE

Germantown Avenue in Chestnut Hill is just "the Avenue" to locals of the upscale neighborhood in Northwest Philadelphia. The only business district in an otherwise residential area, it feels like a small-town Main Street with its attractive storefronts, Victorian lampposts, cobblestone streets, and shoppers who stop to chat with one another. While selections are varied, you can find a good dose of antiques, upscale home goods, several art galleries, spas, and clothing and jewelry shops. More people from the surrounding neighborhoods and suburbs than from Center City frequent these shops, although a few of the special art, antiques, and furniture stores draw the downtown sect as well.

MAP 8: Germantown Ave. btwn Chestnut Hill and Springfield Ave.

Manayunk Map 8

MUSIC
MAIN STREET MUSIC

The only record store in Manayunk, this independent-music mainstay has a faithful following. Listen to new and used CDs at listening stations, and if you like what you hear, buy or trade for some of your own old music. For a small space, it's well stocked with plenty of indie, local bands, new releases, and random oldies of whatever other people have traded. The helpful and well-versed staff will order anything you want at no extra charge. They also host intimate live acts in the store; check the website for details and upcoming events.

MAP 8: 4444 Main St., 215/487-7732; Mon.-Thurs. 11am-7pm, Fri.-Sat. 11am-9pm, Sun. noon-6pm

SHOPPING CENTERS AND DISTRICTS

MANAYUNK

Formerly a run-down mill town, Manayunk has transformed into one of the city's major business districts in the past few decades. Straddling the Schuylkill River a short drive from Center City, the shops are concentrated on Main Street and include both upscale and vintage boutiques, jewelry, accessories, stylish eyeglasses, and independent music and art galleries. Main Street also claims to hold the largest concentration of furniture and home-goods stores on one street on the entire East Coast.

MAP 8: Main St. btwn Green Ln. and Shurs Ln.

SPA, BATH, AND BEAUTY

SALON L'ETOILE & SPA

Well worth the short drive from Center City, the salon offers excellent hair, nails, and waxing in a beautiful old building with huge windows overlooking Main Street in the heart of Manayunk. It's a lovely multilevel oasis, where you can go to get pretty and to get pampered. Upstairs is a serene spa offering massage, body treatments, and facials, while the downstairs is a bright, high-energy salon. The friendly, talented beauticians and therapists are happy to help you choose the perfect treatment or the best haircut for you. Reflexology, a treatment utilizing pressure points on your feet, can be experienced on its own or added on to another treatment; try it out, it's divine.

MAP 8: 4360 Main St., 215/483-2500, http://manayunk.salonletoile.com; Sun. 10am-4pm, Mon.-Tues. and Thurs. 10am-8pm, Wed. 8:30am-8pm, Fri. 9am-5pm, Sat. 8am-5pm

Hotels

Old City 248

Society Hill 251

Center City East. 252

Center City West. 256

Museum District. 259

South Philadelphia 260

University City. 260

Fishtown 262

Chestnut Hill 262

Fairmount Park 264

PRICE KEY

💲 Less than $100 per night

💲💲 $100–200 per night

💲💲💲 More than $200 per night

Along with all the standard chain hotels you'd expect in a major city, Philadelphia offers plenty of independent and boutique hotels, bed-and-breakfasts, and two youth hostels. In addition, many of the chain hotels have taken up residence in historic buildings, offering way more character than their big, boring names might suggest. Whether you're working with an unlimited expense account or you can barely scrape together change for a cheesesteak, there is a place for you to lay your head in Philly.

The bulk of hotels are located in Center City—convenient considering this is where most visitors spend the majority of their time. You won't be more than a 10-minute drive or about a 30-minute walk from the city's major sights, dining, and nightlife anywhere in Center City. If money is no object, stay at one of Philadelphia's drop-dead gorgeous world-class hotels: the Four Seasons, The Ritz-Carlton, the Park Hyatt at the Bellevue, or the independent, award-winning Rittenhouse Hotel. And if you can't afford to stay in one of these luxury hotels, at least stop in to check out the elegant lobbies, eat or drink at one of their swank restaurants or bars, or use their fancy bathrooms. Or check out the newest hotels to open in Philadelphia: Hotel Monaco, Hotel Palomar, Le Méridien, or The Independent, each offering a brand-new look in distinctive settings.

At the other end of the spectrum, budget travelers have several options, including the Apple Hostel in Old City, the Chamounix Mansion hostel in Fairmount Park, and the International House in University City. In the midrange, there are plenty of chain and independent hotels, bed-and-breakfasts, and rooms in private homes.

Previous: Hotel Monaco; Rittenhouse Hotel.

Highlights

★ **Best Place to Make Friends:** The closest thing Philly has to a European-style hostel, **Apple Hostels of Philadelphia** offers budget accommodations in the heart of Old City to a mostly international clientele (page 248).

★ **Most Colonial Digs:** Two of Benjamin Franklin's contemporaries owned impressive homes that have since been converted to bed-and-breakfasts named in their honor. Immerse yourself in colonial history at the **Thomas Bond House Bed and Breakfast** (page 250) in Old City or the **Morris House Hotel** (page 251) in nearby Society Hill.

★ **Most Distinctive Bed-and-Breakfast:** At **Madame Saito Bed & Breakfast** near South Street, the multitalented innkeeper cooks Japanese, Thai, and French cuisine and teaches sushi-making classes out of the attached restaurant (page 251).

★ **Best Hotel Lobby:** Even if you can't afford to blow a week's salary to stay at **The Ritz-Carlton of Philadelphia,** be sure to stop in to see the elegant domed lobby. Enjoy tea, lunch, or drinks in the grand space, or just sneak a peek (page 254).

★ **Most Environmentally Friendly:** The **Hotel Palomar** opened in 2009 in the heart of Rittenhouse Row. Philadelphia's first LEED Gold-certified hotel, it has received the highest awards for its eco-friendly design (page 256).

★ **Best Place to See Stars:** The ultra-elegant, independent **Rittenhouse Hotel** is popular with celebs who visit Philly or stay long-term while filming movies. It's easy to see why, considering its plush amenities and prime location overlooking Rittenhouse Square (page 256).

★ **Cheapest Way to Sleep in a Historic Mansion:** Just because you're traveling on a budget doesn't mean you can't do it in style. The **Chamounix Mansion** hostel, a converted 18th-century mansion in Fairmount Park, offers private and dorm-style accommodations at the lowest rates in town (page 264).

It is wise to reserve a room well in advance when visiting at peak times, namely summer and during festivals and holidays. Independence Day is a huge event in Philadelphia, so if you plan to be here for the weeklong festivities, be prepared to pay a premium.

CHOOSING A HOTEL

Old City is the place to be if you're visiting primarily to experience the historic attractions in and around Independence National Historical Park, but with few exceptions it is expensive. It is jam-packed with families in summertime but isn't quite as crowded—or pricey—during other times of the year. If you can't find a room in Old City, anywhere in Center City is convenient for visiting the historic area as well as the museums of the Benjamin Franklin Parkway and the rest of downtown Philadelphia.

Bed-and-breakfasts can be found scattered throughout Center City, especially in and around Washington Square West, Society Hill, and University City. Wash West is a great central location, popular with gay visitors especially, since it is the center of the city's gay culture. Rooms in the area fill well in advance during the annual Equality Forum in May.

The Museum District is lovely during the day but can be a bit desolate at night; home to mostly chain hotels, it is also very close to Center City. Just across the Schuylkill River, University City is a bit less expensive but still close to Center City. Home to University of Pennsylvania and Drexel University, this area is student-friendly, with a bustling college scene and affordable bars and restaurants. The quieter Chestnut Hill, near Fairmount Park and historic Germantown but farther from the city's main attractions, offers several options near its main business district.

Since chain hotels are so easily found with a few clicks of a mouse, the majority of this chapter is devoted to the lesser-known unique Philadelphia establishments. Chains are, however, included when there are limited options in a particular area or in some cases because the chains are in historic buildings that are too beautiful or the location is simply too convenient to leave out. In addition to Center City, you'll find plenty of chain hotels near

Save with the Philly Overnight Hotel Package

The Philly Overnight Hotel Package is available through the Independence Visitor Center's website (www.visitphilly.com). It will buy you two nights of accommodations with free parking for both nights (a $75-plus value at some Center City hotels) and a free gift when you check in. Additional promotions are sometimes included, like tickets to attractions and exhibits, so it's always worth checking the website for details when planning your visit. The deal is available seven days a week for any two-consecutive-nights' stay; the site connects with a Travelocity search so that you can select from participating hotels. Most local hotels participate.

the airport, including the Philadelphia Airport Marriott, directly connected to the airport. There is also a Holiday Inn near the stadium—convenient for those attending events at the sports arenas.

All rates listed are based on double occupancy in summer (high season). Most hotels offer parking on-site or in a nearby lot, usually for around $20 a day. The Official Visitor Site for Greater Philadelphia (www.visitphilly. com) is another excellent resource for additional hotels, reservations, and discounts, including the **Philly Overnight Hotel Package,** which includes hotel accommodations for two nights, free parking, and a gift and coupon book upon check-in. **Bed and Breakfast Connections of Philadelphia** (800/448-3619, www.bnbphiladelphia.com) has additional offerings if you're looking for something cozy and special. There is also **Airbnb,** which offers some unique accommodations—everything from a historic townhouse in Rittenhouse Square to a warehouse loft in Fishtown.

Old City Map 1

If you're visiting for the historical attractions of Independence National Historical Park, Old City is the ideal place to stay. The area is also great for shopping, dining, entertainment, and nightlife, and is also one of the prettiest areas of the city. With the exception of Apple Hostels and a few of the midrange chains, this is an expensive area, and rooms tend to fill quickly, especially in summer. Society Hill is Old City's neighbor to the south, offering proximity to the main historic attractions in a somewhat quieter, more residential setting. The waterfront Hyatt Regency at Penn's Landing and the Sheraton Society Hill are both fully equipped chain hotels in excellent locations. Several character-filled bed-and-breakfasts provide nearby alternatives at lower prices.

★ APPLE HOSTELS OF PHILADELPHIA ⑤

Formerly Bank Street Hostel, the only Center City Philadelphia hostel came under new ownership in 2008. This is a good thing. Now renamed Apple, the hostel was upgraded in the process and even voted second best hostel in the United States by Hostelworld.com. Perhaps the best change of all is that there is no longer a curfew, which is a great thing considering the prime location in the heart of Old City. On a quiet street but just steps from the historic attractions, restaurants, and nightlife, this is the place to stay for budget-conscious travelers. The vibe is friendly, laid-back, young, and communal, so if you're not any of those things, this probably isn't the place for you. But if you don't mind dorm-style beds or shared bathrooms, and perhaps are looking to make new friends, this is the place for you.

It's an excellent—and pretty much the only—budget option in Old City: High season (summertime) rates are $35-38 for a dorm bed, with a few private and semiprivate rooms available for $79-94. Weekly rates and other specials can be found online. The hostel caters to students and international travelers; locals are not allowed to stay—in fact, ID proving that you live outside of a 100-mile radius is required. Linens and towels are provided, and a communal kitchen, dining area, and lounge with foosball table and Wii are available. Free Internet access, lockers (bring your own padlock), and laundry are available. Tours and other communal events are sometimes offered, including an open-mike night on Fridays. Check-in is at 2pm and checkout is 11am, but bags can be stored until 8pm, and you are free to use the common areas and Internet after you check out. All guests must be 18 or older, or accompanied by a guardian.

MAP 1 DETAIL: 32 S. Bank St., 215/922-0222, www.applehostels.com

BEST WESTERN INDEPENDENCE PARK HOTEL $$

You'd never guess that this building—listed on the National Register of Historic Places—is part of the Best Western chain. Combining modern hotel amenities with plenty of character, the comfortable high-ceilinged guest rooms ($180-400) are decked out in Victorian-era furnishings. It's in a prime spot among Old City's most popular restaurants and bars and just across the street from Independence National Historical Park. Prices at this popular hotel are considerably higher on weekends in summertime than at other times, but be sure to check the website for discounts, including AAA, military, extended stay, and advance booking. A complimentary continental breakfast with a make-your-own-waffle station is included.

MAP 1 DETAIL: 235 Chestnut St., 215/922-4443, www.independenceparkinn.com

HOLIDAY INN EXPRESS PENN'S LANDING $$

The Penn's Landing location and reasonable prices ($99-350) are the primary draws for this basic 10-story, 185-room chain. While the hotel is on a stretch of highway, the attractions of Old City and Society Hill are all within a short walk, and complimentary van service will take you to Old City and Center City. The hotel is clean and offers standard amenities, including wireless Internet, a bar, a small exercise room, laundry service, an airport shuttle, and off-street parking ($30/day). A continental breakfast is included. Request a room on an upper floor facing the river for a view of the Benjamin Franklin Bridge.

MAP 1: 100 N. Columbus Blvd., 800/315-2621, www.hiexpress.com

HOTEL MONACO $$$

The Hotel Monaco has class and character. This four-star boutique hotel is elegant yet boldly modern. Located in the Historic Lafayette Building, each of its 268 guest rooms are individually outfitted with bright colors, wild patterns, and luxury utilities, like Japanese soaking tubs. In addition to the common amenities, like full concierge service and a 24-hour gym, the hotel offers free bicycle rentals, which makes exploring Old City fun and convenient. At the Monaco's Stratus Rooftop Lounge you can get a bird's-eye view of Old City while sipping craft cocktails by the patio fire pit.

MAP 1 DETAIL: 433 Chestnut St., 215/925-2111, www.monaco-philadelphia.com

FRANKLIN HOTEL AT INDEPENDENCE PARK ❸❸

Boasting European-style luxury, the 150 large rooms offer every standard amenity along with great views of Independence National Historical Park. The elegant on-site Azalea restaurant serves modern American cuisine for breakfast, lunch, and dinner, and the on-site bar offers a sophisticated lounge atmosphere. Unwind in the heated indoor pool or enjoy a massage or facial at the Balance Spa.

MAP 1 DETAIL: 401 Chestnut St., 215/925-0000, www.marriott.com/hotels/travel/phlpr-the-franklin-hotel-at-independence-park

PENN'S VIEW HOTEL ❸❸

This elegant medium-size boutique hotel in the heart of Old City is family owned and operated, and it shows in the level of service provided. Built in 1828, the building has been a shipping warehouse, hardware store, and coffeehouse in its long history, and it is on the National Register of Historic Places. The Italian-born Sena family (who also owns the local favorite restaurant La Famiglia) purchased and renovated the hotel in 1989 and opened Ristorante Panorama and Il Bar on-site. Rooms ($180-299) have a touch of European elegance with large mirrors and armoires, and some have unique designs like exposed brick walls. Some of the rooms are equipped with whirlpool tubs, marble fireplaces, and views of the Delaware River. Continental breakfast is included.

MAP 1: 14 N. Front St., 215/922-6600 or 800/331-7634, www.pennsviewhotel.com

★ THOMAS BOND HOUSE BED AND BREAKFAST ❸❸

This charming bed-and-breakfast is in the heart of Independence National Historical Park, adjacent to Welcome Park, where William Penn's home once stood. It has 12 guest rooms, including two large suites with full-size sofa beds, working fireplaces, and whirlpool tubs. Built in 1769, the Georgian-style home was named for its first owner, Thomas Bond, acclaimed surgeon and friend of Ben Franklin, who was a regular guest at the home. With period furnishings and personal touches, including books, games, complimentary sherry, and fresh-baked cookies, a stay here feels like visiting the home of a colonial-era friend. Most rooms are $125-155, with the two suites costing $190 and two smaller rooms going for $105. Continental breakfast is served on weekdays, and a full breakfast is included on weekends. Complimentary wine and cheese is served nightly, and all the restaurants of Old City are steps away, including historic City Tavern just across the street.

MAP 1: 129 S. 2nd St., 215/923-8523, www.thomasbondhousebandb.com

WYNDHAM HISTORIC DISTRICT ❸❸

There are modern renovated rooms ($170-220) in this eight-story Wyndham hotel. The central Old City location is ideal for touring Independence Park.

You can find all the standard amenities, like a fitness center, restaurant, and bar, but the best amenity of all has to be the rooftop pool, which offers much-needed relief from the summer heat and makes it a great place to stay with kids. Parking costs $37 a day, but once you're here, you can leave the car and walk, cab, or take a bus all over the city.

MAP 1: 400 Arch St., 215/923-8660, www.wyndham.com

Society Hill
Map 1

APPEL'S SOCIETY HILL BED & BREAKFAST ⑤⑤

The modern decor of the rooms at this small four-room bed-and-breakfast is a contrast to the historic building dating from 1805. Offering a quieter alternative to the bustle of Old City, with rooms, including an extended continental breakfast, starting at $135 a night, this is a great deal in a pleasant area. It often fills even though the owners do not advertise, so be sure to book in advance, especially in summertime. Each of the basic bedrooms has private bath, air-conditioning, and wireless Internet, and a minimum two-night stay is required. Saturday and Sunday check-in is discouraged but can be arranged for longer stays.

MAP 1: 414 Spruce St., 215/925-5460

★ MADAME SAITO BED & BREAKFAST ⑤

Trilingual Madame Saito, the self-proclaimed queen of sushi, does it all out of two adjoined Society Hill row homes a block north of South Street. In addition to running a five-room bed-and-breakfast, she operates an attached restaurant and catering business specializing in Japanese, French, and Thai cuisine (not fusion, which Madame does not like, just all three cuisines separately). She also teaches ballroom dancing and sushi-making classes in her spare time and is a fascinating woman worth meeting whether you stay here, take a class with her, or come in for dinner. A comfortable private room with one or two double beds ranges $80-120 in summer and a bit lower other times of the year, with discounts available for stays of a week or more. For an additional fee of $10-12, you can enjoy a traditional Japanese breakfast cooked by the fabulous Madame herself.

MAP 1: 124 Lombard St., 215/922-2515, www.queenofsushi.com

★ MORRIS HOUSE HOTEL ⑤⑤

The perfect balance of colonial charm and modern amenities, the Morris House Hotel offers period furnishings and wireless Internet. Built in 1787, this three-story bed-and-breakfast was home to the prominent Morris family for generations. The National Historic Landmark has been beautifully restored; the 15 guest rooms vary in size and price, with doubles starting at $179, suites starting at $199, and extended luxury suites at $249 with the presidential loft going as high as $349 on weekends. Rooms in the new addition next door are attractive and comfortable but quite modern, so if it's colonial ambience you're after, be sure to request a room in the original building. A delicious continental breakfast and afternoon tea are included, and when the weather is nice, you can eat breakfast outside in the pretty walled garden.

MAP 1: 225 S. 8th St., 215/922-2446, www.morrishousehotel.com

Center City East   Map 2

Broad Street divides Center City into East and West. Center City East is home to the Convention Center, Chinatown, and Washington Square West (also called the Gayborhood). Smack dab in the center of the city, it makes a great base for exploring the historic attractions of Old City as well as shopping in Rittenhouse and seeing the museums of the Benjamin Franklin Parkway. There are plenty of chain hotels on and near Market Street that cater to the Convention Center crowds, including the Wyndham, Hilton Garden Inn, Holiday Inn, and the Marriott. Bed-and-breakfasts can be found near Antique Row in Washington Square, along with a few independent, midrange, midsize hotels nearby.

ALEXANDER INN 💲
Popular with gay travelers, this boutique hotel in the heart of the Washington Square West neighborhood is a good deal with double rooms starting at $119 including a continental breakfast buffet. Comfortable rooms, a prime location, and friendly staff make the 48-room hotel a popular choice for returning visitors. The Deco style is a bit outdated, a throwback to cruise ships; but while it's a little cheesy, it's not totally over the top. Some of the rooms are very small, so request a larger one when available. A 24-hour fruit and snack table is available for returning late-night revelers or those in search of a midday snack, and a 24-hour fitness room is here for anyone looking to squeeze in a quick workout.

MAP 2: 12th and Spruce Sts., 215/923-3535, www.alexanderinn.com

CLINTON STREET BED & BREAKFAST 💲💲
This charming bed-and-breakfast occupies a historic 1836 Federal-style townhouse on a tree-lined, primarily residential street near Antique Row. Seven spacious suites ($129-219) each have their own character, and all of them come complete with private baths, kitchens, sitting areas, and Internet access, and most have a fireplace. The emerald suite is the largest, making it ideal for extended stays. Innkeeper Kathleen Rabun provides the makings for a do-it-yourself breakfast (coffee, juice, eggs, bread plate, and more) in your suite, so you can eat at your own pace without leaving your room.

MAP 2: 1024 Clinton St., 215/802-1334, http://1024clintonstreetbb.com/bb

Relocating to Philly temporarily or permanently? You have a few good options for lodging while you make the transition.

For budget travelers, the **International House** in University City is available to students or faculty with valid IDs from any academic institution; stay for a night, a week, a month, a semester, or the entire school year at a reasonable price.

Catering primarily to business travelers staying for a week or more, **AKA Rittenhouse Square** on 18th and Walnut Streets, directly on Rittenhouse Square, and **Windsor Suites** (a bit less luxurious and a bit less expensive) on the Benjamin Franklin Parkway both offer fully equipped apartments close to the Center City business district. The newly built, incredibly hip **ROOST Apartment Hotel** is an excellent choice with locations in Rittenhouse Square and Midtown.

Bed-and-breakfasts or rooms in a private home are also a good bet, offering homey accommodations across a wide range of prices. Many owners encourage long-term visitors with reduced rates for stays of a week or more, and even steeper discounts for stays of a month or more. Try **Madame Saito Bed & Breakfast** for standard rooms at very low rates, or **Bella Vista Bed & Breakfast, Clinton Street Bed & Breakfast,** or **La Reserve Center City Bed and Breakfast** for fully equipped studios with kitchenettes. Visit online or call **Bed and Breakfast Connections of Philadelphia** (800/448-3619, www.bnbphiladelphia.com) for plenty of additional options in neighborhoods across the city. And even if the site doesn't mention discounts for long-term stays, be sure to ask the owner and shop around for rates; since most are privately owned, there is usually wiggle room.

Airbnb (www.airbnb.com) has a wealth of diverse options from townhomes in Rittenhouse, contemporary condos in Old City to South Philly row homes or Fishtown loft apartments. **Craigslist** (www.craigslist.org) is still the ultimate site for finding sublets, temporary, permanent, and shared housing, and pretty much any other arrangement you can imagine.

HOTELS
CENTER CITY EAST

THE INDEPENDENT HOTEL $$

This 24-room boutique hotel opened in a prime location in the heart of Midtown Village in 2008. Occupying a restored Georgian Revival building listed on the National Register of Historic Places, the elegant lobby features a 30-foot hand-painted mural, indicative of many personal touches to come. The rooms are spacious, and the tin-ceilinged bathrooms and hardwood floors lend a modern, clean look. Each room has its own custom-built accents, from fireplaces and exposed brick walls to cathedral ceilings, French windows, and lofts, with luxurious linens and attractive furniture to match the distinctive architecture. All rooms have wireless Internet, a TV, refrigerator, and microwave, and some have a kitchenette. High-season rates start at $154, including a light breakfast in the lobby or delivered to your room, and a wine and cheese reception on weekdays.

MAP 2: 1234 Locust St., 215/772-1440, www.theindependenthotel.com

LE MÉRIDIEN ⓢⓢⓢ

Housed in a 10-story Georgian Revival building that was once a YMCA, Le Méridien opened in 2009. Part of the Starwood Hotels Group, recognized worldwide for the highest service and luxury, it has an air of sophistication and the feel of a unique, independent hotel. Modern, clean lines featuring black, white, and red colors contrast with the elaborate architectural details of the building. Just steps from the Convention Center and Reading Terminal Market and close enough to walk to both Rittenhouse and Old City, the location is popular for both tourists and business travelers. The 202 rooms start at $299 in the high season with Internet deals sometimes available.

MAP 2: 1421 Arch St., 215/422-8200, www.starwoodhotels.com

LOEWS HOTEL ⓢⓢ

The modern, stylish Loews occupies the former Philadelphia Savings Fund Society (PSFS) building, considered the first modern, international-style skyscraper in the country. Designed by George Howe and William Lescaze, it was constructed in 1932, and despite its modern incarnation as a chain hotel today, it retains some original and early details, including Cartier clocks and bank-vault doors. There is a full-service health spa with lap pool, treatment rooms, steam room, and sauna on the 5th floor, and a high-end seafood restaurant and a stylish bar on the first level. The hotel is well equipped for the business traveler with T1 cable lines, modem lines, and electronic safes, and its location a block from the Convention Center makes it a popular choice. But it's cool enough to be chosen by many leisure travelers for its host of amenities, stylish decor, and central location a block from Reading Terminal Market, smack-dab in the middle of Center City. Rates start at $199, though specials and package deals are often available.

MAP 2: 1200 Market St., 215/627-1200, www.loewshotels.com

★ THE RITZ-CARLTON OF PHILADELPHIA ⓢⓢⓢ

In its prime Avenue of the Arts location, The Ritz-Carlton is the epitome of luxury. The five-diamond hotel occupies the historic former Girard/Mellon Bank building, and the lobby—with its domed ceiling, marble floors, and grand columns—is absolutely breathtaking. Each of the 330 guest rooms offers the ultimate in luxury—as it should, with prices starting at $359 a night. The Ritz is home to a state-of-the-art fitness center and the full-service D'Ambra Day Spa & Salon. Aqimero, the Ritz's in-house restaurant, serves Latin dishes with an extensive sushi, ceviche, and raw bar.

MAP 2: 10 Avenue of the Arts, 215/523-8000, www.ritzcarlton.com

Top: Morris House Hotel. **Bottom:** Loews Hotel.

Most of the accommodations in Center City West are near Rittenhouse Square, a lovely area in the heart of the downtown shopping district and an easy walk to the Benjamin Franklin Parkway museums. A popular and pricey part of town, it offers high-end chain hotels along with a few mid-range hotels and bed-and-breakfasts.

★ HOTEL PALOMAR ⑤⑤⑤

This LEED Gold-certified luxury boutique hotel in the Rittenhouse shopping district opened in 2009 and is the first of its kind to receive the ultimate eco-friendly certification in the city. Part of the Kimpton Hotel Group, known for its reuse of historic buildings, the hotel's tagline is Art in Motion. Each of Kimpton's hotels has a theme or a story, and this one pays homage to the arts in all their constantly changing forms with a variety of original artwork placed throughout the hotel's common spaces, including the lobby, restaurant, and fitness center. Boasting an exceptional sustainable design, including water and energy efficiency, eco-friendly materials and furnishings, and high indoor air quality, the hotel offers 230 rooms and suites designed with neutral earth tones, modern lines, and Art Deco details. This is a lovely new hotel in a lovely location. Rooms start around $225 in high season with discounts often available for three nights or more.
MAP 3: 117 S. 17th St., 215/563-5006, www.hotelpalomar-philadelphia.com

LA RESERVE CENTER CITY BED AND BREAKFAST ⑤

This restored 1850s four-story row house sits on a quiet residential block in an idyllic location near Rittenhouse Square. There are 12 rooms to choose from, including 6 fully equipped units (studios and one-bedroom suites), which are intended for people staying a week or longer. Standard rooms that share a bath with one other room are $80-125; deluxe rooms with private bath are $115-150; and studios and executive suites are $120-175. This is an unbeatable deal for the location, especially for long-term stays with discounts of 10-30 percent, depending on length of stay. There are no TVs in the rooms, but a Steinway piano in the parlor and endless activities in nearby Rittenhouse Square keep guests entertained. A continental breakfast is served on weekdays and a full breakfast is served on weekends and holidays, and homemade cookies and afternoon tea are served daily.
MAP 3: 1804 Pine St., 215/735-1137, www.lareservebandb.com

★ RITTENHOUSE HOTEL ⑤⑤⑤

Oprah Winfrey, Bill Clinton, Mark Wahlberg, and Tom Hanks are just a few of the famous guests who have called the Rittenhouse Hotel home during their stays in Philadelphia—and no wonder, considering the ideal location, luxurious accommodations, and perfectly attentive yet unobtrusive service. Nearly all of the rooms, starting at $215 with larger suites at $600 and up, offer a great view of Rittenhouse Square below. The independent luxury hotel is consistently ranked among the top boutique hotels in the world by *Travel + Leisure* magazine and other publications, and has received the esteemed five diamonds from AAA for two decades. With long-term apartment accommodations available for those with fat wallets, everything you want can be found on-site—an indoor pool, health club, salon, and spa. Dining options include the Smith & Wollensky Grill, a steakhouse; Lacroix, one of the most esteemed fine-dining establishments in the city; and a tea room and garden serving afternoon tea and cocktails.

MAP 3: 210 W. Rittenhouse Sq., 215/546-9000, www.rittenhousehotel.com

RITTENHOUSE 1715 $$$

You'll be treated to pure elegance and comfort at this 23-room bed-and-breakfast tucked away on a quiet street just off bustling Rittenhouse Square. With standard rooms starting around $249, junior suites at $309, and the crème de la crème—the deluxe two-level presidential suite—as high as $699, this level of luxury obviously does not come cheaply. But if you've got the cash (or credit) and you're looking for a more intimate alternative to the larger luxury hotels, or you want to splurge for a romantic special occasion like an anniversary, Rittenhouse 1715 cannot be beat. Think plush robes, fireplaces, elegant furniture, dim lighting, plasma TVs, marble baths, and nightly turndown service. A tasty extended continental breakfast is served each morning, and complimentary wine is offered in the drawing room in the evenings.

MAP 3: 1715 Rittenhouse Square St. (btwn Locust and Spruce Sts.), 215/546-6500, www.rittenhouse1715.com

ROOST APARTMENT HOTEL $$$

ROOST Apartment Hotel is a boutique extended stay option that combines the convenience and comfort of your very own apartment with the service and amenities of a hotel. Each of the 27 apartments are fully furnished and feature walk-in rainfall showers, king-size beds and well-appointed kitchens with high-end cookware and utensils. Studios, one, and two bedrooms are available and can be rented on a weekly or monthly basis. Amenities include a bike share program, a lending library, dog walking services, personal training, and a 24-hour front desk and concierge. There is also a second location in the Rittenhouse Square neighborhood (1831 Chestnut St., 217/469-0349).

MAP 3: 111 S. 15th St., 267/737-9000, www.myroost.com

SOFITEL $$$

The sophisticated, French inspired Sofitel is conveniently located less than two blocks from Rittenhouse Square. The hotel has an elegant mid-century modern look and feel. The spacious rooms feature free Wi-Fi, flat-screen TVs, marble bathrooms with soaking tubs, and their patented brand of

Top: ROOST Apartment Hotel. Bottom: Sofitel.

luxurious bedding. The suites have separate living rooms with pullout sofas to accommodate larger parties. On-site amenities include a French brasserie, 24-hour room service, valet parking and a fitness center. The Sofitel is also pet friendly.

MAP 3: 120 S. 17th St., 215/569-8300, www.sofitel.com

WESTIN ⑤⑤⑤

With rooms starting at around $200 a night, this deluxe chain in the heart of the downtown business and shopping district is a top choice for business travelers with expense accounts. With clean lines and soothing colors, both the rooms and common areas are sleek, stylish, and modern. The 294 guest rooms and 19 suites have all the luxury amenities, but the greatest amenity of all has to be the signature Heavenly Bed. It is, quite simply, the most comfortable bed in the world. The hotel is connected to the Shops at Liberty Place with all the Rittenhouse shops just outside your door.

MAP 3: 99 S. 17th St., 215/563-1600, www.starwoodhotels.com

Museum District   Map 4

An easy walk to Center City and Fairmount, and just next door to a few of the city's biggest museums, including the Philadelphia Museum of Art and the Franklin Institute, the area is home to primarily chain hotels, including the Sheraton, Embassy Suites, Crowne Plaza, and the impressive Four Seasons. Popular with business travelers, but also a good base for tourists, the area is bustling during the day but a bit quiet at night.

WINDSOR SUITES ⑤

This 24-story hotel sits directly on the Benjamin Franklin Parkway and is easily recognizable by its curved exterior. Offering spacious apartment-style accommodations and large work stations, it's popular with long-term guests in town for business. But considering the reasonable price for the location (rooms start at approximately $129 per night), it is also a decent option for anyone looking to prepare meals at home and stay near the heart of Center City. A 24-hour fitness facility, free Internet access, a seasonal rooftop pool, and a sundeck are a few of the amenities. Two on-site dining options offer Asian and Irish Pub cuisine.

MAP 4: 1700 Benjamin Franklin Pkwy., 877/784-8379, www.thewindsorsuites.com

Just south of South Street, the Queen Village and Bella Vista neighborhoods are two of the city's most popular areas, with lots of character and plenty of great restaurants. There are no hotels in this part of the city, but a few good, reasonably priced bed-and-breakfasts are available, all within a short walk of Old City. In addition to the excellent one listed here, you can find several more at www.bnbphiladelphia.com.

BELLA VISTA BED & BREAKFAST $

Just a block from the Italian Market, this converted circa-1860 townhouse has nine rooms and seven suites, with rates of $95-150. Rooms vary in size (from small to spacious) and design (from colonial to contemporary), but each has its own charm filled with artwork, antiques, and eclectic touches. All rooms have satellite TV and DSL, and most have private baths. A continental breakfast with homemade muffins is included in the price. Some suites have kitchens and separate living areas; with great deals on long-term stays, they make a great option for long-term visitors or anyone planning to relocate to Philly who wants to feel at home but needs some time to find a place.

MAP 5: 752 S. 10th St., 215/238-1270, www.philadelphiabellavistabnb.com

University City Map 6

An affordable alternative to staying in Center City, especially for college students or anyone visiting Penn or Drexel, University City is easily reached via several car and foot bridges. Numerous Victorian bed-and-breakfasts with loads of character offer alternatives to the two chain hotels, the Hilton Inn at Penn and the Sheraton University City. In addition to those listed, there are plenty of other great options that can be found at www.bnbphiladelphia.com.

CORNERSTONE BED & BREAKFAST $$

This restored 1865 Victorian mansion has six beautifully appointed rooms ($165-230), including two suites. Located near the campuses of the University of Pennsylvania and Drexel, it offers a nice alternative for visiting parents, professors, or students. Rooms have a mix of antique and contemporary furniture and include modern amenities like large flat-screen TVs. A full breakfast is served in the dining room on weekends, and a continental breakfast is available on weekdays. The wraparound porch is surrounded by a lovely garden, offering a picturesque place to sit when the weather is nice.

MAP 6: 3300 Baring St., 215/387-6065, www.cornerstonebandb.com

GABLES $

Built in 1889 by prominent Philadelphia architect Willis Hale, this restored Victorian mansion, with 10 rooms available for guests, is one of the most popular bed-and-breakfasts in West Philadelphia. The innkeepers have created a beautiful and friendly atmosphere with a mix of antique furniture and modern amenities, including air-conditioning, cable TV, and wireless Internet. Most rooms, which range $125-185, have private baths, but visit the website for detailed descriptions of each individual space. A computer station, refrigerator, and microwave are available for guest use in the common area, and a full homemade breakfast is served every day. A large wraparound porch—a classic feature in most large homes in this area—is a great place to meet fellow travelers.

MAP 6: 4520 Chester Ave., 215/662-1918, www.gablesbb.com

THE HILTON INN AT PENN $$

In the heart of the University of Pennsylvania's campus, this is the most popular hotel for visiting parents, faculty, and guests of the university, and it is as comfortable and high-tech as you'd expect from an Ivy League-affiliated establishment. The AAA four-diamond hotel is managed by Hilton but retains its own character. With 238 rooms, including four suites, prices start around $150 when purchased several weeks in advance. The already attractive rooms underwent a multimillion dollar renovation in early 2011. The hotel's on-site dining options include an Italian restaurant, Penne, open for lunch and dinner, and the University Club for breakfast, with plenty of additional dining, shopping, and entertainment options just outside the door. Rooms fill early during the beginning and end of the semester and especially during graduation in May.

MAP 6: 3600 Sansom St., 215/222-0200, www.theinnatpenn.com

INTERNATIONAL HOUSE $

There is a lot going on inside this large, boxy, bland-looking building on the edge of the University of Pennsylvania's campus. The International House offers basic accommodations for a few days, monthly, or long-term. Rooms are rented to students, prospective students, faculty, or anyone with an academic affiliation (ID is required). Singles ($90), private rooms ($125), and efficiency apartments ($150) are rented on a nightly basis when available, but many residents stay for a month ($795-1,350) or more (price is lower with stays of three months or more). This is where many international students studying at Penn live for a semester or a year, for its affordability, community spirit, and for a host of other programs built in that cater to the international community, including the on-site movie theater showing mostly international films, events and parties, and language and other classes. Note that you don't have to stay here to take advantage of all the great programming.

MAP 6: 3701 Chestnut St., 215/387-5125, www.ihousephilly.org

In recent years, Fishtown has become the nightlife epicenter of Philadelphia. Though there is only one hotel here as of printing, there are more planned for the area. This is also the best area to find an interesting Airbnb thanks to the hip, young cohorts that call Fishtown home.

WM. MULHERIN'S SONS ⑤⑤

With just four rooms, Wm. Mulherin's Sons may be the smallest but also the coolest hotel in the city. It's currently the only hotel in Fishtown, so it is a perfect choice if you plan to partake in the area's abundant nightlife. Mulherin's is housed in a newly renovated whiskey blending and bottling facility, located above a chic restaurant of the same name. The rooms themselves are spacious and loftlike, each one with its own design and layout.
MAP 7: 1355 N. Front St., 267/753-9478, www.wmmulherinssons.com

Chestnut Hill   Map 8

Chestnut Hill has one full-service hotel in the heart of the Germantown Avenue business district. It's a lovely part of the city but about a 25-minute drive from downtown, so you'll want to have a car to do ample exploring from here. It's a great base for visiting the historic attractions of nearby Germantown, Wissahickon Park, and the Manayunk business district. The area is filled with mansions, some of which rent out rooms as bed-and-breakfasts. Visit www.bnbphiladelphia.com for more information.

CHESTNUT HILL HOTEL ⑤⑤

Built in 1864, the current building replaced an inn in the same location that dated from 1772. The comfortable 36-room hotel offers modern amenities with antique-looking furnishings that pay homage to its long history, with high-season rates starting around $189. The only full-service hotel in Chestnut Hill, it is an excellent base for exploring the area right in the heart of the business district, which is bustling during the day and relatively quiet at night. The three on-site restaurants happen to be some of the neighborhood's best, but there are a myriad of other options nearby. The AAA three-diamond establishment has hosted its fair share of celebrities, including Kate Hudson, Billie Jean King, and Cuba Gooding Jr.
MAP 8: 8229 Germantown Ave., 215/242-5905, www.chestnuthillhotel.com

Top: Wm. Mulherin's Sons. Bottom: Chamounix Mansion.

There is a youth hostel, Chamounix Mansion, tucked away amidst the trees and trails of Fairmount Park. The location is accessible although a bit out of the way for exploring the major tourist attractions, but the setting is unique and lovely, making it a great option for outdoor lovers or anyone on a budget.

★ **CHAMOUNIX MANSION** ⑤

A one-of-a-kind mansion turned youth hostel, Chamounix (pronounced CHAM-ah-nee) occupies a bucolic setting in the heart of Fairmount Park. Originally built as a country home for Philadelphia merchant George Plumstead in 1802, the restored mansion offers clean air-conditioned dorm accommodations with several private rooms available at an unbeatable price of $22 for Hostelling International members with valid ID and $25 for nonmembers. A public SEPTA bus runs into the city from a stop a short walk from the hostel, but having a car or bike is useful for greater flexibility and safety, especially at night; there are a few free bikes available for guests. Included in the common areas is an Internet kiosk, a TV lounge with a video library, and a recreation room with table tennis, a piano, and foosball. Linens, pillow, and blanket are provided free of charge. A washer, dryer, towels, and lockers are available for a fee. There is a 2am curfew and a daily lockout, 11am-4:30pm. Alcohol and smoking are not permitted on-site.

MAP 9: 3250 Chamounix Dr., 215/878-3676 or 800/379-0017, www.philahostel.org

Excursions

Brandywine Valley 269   Pennsylvania Dutch Country . . . 288
Bucks County 281

Look for ★ to find
recommended Excursions

Highlights

★ **Best Place to See the Brandywine Valley in Still Form:** The **Brandywine River Museum** displays an impressive collection of American art, including many paintings of the local landscape by world-renowned artist Andrew Wyeth (page 271).

★ **Best Historic Gardens:** With more than 1,000 acres of landscaped gardens, **Longwood Gardens,** a local du Pont family legacy, is one of the best horticultural showcases in the world (page 271).

★ **Best Decorative Arts Collection:** One of several local du Pont family estates in the Brandywine Valley, **Winterthur Museum, Garden, and Library** is home to America's most esteemed collection of decorative arts, along with 1,000 lush acres of rolling hills, streams, and gardens to explore (page 278).

★ **Most Charming Town:** An artist enclave straddling the Delaware River, **New Hope** offers shops, restaurants, art galleries, antiques, and bed-and-breakfasts for a bustling culture in a small-town setting (page 282).

★ **Best Castle Museums:** In the early 20th century, Henry Mercer, one of Bucks County's most famous sons, built a castle, a museum, and a factory in Doylestown. The three National Historic Landmarks make up the **Mercer Mile** (page 283).

★ **Best Kids' Theme Park:** Based on the *Sesame Street* television series, **Sesame Place** is hugely popular with kids (page 284).

★ **Best Way to Cool Off on a Hot Day:** Several Bucks County companies offer **water sports on the Delaware River.** For tubing, rafting, canoeing, and kayaking, try Delaware River Tubing Co. on the New Jersey side of the river or Bucks County River Country on the Pennsylvania side (page 285).

★ **Best Market:** Lancaster's **Central Market** is reminiscent of Philadelphia's Reading Terminal Market but with lower prices and even more homemade Amish goods and crafts for sale. Originally an outdoor market in the 1730s, it is the oldest continually operating market in the country (page 288).

★ **Most Historic Theater:** See a show at Lancaster's historic **Fulton Theatre,** built in 1852. The intimate venue has seen many a famous actor grace its stage, including most of the Barrymore family, Sarah Bernhardt, W. C. Fields, and Mark Twain (page 289).

Y ou'll never run out of things to do in Philadelphia, but if you get the chance to take a day or
weekend trip outside of the city, there is even more
to see and do within just a short drive. The Brandywine Valley, Bucks County, and Pennsylvania Dutch
Country are the most popular nearby destinations, all only 45-90 minutes
away by car. While each is unique, you'll find charming towns, villages,
and farms sprinkled amid bucolic landscape in all three. You'll also find
cozy bed-and-breakfasts, a diversity of dining options, opportunities for
recreation, and shopping galore—from outlets to antiques to fine art to
handmade crafts.

While Bucks County and the Brandywine Valley offer museums, gardens, wineries, galleries, and antiques shops, Pennsylvania Dutch Country
beckons visitors to experience the lifestyle of our non-electricity-using,
horse-and-buggy-riding Amish neighbors amid lush, rolling farmlands.

As you explore, you'll learn about the long, rich history of each area—
many aspects of which are linked with Philadelphia's history. For example,
there are several key Revolutionary War sites in the Brandywine Valley
and Bucks County, and the reason that the largest Pennsylvania Dutch
settlement is near Philadelphia is because persecuted Amish communities
came to Pennsylvania from Germany because of William Penn's pledge of
religious freedom.

The three excursions detailed in this chapter are some of the best and
closest year-round destinations, but there is plenty more to do seasonally. In
summertime, follow the stream of locals who head "down the shore"—local

Previous: Longwood Gardens; the Hagley Museum and Library.

Excursions

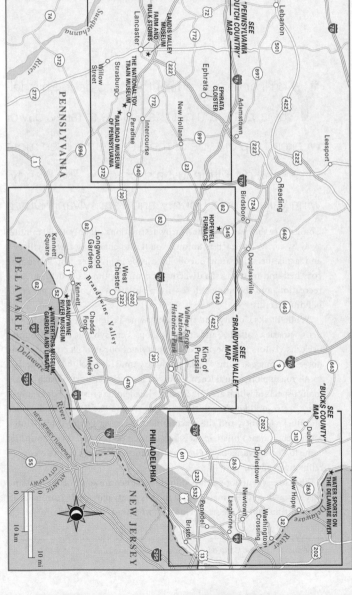

vernacular for the New Jersey beach towns. And for lovers of skiing or snowboarding, no winter trip to the area is complete without a trip to the Poconos in northeastern Pennsylvania, or "up the mountains" as some locals say. And, of course, New York, Baltimore, and Washington, DC are all within a three-hour drive, train, or bus ride. So whether you're just visiting the area or you live here and you're looking for a break from the buzz of the city, be sure to take advantage of the wealth of vastly different areas within reach.

PLANNING YOUR TIME

Each of these destinations can be experienced in a day trip if that is all the time you have, but an overnight—or even better, a weekend—will make for a more relaxing and in-depth experience. The Brandywine Valley is closest to Philadelphia (around 45 minutes), followed by Bucks County (about an hour) and Pennsylvania Dutch Country (90 minutes). Since it is the farthest and also the most spread out, Pennsylvania Dutch Country is the destination in which you'll most want to spend at least a night. The Brandywine Valley and Bucks County are very doable as day trips, although with the great wealth of historic inns in both areas, you'll want to stay overnight if possible.

The best way to travel to any of these areas is by car, although parts of each are accessible by public transportation if you have the patience and no other options. Biking is an excellent option within all three areas when the weather is nice, especially in Bucks County, which is well known for scenic trails and paths. The Brandywine Valley and Pennsylvania Dutch Country are in roughly the same direction, west of Philadelphia, so they may be planned in coordination if you have time to do both.

All are year-round destinations with a climate similar to Philadelphia and plenty to do no matter when you go, but summer is generally busier. There are a multitude of holiday events during the winter season, but you'll miss out on the outdoor attractions, like hiking or tubing on the Delaware River. As with Philadelphia, the most pleasant time to visit is in the spring or fall when the gardens are in bloom, the foliage is colorful, and temperatures are generally mild and pleasant.

Brandywine Valley

Spanning southeastern Pennsylvania and northern Delaware, the Brandywine Valley is around 30 miles southwest of Philadelphia. Home to charming towns, Revolutionary War sites, museums, wineries, and the impressive Longwood Gardens, its central towns include Chadds Ford, Kennett Square, West Chester, and Wilmington, all of which make a fine base for exploring. The area's most popular attractions include several lavish historic estates and gardens of generations of various du Ponts, one

Brandywine Valley

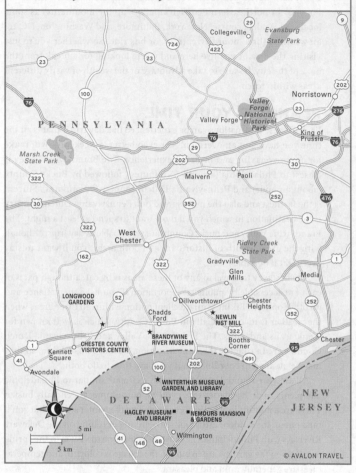

© AVALON TRAVEL

of the wealthiest and most prominent American families in history. The local landscape has been immortalized by the world-renowned painter Andrew Wyeth, and the Brandywine River Museum showcases many of those works.

SIGHTS
Chadds Ford and Kennett Square

Route 1 runs through Chadds Ford and Kennett Square, and the area's main attractions are just a short drive from one another along or near the main road. At the heart of Chadds Ford, at the intersection of Routes 1 and 100, there are about a dozen shops, including boutiques, an art gallery, an inn, and several restaurants. Kennett Square offers plenty of shopping, dining, and entertainment in a small-town setting; be sure to sample some mushrooms while you're in the mushroom capital of the world.

BRANDYWINE BATTLEFIELD HISTORIC SITE

The largest Revolutionary War battle in the Philadelphia area was fought on this site on September 11, 1777. The British won, the American army lost thousands of soldiers, and the remaining American troops retreated to Valley Forge while the British went on to occupy Philadelphia. Despite this devastating outcome, history buffs will enjoy exploring the grounds and visiting the two restored homes that served as headquarters for George Washington and General Lafayette as they camped here. The **Visitor Center** (1491 Baltimore Pike, 610/459-3342, www.brandywinebattlefield. org, Apr.-Dec. Thurs.-Sat. 9am-4pm, Sun. noon-4pm) has a small museum containing artifacts, exhibits, and a gift shop and shows a short film about the history of the site. The grounds are free but there is a fee for admission into the museum ($8 adult, $5 child 6-12, free 6 and under).

★ BRANDYWINE RIVER MUSEUM

This former 19th-century grist mill (100 Creek Rd., 610/388-2700, www. brandywinemuseum.org, daily 9:30am-5pm, $15 adult, $10 senior, $6 student and child 6-12, free child under 6) is now a lovely museum of mostly local art. Among more than 3,000 works are a wealth of still lifes and illustrations from the famous Wyeth family of artists who lived nearby. Andrew, the most famous Wyeth of all, is best known for his moving, realistic portrayals of the Brandywine landscape. As you stroll the galleries, notice the similarities and differences in the works of three generations of Wyeths, including Andrew's father, N. C., and his son Jamie. The Brandywine River can be seen through floor-to-ceiling windows, making it the perfect place to view the works amid the landscape that inspired them. Works of other early American artists are also on display.

★ LONGWOOD GARDENS

In addition to more than 1,000 acres of lush, beautifully landscaped gardens, there is a sprawling multiroom greenhouse, a museum where you can learn about the early history of the gardens and the families that lived here, and a restaurant and gift shop/home and garden store. Dating from 1730, the **Peirce-du Pont House** is the oldest building on the grounds. Inside the house, a short video plays and several rooms contain exhibits about the history of the estate and gardens. While a wealth of trees were planted on this spot by the Quaker Peirce family, the owners of the land from the early 1700s, much of what exists today can be credited to Pierre S. du Pont, who purchased it in 1906 to save it from destruction. Pierre was the great-grandson of Eleuthère Irénée du Pont, a French immigrant who founded the DuPont chemical company when he arrived in the area in 1800. Pierre bought the estate and used it as his weekend residence in 1906-1954, during which time he expanded the corporate empire of his family's business and devoted some of his great wealth to the development of **Longwood Gardens** (1001 Longwood Rd., Kennett Square, 610/388-1000, www.longwoodgardens.org, $20 adult, $17 senior, $10 student and child, free 4 and under). New exhibits and expansions have continually taken place since then, but both the Peirce family and Pierre du Pont laid much of the groundwork for the historic gardens that attract so many visitors today. Like the blooms and the exhibits, the operating hours change seasonally, but the gardens generally open daily at 9am and close at 5pm January-March, at 6pm during the rest of the year, with extended weekend hours in summer (late May-early Sept. Fri. and Sat. until 10pm) and during the winter holidays (open until 9pm late Nov.-early Jan.). While the blooms in winter are obviously not as plentiful, the holiday decorations, massive Christmas tree display, ice-skating performances, and other special events make it a lovely time to visit.

MORE CHADDS FORD SIGHTS

The **Chadds Ford Historical Society** (1736 Creek Rd., 610/388-7376, www.chaddsfordhistory.org, year-round Wed.-Sat. 10am-4:30pm, free) is a nonprofit committed to preserving local history. In addition to a small shop, library, and exhibit room of historic artifacts, the society preserves the **John Chads House,** built in 1725, and the **Barns-Brinton House,** built in 1714, which are occasionally open for tours and offer a glimpse into the lives of early settlers to the area.

Just down the road is the **Christian C. Sanderson Museum** (1755 Creek Rd., 610/388-6545, www.sandersonmuseum.org, Mar.-Nov. Thurs.-Sun. noon-4pm, $5 adult, free 12 and under). Sanderson, born in 1882 in Montgomery County, was an avid collector of early Americana, and his former home contains his 4,000-plus-item collection, including Helen Keller's autograph and Andrew Wyeth's only pastel drawing.

In nearby Glen Mills, the 1704 **Newlin Grist Mill** (Cheyney Rd. and Baltimore Pike, Glen Mills, 610/459-2359, www.newlingristmill.org, office daily 9am-4pm, park daily 8am-dusk) is the only operating 18th-century grist mill in the Commonwealth of Pennsylvania. The 150-acre park is devoted to the history of the people who lived here and the techniques used to power the mill. The park is free, but there is a $5 admission charged for a tour of the historic buildings, including a blacksmith's shop and a smokehouse. Fishing and picnic grounds are also available.

West Chester and Vicinity

This quaint town has a concentrated area of shops and restaurants along with a few interesting sights. The **Chester County Historical Society** (225 N. High St., 610/692-4800, www.chestercohistorical.org, Tues.-Sat. 9:30am-4:30pm, $6 adult, $5 senior, $3.50 student and child 6-17, free under 6), with its modest museum, library, and shop, makes a good starting point to the area. The museum contains over 60,000 items celebrating the area's history, including furniture, clothing, and other artifacts, and the galleries

Top: Longwood Gardens. **Bottom:** the Barns-Brinton House.

Wine Trails of the Brandywine Valley and Bucks County

Both the Brandywine Valley and Bucks County are gaining increasing respect as East Coast producers of quality wine, and visiting just one, or several, of the area's wineries is a lovely way to spend a day. You'll pass rolling farmlands, quaint towns, antiques shops, restaurants, and historic inns and bed-and-breakfasts as you drive between wineries. Each winery is different in size, style, and varieties of wine produced. All are relatively small, and many are family owned and operated, making for an intimate visit.

Most of the area's wineries are part of the **Brandywine Valley Wine Trail** (www.bvwinetrail.com) and the **Bucks County Wine Trail** (www.buckscountywinetrail.com). Their websites offer a lot of information and often discounts. Visit each winery's individual website to learn more about its history, wine, and special events. Most offer tastings and tours for free or for a small fee. Hours change seasonally, with some open only on weekends, and most have longer summer hours, so call or visit the website before visiting.

Brandywine Valley Wine Trail

- **Black Walnut Winery:** 3000 Lincoln Hwy., Sadsburyville, 610/857-5566, www.blackwalnutwinery.com
- **Chaddsford Winery:** 632 Baltimore Pike, Chadds Ford, 610/388-6221, www.chaddsford.com
- **Kreutz Creek Vineyards:** 553 S. Guernsey Rd., West Grove, 610/869-4412, www.kreutzcreekvineyards.com
- **Paradocx Vineyard:** 1833 Flint Hill Rd., Landenberg, 610/255-5684, www.paradocx.com
- **Penns Woods Winery:** 124 Beaver Valley Rd., Chadds Ford, 610/459-0808, www.pennswoodsevents.com

Bucks County Wine Trail

- **Buckingham Valley Vineyards:** 1521 Rte. 413, Buckingham, 215/794-7188, www.pawine.com
- **Crossing Vineyards & Winery:** 1853 Wrightstown Rd., Washington Crossing, 215/493-6500, www.crossingsvineyard.com
- **New Hope Winery:** 6123 Lower York Rd., Rte. 202, New Hope, 215/794-2331, www.newhopewinery.com
- **Peace Valley Winery:** 300 Old Limekiln Rd., Chalfont, 215/249-9058, www.peacevalleywinery.com
- **Rose Bank Winery:** 258 Durham Rd., Newtown, 215/860-5899, www.rosebankwinery.com
- **Rushland Ridge Vineyards:** 2665 Rushland Rd., Rushland, 215/598-0251, www.rushlandridge.com
- **Sand Castle Winery:** 755 River Rd. (Rte. 32), Erwinna, 800/722-9469, www.sandcastlewinery.com
- **Wycombe Vineyards:** 1391 Forest Grove Rd., Furlong, 215/598-9463, www.wycombevineyards.com
- **Unami Ridge Winery:** 2144 Kumry Rd., Quakertown, 215/804-5445, www.unamiridge.com

showcase permanent and rotating collections. Nearby, the **William Brinton 1704 House and Historic Site** (21 Oakland Rd., 610/399-0913, www.brintonfamily.org, May-Oct. Sat.-Sun. 1pm-5pm and by appt., $5 adult, $3 child under 12), a restored home furnished in medieval English style, tells the rich history of its inhabitants, who were some of the early colonists to the area.

For a glimpse into a slice of more recent local history, visit the **American Helicopter Museum and Education Center** (1220 American Blvd., 610/436-9600, www.helicoptermuseum.org, Wed.-Sat. 10am-5pm, Sun. noon-5pm, $10 adult, $8 senior, $7 child and student, free under 2), the premier museum devoted exclusively to helicopters in the country. Pennsylvania is considered the birthplace of the helicopter, and this museum displays more than 35 civilian and military helicopters, autogiros, and convertaplanes, and artifacts and exhibits spanning from the earliest machines to the latest military technology.

Baldwin's Book Barn (865 Lenape Rd., 610/696-0816, www.bookbarn. com, daily 10am-6pm) is more than just a rare and used bookstore and is worth seeing as much for the historic building and grounds as for the fabulous collection of books and antiques inside. The original dairy barn was built in 1822 and has been the headquarters for the Baldwin family's used book and collectible business since they moved here in 1946 (the business was around since 1934, but in a different location). The dairy barn has since been converted to a residence, and the large stone barn is now the bookshop, with five floors filled with more than 300,000 used and rare books, manuscripts, maps, paintings, prints, antiques, and collectibles. Exposed wood ceiling beams, cozy reading nooks, and a wood-burning stove create a lovely atmosphere for perusing the books and antiques.

RIDLEY CREEK STATE PARK

Just 16 miles from Center City Philadelphia and about 20 minutes from West Chester in the suburb of Media, **Ridley Creek State Park** (1023 Sycamore Mills Rd., Media, www.friendsofrcsp.org, sunrise-sunset, free) offers more than 2,600 acres of woodlands and meadows along with seasonal attractions. There are 12 miles of hiking trails and 5 miles of paved biking trails along with fishing, horseback riding, camping, cross-country skiing, and tobogganing. A National Historic Landmark, it is also home to the **Colonial Pennsylvania Plantation** (610/566-1725, www.colonialplantation.org, Apr.-Nov. weekends 11am-4pm, $8 adult, $6 child). At this 300-year-old farming mainstay and small recreated 18th-century village, interpreters in period costume bake bread, mend fences, and card wool. The village aims to recreate the lives of members of the Pratt family, who lived on the Quaker plantation for three generations as early as 1710. Special tours and educational hands-on workshops are often offered.

Forging a Nation

Valley Forge was a pivotal stop on the road to victory during the Revolutionary War, and **Valley Forge National Historical Park** (1400 Outer Line Dr., King of Prussia, 610/783-1077, www.nps.gov/vafo) offers a glimpse into this period in American history. While no battles were fought here, more than 2,000 American soldiers died from disease during the six months the Continental Army spent here during the brutally cold winter of 1777-1778. General George Washington chose Valley Forge because it was close to Philadelphia, which was occupied by the British army at the time, yet far enough away to be relatively safe from surprise attacks. Lacking adequate clothing, food, and medical supplies, the army persevered against all odds and trained and came together as the cohesive and powerful army that went on to defeat the British army and ultimately win the war.

A visit to the park should begin with a stop at the Welcome Center to pick up a map, visit the gift shop, and check out the collection of more than 4,000 exhibits and artifacts. Next, watch the short film shown in the adjacent theater, which provides a visual of the lives of the soldiers at Valley Forge; complete with uplifting music and cannons firing, it's sure to put you in a patriotic mood.

The winding roads and trails of the picturesque 3,600-acre park can be traversed on foot, bike, horseback, or by car. Six miles of pet-friendly, multi-use trails connect the park to Philadelphia and to the Appalachian Trail and are as popular with locals as they are with visitors, but a car (or guided trolley tour in the summer season) is the best way to see all the historic sites. A free cell phone tour is available by dialing a number at key stops along the Encampment Tour trail, which includes Washington's Headquarters; replicas of the Muhlenberg Brigade huts, where the soldiers lived; the Memorial Arch; and the Washington Memorial Chapel, which also has a used-book store, gift shop, and café on the grounds.

WAYNESBOROUGH

Approximately 20 miles from Center City and 5 miles from Valley Forge in Chester County, **Waynesborough** (2049 Waynesborough Rd., Paoli, 610/647-1779, www.historicwaynesborough.org, mid-Mar.-Dec. Thurs.-Sun. 1pm-3pm, $7 adult, $6 senior, $5 student and senior, $5 pp for groups of 10 or more, $14 family, free child 6 and under) was the 18th-century home of Revolutionary War hero General Anthony Wayne. While he was the only commander in chief of the American military that never served as president of the United States, Wayne's contributions to the war were momentous. Nicknamed Mad Anthony as a result of his bravery and mercilessness, the national hero led the Pennsylvania Line in the battles of Brandywine and Germantown and survived the Valley Forge encampment. Wayne spent 10 years at Waynesborough, this classic Pennsylvania farm manor house; he left in 1792 when President Washington asked him to serve as major general and commander-in-chief of the Legions of America. The Georgian-style home was built

Valley Forge National Historical Park

Summer is the best time to visit, because the dogwood trees and lush grounds are in bloom, and options for exploring the park abound. In addition to ranger-led walking tours, guided trolley tours, and bike rentals, Once Upon a Nation (http://historicphiladelphia.org/valley-forge), the same group responsible for the costumed actors in Independence Park, offers special tours and programs, including costumed storytellers, an After Hours tour for a meal with George and Martha Washington, and the Secrets and Spies tour, where kids can be part of the action and learn spy techniques for discovering traitors.

And when you've had your fill of Revolutionary history, you're in luck; the King of Prussia Mall, the largest shopping mall on the East Coast, is only six miles away.

using stone quarried on the property and has been restored and furnished to reflect the Wayne family's life here over seven generations in 1724-1965.

Wilmington and Vicinity

The city of Wilmington, Delaware, and the surrounding area is home to several museums, including the Delaware History Museum, Delaware Center for Contemporary Arts, Natural History Museum, Sports Museum and Hall of Fame, and even the Toy and Miniature Museum. If you have time to do it all, visit the visitor center's website (www.visitwilmingtonde.com) in downtown Wilmington for more details about the many options. If you only have a day or a weekend, the biggest must-see attractions, detailed here, are some of the estates, homes, and gardens of the du Pont family, which has left its mark all over the area, and the world, with its inventions. A tour of any of their remarkable lavish estates and gardens is an experience to remember.

The **Hagley Museum and Library** (200 Hagley Rd., 302/658-2400, www.
hagley.org, daily 10am-4:30pm, $14 adult, $10 student and senior, $5 child
4-16, free under 4) is part of the 235-acre estate along the Brandywine River
belonging to E. I. du Pont, who was responsible for the invention of gunpowder. By 1802, this was home to his mill and the community of workers
that operated it, with his own home perched high on a hill overlooking the
village and operations. In the three-story museum attached to the visitor
center, you can watch a short movie about the du Pont company's many inventions—from gunpowder to pantyhose to countertops—and see exhibits
highlighting the history of the family and the site. A bus makes a continuous loop through the sprawling grounds, allowing you to hop on and off
and explore, with tour guides posted throughout to explain points of interest. Tours of the du Pont home are offered every half hour with the last
tour at 3:30pm, except January-mid-March, when there are only two house
tours a day, at 10:30am and 1:30pm. The library (open weekdays 8:30pm-
4:30pm) contains research collections and is free and open to the public.

NEMOURS MANSION

For a glimpse into the lavish lives of one of the earliest, wealthiest families in America, take a tour of the spectacular **Nemours Mansion** (1600
Rockland Rd., 800/651-6912, www.nemoursmansion.org, May-Dec. Tues.-
Sat. 9am, noon, and 3pm, Sun. noon and 3pm, $15, children under 12 not
allowed). The nearly 50,000-square-foot French chateau-style mansion on a
300-acre estate and gardens was built in the early 20th century by industri-
alist, inventor, and philanthropist Alfred I. du Pont for his second of three
wives, Alicia, in the style that she loved. Alfred, son of E. I. du Pont of the
gunpowder mills you may have seen at the Hagley Museum and Library,
followed in his father's footsteps and was involved in over 200 patents, many
related to gunpowder. He amassed great wealth through many different
inventions and investments, as you will see on a tour of his phenomenal
estate and gardens. The operational Alfred I. du Pont Hospital for Children
also occupies the grounds, and visitors are allowed to enter by guided tour
only. The tours last 2.5-3 hours, so it is probably best that children under
12 are not permitted. Reservations are required and can be made online or
by phone on weekdays until 4pm. On a tour, you'll watch a short film and
then take a bus to explore the formal gardens and lavish mansion. You'll
see countless antiques and works of art, including the family's collection
of antique cars. You'll also learn about the family's fascinating lives, filled
with heartbreak as much as triumph.

★ WINTERTHUR MUSEUM, GARDEN, AND LIBRARY

Another du Pont family gem, **Winterthur** (5105 Kennett Pike, 800/448-
3883, www.winterthur.org, Tues.-Sun. 10am-5pm, last ticket sold 3:15pm
for 3:30pm tour, $17 adult, $15 student and senior, $7 child 2-11, free under
2) was founded and designed by Henry Francis du Pont (1880-1969), an

avid antiques collector and horticulturist, with the help of his father, Henry Algernon du Pont, in the spirit of 18th- and 19th-century European country houses. Part of the estate has been converted into a museum displaying the world's largest collection of more than 85,000 decorative and fine arts made or used in America in 1630-1860. It's organized into categories, including ceramics, glass, furniture, metalwork, paintings and prints, and textiles and needlework, so you can get lost in room after room of American artwork, complemented by pieces from around the world. Henry Francis du Pont added to his original collection until his death in 1969, and Winterthur curators have continued to add new exhibits and artifacts, mostly highlighting local history. Be sure to leave plenty of time to walk or take a trolley ride through the 1,000-acre rolling landscape filled with flowers and streams, including the Enchanted Forest, a three-acre plot complete with a tree house and fairy cottage that is like a dream come true for kids.

RESTAURANTS
Chadds Ford
Just down the road from the Brandywine River Museum, you'll find upscale cuisine in a stylish yet relaxed setting at **Brandywine Prime** (1617 Baltimore Pike, 610/388-8088, www.brandywineprime.com, Mon.-Fri. 5pm-10pm, Sat. noon-2pm and 5pm-10pm, Sun. 10am-2pm and 4pm-9pm). Serving dinner daily and Sunday brunch, the restaurant's specialty is seafood, perfect cuts of meat, and a fresh oyster bar.

If you're looking for a more casual breakfast, lunch, or brunch spot, head just across the street to the quintessential greasy spoon diner **Hank's Place** (Rtes. 1 and 100, 610/388-7061, www.hanks-place.net, Mon. 6am-3pm, Tues.-Sat. 6am-7pm, Sun. 7am-3pm). The near-constant line out the door speaks volumes about its popularity. Once you taste the packed omelets, blueberry pancakes, and the Pennsylvania favorite, scrapple, you'll know why. While breakfast is certainly the star, you can also get plenty of cheap, tasty soups, salads, and sandwiches if you go for lunch.

For an elegant and traditional afternoon tea service ($15.50 pp) or just a cup of tea or coffee and a light meal or snack, visit **The SpecialTeas Tea Room and Gift Shop** (100 Ridge Rd., Chadds Ford, 610/358-2320, www. specialteastearoom.com, Mon. noon-3pm, Tues.-Sat. 11am-4pm), owned by two sisters. All the pastries, including the delicious scones, are made by one of the owners. The shop is part of **Old Ridge Village**, which includes stores selling jewelry, crafts, and quilts, along with several restaurants.

West Chester
In West Chester, **Avalon** (116 E. Gay St., 610/436-4100, www.avalonrestaurant.net, Tues.-Thurs. 4:30pm-10pm, Fri. noon-3pm and 4:30-10pm, Sat. 5pm-10pm, Sun. 3pm-8pm) is a popular rustic Italian BYOB in the heart of town. Chef/owner John Brandt-Lee serves up traditional Italian cuisine with a modern flair out of a bi-level 18th-century townhouse. Be sure to make reservations, as it is one of the area's most acclaimed restaurants.

Or you can head off the main drag about four miles to **Four Dogs Tavern** (1300 W. Strasburg Rd., Marshallton, 610/692-4367, www.marshaltoninn. com, daily 11:30am-10pm) for delicious and reasonably priced salads, burgers, and dinner entrées in an upbeat atmosphere. The bar stays open until midnight on weekdays and 1am on weekends, and there is usually live entertainment on Thursday-Sunday nights. Nab a seat on the outdoor patio when the weather is warm.

Wilmington

Moro (1307 N. Scott St., 302/777-1800, www.mororestaurant.net, Tues.-Thurs. 5pm-9:30pm, Fri.-Sat. 5pm-10pm) is a popular Wilmington restaurant serving cuisine described as inspired rustic Italian. The menu changes often to utilize the freshest ingredients available. From the antipasti to the lamb chops, the presentation is stellar and the wine list is extensive.

HOTELS

There are countless charming inns and bed-and-breakfasts in the area, but one of the very best is the **Inn at Montchanin** (Rte. 100 and Kirk Rd., Montchanin, Delaware, 302/888-2133, www.montchanin.com). Ideally situated for visiting Winterthur, Nemours, and Hagley museums and estates, the award-winning inn was once actually part of the du Ponts' Winterthur estate. Today, it offers every modern convenience in elegant yet cozy rooms and suites. The village-like setting with various buildings amid winding pathways offers loads of character. It has a spa and fitness center and its own fine-dining restaurant, **Krazy Kat's,** offering quality, creative cuisine for breakfast, lunch, and dinner. The 28 rooms and suites start around $200 a night for rooms and around $300 a night for suites, and special packages are sometimes offered online. Among its numerous accolades, it has been named the world's best hotel for under $250 by *Travel + Leisure* magazine.

Sweetwater Farm Bed & Breakfast (50 Sweetwater Rd., Glen Mills, 610/459-4711, www.gracewinery.com) offers a more bucolic experience even though it's just a short drive from the sights of Chadds Ford—and that's exactly the point. Remote country roads lead to the sprawling 50-acre estate, circa 1734, and once you're here, there isn't another property in sight. There are seven rooms in the main house and seven additional private cottages just outside. The decor is country farmhouse with plenty of modern amenities, including refrigerators, fireplaces, and oversized whirlpool tubs in some of the rooms. The main house has comfortable sitting and reading areas, a pool table, and a dining room where gourmet breakfast is served each morning. There is also a pool for use in the warmer months and a barn complete with horses. It's owned by the nephew of Grace Kelly; pictures of the Kelly family as well as the cast and crew of M. Night Shyamalan's *The Village* (who stayed here while filming) are on display in the main lounge. Rates start at $170 on weekdays and $190 on weekends in summer.

The Brandywine River Hotel (1609 Baltimore Pike, 610/388-1200, www. brandywineriverhotel.com) offers a convenient resting place from which to explore the many nearby sights. It's a typical hotel as opposed to the area's bed-and-breakfasts, but it's a nice one with all the standard modern amenities. Weekend rates in summer start at just $139 per night, with king rooms with fireplace and whirlpool tub starting at $199. Complimentary extended continental breakfast and afternoon tea are included.

INFORMATION

Several visitor centers in the area operate useful websites with loads of information about things to do and where to stay. If you're looking for more in-depth information about the area or want to find specific events or special offers, call or visit the websites of the **Delaware County's Tourism Board** (610/565-3679, www.destinationdelco.com) or the **Chester County Conference and Visitors Bureau** (484/770/8550, www.brandywine-valley.com), or visit the conveniently located **Chester County Visitors Center** (300 Greenwood Rd., Kennett Square, 484/770-8550), adjacent to Longwood Gardens. For additional bed-and-breakfasts, the **Brandywine Valley Bed and Breakfast** site (www.bvbb.com) offers information and online booking.

GETTING THERE AND AROUND

The Brandywine Valley is about 30 miles southwest of Philadelphia and easily accessible via major interstate routes I-95 and I-476, by U.S. routes 30 and 322, and the Pennsylvania and New Jersey Turnpikes. The trip should take around 45 minutes from Center City. The major roads running through the area are Routes 202, 1, 100, and 52. A car is the best way to get around, since attractions are spread out. Driving on the country roads is pleasant, and parking is abundant. If that isn't an option, **SEPTA** (215/580-7800, www.septa.org) provides limited bus and regional rail service from Philadelphia to West Chester and some nearby areas. **SCCOOT** (Southern Chester County Organization on Transportation, 610/993-0911, www.tmacc.org) connects with some SEPTA routes and offers service between West Chester, Chadds Ford, Kennett Square, and several other locales. **DART** (800/652-DART, www.dartfirststate.com) offers local service in and around Wilmington, Delaware.

Bucks County

Only about 35 miles north of Philadelphia, Bucks County offers a unique blend of rural countryside filled with farms, creeks, and covered bridges along with a bustling modern arts, cultural, and dining scene. Local towns of interest include New Hope, Lambertville, Doylestown, and Lahaska, all within a short drive from one another along Route 202 and all offering small-town charm with much to see and do. Doylestown has a few wonderful museums that are well worth a visit, and if you are traveling with kids, a visit to Sesame Place in nearby Langhorne is always a hit.

Bucks County

SIGHTS
★ New Hope

Situated along the Delaware River, the town of **New Hope** is easily the most popular destination in Bucks County, drawing loads of visitors from Philadelphia, New York, and well beyond. New Hope, with its rich history and strong artistic roots, is home to charming shops, restaurants, and art galleries in a small-town setting. The action centers on Bridge Street, which connects New Hope with Lambertville, New Jersey, an equally charming town, across a picturesque auto/foot bridge, as well as Union Street in Lambertville and Main Street in both towns. The best way to experience the towns is just to meander around, stopping in shops and galleries and for a bite to eat. While there are specific highlights, the real experience is just in wandering the pretty, lively streets.

In addition to exploring on foot, another great way to see the area (very popular with kids) is to take one of the hourly excursions on the **New Hope and Ivyland Railroad** (32 W. Bridge St., 215/862-2332, www.

Pulled by a steam locomotive, the ride is about an hour from New Hope to Lahaska and back, and it runs daily in summer and on weekends in winter.

Doylestown Museums

Another charming town and cultural center, Doylestown is also home to several impressive museums. Three of them, all National Historic Landmarks, celebrate the life, work, and collections of Henry Chapman Mercer within a short distance of one another in what has become known as Mercer Mile. Another museum is dedicated to another Doylestown native James A. Michener and displays an impressive collection of artwork.

JAMES A. MICHENER ART MUSEUM

The **James A. Michener Art Museum** (138 S. Pine St., 215/340-9800, www. michenerartmuseum.org, Tues.-Fri. 10am-4:30pm, Sat. 10am-5pm, Sun. noon-5pm, $18 adult, $17 senior, $16 college student, $8 youth 6-18, free under 6) is named for the famous Doylestown local and Pulitzer Prize-winning author, philanthropist, and teacher. It displays a collection of 20th-century American art and sculpture, including a world-class collection of Pennsylvania Impressionism. Occupying the former Bucks County Prison, the nonprofit cultural institution is dedicated to preserving, interpreting, and exhibiting the art and heritage of Bucks County. Don't miss the back-yard sculpture garden, set up in a lovely outdoor setting in honor of the local landscape that has inspired many artists.

★ MERCER MILE

Henry Mercer (1856-1930) was an archaeologist, writer, anthropologist, ceramist, scholar, antiquarian, and collector who spent his life in this area. Among his many accomplishments, he designed three distinct poured-concrete structures that make up the **Mercer Mile.** His castle-like home, now **Fonthill Castle** (525 E. Court St., 215/348-9461, www.mercermuseum. org, Mon.-Sat. 10am-5pm, Sun. noon-5pm, guided tour only, last tour 4pm, reservations advised, $14 adult, $12 senior, $8 youth 6-17), was built in 1908-1912 and modeled after a 13th-century Rhenish castle. It is a mix of medieval, Gothic, and Byzantine styles and constructed of poured rein-forced concrete. The ornate, mazelike interior contains 32 stairways and 44 rooms, each in a different shape. Mercer's collections of books, prints, and Victorian engravings are on display, and the ceilings and walls are embedded with handcrafted tiles made in Mercer's kilns.

For a more in-depth look at Mercer's famous tiles, produced during the American Arts and Crafts movement, stroll over to the **Moravian Pottery and Tile Works** (130 Swamp Rd., 215/348-6098, www.buckscounty.org, daily 10am-4:45pm, $5 adult, $4 senior, $3 youth 7-17). The working his-tory museum continues to produce tiles and mosaics in a similar man-ner to Mercer's original works. Tours of the 1912 factory are offered every half hour and consist of a 17-minute video and a self-guided walk, where you can see original installations and displays about the production of the beautiful tiles.

In 1916, Mercer built another six-story concrete castle nearby, now home to the **Mercer Museum and Library** (84 S. Pine St., 215/345-0210, www. mercermuseum.org, Mon.-Sat. 10am-5pm, Sun. noon-5pm, $14 adult, $12 senior, $8 youth 6-17, free under 5). The impressive structure is filled with themed rooms containing Mercer's collection of tools, folk art, and articles from early America. Mercer collected more than 40,000 items in all, fearing that the advance of industrialization would wipe out original tools. His mission was to preserve evidence of America's early productivity, when everything was made by hand. If you plan to visit both Fonthill and the Mercer Museum, purchase the Mercer Experience ticket for reduced admission to both (adult $24, youth 6-17 $15).

More Bucks County Sights
HISTORIC FALLSINGTON

Described as the village that time forgot, **Historic Fallsington** (4 Yardley Ave., Fallsington, 215/295-6567, www.historicfallsington.org, mid-May-mid-Oct. Tues.-Sat. 10:30am-3:30pm, mid-Oct.-mid-May Tues.-Fri. by appt. only, tours $7 adult, $6 senior, $3 child, free under 5) is a 300-year-old preserved Quaker village on the National Register of Historic Places. It evolved around a central Quaker meeting house built in 1690 and includes nearly 90 outlying structures of mostly simple design. You can wander around the village on your own, but to enter some of the structures and get a feel for the way of life on the village, take a guided tour. The site really comes alive during special events, so check the website for the calendar.

PENNSBURY MANOR

Pennsbury Manor (400 Pennsbury Memorial Rd., Morrisville, 215/946-0400, www.pennsburymanor.org, Mar.-Dec. Tues.-Sat. 9am-5pm, Sun. noon-5pm, call ahead in other months, $9 adult, $7 senior, $5 child 3-11, $3 grounds pass) was William Penn's personal estate. Penn preferred the tranquility of country living to more crowded urban dwellings, and at the peaceful 43-acre Pennsbury Manor, it is easy to see why. At the recreated 17th-century country manor and farm, visitors can tour the manor house, brew house, workman's cottage, smokehouse, blacksmith shop, and barn, and see farm animals, including oxen, horses, and sheep. Guided tours make it easy to imagine life on the working colonial farm, which has been beautifully restored to look as it did in Penn's time.

★ SESAME PLACE

Sesame Place (100 Sesame Rd., Langhorne, 215/752-7070, www.sesame-place.com, all-day pass $65 adult and child, free child under 2) is the only theme park in the world based on the popular television series *Sesame Street*. Catering to children ages 2-13, it offers amusements, a three-story netted jungle gym, live stage shows, and a 14-plus-acre water park.

Costumed Sesame Street characters wander around and interact with kids. Because most attractions are outside, the park is only open June-September. It opens daily at 10am and closes anywhere from 5pm to 9pm depending on the day and time of year. Check online for discounted rates.

WASHINGTON CROSSING HISTORIC PARK

Washington Crossing Historic Park (1112 River Rd., 215/493-4076, www. washingtoncrossingpark.org, always open for self-guided tours, guided tours Fri.-Sun. 10am-4pm seasonally, call for prices), a historic site and nature area, commemorates the spot where General George Washington and his troops crossed the Delaware River on Christmas night in 1776, which was considered a pivotal moment in the Revolutionary War. The troops marched on to win a battle at Trenton, which paved the way for the subsequent victories that would lead to the defeat of the British army and, hence, the forming of the United States as an independent nation. Stop at the visitor's center (daily 10am-5pm) to get oriented to the park. Don't miss the 125-foot-tall Bowman's Hill Tower, built in 1931 to commemorate Washington and his army. Climb to the top for a beautiful panoramic view (daily, weather permitting 10am-4pm).

RECREATION

★ Water Sports on the Delaware River

Tubing, rafting, canoeing, or kayaking along the Delaware River is a lovely way to spend a hot summer day. The Delaware River moves at an average speed of 1.5 miles per hour, is about five feet deep, and usually near 80 degrees in summer. There aren't many rapids in the area, so be prepared for more of a lazy, gentle float than an adrenaline-pumping journey. There are two excellent options following similar routes; the **Delaware River Tubing Co.** (2998 Daniel Bray Hwy., Frenchtown, New Jersey, 908/996-5386, www. delawarerivertubing.com) departs from the New Jersey side of the river, and **Bucks County River Country** (2 Walters Ln., Point Pleasant, 215/297-5000, www.rivercountry.net) departs from the Pennsylvania side. The Delaware River Tubing Co.'s packages include a meal plan good for food at the Hot Dog Man stand on the way, for hot dogs, burgers, chips, candy, and drinks. Although, the hot dog man does not discriminate: If you go with the other company, you can still buy food from him à la carte.

SHOPS

One of the biggest draws to Bucks County is the shopping. New Hope and Lambertville have shops galore lining Main Street in both towns, Union Street in Lambertville, and Bridge Street, which traverses both towns. Shops include antiques, art galleries, and collectibles, along with contemporary clothing, furniture, and home accessories.

Just outside of New Hope in Lahaska, **Peddler's Village** (U.S. 202 and Rte. 263, 215/794-4000, www.peddlersvillage.com, Mon.-Wed. 10am-6pm, Thurs.-Sat. 10am-8pm, Sun. 11am-6pm) is a local favorite that has around

75 shops connected by brick walkways spread over a quaint 42-acre village, where you can also stay overnight in the **Golden Plough Inn** and keep kids entertained on the Grand Carousel and in a children's play area, **Giggleberry Fair.**

Just across the street from Peddler's Village, **Penn's Purchase Factory Outlet Stores** (5860 York Rd. at U.S. 202, www.pennspurchase.com, Mon.-Sat. 10am-6pm, Sun. 11am-6pm) offers more than 40 name-brand shops with discount prices.

Rice's Market (6326 Greenhill Rd., New Hope, 215/297-5993, www.ricesmarket.com, Mar.-Dec., Tues. and Sat. 7am-1:30pm) is a 30-acre open-air market selling antiques, collectibles, new and used clothing, and gourmet treats.

The **Golden Nugget Antique Market** (1850 River Rd., 609/397-0811, www.gnflea.com/, Wed. and weekends 6am-4pm) is a 40-year-old indoor/outdoor market. Sunday, the busiest day, often has as many as 400 vendors selling a wide variety of antiques, crafts, and more.

RESTAURANTS

In a town packed with excellent restaurants, it's hard to have a bad meal. Here are a few fine choices.

Marsha Brown (15 S. Main St., New Hope, 215/862-7044, www.marshabrownrestaurant.com, Mon.-Thurs. 5pm-10pm, Fri. 5pm-11pm, Sat. 4:30pm-11pm, Sun. 4:30pm-9:30pm) occupies a large former church. More than 125 years old, the stone structure features many stunning original details and furnishings. Despite the stylish, bustling atmosphere, it is easy to imagine its former incarnation, especially on the 2nd floor, with its two-story cathedral ceilings, original woodwork, large stained-glass windows, and a step-up dining area, where services were once led. Louisiana-bred owner Marsha Brown's sophisticated New Orleans-inspired menu features upscale versions of classics like jambalaya and inventive new creations using the best cuts of meat and fresh seafood, including an ample raw bar. A happening downstairs bar serves a variety of cocktails.

Sprig & Vine (450 Union Square Dr., New Hope, 215/693-1427, www.sprigandvine.com, Tues. 5pm-9pm, Wed.-Thurs. 11:30am-2:30pm, and 5pm-9pm, Fri.-Sat. 11:30am-2:30pm and 5pm-10pm, Sun. 10am-2pm) is a popular vegan restaurant that will satisfy strict vegetarians and meat eaters alike. The casual, cozy BYOB is affordable yet elegant. The strictly vegan menu uses organic seasonal ingredients.

Lambertville Station (11 Bridge St., Lambertville, 609/397-8300, www.lambertvillestation.com, Mon.-Thurs. 11:30am-10pm, Fri.-Sat. 11:30am-11pm, Sun. 10:30am-10pm) occupies a restored former train station with tracks lining one side of the restaurant. Just across the bridge from New Hope, it is a local favorite for breakfast, lunch, and dinner, serving excellent New American cuisine. Lunch is casual with alfresco dining that's great for people-watching while dinner offers a more upscale environment. It is attached to the popular **Inn at Lambertville Station,** where rooms are decked out in antiques in themes of different cities from around the world—some offering lovely river views.

HOTELS

There are so many great bed-and-breakfasts in Bucks County that choosing one can be difficult. One of the most luxurious is about 2.5 miles from the center of town. The **Inn at Bowman's Hill** (518 Lurgan Rd., New Hope, 215/862-8090, www.theinnatbowmanshill.com) has just four romantic rooms and two extended suites on a private five-acre estate. The inn is consistently awarded the AAA Four-Diamond Award among many other accolades. When the weather is warm, a pool offers a lovely place to swim, and when it's colder, the in-room fireplaces and in-room and outdoor whirlpool tubs offer luxurious warmth. A gourmet breakfast is included in the rate, and in-room massage is available for a fee. With rooms and suites $395-585 per night, a stay does not come cheap, but for a romantic getaway or special occasion, there is no better place.

The Lambertville House (32 Bridge St., Lambertville, 609/397-0200, www.lambertvillehouse.com), located in the heart of Lambertville just steps from the bridge into New Hope, has 26 rooms offering every modern amenity. Most rooms have in-room fireplaces, some have oversized whirlpool tubs, and all have ultra-comfy beds. Listed on the National Register of Historic Places, it was built in 1812 and has provided rest to Presidents Andrew Johnson and Ulysses S. Grant, among other notable guests on their travels between New York and Philadelphia. Have a drink on the pretty front porch of the cozy bar, **Left Bank Lounge,** perfect for people watching. Rates including breakfast start at $210 and go as high as $330 for the best room in the attached carriage house.

Hotel du Village (2535 River Rd., New Hope, 866/683-3586, www.hotelduvillage.com) is a unique, affordable alternative about a mile outside New Hope. There are 20 rooms on the grounds of what was formerly a prep school for young girls and boys. A cozy, upscale French restaurant is on-site. Rates range $145-300 with continental breakfast included.

The **Doylestown Inn** (18 W. State St., 215/345-6610, www.hattery-doylestown.com), on a central corner in the heart of town, was built in 1902 but has been updated for a modern look with plenty of amenities. The 11 comfortable rooms, all on the 3rd floor of the historic building, have jetted tubs, and some have fireplaces. A bar offers a nice place to grab a drink or snack. Rates range $170-230 in the high season.

There are campgrounds nearby; **Tinicum Park** (901 E. Bridgetown Pike, Langhorne, 215/348-6114, $20/day) is a popular spot for camping, hiking, and other outdoor activities.

INFORMATION

The **Bucks County Visitor Center** (800/836-2825, www.visitbuckscounty.org) offers downloadable maps and loads of information about the area's attractions, lodging, dining.

GETTING THERE AND AROUND

About 30 miles north of Philadelphia, Bucks County is easily accessible by I-95, Routes 1 and 13, and the Pennsylvania Turnpike. Traffic permitting, you can be there in just under an hour by car. **Amtrak**'s (800/872-7245, www.amtrak.com) regional rail lines travel through Bucks County with stops in Trenton, New Jersey, and other nearby locations. **SEPTA** (215/580-7800, www.septa.org) has regional rail lines throughout Bucks County with stops in Doylestown and Trenton. Once in Bucks County, it is possible to get between major points on public transportation, but most people prefer to drive or bike, which is essential for getting to some of the more off-the-beaten-path sights. If you plan on staying in New Hope or Lambertville, you can get here on public transportation, and once here most attractions are within an easy walk, but a car is best for exploring outside of these towns.

Pennsylvania Dutch Country

As the largest Amish and Mennonite settlement in the world, Pennsylvania Dutch Country's people and culture are the primary tourist draw, so plenty of attractions have been created to allow visitors a glimpse into their way of life. It can be difficult to sift through the tourist traps and find more legitimate cultural experiences, so it always helps to ask a local, like a friendly innkeeper, to point you in the right direction. Taking a horse-and-buggy ride with an Amish or Mennonite guide is a good way to have your questions answered and take in the lovely landscape. And while the Amish are the primary draw, the area also offers more contemporary attractions like theaters, dining, and antiques. The city of Lancaster makes a good base for exploring, or if you prefer a more quintessential small-town experience, check out the quaint towns of Lititz, Ephrata, Bird-in-Hand, Adamstown, Paradise, Strasburg, or Intercourse.

SIGHTS
City of Lancaster

Quaint and quiet in comparison to Philadelphia, **Lancaster** is bustling and lively compared to the rest of rural Lancaster County. It also has museums, theater, and attractions that pay homage to the Amish experience while offering the largest concentration of accommodations and dining.

★ CENTRAL MARKET

The **Central Market** (23 N. Market St., www.centralmarketlancaster.com, Tues. and Fri. 6am-4pm, Sat. 6am-2pm) is an excellent place to stop for a bite or shop for locally made goods and food. The red brick building that houses it was built in 1889, but the market's history goes back much further than that; it began as an outdoor market in the 1730s, and is the oldest continually operating market in the country today. Reminiscent of Philadelphia's Reading Terminal Market, but (for obvious reasons) with a

Pennsylvania Dutch Country

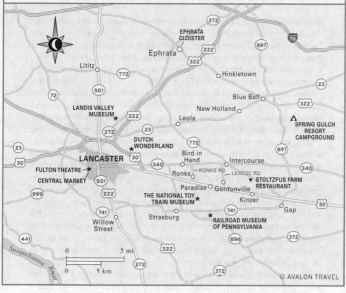

greater array of Amish goods and food, it has over 60 stalls, including a variety of fresh produce and meat, fresh-cut flowers, seafood, handcrafted quilts, handmade fudge, baked goods, and international cuisine. Examples of the great prices: A bag of fruit costs around $1, apple fritters are $0.60, and empanadas cost $1.50 each.

★ FULTON THEATRE

While you're in town, see a show at the historic **Fulton Theatre** (12 N. Prince St., 717/397-7425, www.thefulton.org) if you get the chance. The Victorian gem, built in 1852, is the oldest continuously operating theater in the country and one of just eight National Historic Landmark theaters. Quality musicals, comedies, and dramas are shown in the elegant venue, which has seen many a famous actor grace its stage, including many Barrymores, Sarah Bernhardt, W. C. Fields, and Mark Twain.

Nearby Sights
DUTCH WONDERLAND

While there is nothing very Dutch about **Dutch Wonderland** (2249 Lincoln Hwy. E., 866/386-2839, www.dutchwonderland.com, early June-late Aug. daily 10am-8:30pm, reduced hours in other seasons, $40.99, free under 2) other than the Dutch Country location, kids don't care about that. The self-proclaimed kingdom of kids is a small amusement park with about 40 rides, mini-golf, and live entertainment. Geared toward children 12 and under, it's a pleasant and easy-to-navigate park.

Pennsylvania Dutch Culture

The Pennsylvania Dutch (also called Pennsylvania Germans or Pennsylvania Deutsch) are descendants of early German immigrants to Pennsylvania who arrived in droves, mostly before 1800, to escape religious persecution in Europe. Like so many other persecuted groups, they came for William Penn's promise of religious freedom. Today, most speak a variation of their original German language as well as English, and they are made up of Amish, Mennonite, Lutheran, German Reformed, Moravian, and other groups that share some beliefs while differing in others. While there are other such communities in many parts of the United States and Canada today, the largest settlement is here in Pennsylvania, concentrated in and around Lancaster County.

It is unusual in the United States for the people and culture to be the primary tourist draw, as it is in the area often referred to as Amish Country, but it is no surprise that visitors want to witness a lifestyle so different from their own. Observing the culture, free from modern technology like telephones, computers, and cars, offers a window into a time long past. And while many local Pennsylvania Dutch welcome and have come to rely on the tourist industry for their livelihood, it is important to also be respectful of their privacy; remember that they are real people going about their daily lives. It is important for all visitors to know that among their many beliefs, most Pennsylvania Dutch do not believe in having their photograph taken, as they believe it is a sign of vanity.

The many different sects of Pennsylvania Dutch vary from strict followers of the Old Order to more modern groups who have allowed certain aspects of modernity into their lives. Some do not use battery-powered electron-

EPHRATA CLOISTER

The **Ephrata Cloister** (632 W. Main St., Ephrata, 717/733-6600, www.ephratacloister.org, Mar.-Dec. Mon.-Sat. 9am-5pm, Sun. noon-5pm, Jan.-Feb. Wed.-Sat. 9am-5pm, Sun. noon-5pm., $10 adult, $9 senior, $6 youth 3-11, free under 3) was founded in 1732 as the home of a German religious community, one of the first of its kind. Today it is a National Historic Landmark managed by the Pennsylvania Historical and Museum Commission to highlight the history of the people who lived and worshipped here. At its peak in the 1740s and 1750s, about 300 people lived and worked here. The group believed in spiritual rewards and shunned earthly pleasures, including sexual intercourse. The community is known for creating self-composed a cappella music; developing a form of Germanic calligraphy, Frakturschriften; and building a publishing center that included a paper mill, printing office, and book bindery, among other accomplishments. Some parts of the cloister are open for self-guided tours, but to see all of the buildings and to learn more about this interesting group, take a guided tour, included with the price of admission and offered on the hour beginning at 10am or 1pm depending on the time of year, so call ahead to confirm.

ics, while others now use phones or cars. Some do not allow phones in their home but have them in their place of business, as it can be essential to making a living. Each sect has its own rules, ranging from guidelines for dress and hair length to buggy styles and farming techniques. Most Pennsylvania Dutch wear traditional clothing that is simple, unadorned, and made by hand. Jewelry is not worn—not even wedding bands; unmarried men are usually clean-shaven while married men have beards to distinguish them. The Amish are generally averse to anything that could chip away at the family or close-knit community structure, which is of the highest importance. This includes most modern technology as well as education beyond the eighth grade, which they feel can lead to unnecessary egoism and separation. Mennonites hold many of the same beliefs but tend to be somewhat less conservative in dress codes and in the use of technology.

It would take an entire book to delve into the fascinating heritage of the Pennsylvania Dutch and the unique code the different groups live by, but there is no better way to get a glimpse into their unusual way of life than to visit the area. You'll learn much through your own observation and through the many museums and sites dedicated to preserving local culture. Most Pennsylvania Dutch tour guides are very open and willing to answer any questions. Many constantly have to reassess their beliefs and choose what to incorporate from the modern world without sacrificing their core values. It is best not to generalize, as every family and sect is different. Times have changed, and continue to change, for the Pennsylvania Dutch, if at a much slower pace than for the rest of the world.

LITITZ FOOD TOURS

In the quaint town of Lititz, you can visit two different historic food institutions. The **Wilbur Chocolate Company's Candy Americana Museum & Store** (48 N. Broad St., 717/626-3249, www.wilburbuds.com, Mon.-Sat. 10am-5pm, free) is open for tours. Get your Willie Wonka fix and learn about the chocolate-making process, try delicious samples, and check out the display of antique candy molds and paraphernalia.

Then for a little salt to go with your sugar, walk over to the **Julius Sturgis Pretzel Bakery** (219 E. Main St., 717/626-4354, www.juliussturgis.com, tours mid-Mar.-Dec. Mon.-Sat. 9:30am-4:30pm, Jan.-mid-Mar. Mon.-Fri. 10:30am-3:30pm, $3.50 adult, $2.50 child). It was established in 1861 as America's first commercial pretzel bakery. Most of the production has since moved into a larger facility, but you can still tour its original location. You'll learn about the history and symbolism (yes, there is symbolism in the shape of the pretzel) involved in pretzels, and you'll even get to twist your own. Stop in the attached store on the way out to pick up an array of pretzels, including the best pretzels of all—chocolate-covered—and other tasty treats.

Top: a farm in Amish Country. Bottom: Strasburg Railroad.

Founded in 1832, the **Strasburg Railroad** (301 Gap Rd., Ronks, 866/725-9666, www.strasburgrailroad.com, seasonal hours, tickets start at $20 adult, $20 child 2-11, free under 2) is America's oldest short-line railroad. Visit the historic station to ride the Victorian-style wooden passenger train pulled by a coal-burning steam locomotive. On a 45-minute ride to the town of Paradise and back, you'll pass quintessential scenic rolling Amish farmlands and hear stories about the history of the train, and for an additional fee, you can have lunch on board. There are several displays and souvenir shops at the station, including one that takes old-fashioned photographs.

Strasburg is home to two more stops you'll want to check out while you're here. Just across the street from the railroad, you can see more historic trains, locomotives, and engines at the **Railroad Museum of Pennsylvania** (300 Gap Rd., Strasburg, 717/687-8628, www.rrmuseumpa.org, Apr.-Oct. Mon.-Sat. 9am-5pm, Sun. noon-5pm, Nov.-Mar. closed Mon., $10 adult, $9 senior, $8 youth 3-11, free under 3). And not far from that, the **National Toy Train Museum** (300 Paradise Ln., Ronks, 717/687-8976, www.nttmuseum.org, May-Oct. Fri.-Mon. 10am-5pm, Apr. and Nov.-Dec. Sat.-Sun. 10am-5pm, closed Jan.-Mar., $7 adult, $6 senior, $4 child 6-12, free under 6, $22 family), home to a huge collection of toy trains, is especially popular with kids.

WHEATLAND

Wheatland (1120 Marietta Ave., Lancaster, 717/392-8721, www.lancaster-history.org, Apr.-Oct. Mon.-Sat. 10am-4pm, Feb.-Mar. Fri.-Sat. 10am-3pm, closed Nov.-Jan., $12 adult, $10 senior, $6 student, free under 11) was the home of President James Buchanan for 20 years, and it served as Democratic headquarters during the 1856 presidential campaign. Buchanan gave his first campaign address on the front lawn. On a tour, offered hourly, you'll see the restored home and expansive grounds and learn about the era in American history when Buchanan served as president.

WORKING AMISH VILLAGES

The **Amish Farm and House** (2395 Lincoln Hwy. E., Lancaster, 717/394-6185, www.amishfarmandhouse.com, daily 9am-6pm, $9.50 adult, $8.50 senior, $6.50 child 5-11, free under 5) is a replicated traditional Amish village. On a self-guided or guided tour, you can see the working barn, built in 1805, the stone farmhouse, and the blacksmith shop, among other structures, and learn about the customs, history, and religion of the Old Order Amish.

The **Landis Valley Museum** (2451 Kissel Hill Rd., 717/569-0401, www.landisvalleymuseum.org, Mon.-Sat. 9am-5pm, Sun. noon-5pm, $12 adult, $10 senior, $8 youth 3-11, free under 3) is another recreated Pennsylvania Dutch village with more than 40 historic structures on 100 acres. The buildings have docents stationed to explain and demonstrate a village at work, including a blacksmith shop, gun shop, tavern, and homes showing pottery, weaving, cooking, and quilting demonstrations in realistic settings. There are also tours, wagon rides, and a short film that runs in the visitor center explaining the site.

SHOPS

There are plenty of places to shop for authentic Amish goods and foods, which is what most people are looking for when they visit the area. **Kitchen Kettle Village** (3529 Old Philadelphia Pike, Intercourse, 800/732-3528, www.kitchenkettle.com, May-Oct. Mon.-Sat. 9am-6pm, Nov.-Dec. and Mar.-Apr. Mon.-Sat. 9am-5pm) offers a special shopping experience with more than 40 shops featuring mostly locally made products, 2 restaurants, and 17 lovely guest rooms. The quaint village and shopping center has grown out of a canning business that the Burnley family started out of their garage in 1954. Still run by the same family, the village sells Amish and Mennonite canned goods and treats, quilts, ironwork, folk art, pottery, and designer leather, among other local crafts and food. Don't miss the Jam & Relish Kitchen, where you can see the products get made and prepared. Lodging starts at $139 per night in summer.

Olde Mill House Shoppes (105 Strasburg Pike, Lancaster, 717/299-0678, www.oldemillhouse.com, hours vary seasonally but usually are Mon.-Sat. 9:30am-5pm or later) offers more handcrafted home accessories and arts and crafts from local and national artists, along with all manner of home goods and lighting from national retailers.

Antiques lovers will not want to miss the town of **Adamstown** (just off exit 286 of the Pennsylvania Turnpike, www.antiquescapital.com, hours vary). The self-proclaimed antiques capital of the United States is home to thousands of vendors and dealers of furniture, collectibles, dolls, and all manner of antiques in a concentrated area, mostly along Route 272 just off the turnpike. Check the website for special events.

If you prefer name-brand clothing, jewelry, and shoes at rock-bottom prices, you're also in luck in this area. There is extensive outlet shopping at both **Tanger Outlets** (311 Stanley K. Tanger Blvd., Lancaster, 717/392-7260, www.tangeroutlet.com, Mon.-Sat. 9am-9pm, Sun. 10am-7pm) and **Rockvale Outlets** (35 S. Willowdale Dr., Lancaster, 717/293-9595, www.rockvaleoutletslancaster.com, Mon.-Sat. 9:30am-9pm, Sun. 11am-5pm).

RESTAURANTS

There are many traditional Pennsylvania Dutch restaurants, where you'll eat family-style all-you-can-eat meals that are hearty and plentiful, with stick-to-your-ribs meat, potatoes, and delicious home-baked bread. Two to try are **Amos' Place Restaurant** (14 Center St., 717/768-7287, Intercourse, www.stoltzfusmeats.com, Mon.-Thurs. 6am-6pm, Fri. 6am-8pm, Sat. 6am-5pm), which is great for breakfast and lunch, or **Plain and Fancy Farm Restaurant** (3121 Old Philadelphia Pike/Rte. 340, Bird-in-Hand, 800/669-3568, www.plainandfancyfarm.com, usually daily 11:30am-7pm, hours subject to change so call ahead), which offers an all-you-can-eat feast or an à la carte menu, as well as lodging and tours.

John J. Jeffries (300 Harrisburg Ave., Lancaster, 717/431-3307, www.johnjjeffries.com, Mon.-Sat. 5:30pm-10pm, Sun. 5:30pm-9pm) is a popular Lancaster spot located inside The Lancaster Arts Hotel, a converted 1800s tobacco warehouse that's decorated and furnished with work from local artists. The upscale restaurant makes use of Lancaster's abundant farm goods. The menu is all locally sourced, seasonal, and organic. The extensive wine menu also showcases the best of Pennsylvania wineries.

HOTELS

There are many distinctive accommodations in the area, including numerous bed-and-breakfasts. **King's Cottage Bed and Breakfast** (1049 E. King St., Lancaster, 717/397-1017, www.kingscottagebb.com), a distinguished Select Registry Inn, is one of the best. Just a short drive from the heart of the city, the Spanish-style 1913 mansion is a National Historic Landmark offering many modern amenities. Each of the eight luxury rooms has been tastefully decorated with its own special charm; most have fireplaces and some have large whirlpool tubs. The friendly innkeepers, Janis and Ann, know all there is to know about the area, and they are happy to help you plan your visit. Rates range $175-270, with the private carriage house for $295. A delicious homemade gourmet breakfast is included.

For a unique modern hotel in the heart of the city of Lancaster, try the **Lancaster Arts Hotel** (300 Harrisburg Ave., Lancaster, 717/299-3000, www.lancasterartshotel.com). Housed in a former tobacco warehouse on a bustling corner, this boutique hotel has tons of character, including original brick and stone walls, exposed wood beams, and locally made furniture and artwork. The first floor has an art gallery and a restaurant and bar. Rates for the 63 rooms, including 16 suites, start around $169 in summer.

The **General Sutter Inn** (14 E. Main St., Lititz, 717/626-2115, www.generalsutterinn.com) is a popular spot in the heart of Lititz. Built in 1764, it has been a local institution at the intersection of the two main drags of the town for 250 years. An elegant restaurant and tavern on the first floor draws a steady stream of locals, while the rooms decked in Victorian antiques draw overnight guests. Despite a few creaky floorboards and windows, the hotel is clean, comfortable, and in great shape despite its old age. Weekend rates for a queen room start at around $125 per night, and with several connecting rooms and larger apartments, it is a great place for families.

For those who prefer the outdoors, check out the RV and tent campground, **Spring Gulch Resort Campground** (475 Lynch Rd., New Holland, 717/354-3100, www.springgulch.com). Highly rated by camping publications, it has 450 sites over 115 acres, and there are activities and special events planned throughout the year.

INFORMATION AND TOURS

The **Pennsylvania Dutch Visitors Center** (501 Greenfield Rd., 800/723-8824, www.padutchcountry.com, Memorial Day weekend-Oct. Mon.-Sat. 9am-5pm, Sun. 10am-4pm, rest of year daily 10am-4pm) is an excellent source of information about the area. The website lists attractions, accommodations, dining, shopping, discounts, and more, along with suggested itineraries and a function to create your own itinerary. You can also stop by in person to ask questions, pick up maps, or take the one-hour guided **Amish Farmlands Tour,** which departs from the visitor center daily in late May-October and some weekends in November.

There are many other walking, buggy, and bus tours to get you oriented to the area and give you an up-close look at Amish life. Led by knowledgeable guides in colonial garb, the **Historic Lancaster Walking Tour** (5 W. King St., 717/392-1776, www.historiclancasterwalkingtour.com, departs Apr.-Oct. daily 1pm, Tues., Fri., and Sat. 10am and 1pm, $8 adult, $7 senior, $6 college student, $1 child 6-18, free child under 6) departs from the visitor center in the city of Lancaster.

The **Amish Experience** (3121 Old Philadelphia Pike/Rte. 340, Bird-in-Hand, 717/768-3600, ext. 210, www.amishexperience.com) offers tours of an Amish Country homestead and guided bus tours of the area, which can be combined with other attractions at a discount. They also have an "experiential" theater that features scenes from Amish history recreated with multiple projection screens, special effects, and a three-dimensional set.

The **Mennonite Information Center** (2209 Millstream Rd., Lancaster, 800/858-8320, www.mennoniteinfoctr.com) offers personal tour guides who have Amish or Mennonite heritage and will ride in your car, van, or group tour bus with you while telling you everything you ever wanted to know about local culture. Price varies depending on the number of people, and note that the vehicle is not provided.

There are many different companies and individuals offering buggy rides of the countryside, usually led by an Amish or Mennonite guide. Try **Abe's Buggy Rides** (2596 Old Philadelphia Pike/Rte. 340, Bird-in-Hand, 717/392-1794, www.abesbuggyrides.com, seasonal Mon.-Sat. 9am-5pm). They are not available in winter and on Sundays, but that goes for most buggies (too cold in winter) and most authentic Amish guides (because Sunday is a day of worship).

And last, for an exhilarating tour experience, take in the beauty of Pennsylvania Dutch Country from above in a hot-air balloon. The **United States Hot Air Balloon Team** (2737 Old Philadelphia Pike, 800/763-5987, www.ushotairballoon.com) offers flights throughout southeastern Pennsylvania that depart from several locations, including Bird-in-Hand; call for details, prices, and reservations.

GETTING THERE AND AROUND

The heart of Dutch Country is about 65 miles from Philadelphia. It can be reached via I-76 West (Schuylkill Expressway) to U.S. 202 South to U.S. 30 West, or by taking I-76 to the Pennsylvania Turnpike. The drive should take about 90 minutes. Since much of the area is wide-open roads and farmland, it is best to have a car for a leisurely tour of the area. However, there is a train that runs from Philadelphia into the city of Lancaster via **Amtrak** (800/872-7245, www.amtrak.com), as well as local **bus service** (Red Rose Transit Authority, 717/397-4246, www.redrosetransit.com) within Lancaster and nearby towns, including Ephrata and Lititz.

Background

The Setting 298
History 299
Government and Economy 316
People and Culture 317
Art and Architecture........... 325

The Setting

GEOGRAPHY

The second-largest city on the East Coast and the fifth-largest in the nation in terms of population, Philadelphia is conveniently located in the middle of the Northeast Corridor. By car, Philadelphia is approximately 2 hours from New York City and 2.5 hours from Washington, DC. It is an hour's drive from Lancaster County, also known as Amish Country, and an hour from Atlantic City, New Jersey, with the rest of the New Jersey Shore points just beyond. The area known as the Greater Philadelphia region consists of five counties in southeastern Pennsylvania (Bucks, Chester, Delaware, Montgomery, and Philadelphia). The four counties in southern New Jersey (Burlington, Camden, Gloucester, and Salem) and New Castle County in Delaware are also sometimes included when referring to the Greater Philadelphia region.

The original city of Philadelphia as outlined by founder William Penn consisted only of the area that is today known as Center City. The rectangular grid occupies approximately two square miles bordered by the Delaware and Schuylkill Rivers to the east and west, Vine Street to the north, and South Street to the south. It wasn't until 1854 that the city consolidated,+ and all the boroughs, townships, and districts of the County of Philadelphia were incorporated into the city. Today, the city and county are one and the same, covering approximately 135 square miles. In addition to the neat grid of the Center City blocks, the city proper now also includes hills, valleys, winding roads, rivers, creeks, and woodlands.

Water occupies just over 5 percent of the total area of Philadelphia, and parks and woodlands cover around 10 percent of the land area. The lowest point of the city is 10 feet above sea level at the meeting of the Delaware and Schuylkill Rivers in Southwest Philadelphia. The highest point is in Chestnut Hill, at 444 feet above sea level. In addition to the two major rivers, the Delaware and the Schuylkill, smaller bodies of water include the Wissahickon, Cobbs, and Pennypack Creeks.

Covering more than 9,200 acres, Fairmount Park is the largest urban municipal park in the world. The largest continuous sections of the park are East and West Fairmount Parks, on either side of the Schuylkill River, the Wissahickon Valley Park in the northwest section of the city, and Pennypack Park in the northeast, but the entire park system includes a total of 63 regional and neighborhood parks, including Franklin Square, Logan Square, Rittenhouse Square, and Washington Square. In fact, pretty much every patch of green in the city is technically part of Fairmount Park.

Previous: the Delaware River; Walnut Street Theatre.

CLIMATE

Philadelphia's four distinct seasons offer very different experiences and activities. Summers can be hot and humid, while winters can be extremely cold, and fall and spring are generally mild and pleasant. While each season offers advantages, you'll need to plan your day and dress accordingly if you visit in one of the more extreme seasons. Average temperatures in July range 67-86°F (20-30°C), but severe heat waves can bring temperatures upward of 95°F (35°C) with the heat index as high as 110°F (43°C). While this usually lasts only a few days each summer, it is unpleasant to do anything outdoors during a heat wave. Fortunately, most attractions are indoors and air-conditioned. In January, the average temperature is 23-38°F (3-5°C), with occasionally frigid temperatures, severe snowfall, and icing that can make driving dangerous. This is the exception rather than the rule, however, and on most winter days, bundling up in warm clothes will make it possible to get between destinations without too much trouble. The classic northeastern fall is quite beautiful in Philadelphia, complete with leaves changing colors and falling from the trees as the heat of summer gives way to cooler weather, while spring is filled with many perfectly comfortable, pleasant days. Rainfall is moderate with 41 inches annually. Seasonal snowfall varies from a light dusting to the occasional blizzard with an average of 21 inches a year; the snowiest winter ever was 2009-2010, with a whopping 78.7 inches.

History

Philadelphia has one of the oldest and richest histories of any U.S. city, with a wealth of monuments and attractions that keep that history alive. Considered the birthplace of the nation, Philadelphia is most famous for its central role in the Revolutionary War. Major battles and the drafting of the Declaration of Independence and Constitution took place here, and Philadelphia was the nation's capital for the first 10 years before it moved to Washington, DC.

But while the late 18th century was undeniably one of the most fascinating and most discussed periods in Philadelphia's history, it's only part of the story. Beginning even before William Penn arrived and founded Philadelphia and continuing today, the city's tumultuous and storied history spans more than 300 years. Visiting the city's many historic sites will reveal much, but hardcore history buffs should read *Philadelphia: A 300-Year History* for much more background. In the meantime, here are some of the highlights.

WILLIAM PENN'S VISION

William Penn negotiated to take ownership of the land west of the Delaware from King Charles II of England as partial payment for a debt the king owed to Penn's deceased father, a wealthy high-ranking naval officer, admiral, and courtier. The 45,000 square miles that would become Pennsylvania were primarily woodlands stretching from the Allegheny Mountains to the Delaware River. The king was happy to hand over land that was not of major importance to him, but perhaps even happier to see the rebellious young Quaker and many of his followers leave England.

Quakers were not generally well regarded by proper English society because their rejection of a hierarchal system clashed with the lavish wealth and strict monarchy of English society and government. William Penn was actually imprisoned several times in England for expressing his religious beliefs and insisting on religious freedom as a moral right. In 1661, Penn was expelled from Oxford for failing to properly honor the Church of England, and shortly thereafter, he became a Quaker, much to the displeasure of his wealthy, traditional family. The young rebel was purportedly beaten by his father, whom he fiercely battled with over matters of religion among other things.

Penn set out to found a society where not only Quakers, but also people of all religions, could practice without persecution. This was an unprecedented idea for the colonies of the time and a stark contrast to the puritanical zeal of the settlers in Boston and New England who longed for stricter religious control over settlers in their communities. Penn began to carry out his "holy experiment" in his new city of Philadelphia when he arrived with his ship, the *Welcome,* one of 23 shiploads of immigrants to arrive in 1682, the first year of Philadelphia's founding.

Penn had hired his cousin William Markam to help him plan "a large Towne or City in the most Convenient place upon the [Delaware] River for health & Navigation." He hoped for a "greene Country Towne, which will never be burnt, and always be wholesome." Penn envisioned a city that bore a closer resemblance to some of the rural towns of England, which he preferred to the overcrowded cities he knew well, such as London, which was more susceptible to disease and fire damage because people lived in such close proximity. Exhibiting one of the first examples of thoughtful city planning in the New World, Penn and his assistants laid out a grid with large lots, wide streets, and space for gardens and orchards, including the five central city parks that remain an important part of life in Philadelphia today. His design served as an example for numerous cities to follow.

THE COLONIAL ERA

Before Penn arrived, the area that would become Philadelphia was inhabited by Native Americans. The Lenni-Lenapes, known as the Delaware Indians, were the earliest known residents, and many of them were pushed west by the advance of Swedish, Dutch, and English settlers in the early 1600s. In the 1630s and 1640s, the Swedes and Dutch spent approximately 17 years arguing over claims to land along the Delaware River, but the dispute over ownership was never resolved, and the area ultimately fell under British rule.

When Penn arrived, many early settlers were living in caves dug out of the Delaware River banks. Penn made an unprecedented move in

Five Squares

Logan Square

In one of the earliest examples of thoughtful city planning, William Penn and his surveyor, Thomas Holme, laid out a detailed plan for Philadelphia. Drawn more than 300 years ago, much of it remains in place today. That is because it not only factored in the conditions of the time, but also considered the effects of the growth and expansion that would ultimately occur. The area we now know as Center City was originally the entire city of Philadelphia. Its symmetrical grid of streets between two rivers also contained five strategically placed squares, or parks. There was one at the center of the city and one in each of the four quadrants. Penn recognized the importance of having preserved green spaces to break up the expanses of buildings long before that concept came into vogue. While their names and appearances have changed over time, his five original squares continue to anchor the city and play an important role in Philadelphia today.

Center Square is now where City Hall resides. While it's the only square that is no longer mostly green, it is perhaps the most important one of all. It is home to the main offices of city government, including the mayor's office, and is fittingly located at the geographic center of the city, where its two main thoroughfares, Market Street and Broad Street, intersect. While the current City Hall structure wasn't built until about a century later, it fulfilled Penn's intentions. The city government offices were originally in Old City at the State House (now Independence Hall), but Penn thought they should move when the city grew westward, and this became the new center, as he predicted it would. (He was a smart guy.)

The other four well-landscaped squares are primarily spots for rest and relaxation, and each has plenty of green space, park benches, sculptures, and monuments. Originally named for their locations—Southwest, Southeast, Northwest, and Northeast—the squares have all been renamed over time, and today they are, respectively, **Rittenhouse Square, Washington Square, Logan Square,** and **Franklin Square.** Each of these lovely landscaped parks is well worth a visit for a picnic lunch, people watching, or a photo op. In addition, Franklin Square underwent a massive makeover in 2006 and is now a popular Old City attraction complete with an old-fashioned carousel and Revolutionary-themed mini-golf course.

Philly Firsts

In addition to being considered the birthplace of the United States of America, Philadelphia claims countless landmark firsts, among other distinctions in American history. Listed here are just a few of the city's many distinguished accomplishments.

Firsts

· 1681: First parks created for the pleasure of people—three of Penn's original squares

· 1690: First paper mill in North America, built near Germantown by William Bradford

· 1685: First almanac: *America's Messenger,* by William Bradford

· 1698: First public school in the American colonies

· 1728: First botanical gardens, by John Bartram on the Schuylkill River

· 1731: First lending library: the Library Company of Philadelphia

· 1736: First voluntary fire squad in the United States: Union Fire Company

· 1743: First institution devoted to science and philosophy in North America: the American Philosophical Institution

· 1751: First hospital: Pennsylvania Hospital

· 1752: First fire insurance company: Philadelphia Contributionship

· 1776: First reading of the Declaration of Independence

· 1777: First United States flag on record and first Fourth of July celebration

· 1780: First bank: Pennsylvania Bank

· 1790: First stock exchange: Philadelphia Exchange

· 1790-1800: First capital of the United States: Philadelphia

· 1799-1802: First row houses: Carstairs Row (now Jewelers' Row)

· 1802: First public water supply project: Philadelphia Water Works

· 1805: First art museum/art school: Pennsylvania Academy of the Fine Arts

· 1812: First natural history institution: Academy of Natural Sciences

· 1854: First Consolidation Act by a city and its townships, thereby expanding the city's boundaries

· 1874: First zoo

· 1876: First department store: Wanamaker's

· 1920: First Thanksgiving Day Parade

- 1934: First professional football game (for the record, the Philadelphia Eagles beat the Cincinnati Reds, 64-0)

- 1946: First computer (ENIAC), constructed at the University of Pennsylvania

- 2015: First World Heritage City in the United States

Other Distinctions

- Oldest street in continuous use: Elfreth's Alley (since 1702)

- Most murals (more than 3,000) in any city in the world

- Oldest theater in continuous use in the English-speaking world: Walnut Street Theatre (since 1809)

- Oldest and largest outdoor market: the Italian Market

- Largest landscaped city park: Fairmount Park (9,200 acres)

- Oldest African American newspaper: *The Philadelphia Tribune* (since 1885)

- Largest masonry building in the world: City Hall

- Longest-running parade: the Mummers New Year's Day Parade, since 1901

Mummers New Year's Day Parade

attempting to buy, rather than take, their land, aiming to set a new standard for treatment of indigenous peoples. Popular legend has it that Penn made a treaty of friendship with the Lenape chief Tammany under an elm tree at Shackamaxon (the present-day neighborhood of Kensington and home to Penn Treaty Park in memory of the event). The famous painting *Penn's Treaty with the Indians,* by Benjamin West, immortalized the scene, and the giant statue of William Penn atop City Hall was positioned to point to the location of the signing of the treaty. Some historians debate whether the exact event took place, but what it represents—Penn's peaceful relationship with the natives—is well supported. Documents show that Penn wrote to the Indians, asking for peaceful relations and acknowledging the mistakes of previous European settlers, and even learned their language so he wouldn't need a translator.

To attract people to his new colony, Penn advertised all over Europe for the purchase of large tracts of land at reasonable prices. In 1683, there were just a few hundred inhabitants; by 1701, there were around 2,500. The promise of religious freedom and economic opportunity brought not only English, Welsh, German, and Dutch Quakers, but also Huguenots (French Protestants), Mennonites, Amish, Lutherans from Catholic German states, Irish Catholics, and Jews, among others. A group of German Quakers established the first German settlement in America in present-day Germantown.

The vast majority of those first land purchasers settled along the Delaware River in what is today known as Old City and Society Hill. Despite Penn's hope for westward expansion and plans for large lots surrounded by gardens, nearly all of the lots in that area eventually were subdivided and resold, and smaller alleys were built in between the main streets to accommodate additional homes and people. While Penn's goals were admirable, he had to compete with the reality of a city's natural growth and immigrants from other large cities who were inclined to replicate what they were accustomed to. Until 1704, few people lived west of 4th Street, and it would be many years before they spread west toward the Schuylkill River.

In the spring of 1682, Penn wrote the Frame of Government for Pennsylvania. He consulted with Algernon Sidney and John Locke in drawing out the details; the former complained he was keeping too much power for himself and the latter that he was giving too much to the people. Penn's Frame survived and was studied by Benjamin Franklin, Thomas Paine, and others. Parts of it were used as a model for many state governments to follow, and many of its principles influenced the content of the original United States Constitution, including the call for religious liberty, an assembly elected by the people to make laws, trial by jury, and a penal system designed to reform, not just to punish. In short, Penn was way ahead of his time.

While Penn was largely responsible for the way Philadelphia would eventually develop due to his careful, conscious planning, he barely spent any time here. While certainly a visionary, he was not the best businessman, and he ultimately spent much of his life trying to get his finances in order in England. Penn's final significant act before returning to England for good on October 25, 1701, was issuing the Charter of Privileges, also known as the Charter of 1701. It established Philadelphia as a city and gave the mayor, aldermen, and councilmen the authority to issue laws and ordinances and to regulate markets and fairs, and it officially granted the religious freedom that was already practiced. In his later years, Penn actually attempted to sell Pennsylvania back to the English Crown, but in 1712 he had a stroke and could no longer speak. The deal was never made, and the colony remained his property under the control of his mostly ineffective, uninvolved offspring until the Revolutionary War, when, once again, strong leaders would take over the city.

SEEDS OF REVOLUTION

The city prospered in the first half of the 18th century. Streets were paved and gas lights installed, making the streets brighter and safer. Schools and theaters were formed, and by the 1750s, Christ Church and the Pennsylvania State House, now Independence Hall, had been built. Philadelphia had developed into a true city, but as it became increasingly established, accomplished, and self-sufficient, a need for change also became evident.

In the 1760s, resentment toward British rule was mounting among many residents. England incurred a large debt during the Seven Years War and attempted to impose unprecedented taxes on the colonies to help pay those debts without the consent of the colonials. The British felt that since the outcome of the war was beneficial to the colonies, they should bear some of the tax burden, but under the Magna Carta, colonies were entitled to a vote on the policies that affected them.

By 1764, the British Parliament was realizing the increasing importance of the colonies and attempted to gain more control. Meanwhile, many colonists were increasingly frustrated that they had no voice in the governmental decisions of a distant ruler and were starting to wonder if their relationship with the crown did them more harm than good. Tensions escalated with the Stamp and Townshend Acts of 1765 and 1767, respectively, in which the British imposed a direct tax on stamps and an import tax on products including lead, paper, paint, glass, and tea. In both cases, colonists revolted and successfully boycotted the importation of British goods until the acts were repealed. The phrase "no taxation without representation" became popular during this time.

After the boycotts, the only remaining food tax imposed by England was on tea—but not for long. In 1773, the famous Boston Tea Party took place in Boston Harbor. The massive protest was a response to the Tea Act, which allowed England to sell tea in the colonies with no import taxes. Revolutionaries broke into a British ship the night before it was scheduled to arrive in Boston and dumped an estimated 90,000 pounds of tea overboard. The radical act of defiance further inspired revolt among colonists along the eastern seaboard.

The British government was outraged and responded by passing five acts that became known to colonists as the Intolerable Acts. While their

What's in a Name?

There is an interesting story behind the names of both Pennsylvania (Penn's Woods) and Philadelphia (City of Brotherly Love). Can you guess which one was named by William Penn? If you guessed Pennsylvania, you're wrong. William Penn was given the colony of Pennsylvania by King Charles II of England to repay a debt the king owed to Penn's deceased father, the wealthy, high-ranking naval officer Admiral Penn. The 45,000-square-mile tract of land consisted primarily of woodlands stretching from the Allegheny Mountains to the Delaware River. William Penn wanted to name the colony Sylvania after the woods, but the king insisted on adding Penn to the name, in honor of the elder Admiral Penn. William Penn wasn't crazy about the name. The young Billy Penn was part of the Society of Friends, or Quakers, a religious group that denounces excess and self-promotion, and Penn considered it egotistical to name land after oneself. He was embarrassed, knowing that people would assume the colony was named after him, and he was right; many do assume that to this day.

The young William Penn, however, did choose the name for the city that would shape his colony, a name rooted in his own ideals and plan for the city. He set out to found a society where not only Quakers, but people of all religions could practice without persecution, an unprecedented idea at the time. Philadelphia was his "holy experiment," and he named it based on the Greek *philos* for "love" and *adelphos* for "brother," which is why Philadelphia is called the City of Brotherly Love.

action was an attempt to regain power and order and scare the colonists into submission, it backfired, inciting the colonies to unite in support of Massachusetts and resolve not to be taken advantage of by England any longer. Benjamin Franklin, who considered himself a loyal British subject until that time, was staunchly against what he called the capricious English policy.

The tide was quickly turning, and there was a call for a general congress of the colonies to meet and discuss the issues. The First Continental Congress was held in September 1774 in Carpenters' Hall in Philadelphia, chosen because it was centrally located. The 55 delegates in attendance represented all the colonies except for Georgia. As a result of the meeting, the Articles of Association, a formal agreement to boycott British goods, was drafted on October 20, 1774. It was wildly successful, and imports from Britain dropped 97 percent the following year, showing that the colonies could be powerful when they banded together. The Congress agreed that if the Intolerable Acts were not repealed, the colonies would cease to provide exports to Britain after a certain date. They also planned for a Second Continental Congress to meet in Philadelphia on May 10, 1775.

REVOLUTIONARY WAR

Most members of the First Continental Congress hoped a commercial boycott would persuade the British government to grant their demands and that the colonies would remain part of the British Empire, but this was not to be. Instead, they were quickly thrust into the Revolutionary War. The king of England declared Massachusetts in a state of rebellion due to its boycott of the Intolerable Acts, and trade was severely restricted throughout New England. Acts of protest, picketing, and even the burning of several British ships took place. On April 19, 1775, British troops advanced at Concord and Lexington in Massachusetts and fired at colonists; this became known as the shot heard around the world. Word quickly spread, marking the unofficial beginning of the Revolutionary War.

When the Second Continental Congress met as planned in 1775 at the Pennsylvania State House, now Independence Hall, they declared war and formed the Continental Army with George Washington as commander. During the war, this Congress essentially acted as the government of the country-to-be, making all the leadership decisions for the now-united colonies.

In March of 1776, the British began a blockade of the Delaware Bay and moved south through New Jersey. By December, half of Philadelphia's population had fled, and the Continental Congress went to Baltimore for fear the city was about to be invaded. But American troops pushed back the British at the Battles of Princeton and Trenton, and most refugees as well as Congress returned to the city. By late spring of 1776, the Americans forced the British to evacuate Boston, and by July all of the British Royal officials had fled, and the patriots were ready to declare victory—but the British weren't ready to give up.

DECLARATION OF INDEPENDENCE

Meanwhile, while the war was still raging, a committee including John Adams, Benjamin Franklin, and Thomas Jefferson was assigned to draft a Declaration of Independence. It declared that the 13 colonies in North America were "free and independent states" and that "all political connection between them and the State of Great Britain, is and ought to be totally dissolved." The final document that we know today was the result of much debate and multiple drafts, and while it is believed that Adams wrote the bulk of it, Franklin made several key edits. The delegates voted, and the document passed in Congress on July 4, 1776. As legend has it, the Liberty Bell sounded to summon citizens to hear the first public reading of this revolutionary document on July 8, 1776.

In September 1777, American troops could no longer hold off the British, who invaded Philadelphia from the south. Washington tried to stop them at the Battle of Brandywine but was driven back. Residents fled into other parts of Pennsylvania and New Jersey, and Congress fled to Lancaster and later to York. British troops went on to claim Philadelphia, abandoned by all residents who had the means to flee, for 10 months.

There was a change of tide when the French Army joined the American cause and gave them the extra help they needed to begin to win battles. After several key victories, the British troops eventually pulled out of Philadelphia on June 18, 1778, to try to defend New York City. American troops began to reoccupy Philadelphia and the Continental Congress

Ben Franklin: Philly's Favorite Son

When Benjamin Franklin arrived in Philadelphia in October 1723 as a 17-year-old runaway from Boston, no one could have possibly guessed at the significant contributions he would make to the development of the city, the nation, and the world. A man of many talents in his lifetime, Franklin was an author, political theorist, politician, printer, scientist, inventor, civic activist, and diplomat. As a scientist, he is best known for his discoveries and theories regarding electricity, by way of experimenting with lightning and a kite. As a political writer and activist he was one of the major players to fight for and articulate the hopes and meaning of an independent American nation. As a diplomat during the American Revolution, he was largely responsible for securing the support from France that ultimately led to victory.

Among Franklin's many accomplishments in the city of Philadelphia, he established postal routes between Philadelphia, New York, Boston, and several other locations; founded the Union Fire Company to help protect the city from destruction by fire; set up a volunteer group for defense; built two batteries in case the city should be attacked; raised money to build the first hospital in the colonies; and founded the first lending library and the oldest philosophical society. His accomplishments are too great to list because Franklin was involved in practically every significant accomplishment, decision, and invention that took place in Philadelphia during the most critical time in the city's—and ultimately the nation's—history.

returned in early July when the city was no longer under serious threat. The war was essentially won, though it wasn't official until 1783, when the Treaty of Paris recognized U.S. sovereignty.

THE CONSTITUTION

Under the Articles of Confederation, Congress only had power over colonial governments but not the citizens themselves. After the war ended, this system grew problematic, especially since any change to the Articles of Confederation required a unanimous vote by representatives of all of the colonies. This was nearly impossible since each acted independently and there was often refusal to participate for the common good. The country could not pay the debts it accrued over the war while each colony was busy issuing independent and conflicting laws and rules. In 1787, delegates of the 13 colonies held the Constitutional Convention in Philadelphia and immediately voted to drop the Articles of Confederation. They spent many months debating the form that their new government should take, until they finally found a compromise and drafted and adopted the U.S. Constitution.

This seminal document unified and guided the laws and principles of the new country's government as it does to this day. Philadelphia was the U.S. capital from 1790 to 1800, and George Washington served as the nation's first president. The northern colonies petitioned Congress to keep the capital in Philadelphia or New York, but—after a debate that Thomas Jefferson called the "most bitter and angry contest ever known in Congress, before or since the Union of the States"—the northerners were forgiven heavy debts in return for agreeing to move the capital city to a site along the banks of the Potomac River in what is now Washington, DC, in 1800.

POST-REVOLUTIONARY ERA

The city's economy and population experienced rapid growth as the country stabilized and had more time to focus on things other than war. However, two massive yellow fever outbreaks in the 1790s caused thousands to flee, virtually shutting down trade and commerce. The yellow fever epidemic of 1793 killed nearly 1 in 10 residents, while most of the upper class fled to the suburbs to be safer from the disease plaguing cities. Benjamin Rush, the most famous American physician of his time, gained renown during the epidemics when he refused to flee the city and insisted on treating as many patients as possible. The work of Rush, along with that of Philip Syng Physick (the father of American surgery) and the success of Pennsylvania Hospital, contributed to making Philadelphia the leading center for the study and practice of medicine in the United States. By 1800, Philadelphia had largely recovered from the epidemic and became one of the United States' busiest ports and the country's largest city with almost 68,000 people in the city and nearby suburbs.

However, as the largest city in the country, Philadelphia was among the most heavily affected by international events. As the British and French warred against each other, the United States tried to stay neutral but could not. Maritime trade was interrupted by the Embargo Act of 1807, when the United States tried to stop trading with both Britain and France, and by the War of 1812, when the United States went to war against the British in an effort to reassert its independence. Philadelphia's shipping industry never recovered, and New York soon became the United States' busiest port and largest city.

While the embargo was initially bad for the city, it ultimately helped shape Philadelphia into the United States' first major industrial and cultural city. Many goods were not available due to trade embargos, so factories were established to make those goods at home. Manufacturing plants were built, and the city became an important center for paper, leather, shoes, and boots. Coal and iron mines and the construction of new roads, canals, and railroads helped the city grow into an industrial power. Major projects included the Water Works, a gasworks, and the U.S. Naval Yard. Philadelphia became the financial and cultural center of the country; chartered and private banks (including the First and Second Banks of the United States) and the first U.S. Mint opened. The Pennsylvania Academy of the Fine Arts, the Academy of Natural Sciences, the Athenaeum, and the Franklin Institute were created, and public education became available after the Pennsylvania General Assembly passed the Free School Law of 1834. Philadelphia was booming.

CRIME AND CONSOLIDATION

The population grew rapidly as immigrants, mostly from Germany and Ireland, continued to arrive. The wealthy moved west of 7th Street, and the poor moved into their former homes near the Delaware River, many of which were now converted into tenements and boarding houses. With crowded row houses filling tiny streets and alleys, the area grew filthy and smelly—like areas of London that Penn hoped his city would never resemble.

During the 1840s and 1850s, hundreds of people died each year from malaria, smallpox, tuberculosis, and cholera. The poor were affected the worst because when disease broke out in the city, the rich found respite in areas outside the city. Violence, lawlessness, and gangs became serious problems during these years. Many of the volunteer fire companies were infiltrated by gangs, and brutal fights broke out between rival gangs at fire sites, all wanting to be paid for putting out the fire.

As the city grew into an industrial metropolis, ethnic tensions also grew. In addition to Swedish, German, and British immigrants who had first established homes in the city, Philadelphia was home to strong Irish Catholic and African American communities in the early part of the 19th century. These communities established mutual aid societies, churches, and other institutions, while facing a great deal of opposition from the "Nativists." Rampant racism and violence against immigrants, especially Irish Catholics, was common in the 1840s and 1850s. The Nativist Riots between Protestant Nativists and Irish Catholic immigrants began in 1844 over a question of religious practice in public schools and resulted in injury, death, and much property damage. Violence against African Americans was common, and African American homes and churches were sometimes burned.

The city didn't have the structure or government in place to handle all its problems, and additional tax revenue was required to put programs and institutions—including a police force—in place. As a result, the Act of Consolidation was passed on February 2, 1854, which united all of Philadelphia County's districts, townships, and municipalities into one big city. Through this act, 5 of the 30 largest cities in the country at the time were formed into a single municipality. This dramatically increased the size and tax base of the city, and the population grew from about 125,000 to more than 500,000 while the total area of the city grew from 2 to 129 square miles. In addition to the crowded area along the Delaware, there were now more than 1,500 farms, woods, and wetlands in Philadelphia's new boundaries, and the city now included the townships and villages (which we now know as neighborhoods) of Germantown, Manayunk, Roxborough, Frankford, Northern Liberties, and Kingsessing. The act meant that enough money could be generated to pay the new and much-needed police force, as well as many other public services, including water, streets, and transportation.

CIVIL WAR

When the Civil War began in 1861, Philadelphia was initially divided over allegiances. The number of blacks living in the city was just 4 percent, or 22,000—small by modern standards but far greater than in any other northern city at the time. Philadelphia served as an important stop on the Underground Railroad, housing the largest free black population in the north. Large networks of African Americans and whites, especially among the fiercely abolitionist Quakers, assisted many slaves on the way to freedom. However, many Philadelphians were against the antislavery movement, and abolitionists were sometimes the target of violence. Some Quaker meetinghouses were burned to the ground.

Ultimately, Philadelphia joined the Union and the city went on to play an important role in the war by supplying soldiers, ammunition, war ships, and army uniforms. More than 157,000 soldiers and sailors were treated within the city—many at Satterlee Hospital, the largest army hospital in the world at the time, which stood in West Philadelphia near the site of today's Clark Park. The Mower General Hospital in Chestnut Hill also treated hundreds of thousands of injured soldiers. Philadelphia began to prepare for invasion in 1863, but the southern army was held off at Gettysburg and ultimately the war was won. Philadelphia was less impacted by the Civil War than many other places involved in the war because it avoided the major physical destruction that many cities in the south suffered, as well as the major political and social upheavals that took place in other northern cities.

A GROWING CITY

After the Civil War, immigrants continued to arrive in the city, and by 1870, 27 percent of the population was foreign born. By the 1880s, immigration from Russia, Eastern Europe, and Italy rivaled immigration from Western Europe. By 1881, there were around 5,000 Jewish people in the city, and by 1905, the number grew to more than 100,000. The Italian population increased from around 300 in 1870 to 18,000 in 1900, and the majority settled in South Philadelphia, which remains an Italian stronghold today. In 1876, there were 25,000 blacks in the city, and by 1890, there were nearly 40,000. During the 1880s, the people moving into the city were mostly poor, working-class immigrants, and the wealthy were beginning to leave. The suburbs along the Main Line of the Pennsylvania Railroad just west of the city became a popular destination, and the area remains one of the wealthiest and most elite suburbs in the region today.

Over the course of the late 19th century, industry grew in the modern metropolis despite a great deal of political corruption and setbacks. Philadelphia became a city of homeowners, distinct from cities like New York and Chicago, where large groups of people rented tenements. The city developed to include row after row of single-family homes, which provided affordable housing for the middle class. The police department improved, and volunteer fire companies were finally replaced by a paid fire department. Education reforms were implemented that served to protect the education system from corruption in politics. Opportunity for higher education improved when the University of Pennsylvania moved to West Philadelphia and Temple University, Drexel University, and the Free Library were founded.

One of the biggest events in the history of the country took place in Philadelphia in 1876. The Centennial Exposition was a World's Fair held in Fairmount Park to celebrate the United States' Centennial. Nine million people came to the city over a six-month period to take part in the carnival atmosphere and to see the landmark science exhibits, including Alexander Graham Bell's telephone and the Corliss Steam Engine. Millions of dollars went into planning the incredible event, but unfortunately many of the buildings constructed for it were left abandoned with no real purpose once the fair ended. (One of these buildings was Memorial Hall in Fairmount Park, which opened as the new site of the children's attraction the Please Touch Museum in 2008.)

Other major developments of the growing city included the construction of City Hall at the center of the city at Broad and Market Streets. The architectural marvel took 23 years to complete, and for 100 years it was the tallest building in Philadelphia. An unofficial agreement kept it the tallest building until the 945-foot One Liberty Place snatched that crown in 1987, soon to be followed by many other skyscrapers, all of which make City Hall look tiny in comparison.

Another key element to the city's growth was the Pennsylvania Railroad, which expanded westward to connect Philadelphia with the entire East Coast and the Midwest. This was also the era when major department stores, including Wanamaker's and Strawbridge & Clothier, came to the city. As automobile use increased, new roads and bridges were built, including the Northeast (now Roosevelt) Boulevard in 1914, the Benjamin Franklin Parkway in 1918, and the Delaware River (now Benjamin Franklin) Bridge—which connects the city to Camden, New Jersey—in 1926. New skyscrapers were built and wired for electricity, and the first subway was constructed in 1907. The Philadelphia Museum of Art opened in 1928. The city was growing in every way imaginable.

THE GREAT DEPRESSION AND WORLD WAR II

While several economic depressions and recessions of the 19th and early 20th centuries certainly hurt the city, their effect was somewhat hampered in Philadelphia compared with other cities because of its variety of industry. But in 1929, when the Great Depression hit, Philadelphia—like the rest of the country—could not withstand the blow. The effects were devastating to the functioning of commerce and the well-being of residents. In the three years that followed the stock market crash, 50 banks closed and thousands of residents couldn't pay their mortgages, making foreclosures commonplace. More than half of the savings and loan associations went out of business. In 1933, the unemployment rate was at its highest; blacks were affected worse than whites, and immigrants worst of all.

The mayor at the time, J. Hampton Moore, was considered

unsympathetic to the plight of the people, blaming them for laziness. He fired 3,500 city workers, instituted pay cuts, forced unpaid vacation, and reduced the number of contracts. Many groups of workers united, and not long after, Philadelphia became a strong union city, which it remains to this day.

There was a great deal of corruption and fraud in the city government throughout this period, and many had no faith in what they saw as the GOP machine. Mob activity was high, especially during Prohibition, and the city slowly started to shift toward the Democratic Party in hopes of change. The government was exposed on multiple counts of corruption and stealing, and in the 1951 election, Joseph S. Clark became the first Democratic mayor in 80 years. Philadelphia has remained staunchly Democratic ever since, with not a single Republican mayor or congressman elected in Philadelphia in more than 60 years.

The beginning of World War II helped bring Philadelphia out of the Depression as new jobs, many in the defense industry, offered new opportunity. More than 30,000 workers found jobs at the Naval Ship Yard. When the United States became involved in the war in 1941, many Philadelphia men went to serve, while women, African Americans, and workers from outside the city, who had been excluded by unions, filled in for the missing local labor force. At the end of the war in 1945, there were around 184,000 Philadelphians in the U.S. armed forces.

A SHRINKING CITY

The city's population peaked at over two million residents in 1950, and ever since the numbers have declined while those of suburban counties have grown. After World War II, Philadelphia experienced a serious housing shortage, with many of its homes more than 100 years old and in poor condition. The phenomenon known as white flight began, and has continued ever since, in Philadelphia as in many other U.S. cities. Many economically disadvantaged African Americans, Puerto Ricans, and other groups moved into the city, while middle- and upper-middle-class families, mostly white, moved out. Between 1950 and 2000, the city lost 26.7 percent of its population, in keeping with national trends. (Chicago lost 20 percent and Baltimore lost 31.4 percent during this time, according to U.S. census data.) Philadelphia was shrinking at a startling rate, and many manufacturing and other businesses were leaving the city or shutting down entirely, so there were no jobs for the people coming in.

The 1960s were a turbulent decade in Philadelphia, as they were across the nation. Crime had become a serious problem with drug-related gang warfare plaguing the city. A 1970 City Planning Commission survey noted crime as the city's number one problem. Police Commissioner Frank Rizzo was a controversial and polarizing figure; he was both loved and hated, depending on whom you asked. He had a reputation as an aggressive police officer—quick to use force, especially against African Americans, some said—but also as a strong proponent of law and order. He was elected mayor in 1971, after serving four years as police commissioner, and was given credit for keeping violence in check, if only by comparison to other cities at the time. He was reelected in 1975, and police and fire departments and some cultural institutions were well taken care of. Meanwhile, other areas, including the Free Library, the Department of Welfare and Recreation, the City Planning Commission, and the Streets Department experienced major cuts. Mayor Rizzo divided the city perhaps more than any other mayor in its history.

Crime continued through the 1980s, with mafia warfare taking place, mostly in South Philadelphia. Drugs, gangs, and crack houses existed in many of the city's poorest neighborhoods, and the murder rate skyrocketed. In 1984, Wilson Goode became Philadelphia's first African American mayor. Throughout the decade, development continued in some areas of the city, including Old City, South Street, and Center City, which saw several massive skyscrapers built. But due to a combination of massively reduced federal spending on cities, a shrinking tax base, and generous labor contracts, among other things, the city finances worsened throughout the 1970s and 1980s. When Goode left office at the end of the 1980s, the city was nearly bankrupt.

The very least shining moment of the entire Goode administration and perhaps all of Philadelphia municipal politics was the highly publicized MOVE incident. The police had several prior run-ins with the radical group MOVE, and a major clash in 1978 resulted in the tragic death of a police officer and nine MOVE members going to prison. The second major incident occurred in 1985 during a standoff at the group's headquarters in Southwest Philadelphia. The police had no idea how to handle the situation and eventually dropped a satchel bomb from a helicopter onto the house, setting off a fire that killed 11 MOVE members, including five children, and destroyed 62 neighboring houses. The handling of this unbelievable event was a shameful disgrace to the police, the administration, and the entire city.

A CITY REBORN

When Ed Rendell, who went on to serve two terms as governor of Pennsylvania, was elected mayor in 1992, he had a hard road ahead to fix the financial and social mess the city was in at the time. The vast problems included numerous unpaid bills, the lowest bond rating of the top 50 largest U.S. cities, and a budget deficit of $250 million. With charm and determination, Rendell somehow attracted investment in the city, stabilized finances, and even produced small budget surpluses.

Revitalization took place in many parts of the city through the 1990s, and in 1993, the new Convention Center was built and 17 new hotels followed between 1998 and 2000. The city began to work harder to promote its historic sites, festivals, and entertainment, and it worked; increasing numbers of visitors came to the city.

Former city council president John F. Street was elected mayor in 1999, and many aspects of the city's revitalization continued into the 21st century, although some locals don't give Street much credit for the momentum created by the Rendell administration. There were accusations of typical Philadelphia-style scandals in Street's administration, including awards, insider deals, and poor money management. There was also once again a rise of violent crime after a decline for a short time in the 1990s; it should be noted, however, that both the decline and increase have matched changes in cities throughout the country.

Many neighborhoods continued to revitalize during Street's two terms in office, and the city saw considerable progress in many areas, while it suffered in other areas. There was a condominium boom, created in part by tax breaks for new construction.

PHILADELPHIA TODAY

To look around Center City Philadelphia today is to have no doubt that the city is still growing and improving and that the revitalization that began during the Rendell era continues today. The skyline continues to expand, with the Comcast Center, built in 2005, standing 975 feet high as the tallest building between Chicago and New York. The city has seen a rebirth in arts and culture as well in recent decades, with newer additions to the Avenue of the Arts like the modern Kimmel Center and the Suzanne Roberts Theatre. As a result of updating, expanding, and marketing our many historic attractions, tourism has become a major industry, and Philadelphia has garnered much national attention.

Construction projects are still taking place around the city, and fewer people are leaving the city, while new people, many of them young, are moving in. Many neighborhoods, including Fairmount, University City, Northern Liberties, Graduate Hospital, Manayunk, and Fishtown, continue to experience a rebirth, as empty lots become homes and condominiums, and new businesses open in economically underdeveloped areas. As is typical with gentrification, there is concern over long-term residents being priced out of their homes, as well as other concerns that fall in line with the division of the city along class lines. Yet most Philadelphians have felt a change was long overdue, and there is generally great enthusiasm around the development.

Michael Nutter, endorsed by local media and elected in a landslide, became mayor in 2008. The West Philadelphia native was a true reformer as a city councilman and a key leader in instituting the citywide smoking ban and fighting proposed cuts to hours of city libraries and other important community resources. He accomplished much as a councilman in the face of a lot of opposition, including frequent clashes with former mayor Street, who many felt was comfortable with the status quo whereas Nutter wanted to make a real change. Nutter was elected with enthusiasm and served two eventful terms in office leaving his successor Jim Kenney a more prosperous and cosmopolitan city to govern in 2016.

According to the 2010 census, the population of Philadelphia has finally stopped shrinking, and in the years 2000-2009, it actually grew by 2 percent; this was the first time the population had grown since 1950. The reasons some cite include an increase in new transplants from foreign destinations and from pricier nearby Northeast cities, the 10-year tax abatement on some types of new housing, a historically undervalued housing market, improvements to the waterfront, and continuing redevelopment throughout the city.

Government and Economy

GOVERNMENT

Philadelphia is by far the most Democratic county in Pennsylvania, with Democrats making up about 75 percent and Republicans just 15 percent of registered voters. Since 1932, Philadelphia has voted Democrat in every presidential election and has often been the only county in the entire state to do so, as Pennsylvania is by and large Republican. Philadelphia once had six congressional districts, but as a result of the city's declining population it now has only four—all of which are Democratic. A Republican has not represented a significant portion of Philadelphia in any office since 1983.

From the Civil War until 1951, Philadelphia was staunchly Republican, and for many years, Philadelphia was dominated by what many considered a corrupt political machine. The Republican Party rode the successes of Lincoln and the Civil War to hold onto the mayor's office through the 1950s despite wave after wave of reform movements by city activists. The machine controlled the city through voter fraud and intimidation and through extensive patronage. Reform efforts slowly changed city government, with the most significant change in 1950 when a new city charter strengthened the position of mayor and weakened the Philadelphia City Council. Other northern industrial cities elected Democratic mayors in the 1930s and 1940s, but Philadelphia didn't join the trend until 1951. While the city switched allegiances to the Democratic Party in the 1950s, the reputation of Philadelphia as a city that is "corrupt but contented" survives to this day in some minds.

ECONOMY

Philadelphia was a leading agricultural center early in its history, surrounded by rich Pennsylvania farmlands. Due to its location at the meeting of the Delaware and Schuylkill Rivers, shipyards were very successful. Farm goods were traded for sugar and rum in the West Indies, and these products were in turn exchanged for goods from England and elsewhere. Abundant natural resources, including coal and iron, helped Philadelphia become an early industrial leader, and by the 1770s Philadelphia was one of the most important business centers in the British Empire, with printing, publishing, papermaking, and textiles leading the way. Despite the national government leaving Philadelphia in 1800, the city remained the cultural and financial center of the country for some time. It also became one of the first and strongest industrial powerhouses.

The face of industry has changed drastically since its early days in Philadelphia as in other parts of the world. The private-services-providing sectors, which are now the leading industries (including trade, transportation and utilities, information, financial activities, professional and business services, education, health, leisure, and hospitality), continue to grow, while the goods-producing sectors (including natural resources and mining, construction, and manufacturing) fall as we continue to move away from the traditional manufacturing economy. Today, Philadelphia has some of the very best education and health systems in the world, with a wealth of top-rated universities and hospitals. The tourism industry also continues to grow, and new businesses from hotels to restaurants to museums form each year to meet the needs of the increasing numbers of visitors.

People and Culture

DEMOGRAPHICS

Philadelphia is the fifth most populous city in the country, with approximately 1.55 million people as of the 2010 census, and Center City has the third-largest residential downtown population in the entire country after New York and Chicago. The Greater Philadelphia region is the fifth-largest metropolitan region in the United States and is home to more than 6 million as of 2010, with a total of 46.1 million people living within just 200 miles of Philadelphia—a close second only to New York City for this statistic. This means that approximately one-fourth of the total U.S. population lives within a six-hour drive of Philadelphia.

As of the latest census, the population of the city of Philadelphia is 48.6 percent white, 43.7 percent African American, 11.7 percent Hispanic or Latino, and 5.7 percent Asian. It is interesting to note that while Philadelphia has almost equal numbers of Caucasians and African Americans, the statistic is drastically different for the state of Pennsylvania, where African Americans represent only 10.9 percent and whites 85.2 percent.

It is also worth noting that two of the most subjugated ethnic groups in the city during the mid-19th century, African Americans and Irish Americans, today make up the largest groups in the city. While Philadelphia has long been considered a largely black and white city compared with other major cities, the number of Hispanics and Asian Americans has begun to increase over the past two decades. Philadelphia also has the second-largest Irish, Italian, and Jamaican American populations in the entire United States. The number of foreign-born residents represents about 10 percent of the city's population.

Philly-Speak

Philly-speak is one of a kind. You'll surely notice the unique dialect—unless, of course, you were born here; many locals aren't aware that we say things a little differently until we leave town and someone tells us. There are many variations among neighborhoods, classes, and ethnic groups, but many of our terms cut across boundaries and are just distinctively Philly. Here are some of the most common:

- **down the shore:** the New Jersey beach towns, including Ocean City and Wildwood, where many Philadelphians go in summer. Usage: "I'm going down the shore this weekend" (not to be confused with going "up the Poconos" to ski in winter).

- **The Blue Route:** I-476, the highway that cuts through Philadelphia's suburbs, including Delaware and Montgomery Counties.

- **The Drive:** Kelly Drive or East River Drive.

- **The Expressway:** the Schuylkill Expressway (pronounced SKOO-kil), the section of I-76 that runs through Philadelphia.

- **hoagie:** a sandwich (or samwich) on a long roll filled with meat, cheese, and toppings; referred to as a sub in many other places.

- **Iggles:** the Philadelphia Eagles professional football team.

- **jawn:** any person, place, or thing. Usage: "Pass me that jawn" (anything from a beer to the remote control); "You goin' to that jawn?" (often a party or club, but works for any event); or "That jawn is fly" (the jawn being an attractive person).

- **jimmies:** small chocolate or rainbow-colored candy that you sprinkle onto ice cream, known in most places as sprinkles.

- **lager:** Yuengling lager. When you order a lager in Philly, it implies the locally brewed Yuengling brand.

- **wit/witout:** When ordering a cheesesteak, "wit" (with) means with onions and "witout" (without) means no onions, so "Whiz wit" is a cheesesteak with Cheez Whiz and onions.

- **wooder:** local pronunciation of water, as in "I'll have a cherry wooder ice," when ordering the sweet, flavored, slushy ice treat popular in Philly.

- **youse** or **yiz:** plural for you, when addressing more than one person, as in "What're youse/yiz doin' tonight?"

RELIGION

Since its founding, the only colony that practiced religious tolerance has attracted a wide diversity of religious sects. Many Quakers followed William Penn to his new city, where they could practice their religion without persecution, and the Quaker influence can be seen today in the many Quaker Friends' schools and meeting houses that still exist.

However, today Christianity is the dominant religion in the city, with

Protestants and Roman Catholics making up the two largest sects in similar numbers. There is a significant Eastern Orthodox population, and since the early 1800s, there has been a large Jewish population that has continued to grow as Eastern European Jews immigrated to Philadelphia. However, many of the Jewish communities left the city for the suburbs during the period 1950-2000, and some synagogues were converted to mosques and Baptist churches.

Smaller religious communities include Islam and Hinduism, which have seen an increase as immigration from the Middle East, Pakistan, Bangladesh, and India has increased. The small Muslim community is about 85 percent African American.

FESTIVALS AND EVENTS

Philly has a variety of festivals and special events throughout the year; the majority are in spring and summer and around major holidays. The winter holiday is kicked off with a Thanksgiving Day parade, and soon after signs of Christmas light up Center City. The last hurrah of the year is the New Year's Eve fireworks display. Here is a sampling of some of the best and biggest annual events, but be sure to visit www.visitphilly.com/events, www.phillyfunguide.org, and the festivals' individual websites for more comprehensive listings and exact dates. The free weekly newspaper *PW* is also an invaluable event resource.

Winter
WING BOWL
Fans of chicken wings, drinking, and scantily clad women will find their own strange heaven at this popular event. The **Wing Bowl** (Wells Fargo Center, 800/298-4200, www.610wip.com) was founded by AM radio staple WIP 610 as a promotion to compensate for the Philadelphia Eagles' losing ways. The city needed something to get excited about since the team kept losing, and somehow the Wing Bowl has partially lived up to that strange expectation, garnering much local fanaticism in its own right. It's traditionally held the Friday before the Super Bowl at the Wells Fargo Center, and crowds form outside well before dawn, enjoying beer and wings for breakfast. More than 150 contestants compete in the wing-eating contest, and more than 20,000 attend to watch the intensely competitive gorge fest. Tickets are required, and the event often sells out within 24 hours.

Spring
DAD VAIL REGATTA
Over 100 universities from North America participate in this rowing classic on the Schuylkill in early May. One of the nation's oldest student athletic events, the **Dad Vail Regatta** (Schuylkill River along Kelly Dr., 215/542-1443, www.dadvail.org) brings thousands of students and families to Philadelphia each year, while hordes of locals and visitors come out for the festivities. The 6,000-foot race winds along the Schuylkill River; the

Philly 'Tude

A nasty rumor has somehow spread that Philadelphians are unfriendly, boorish, and sometimes even downright mean, and I'd like to set the record straight. Many locals are a little rough around the edges, but that is part of the local charm; this is a traditional blue-collar town, after all. But unless you insult our sports teams, loudly root for another team in front of us, or play for one of our sports teams and blow the season, you shouldn't be the target of any more rude behavior than you would in any other East Coast city.

Granted, we can be loud, and maybe a little impatient—especially if you're holding up traffic while staring at a map—but beneath the tough exterior, Philadelphians are, by and large, warm, helpful, and down-to-earth people. We like to think we're just more honest here. At least you'll always know where you stand. If people are being nice to you, they probably really like you, and if not, they're just not in the mood, so move on to ask someone else for directions.

And just to be safe, anything negative you have to say about Philly should be said in private. While locals insult the city (and the sports teams) quite freely, visitors rarely earn the right. Oh, and one last thing—you might want to learn how to order a cheesesteak at the fast-lane cheesesteak joints so you don't hold up the line.

best seats are at the Grand Stand finish line beyond Boathouse Row coming from the Art Museum. The packed bleachers afford a great view, and the atmosphere is bustling with cheering onlookers.

EQUALITY FORUM

It's fitting that **Equality Forum** (various locations in the Gayborhood, 215/732-3378, www.equalityforum.org), the country's largest gay-lesbian-bisexual-transgender civil rights organization, hails from the city where American democracy began. What began as weekend-long PrideFest Philadelphia in 1993 is now a full week of programs, panels, screenings, and social events around the city in June. It is capped off by SundayOUT, which is certainly Philly's, but also one of the country's, largest and most fabulous gay pride events. During its off-season, the Equality Forum organization keeps busy by producing gay-themed documentaries, advocating for same-sex marriage, and lobbying Fortune 500 corporations for nondiscrimination policies and domestic-partner benefits.

ITALIAN MARKET FESTIVAL

The **Italian Market** (9th St. btwn. Fitzwater and Federal Sts.) has a festive atmosphere on any Saturday afternoon, but on one weekend each May, it closes to car traffic and an all-out party ensues. As if the market wasn't tempting enough with its delicious smells and tastes, vendors set up shop outside their businesses with foods that are simply irresistible. Stroll and shop, sample goodies along the way, and don't miss the stage featuring live music and chef demonstrations. Check the festival website (www.italian-marketfestival.com) for more information.

KINETIC SCULPTURE DERBY AND TRENTON AVENUE ARTS FESTIVAL

The **Kinetic Sculpture Derby and Trenton Avenue Arts Festival** (Trenton Ave. and Norris St., www.kensingtonkineticarts.org) is a design competition that celebrates art and ingenuity. It's a truly exceptional event. Competitors make their own human-powered floats and parade them through the streets of the Fishtown and Kensington neighborhoods. The floats, which are both beautiful and in many cases comical, make their way to a mud pit finish line, where they are judged on their merits. Meanwhile, artists and food vendors line cobblestoned Trenton Avenue selling their goods, and revelers celebrate in the streets.

PENN RELAYS

Penn Relays (235 S. 33rd St., Franklin Field, 215/898-6151, www.thepennrelays.com) dates back more than 100 years, making it the oldest recognized relay meet in the world. Each year in late April, massive crowds come to the University of Pennsylvania's Franklin Field to watch the world's top track athletes compete. The highlight and most popular event is the USA vs. World races on Saturday. In addition to the action on the field, there is a carnival atmosphere around the entire campus, with food, crafts, and entertainment.

PHILADELPHIA INTERNATIONAL FESTIVAL OF THE ARTS (PIFA)

The **Philadelphia International Festival of the Arts** (various locations, www.pifa.org) is a month-long event, usually held in April, that brings visual and performing artists from around the world to Philadelphia. Events include art installations, concerts, theater, and fashion shows. The grand finale is a giant street fair that shuts down Broad Street to traffic, complete with a 70-foot-tall Ferris wheel.

PHILADELPHIA SCIENCE FESTIVAL

The 10-day **Philadelphia Science Festival** (various locations, 215/448-1346, www.philadasciencefestival.org) is an interactive exploration of science, technology, and engineering. Events take place throughout the city and include lectures, debates, carnivals, and cocktail parties, each with their own science-related theme. Experts illuminate various topics from sports science to spy technology to the chemistry of cocktails. Science buff or not, this festival has plenty of fun and fascinating events for children and adults.

RITTENHOUSE ROW FESTIVAL

The huge **Rittenhouse Row Festival** (Walnut St. btwn. Broad and 19th Sts., www.rittenhouserow.org) takes place on a Saturday in May, rain or

Wawa Welcome America Festival

fireworks at the Wawa Welcome America Festival

It's fitting that Philadelphia is quite possibly the best place on earth to celebrate Independence Day. It was here that the Declaration of Independence was conceived and signed by the founding fathers. The **Wawa Welcome America Festival** (various locations, www.welcomeamerica.com), held each year during the week of July 4th, brings an action-packed lineup of free events, including block parties, concerts, and multiple fireworks displays throughout the city.

Each year is different, but one consistent festival highlight is a free performance by the Philadelphia Orchestra on the Delaware River, followed by a spectacular fireworks display (very romantic). The Historic Philadelphia Block Party Experience, an outdoor block party at the foot of Independence Hall, is another annual standout event. Extending between 5th and 6th Streets and from Market to Chestnut, you'll find some of the city's best food trucks, two performance stages, and free activities for kids. Many museums, including the Constitution Center and the Barnes Museum, are free for the duration of the festival.

The celebration culminates on the 4th of July with The Party on the Parkway, the largest free concert in the United States. The Welcome America stage has featured a diverse medley of performances from hip-hop artists, The Roots, to 70s crooners, Hall and Oates (both groups happen to be comprised of Philly natives). The show is capped off with a massive fireworks display above the Art Museum that is so large it can be seen from miles away in every direction. More information about the festival, including a full talent lineup, can be found at www.welcomeamerica.com.

shine. Vendors set up in and around Rittenhouse Square and several blocks of Walnut Street, which is closed to car traffic. Enjoy samples of five-star dining at great prices in front of the restaurants along with other special offers from many local businesses. There is music and people galore, and when the weather is nice, the event is that much better.

SUBARU CHERRY BLOSSOM FESTIVAL

Named for *sakura*, the pretty pink cherry blossoms that come out in March and early April and hold deep significance in Japanese culture, the **Subaru Cherry Blossom Festival** (various locations, 215/790-3810, www.subarucherryblossom.org) welcomes spring with several weeks of events around the city. Watch taiko drumming or martial arts demonstrations, learn to make origami or sushi, or take part in a traditional tea ceremony. Sakura Sunday is the highlight—this festival at the Japanese House and Gardens in Fairmount Park takes place toward the end of the festival in early April. Even if you miss the organized events, be sure to make time to take in the cherry blossoms throughout the city, especially in Fairmount Park.

Summer
CONCERTS IN THE PARK

On a series of summer Wednesdays, usually during the month of August, *Philadelphia Weekly* sponsors free concerts in **Rittenhouse Square** (18th and Walnut Sts., www.philadelphiaweekly.com). Everyone comes out with blankets, food, and drinks to sit on the grass and listen to live music, usually 7pm-9pm. The acts are varied and generally good but often take second stage to the socializing happening around them.

ODUNDE AFRICAN AMERICAN STREET FESTIVAL

The **Odunde African American Street Festival** (23rd and South Sts., www.odundefestival.org) takes place the second weekend in June in one of Philadelphia's oldest, historically African American neighborhoods in Center City South. In existence for more than 30 years, it has become a three-day event filled with festivities and cultural events, culminating with a large street festival on Sunday featuring African music, food, and crafts. Around the same time, mid-June, there are often other events throughout the city in honor of Juneteenth, the holiday that celebrates the official end to slavery.

PRO CYCLING TOUR

Known locally as the Bike Race, the **Pro Cycling Tour** (Kelly Dr. and other locations, www.procyclingtour.com), one of the biggest sporting events in the United States, is, for most Philadelphians, just another excuse to party. On a Saturday in June, cyclists complete 10 laps of a scenic 14.4-mile circuit, passing over the Benjamin Franklin Parkway, Kelly Drive, through Fairmount Park, and up the infamously steep Manayunk Wall. Watch from the Benjamin Franklin Parkway, the steps of the Philadelphia Museum of

Art, Main Street in Manayunk, or near the Manayunk Wall. Many neighborhood households along the route hold parties on their front porches to cheer the athletes on and drink the day away.

WAWA WELCOME AMERICA FESTIVAL

The 11-day **Wawa Welcome America Festival** (various locations, www.welcomeamerica.com) is filled with fun, family-friendly concerts, museum events, outdoor screenings, street festivals, fireworks, discounts at many businesses, and a big parade, concert, and fireworks on the Benjamin Franklin Parkway, which has featured Hall and Oates, Elton John, the Roots, and the Goo Goo Dolls, among other stars. While some locals try to escape the mayhem and the heat by heading to the Jersey Shore, others embrace the revelry and join the throngs of tourists in the action.

Fall
FILM FESTIVALS

Film lovers should take advantage of the **Philadelphia Film Festival** (various theaters, www.phillyfests.com) in October, the spring preview in April, or its midsummer sibling, the **Philadelphia International Gay and Lesbian Film Festival** (www.qflixphilly.com). These festivals are huge affairs with hundreds of screenings across multiple venues, guest stars, VIP meet and greets, and, of course, loads of parties and events.

FRINGE FESTIVAL

There's a lot to love about the **FRINGE Festival** (various locations, 215/413-1318, www.fringearts.com). The early fall extravaganza is a tribute to theater, dance, music, spoken word, and other arts and performance mediums. The FringeArts organization brings the best performers from around the world to Philly. However, it's the "Fringe" part that gets really wild, since anyone with a venue and a dream can include a show in the program. And, yes, "venue" occasionally means the sidewalk. It's a thrilling and unpredictable artistic ride, and the no-cover fringe cabaret promises good times and often hungover mornings. Visit the website for details and to learn about some year-round events organized by the organization.

TERROR BEHIND THE WALLS AT
EASTERN STATE PENITENTIARY

The place is creepy enough on a regular tour, but every October, the former prison hosts **Terror Behind the Walls at Eastern State Penitentiary** (2124 Fairmount Ave., 800/745-3000, www.easternstate.org/Halloween, $20-40 depending on day), Philadelphia's most frightening tradition. Eastern State Penitentiary's haunted-house tour lets guests walk through long, shadowy corridors and past dark and (seemingly) empty cells. Enhanced by realistic cosmetics, deformed and decaying monsters are everywhere and eager to greet you. Tours begin at 7pm every night and continue every 30 minutes. Be warned: There is often a line around the block to get into this popular event. Ask about the more subdued Family Night, which offers a somewhat less terrifying alternative for the easily frightened and younger crowds.

325

Art and Architecture

Philadelphia is one of the artistic and cultural capitals of the country and has been since its earliest days. In the 19th century, while New Yorkers flocked to dime museums and tawdry circus acts, Philadelphians attended art galleries and public libraries. Once referred to as the Athens of America, Philly was North America's first nexus of culture. The bustling cosmopolitan center in a rapidly growing young country was home to dozens of arts and cultural innovations such as America's first library, art school, museum, university, hospital, and much more. The evolving artistic and cultural scene continues to thrive in the 21st century, from the sparkling Avenue of the Arts to the vibrant independent arts scene.

ARCHITECTURE

Philadelphia is a living gallery for more than 300 years of architectural history—and not all of it is made from the ubiquitous red brick. More than 100 buildings are designated National Historic Landmarks, with outstanding examples of practically every notable style represented. Renowned architects who have left their marks on the city include William Strickland, Frank Furness, Daniel Burnham, George Howe, Louis I. Kahn, Robert Venturi, I. M. Pei, Frank Lloyd Wright, and César Pelli.

Those who are interested in learning more about the city's architecture should take one of the Open House tours offered by the Friends of Independence (www.friendsofindependence.org), or the Architectural Landmarks tours offered by the Philadelphia Society for the Preservation of Landmarks (www.philalandmarks.org). And anyone who appreciates architecture should visit the Athenaeum, the world's premier landmark devoted to American architecture 1800-1945. For still more information and background, Philadelphia Architects and Buildings maintains an excellent online database (www.philadelphiabuildings.org/pab) with a wealth of information about the city's architectural gems and the innovative architects responsible for them.

17th Century

Many of the city's first settlers lived in caves built into the riverbanks, followed by log cabins, which were introduced by early Swedes. People soon began building with wood and brick, with the first brick house completed in 1684. Old Swedes' (Gloria Dei) Church, completed in 1700, is the oldest surviving building in Philadelphia today. The church reflects the Quaker aesthetic for simplicity and symmetry, as do many of the city's surviving first buildings; the largest of these Quaker-style buildings is the Arch Street Friends Meeting House in Old City.

18th Century

The 18th century brought an array of more elaborate styles in architecture, including Georgian and Federal, and many of the structures in Old City and Society Hill today represent some variation of these styles. Named after several generations of kings of England named George, the Georgian style was characterized by proportion and balance. Classic examples are red brick with white trim, including Independence Hall and Christ Church. The Carpenters' Company was formed in 1724 to instruct builders on these new styles of architecture.

After the Revolution, there was a deliberate move away from the English ways in many regards, including architecture. An influx of new styles came to Philadelphia, including Classical Revival, as seen in the First Bank of the United States, and Romanesque Revival, as can be seen in Mother Bethel A.M.E. Church.

The Federal style was named for the Federal period in American history, when it gained popularity. During the late 18th century, the founders of the United States, after rejecting the authority of the English crown, were inspired by the ancient democracies of Greece and Rome. Marked by an intricate interior and a simple, conservative exterior, one of the city's best examples of Federal architecture is the Central Pavilion of Pennsylvania Hospital, completed in 1805. The American eagle was a popular emblem, and many buildings you'll see with this mark were built during this period; the style became a symbol for the nation's wealthy and elite class.

19th Century

The beginning of the 19th century brought the Greek Revival style to Philadelphia, along with leading architects William Strickland and Robert Mills. Strickland was responsible for the Second Bank of the Unites States, modeled on the Parthenon, and the impressive Merchants' Exchange, which offered a modern twist on classic Greek styles.

The early 1800s also saw the start of a new housing innovation: the inexpensive and efficient row house. The first row houses in the United States were part of Carstairs Row (now Jewelers' Row), named for their builder and architect Thomas Carstairs. They provided a new type of housing that was not yet available in cities like New York and Boston. The style became known as Philadelphia rows. As the city industrialized in the 1830s and 1840s, the Delaware riverfront was lined with tenements, warehouses, and factories, some of which survive today as converted luxury lofts.

John Haviland also worked during this period. His 1829 Eastern State Penitentiary was the first structure that so deliberately melded structure and function, and he is also credited for the design of the Philadelphia History Museum (formerly the Atwater Kent Museum), Walnut Street Theatre, St. George's Episcopal Church, and the University of the Arts' Hamilton Hall.

As the 19th century progressed, commercial buildings increased in size and splendor, and architects like William L. Johnson and G. P. Cummings made their marks. Heavily ornamented Victorian and Gothic revival architecture came into vogue, bringing ornate homes especially to West Philadelphia and Center City. A large-scale example of the style includes the Pennsylvania Academy of the Fine Arts' main building, designed by architect Frank Furness.

City Hall deserves a paragraph of its own in Philadelphia's—and the world's—architectural history. Designed by John MacArthur Jr., the mammoth structure is one of the finest examples of French Second Empire architecture in the world. It is the country's largest governmental building and the world's tallest masonry building. Sculptor Alexander Milne Calder created more than 250 statues to adorn the edifice, including the 37-foot-tall statue of William Penn atop the building. Construction of City Hall took 30 years (1871-1901) due in part to municipal corruption and cost overruns. Originally intended to be the world's tallest building at 548 feet, it had already been superseded by the Eiffel Tower and Washington Monument by the time it was completed. Just north of it stands the Norman-Romanesque-style Masonic Temple and the Gothic Revival-style Arch Street United Methodist Church, also built during this period.

20th Century

The 20th century brought much new and notable architecture to Philadelphia. The Benjamin Franklin Bridge, designed by Paul Philipe Cret and built in 1926, was the largest suspension bridge in the world at the time. The building that now houses the Philadelphia Museum of Art was built 1919-1928 and was designed by Horace Trumbauer and Julian Abele. Abele was a Philadelphia native and the first African American to graduate from the University of Pennsylvania's School of Architecture. He drew inspiration for the design while traveling in Greece, as can be seen in many of the details. Abele also played a role in the Beaux Arts-style Free Library, constructed on the Benjamin Franklin Parkway in 1927. The 30th Street Station and the Franklin Institute were also built in the 1930s.

The Philadelphia Savings Fund Society building, which now houses the Loews Hotel, was built in 1932 and designed by William Lescaze and his partner George Howe. It is considered America's first International-style skyscraper. West of City Hall, the office mega-complex Penn Center rises on the site of former train tracks (and Furness's Broad Street Station), while I. M. Pei's 1963 Society Hill Towers stand as modernist beacons in colonial Society Hill. No building could be built taller than the head of the William Penn Statue atop City Hall until 1987, when City Council granted permission for the skyscraper One Liberty Place, and by the end of the 20th century, there were already seven skyscrapers taller than City Hall.

21st Century

Philadelphia remains at the cutting-edge of architecture. The magnificent, modern Kimmel Center on the Avenue of the Arts opened in 2001, designed by architect Rafael Viñoly. And west of the Schuylkill, the 28-story glass

Cira Center, by César Pelli, was completed in 2005. The Comcast Center is the tallest in Philadelphia at 975 feet, notable for its sustainable, LEED platinum design. Projected to open in 2017, a second building, the Comcast Innovation and Technology Center will be one of the largest in the country.

FINE ARTS

Philadelphia's fine arts tradition can be traced back to its earliest days. Before the American Revolution, the wealthy merchant class began to patronize the arts, especially the portrait painters; no proper high-society home was complete without a portrait of its owners hanging on the walls. Due to high demand, fine artists, including William Williams, his son William Joseph Williams, Benjamin West, Gilbert Stuart, and Charles Wilson Peale, gravitated to the burgeoning city. Peale painted portraits of many notable historic figures, including George Washington, John Hancock, Thomas Jefferson, and Alexander Hamilton, and many of them are on display in a gallery housed in the Second Bank of the Unites States.

In 1805, the Pennsylvania Academy of the Fine Arts was founded by Charles Wilson Peale, sculptor William Rush, and others in the city's arts and business communities. One of the nation's leading art schools, it is known for its vast holdings of 19th- and 20th-century paintings and for playing a central role in the education of generations of American artists.

The Philadelphia Museum of Art, one of the world's greatest art museums, was founded as the Pennsylvania Museum and School of Industrial Art. It opened its doors in Memorial Hall in Fairmount Park in 1876 as part of the World's Fair. The landmark building that now houses it dates from 1919, and today its collection includes almost a quarter of a million pieces. The Art Museum (as it's locally known) is also the starting point for two local institutions of higher education. Philadelphia University, formerly the Philadelphia Textile School, began in its early days by offering textile manufacturers a polished education, while the University of the Arts traces the origins of its fine arts program to the Art Museum's original school.

Public art is a major part of the Philadelphia landscape. The Fairmount Park Art Association ensures that the main municipal park is a showcase for sculpture and architecture, and the much-copied One Percent for Art program requires any construction project with city funding to include public art. Meanwhile, the landmark Mural Arts Program has created more than 3,000 murals across the city—more than in any other city in the world.

LITERATURE

Philadelphia has had an important presence in the literary world dating all the way back to Benjamin Franklin. The statesman, printer, inventor, scientist, political theorist, and author published his *Poor Richard's Almanack* annually during 1732-1758. It contained the standard information normally found in an almanac, as well as Franklin's own doses of wit and wisdom, much of which has resulted in sayings that still exist in American vernacular (e.g., "A penny saved is a penny earned").

The 19th century transformed Philadelphia into a center of publishing, with major publishers like J. B. Lippincott playing a major role in local industry for decades. Philadelphia writers at the time included Charles Brockden Brown, a pioneer in the development of the American novel. Meanwhile, interlopers such as Edgar Allan Poe and Louisa May Alcott made brief stops here during their illustrious careers. Noted African American scholar, activist, and historian W. E. B. Du Bois wrote his social history *The Philadelphia Negro* in 1899, and Walt Whitman, the father of American poetry, spent much time in the city, just a quick trip from his native Camden, New Jersey, across the Delaware River.

The Curtis Publishing Company was one of the largest publishers in the country during the early 20th century. It ran its magazine empire from its historic Curtis Center building in Society Hill, publishing the *Ladies' Home Journal* and *The Saturday Evening Post,* the country's oldest magazine. Though the major publishing houses today are largely centered in nearby New York City, some domestic and international publishers still have outposts in Philly.

PERFORMING ARTS

Philadelphia's most famous performing arts space is the Walnut Street Theatre, America's oldest surviving and the world's most-subscribed-to theater. The building at the corner of 9th and Walnut Streets opened as a circus in 1809 and went through several incarnations before becoming the nonprofit regional theater it is today. Other historical theaters include Forrest, Plays & Players, and Merriam, which all date from the beginning of the 20th century, when powerful national theater syndicates like the Shubert controlled the country's live entertainment.

In the music world, the Philadelphia Orchestra, founded in 1900, has established its reputation as one of the United States' Big Five orchestras. Several opera companies competed for attention, and in 1975, two merged into the current Opera Company of Philadelphia.

After Broadway tryouts left Philadelphia in the 1960s, innovative young theater companies, including the Wilma Theater and the Philadelphia Theatre Company, began filling in the gaps. In the 1990s, Mayor Ed Rendell spearheaded the Avenue of the Arts initiative, which focused on turning the stretch of Broad Street spanning out from City Hall into a true center for performing arts. At the time, the Academy of Music was essentially a loner, but since then, theater groups have flocked to the new and renovated theater spaces, including the Arts Bank in 1994, Clef Club in 1995, Wilma in 1996, and the Prince Music Theater in 1999. And, of course, the Kimmel Center opened in 2001, giving a grand home to the Philadelphia Orchestra and several other resident companies, followed by the modern Suzanne Roberts' Philadelphia Theatre Company in 2007.

BACKGROUND
ART AND ARCHITECTURE

Essentials

Getting There 331

Getting Around............... 332

Conduct and Customs 337

Travel Tips.................... 338

Health and Safety.............. 341

Information and Services 342

Getting There

AIR

The **Philadelphia International Airport** (800/745-4283, www.phl.org) is approximately seven miles from Center City and offers frequent service for more than 25 major airlines and several discount airlines. It is a major hub for American Airlines (www.aa.com), and Southwest Airlines (www.southwest.com) offers daily nonstop flights from Philadelphia to numerous cities, including Chicago, Las Vegas, Orlando, Phoenix, Providence, and Tampa. Millions of dollars in renovation projects in the past decade have resulted in a generally pleasant airport experience. The Marketplace now consists of more than 150 national and local shops offering food, beverages, and merchandise, so there is plenty to do while you wait for your flight—which you often will, as delays occur frequently.

Getting to and from the airport on public transportation is easy enough on Airport Regional Rail Line, which directly links the airport to Center City for around $7 one way. The train runs every 30 minutes daily 5am-midnight and takes approximately 25 minutes either way. It connects with other rail lines that can get you practically anywhere within the city and nearby suburbs. Taxis charge a flat rate of $28.50 for travel to and from Center City from the airport and are always waiting just outside the baggage claim area. The drive should take about 20 minutes.

Alternative airports include Newark International (Newark, New Jersey, 85 miles), Baltimore-Washington International (Baltimore, Maryland, 109 miles), JFK International (Jamaica, New York, 105 miles), La Guardia (Flushing, New York, 105 miles), and Atlantic City International Airport (Atlantic City, New Jersey, 55 miles). You'll often find the best fares by coming directly to Philadelphia, especially once you factor in time and money spent traveling from the other airports, but it is worth investigating airfares from these nearby cities, especially if you're planning a multi-city visit in the area.

TRAIN

Since the early days of rail transport in the United States, Philadelphia has been a hub for the Pennsylvania Railroad and the Reading Railroad. Today, Philadelphia is a hub of the nationalized **Amtrak** (30th and Market Sts., 800/872-7245, www.amtrak.com). The station is a primary stop on the Washington-Boston Northeast Corridor route and the Keystone Corridor, which connects to Harrisburg and Pittsburgh. It also offers direct or connecting service to Atlantic City, Chicago, and many other cities in the

United States and Canada. All trains traveling outside the city depart and arrive at Amtrak's 30th Street Station (30th St. and JFK Blvd.). The train is the most pleasant, and most expensive, method of public transportation to nearby cities like New York and DC, although the website often offers fare specials, and there are discounts for seniors and people with disabilities.

The Southeastern Pennsylvania Transportation Authority, or SEPTA (215/580-7800, www.septa.org), has regional lines serving the suburbs of Philadelphia. It also connects to New Jersey Transit in Trenton, which continues to Newark, New Jersey, and New York City. Regional rail also extends south of the city to Wilmington, Delaware.

BUS

The **Greyhound Bus Terminal** (10th and Filbert Sts., 215/931-4075 or 800/231-2222, www.greyhound.com) offers direct and connecting service all over the country. **NJ Transit** buses (973/275-5555, www.njtransit.com) travel between Philadelphia and South Jersey, including the Jersey Shore as far as Cape May at the southernmost tip. **SEPTA** (215/580-7800, www.septa. org), in addition to providing extensive local service, also offers service to some parts of southeastern Pennsylvania.

CAR

Philadelphia is easily accessible by car and connected to several major highways, including the Pennsylvania Turnpike (I-276), I-76, I-476, I-95, U.S. 1, and the New Jersey Turnpike. I-676 is the section of I-76 that runs through Center City and continues across the Ben Franklin Bridge into New Jersey. The Walt Whitman Bridge and the Tacony-Palmyra Bridge also connect Philadelphia to New Jersey. It usually takes just under 2 hours to reach Philly from New York City and about 2.5 hours from Washington, DC. The usual car rental agencies, including Avis, Hertz, and Enterprise, can be found at the airport or in Center City.

Getting Around

You have plenty of options for getting around in Philadelphia, including public transportation; hop-on, hop-off tour buses and trolleys; taxis; and easy-to-navigate, grid-like streets that are great for walking and biking. Ride share apps, Uber, and Lyft, are still unregulated in the city of Philadelphia as of printing and are an affordable and convenient option, though their future legality remains uncertain. There is rarely a reason to drive your car in Center City when you factor in the difficulty of parking in the busiest parts of town. It's usually best to ditch the keys unless you're traveling outside of Center City, where limited public transit and ample parking make driving convenient.

Philadelphia to New York on the Cheap

Locals and visitors alike regularly make the short trip to our nearby neighbor, the Big Apple. The most luxurious way to get there in a hurry is to take the Amtrak train. With trips just 1-1.5 hours, tickets start at $55 each way and are much higher at peak times, so the only people who regularly use Amtrak are those with business accounts and the wealthy. The good news is you can get to New York for as little as $20 round-trip by bus in about 2 hours.

The cheapest way to go, and the method preferred by many locals, is to take **the Chinatown bus,** starting at just $10 one-way and $20 round-trip and taking about 2 hours depending on traffic. Originally used primarily by Chinese food purveyors buying products in New York to sell in Philly, today it is used by commuters, students, and just about everyone on a budget. Service is from Chinatown in Philly (most buses depart 55 N. 11th St., between Arch and Race Sts.) to Chinatown in New York. Service to Washington, DC ($15 one-way, $28 round-trip, 2.5 hours) and Baltimore, Maryland ($16 one-way, $28 round-trip, 2 hours), is also offered. The buses are run by a variety of different companies, and you can find schedules and buy tickets at the following websites: www.chinatown-bus.org and www.gotobus.com.

Another option is the **BOLT Bus** (877/BOLTBUS, www.boltbus.com) or the **Megabus** (877/462-6342, us.megabus.com). Both depart from outside Amtrak's 30th Street Station (30th and Market Sts.) and drop off near New York's Penn Station. Tickets start at $10 each way, and the buses are definitely nicer than the Chinatown buses but often sell out, so be sure to book a few days in advance. In an effort to compete, **Greyhound** (10th and Filbert Sts., 215/931-4075 or 800/231-2222, www.greyhound.com) offers $11 web fares (standard fare is $17) and drops off at Port Authority and Penn Station.

If you'd rather travel by rail but can't afford Amtrak, another option is to take a local **SEPTA** train to Trenton and connect with the **NJ Transit** light rail. SEPTA departs from the major downtown stops, including 30th Street, Suburban Station, and Market East; once in Trenton, you'll wait about 20 minutes and transfer onto NJ Transit's light rail to Penn Station in New York, for a total travel time of about 2.5 hours. The trip costs around $20 one-way depending on the time of day—a bit more than the bus, but the advantage, aside from being on rails (which means no traffic and no bumps), is more flexibility in departure stations and times and arriving in Penn Station.

PUBLIC TRANSPORTATION

The extensive public transportation network includes buses, subways, trolleys, and regional rail lines, all operated by **SEPTA** (215/580-7800, www.septa.org). While locals are quick to complain about increasing fares and delays, and the public transit system certainly has its flaws, it will generally get you to most places you need to go in the city without any major trauma. However, it can be confusing, as some trips in Philly may require a combination of bus, subway, and/or regional rail lines. The farther away from Center City you travel, the fewer direct routes you'll find, but within the central areas it is generally quick and easy. All you need is a little patience

Important Contacts

- **Amtrak** (train): 30th and Market Sts., 800/872-7245, www.amtrak.com

- **Greyhound** (bus): 10th and Filbert Sts., 215/931-4075 or 800/231-2222, www.greyhound.com

- **Philadelphia Airport:** 215/937-6937, flight/gate 800/745-4283, www.phl.org

- **SEPTA** (bus, subway, and regional rail): 215/580-7800, CCT connect (paratransit service) 215/580-7145, www.septa.org

- **Taxis:** Liberty Cab, 215/389-8000; Olde City Taxi, 215/247-7678; Quaker City Cab, 215/298-1088; Philadelphia Taxi Co.

and willingness to figure out the system or to ask for help. The SEPTA website lets you enter departure and arrival information with the "Plan My Trip" feature and will give you the best way to get from A to B—a good idea if you have Internet access and time to plan. Service begins around 5am. A few SEPTA Night Owl routes run all night but with a limited schedule after 8pm. Many lines, including the regional rail, stop running at midnight.

Buses, trolleys, subways, and subway surface cars cover the city, especially in Center City. Regional rail lines run within the city to the northeast and northwest sections, including Germantown, Manayunk, and Chestnut Hill, and to many suburbs. The eight rail lines can all be accessed through Center City stations at Market East, Suburban, and 30th Street, and all connect with the airport. These routes connect with many of the subway and bus lines, but fares for different modes of transport must be paid separately, and cost is dependent on distance or number of zones traveled. Fares increase during peak hours: weekdays 6am-9:30am on trains heading toward Center City and 4pm-6:30pm on all trains leaving from Center City.

Those doing the tourist circuit in summertime will find the **Philly PHLASH** bus (484/881-3574, www.phlvisitorcenter.com, $2 per trip) a convenient option. Offering continuous service every 15 minutes 10am-6pm May-October, it stops at 22 attractions throughout the city. Another option is the **One-Day Independence Pass** ($12, $29 for family up to five people, available at SEPTA ticket offices or online at http://shop.septa.org). This comprehensive ticket allows you to travel on all SEPTA buses, trolleys, subways, and trains, so you can get all over the city and suburbs.

Fares

Buses, trolleys, and subways cost $2.25 per ride and an additional $1 for a transfer, good for an additional ride on a different line continuing in the same direction. Up to two transfers can be purchased for any one trip;

transfers are not required when transferring from one subway line to another but are required between buses or when switching between bus and subway. If you'll be using a lot of public transportation, consider the One-Day Convenience Pass, which will get you eight trips on any bus or subway in one day for $8. Buying tokens also saves money ($1.80 each). They can be purchased in any major subway station, including Suburban, 30th Street, and Market East, and at over 400 retail locations in the city, including some newspaper stands. A weekly TransPass gets you unlimited rides on all modes of public transit in a calendar week for $24; a pass for unlimited rides in a calendar month is $91. Trips on some regional rail lines require a surcharge if used with a pass. Discounts are available for seniors, riders with disabilities, children, K-12 students, some college students, families, and groups.

Accessibility

Every SEPTA bus line is equipped with some vehicles with a wheelchair lift or ramp that can be lowered by the driver. The majority of vehicles include automated route and stop announcements that can be heard inside and outside of the bus. Route information is displayed electronically on the front and side of buses.

Regional rail cars are accessible to those with mobility devices, and many stations are ADA accessible. Many of the major regional rail stations, including Temple University, Market East, Suburban, 30th Street, and University City, are ADA accessible. Primary subway and trolley stations, including Frankford Transportation Center, 69th Street Station, Fern Rock, and Olney, are accessible and provide easy connections to many bus routes. More than 70 stations have elevators, and a toll-free 24-hour elevator-status number (877/737-8248) is updated when changes in elevator service occur; an Alternate Accessible Service list on the SEPTA website provides alternative options.

SEPTA also runs **Customized Community Transportation** (CCT Connect, 215/580-7145), which provides ADA paratransit services to individuals with disabilities who are unable to use regular services, along with a shared-ride paratransit program for senior citizens.

Getting to New Jersey

For travel to nearby New Jersey, including Collingswood and Haddonfield, **PATCO** (856/772-6900, www.ridepatco.org) offers regular service from several Center City stations. **Camden RiverLink** (215/928-8804, www.riverlinkferry.com) offers a scenic option for getting across the river to Camden in summer, departing every hour on the hour from Philadelphia and on the half hour from Camden, with additional departures during events at the Susquehanna Bank Center. It runs May-September and costs $7 general admission, $6 for seniors and active military, free for children 3 and under.

Car Share

If you're relocating to the area and you don't own a car, never fear; Philadelphia has another option. Since most city dwellers only drive occasionally—to the supermarket, suburban malls, or for day and weekend trips outside the city—there is no need for many to own a car. You can save tons of money on insurance and maintenance, avoid the nightmare of parking in some of the more crowded neighborhoods, and still have a car at your fingertips. Environmentally friendly car-sharing programs are sweeping the world, and Philly has two options, Enterprise Car Share and Zip Car.

Enterprise Car Share (888/989-8900, www.enterprisecarshare.com) has plans starting as little as $5 per month, and rental rates start at $3.25 per hour or $44 per day. Zip Car (215/735-3695, www.zipcar.com) starts at $7 per month and $8 per hour. Both programs include gas and insurance and use key fab technology that allows you to reserve and drive a car without ever going into an office to pick up a key. The numbers of users, vehicles, and designated Car Share parking spaces are constantly increasing, so no matter where you live, you're never far from a car or parking spot.

BICYCLING AND WALKING

Center City is compact and the grid-like streets are easy to navigate on foot or by bike. Bicycling is a quick way to get around without having to worry about parking or traffic. As in any major city with car traffic, bicyclists should exercise caution when riding on busy city streets, and a helmet should always be worn. There is an increasing network of wide bike-friendly streets with designated bike lanes. A map of routes can be found at the Independence Visitor Center or through the website of the **Bicycle Coalition of Greater Philadelphia** (www.bicyclecoalition.org/resources/maps). **Indego Bike Share** has stations throughout the city, where you can quickly and cheaply grab a rental bike (844/446-3346, www.rideindego.com).

DRIVING AND PARKING

While driving and parking in Center City can be difficult, you'll usually find a parking meter even in the busiest parts of town if you're willing to search for up to 15 minutes and walk a few blocks. The Philadelphia Parking Authority's website (www.philapark.org) provides a directory of parking lots and garages. There are garages all over Center City, especially near the Convention Center and the Avenue of the Arts, but they can be expensive. Metered parking in Center City is $2 per hour. Garages vary depending on the day and time, with prices generally lower after 5pm. A day rate (24-hour period) is generally in the $25-35 range.

Most central areas have metered street parking. The time limit varies depending on the area but is usually 1-4 hours. Meters accept Smart Cards (prepaid parking cards the size of a credit card) and coins, and many major areas now have machines so you can pay for parking with a credit card.

Smart Cards are available in $20 and $50 denominations and can be purchased at any Shop Rite or 7-Eleven, or online from the Parking Authority (www.philapark.org). Be aware that some areas that have no meters still have time limits. Pay close attention to signs, especially in Center City, or you may get a ticket.

TAXIS

It's usually easy to hail a taxi anywhere in Center City, but the best place to find one is in front of a hotel or on any busy corner. Rides are metered, with the exception of the flat fee of $28.50 for trips between Center City and the airport. The flag drop rate is $2.70 and it will cost you $2.30 for every mile you travel as well as additional wait-time fees. If you're in an area without a lot of activity, it's best to call a cab and go outside when it arrives. It generally shouldn't take more than 15 minutes, except during rain showers or at 2am when the bars close and everyone is clamoring for one. Fares are regulated, and taxis should always have a meter running so you can see how much you're paying. Your driver should be able to give you an estimate of how much it will cost to get to a specific destination.

Conduct and Customs

ALCOHOL

The drinking age is 21 in Pennsylvania, and it is strictly enforced in most bars in the city. If you look young, you will get carded, with the exception of a few complete dives (which will remain unnamed for their sake). Purchasing alcohol in Pennsylvania is not always simple. Beer distributors and state-run Wine & Spirits shops are located throughout the city and keep limited hours. Most bars will let you buy take-out beer but at a steep price.

SMOKING

In 2007, a smoking ban went into effect in all restaurants and bars in Philadelphia. There is the occasional dive bar, remote neighborhood bar, or private club where smoking is still allowed, but they are the exception. It is still acceptable for smokers to light up at most alfresco bars, restaurants, and coffee shops, as well as in subway stations and in parks. Smoking is not as taboo here as in many West Coast cities, but the ban has certainly changed the bar culture—for the better, according to most.

BUSINESS HOURS

Most offices, including banks, are open 9am-5pm or 5:30pm on weekdays. Shop hours vary greatly, but with the exception of smaller boutiques or antiques stores, which often have limited hours, most stores are open from at least 10am or 11am to 6pm or 7pm Monday-Saturday, and are closed or have very limited hours on Sunday. Many Center City shops stay open as late as

8pm or 9pm on Wednesday evening. Most restaurants serve food until 9pm or 10pm on weeknights and until 10pm or 11pm on weekends, with some restaurants in the most active parts of town (like Rittenhouse Square, Old City, South Street, Northern Liberties, and Manayunk) offering late-night menus. Many bars serve food until midnight or 1am, and some Chinatown restaurants stay open until 3am. Other than that, late-night dining is generally limited to diners and cheesesteak and pizza joints—some of which are open 24 hours. With the exception of a few private clubs and after-hours clubs, bars in Philadelphia close at 2am sharp.

TAXES AND TIPPING

There is a hotel tax of 14 percent, with 6 percent going to state tax and 8 percent to city tax. There is an 8 percent tax on dining out and most general sales and a 10 percent tax on liquor, but there is no tax on items considered essential, including clothing and groceries.

Philadelphians have a reputation for being excellent tippers. A 15 percent tip is usually the minimum, even when people are not particularly impressed with service. When all is good, most locals drop 20 percent. The 15-20 percent tipping rule usually applies to taxi cabs, although with more flexibility; a $2-3 tip will cover most rides within the city. For a ride to the airport, especially when luggage handling is involved, the standard is closer to $5. Bell hops and valet parkers generally get $1-2 per bag or per vehicle, and slightly more at the city's ritzier establishments.

Travel Tips

BUSINESS TRAVELERS

For the increasing numbers of travelers who come to the city for business, most hotels have on-site facilities like fax machines and in-room Internet access. There are various **FedEx print centers,** including those at 1201 Market Street (215/923-2520) and 2001 Market Street (215/561-5170). For shipping, call the local **UPS service** (215/567-6006, www.ups.com).

INTERNATIONAL TRAVELERS

Philadelphia has become an increasingly popular destination for international travelers. It is in the eastern time zone, the same as New York, and three hours ahead of the West Coast. English is the language spoken and U.S. dollars are the currency. There is a **Travelex Currency Services** office at 18th Street and John F. Kennedy Boulevard (215/563-7348), where you can cash travelers checks or change money. The **International House** (3701 Chestnut St., 215/387-5125, www.ihousephilly.org) on the University of Pennsylvania campus also serves as a great resource for international visitors. It offers information, social and cultural programming, language

Gay Philly

Though it's not as large or visible as in New York or San Francisco, there has long been a thriving gay community in Philadelphia. As far back as the 1930s and '40s, underground gay house parties and social networks existed not only in Center City but in West Philadelphia, Germantown, and other areas. There was also a group of mob-owned gay bars centered around 13th and Locust Streets—the area that remains the nexus of gay culture in Philly today. This east-of-Broad, south-of-Market neighborhood, also called Washington Square West, is most commonly called the Gayborhood.

A pivotal change occurred in Philadelphia in 1965 when a group of protesters began an annual July 4 march in front of Independence Hall. Four years before the Stonewall Riots in New York ignited the worldwide modern gay rights movement, this period began the era of openness in the city. Gays and lesbians began to come out in increasing numbers and to claim their rightful place in the community.

Today, Philly's gay community is a highly visible and important part of the city, with several dozen clubs, bars, lounges, bookstores, boutiques, restaurants, and shops catering to it. Local politicians court the LGBT crowd for support and dollars, and the media gives wide coverage to various pride festivals and events, including Equality Forum in late April and early May, the Pride Parade in June, and OutFest in October.

The Tourism Board website has a section geared toward gay visitors to the city (www.visitphilly.com/gay-friendly-philadelphia), including gay-friendly hotel accommodations and special event packages. There are several hotels and bed-and-breakfasts in the Gayborhood, with plenty of others nearby. The **William Way LGBT Community Center** (1315 Spruce St., 215/732-2220, www.waygay40.org) is the city's largest gay and lesbian center and is filled with resources and information, and the online calendar (www.phillygaycalendar.com) has the most comprehensive guide to gay-friendly events, venues, organizations, and clubs. The *Philadelphia Gay News* is a publication that offers a calendar of events and articles and is available in print or online (www.epgn.com).

lessons, and affordable short- and long-term accommodations for students or anyone affiliated with a university.

SENIOR TRAVELERS

Philadelphia is a hospitable destination for older travelers, although some may choose to avoid the hottest summer months and the coldest winter months. Senior citizens with proof of age (65 and older) ride buses and subways for free all the time and regional rail for free during off-peak hours (before 6am, 9am-3pm, and after 6pm). Discounts are available at many attractions and AARP discounts are available at many hotels. The **Independence Visitor Center** (6th and Market Sts., 800/537-7676, www.independencevisitorcenter.com) offers additional resources and information for seniors.

STUDENTS

The Greater Philadelphia region has the second-largest number of colleges in the nation and the second-largest concentration of college students living on the East Coast. There are around 120,000 students attending college in the city and over 300,000 in the entire metropolitan area. Including colleges, universities, and trade and specialty schools, there are more than 80 schools in the region. The biggest colleges and universities include the University of Pennsylvania, Temple University, Drexel University, The Art Institute of Philadelphia, Villanova University, Arcadia University, Bryn Mawr College, Haverford College, La Salle University, and St. Joseph's University.

Students should check for student discounts at many sights and movie theaters throughout the city. If you're considering studying in the area, be sure to check out **Campus Philly** (www.campusphilly.org) for a wealth of information and resources for students.

TRAVELERS WITH DISABILITIES

Those using a wheelchair or who have difficulty walking should exercise caution on Philadelphia's sometimes older, cracked, or bumpy sidewalks and walkways. Most of the major streets in Center City have curb cuts and handicapped parking, although parking spaces can be limited near major attractions so allow extra time to find one. Most attractions, theaters, and all the stadiums and newer, larger hotels in Philadelphia have elevators or ramps, but due to their old age, some of the historic buildings are ill equipped. When in doubt, call ahead before arriving to be sure a location is accessible.

The **Mayor's Commission on People with Disabilities** (215/686-2798, www.phila.gov/mcpd) offers resources and a wealth of information, including help finding accessible parking, ATMs, health centers, and cultural events. **ARTREACH, Inc.** (215/515-6720, www.art-reach.org) connects people with disabilities to services and arts in the area and offers an online and print access guide with information on more than 75 of the region's theaters, performing arts centers, and museums. Listings include wheelchair accessibility of entrances and restrooms, phone numbers, and information on large-print or braille materials or assistive listening devices. The guide is also available on audiocassette for the blind.

SEPTA provides detailed information on their website (www.septa.org). The **Independence Visitor Center** (6th and Market Sts., 800/537-7676, www.independencevisitorcenter.com) is helpful in providing additional information and resources.

TRAVELING WITH CHILDREN

Philadelphia is an extremely popular destination for families with children. The many kid-friendly, interactive attractions make it a favorite for school trips or for parents to teach their kids about history. With the exception of the very high-end restaurants, kids can be found dining out with parents in most of the city's restaurants. When traveling with children in the hot summer months, consider booking a hotel with a pool or visit one of the city's public pools.

TRAVELING WITH PETS

Philadelphia is a pet-friendly town, especially in Center City and in the northwest section of the city. With plenty of green spaces, and several specifically designated dog parks, there are plenty of places to walk your dog. Some hotels also allow pets, but you should always check in advance, as there may be a surcharge or limited rooms available. Some restaurants and bars with outdoor seating allow well-behaved pets to sit with you while you eat and drink. Friendly servers will often offer your dog water. Visit www.dogfriendly.com for listings of dog parks and dog-friendly accommodations and businesses.

WOMEN TRAVELING ALONE

As in most places, women traveling alone should exercise extra caution, especially at night. Most, but not all, parts of Center City are generally well lit and filled with people except very late at night. When venturing out after dark, it's always best to travel in groups or take a cab. Muggings and purse snatchings do occur, so be alert and hold your purse tightly, or, better yet, don't carry one at all at night if you can avoid it. As a general rule, whenever you don't feel safe for any reason, step inside the nearest open business and wait there while you call a cab.

Health and Safety

HOSPITALS AND PHARMACIES

Philadelphia is home to several of the world's best hospitals and medical research facilities. For medical emergencies or short- or long-term care, you will find as good treatment in Philadelphia as anywhere. There are too many to name them all here, but just a few of the most renowned hospitals include Pennsylvania Hospital, University of Pennsylvania Hospital, Thomas Jefferson University Hospital, Hahnemann University Hospital, Wills Eye Hospital, and Temple University Hospital. Most hospitals are located in Center City and University City. Independent and chain pharmacies can be found everywhere in the city, and you're never very far from a Rite Aid, CVS, or Walgreens. Among others, there is a 24-hour **CVS** in Center City West (1826 Chestnut St., 215/972-0909).

CRIME

If there is one statistic that Philadelphia is least proud of and most in need of changing, it is crime. Criminologists blame the high crime rate on many social and economic problems, including unemployment, gang activity, increased illegal gun trafficking, reductions in youth programs, poverty, and single-parent households. While it is impossible to pinpoint the cause or predict the future, it is a dire situation in some parts of the city, and we can only hope that this trend will change soon.

It would be remiss to say that tourists are completely safe from the violence that plagues some parts of Philadelphia, but it also must be noted that the vast majority of these crimes, especially murders, are taking place in areas most visitors and many locals never visit. While infrequent murders have taken place in practically every area of the city, most are in economically downtrodden pockets of North, Southwest, and West Philadelphia. Many of the crimes involve drugs, and innocent people who live in drug-infested areas have fallen victim.

The most likely crimes that people outside of these areas encounter are muggings, purse snatchings, and car thefts, which happen mostly at night in desolate areas. You should always exercise caution and be alert to your surroundings, especially when leaving bars, clubs, and parking garages. When in doubt, always take a cab to your destination. If you don't feel safe, get to a well-lit, populated area or step inside the nearest business and wait for a cab. Trust your instincts and travel in groups whenever possible at night.

Information and Services

COMMUNICATIONS AND MEDIA
Phones
When the number of phone numbers in the city got too large for the 215 area code to accommodate, the 267 area code became a second Philadelphia area code. The number of public pay phones has decreased dramatically as it has in most places with the advent of cell phones. The few that still exist cost $0.50 for local calls, and most accept coins and calling cards. Dial 1 before calling toll-free numbers (those starting with 800, 888, 877, etc.). Prepaid phone cards are available at many convenience stores and cell phone stores.

Internet Services
It isn't difficult to find free wireless access at many coffee shops and libraries throughout the city. If you don't have your own computer, public libraries are a good option for residents but aren't much help to nonresidents since you need a library card to access the system and only residents can obtain one. Many hotels and youth hostels have a computer available for free or cost for short-term use. The **ING Direct Café** (17th and Walnut Sts., 215/731-1410) has computers available for free Internet surfing.

Post offices are located all over the city, and the **main branch** (3000 Chestnut St., 215/895-8956) across from 30th Street Station stays open nightly until 9pm, except for Sundays when it closes at 6pm.

Newspapers and Periodicals

Philadelphia has two main daily newspapers, the *Philadelphia Inquirer* (www.philly.com) and the *Daily News* (www.philly.com/dailynews). The *Inquirer* is considered the more serious paper, offering balanced coverage of local, national, and international news. While its popularity and ratings wax and wane, it is often considered in the top tier of daily papers in the country. Check out the Friday "Weekend" supplement for listings of entertainment and events. The *Daily News*, not generally regarded as serious journalism, is concentrated mostly on local news, with extensive sports coverage; some locals are avid fans of the easy, fun read. The *Metro* (www.metro.us/philadelphia), a free daily available at many SEPTA stations, is filled with short snippets of news and entertainment that range from important to entertaining to completely inane.

Many locals, especially the younger set, get their information and news from the free alternative weeklies *PW* (www.philadelphiaweekly. com). Most stories are locally based, and both offer good listings of events, concerts, restaurants, bars, and more. You'll find them in newspaper boxes all over Center City. *Philadelphia* **magazine** (www.phillymag.com) is the award-winning glossy monthly lifestyle magazine for the city and suburbs, sold at bookstores and newsstands. It is an entertaining read, offering a mix of interesting features, sensational local-interest stories, and useful service journalism. Many read it for its local style, dining, and arts and entertainment coverage. The *Philadelphia Gay News* is geared toward issues, news, and events affecting the gay community, and the *Philadelphia Tribune* is an African American weekly newspaper, the oldest of its kind in the country.

Radio

The independent and world music station WXPN (88.5 FM) is a very popular local station operated out of World Café Live in University City. Here are some of the other local stations:

- classical and jazz: WRTI 90.1 FM
- sports radio: WYSP 94.1 FM
- classic rock: WMGK 102.9 FM
- country: WXTU 92.5 FM
- hip-hop and R&B: WUSL 98.9 FM and WRNB 107.9
- National Public Radio: WHYY 90.9 FM
- news: KYW 1060 AM

- oldies: WOGL 98.1 FM
- R&B and classic soul: WDAS 105.3 FM
- rock: WMMR 93.3 FM
- smooth jazz: WJJZ 106.1 FM
- top 40: WIOQ 102.1 FM

MAPS AND INFORMATION

The best place to find maps and a wealth of information about what to do and where to go in Philadelphia is at the **Independence Visitor Center** (6th and Market Sts., 800/537-7676, www.independencevisitorcenter.com), conveniently located in Old City near the major historic attractions. The large facility has knowledgeable staff and volunteers, as well as exhibitions, a small film theater, café, gift shop, and bookstore.

Resources

Suggested Reading

Barra Foundation. *Philadelphia: A 300-Year History*. New York: W. W. Norton & Company, 1982. This is the most comprehensive account of the history of Philadelphia ever written, produced over 15 years from conception to publication. The mammoth 800-plus-page volume is a collaboration of more than 20 scholars and historians. Each chapter is written by a different expert and offers a compelling and colorful narrative of a slice of Philadelphia's history, beginning with "The Founding, 1681-1701," and culminating with "The Bicentennial City, 1968-1982." It is considered required reading for anyone really interested in local history.

Bissinger, Buzz. *A Prayer for the City*. New York: Vintage, 1998. Written by Pulitzer Prize-winning author and former *Philadelphia Inquirer* journalist Buzz Bissinger, this book intimately follows Ed Rendell, arguably Philadelphia's most esteemed and fascinating mayor both personally and politically (who went on to become governor of Pennsylvania), through his first four-year term in the mayoral office. The author was granted behind-the-scenes access to city government, and he provides a candid account of the mayor, city politics, and the lives of other diverse Philadelphians in the 1990s. A compelling read for anyone interested in the complex problems facing American cities in general and certainly for anyone interested in Philadelphia, the book is disturbing, hopeful, and very real. It is, however, more than a decade out of date, so it serves as a slice of Philadelphia history rather than a current report; fortunately, many improvements have taken place since it was published.

Booker, Janice L. *Philly Firsts: The Famous, Infamous and Quirky of the City of Brotherly Love*. Philadelphia: Camino Books, Inc., 2007. This fun, entertaining little book reveals much about Philadelphia's history through its many firsts. The city was the first in so many landmark accomplishments, from major achievements like the first hospital and first university, to the more inane, like its claim as the birthplace of bubble gum and licorice.

Du Bois, W. E. B. *The Philadelphia Negro*. Philadelphia: University of Pennsylvania Press, 1995. Originally published in 1899, this sociological study was the first of its kind to look closely at black urban Americans by examining the lives and communities of blacks in Philadelphia at the end of the 19th century. A novel concept at the time, the study did not presume that blacks lived in poor conditions due to an innate shortcoming of the race. The writer was a civil rights activist and scholar and the first black man to receive a PhD from Harvard University. A cofounder of the NAACP, Du Bois also wrote *Black Folk, Then and Now* (1899) and *The Negro* (1915).

Isaacson, Walter. *Benjamin Franklin: An American Life*. New York: Simon & Schuster, 2003. In nearly 600 pages, you will learn more than you may have ever wanted to know about Benjamin Franklin. The detailed, entertaining account of Philadelphia's favorite son portrays the complex figure's shortcomings, as well as his numerous accomplishments over his fascinating lifetime. Franklin spent much of his life in Philadelphia and played a key role in many monumental events in the city's history, so you will learn much about the history of the city through the life of its most prominent historical figure.

Internet Resources

INFORMATION AND EVENTS

Campus Philly
www.campusphilly.org
With more than a quarter million students attending more than 80 local colleges and universities, there are lots of resources to support the student population and enhance the college experience; Campus Philly is one of the best. The nonprofit's mission is to "fuel economic growth by encouraging college students to study, explore, live, and work in the Greater Philadelphia tri-state region." Initiatives include sponsoring career fairs and networking opportunities, a student discount program, and helping prospective students and families visit local schools. The website, geared toward current and prospective students, includes information, articles, and job and internship listings.

City of Philadelphia
www.phila.gov
The official website of the City of Philadelphia is a useful resource for new residents. This is the place to go to find out where to sign up for gas and electricity or how to find hospitals and other emergency services. A news section offers announcements, and the site offers links to many other useful sites, including public transportation, education, and employment resources.

Greater Philadelphia Tourism Marketing Corporation
www.visitphilly.com
www.uwishunu.com
Philadelphia's tourism and marketing board is the ultimate online resource for visitors to the city and surrounding region, including Bucks, Chester, Delaware, and Montgomery Counties. The primary website offers information

about historic sites, tours, restaurants, nightlife, shopping, and more. It also offers suggested themed itineraries for visitors with varied interests, including couples, families with children, gay travelers, and African American visitors as well as discounts for booking hotels, events, and travel packages. Their blog, www.uwishunu.com, offers detailed descriptions of upcoming events.

Philly Fun Guide
www.phillyfunguide.com

For nearly comprehensive entertainment and other event listings in the area, this is the place. Offering a wide range of leisure activities, including music, dance, sports, fairs, festivals, outdoor activities, tours, parades, dining, and more, it is coordinated by the Greater Philadelphia Cultural Alliance, whose mission is to increase participation and support for arts and cultural organizations in the area. Sign up online to receive FunSavers and half-price discounted ticket offers for many of the best visual and performing arts shows, exhibits, and museums delivered to your email inbox every Thursday.

NEWS

PW
www.philadelphiaweekly.com

These free alternative weekly newspapers have news, event listings, restaurant and movie reviews, and more, and are written with opinion and personality. They can be found in news boxes and coffee shops across Center City or read online.

Flying Kite
www.flyingkitemedia.com

This weekly online magazine launched in 2010 and quickly became a leading source for development-related news affecting the city and suburbs.

Metro
www.metro.us/philadelphia

This free paper has a mix of local, national, and international news and a good dose of fluff; it can be found in SEPTA stations and newspaper boxes across the city and online.

Philadelphia Gay News
www.epgn.com

Available online or in print, it has personals, classifieds, and event listings for the gay community. Plenty of additional events can be found at www.phillygaycalendar.com.

Philadelphia Inquirer and Daily News
www.philly.com

Philadelphia's two main daily newspapers can both be read online or purchased from newspaper boxes and stands.

Philadelphia Magazine
www.phillymag.com

The main glossy city magazine covers arts, events, restaurants, politics, and more. Popular annual issues include those of top schools, top doctors, and a general "Best of Philly" issue. With an upscale readership, the magazine caters to the suburban community and the Center City elite and can be purchased at newsstands or read online.

The Philadelphia Tribune
www.phillytrib.com

Published five days a week, this award-winning newspaper geared toward the African American community can be found online or in print.

HISTORY AND ARCHITECTURE

Philadelphia Architects and Buildings Project (PAB)
www.philadelphiabuildings.org

It's the ultimate resource for architectural scholars, but the easy-to-use, accessible website is also an excellent resource for anyone interested in architecture. It brings together the collections, data, and images of the Athenaeum of Philadelphia, the University of Pennsylvania Architectural Archives, the Philadelphia Historical Commission, the Pennsylvania Historical and Museum Commission, and other architectural organizations. As of 2011, the website contains more than 131,000 images and 25,000 architects, engineers, and contractors, with an ever-growing database. If there is a local building you want to know more about, look here.

Philadelphia Society for the Preservation of Landmarks
www.philalandmarks.org

The group began in 1931, when the historic Powel House was set to be demolished and Frances Anne Wister and other supporters set out to save it. They later acquired Grumblethorpe, the Physick House, and Waynesborough, and today the organization manages the four historical museum homes and is involved in other programs that support historic preservation.

Philly History
www.phillyhistory.org

This award-winning site contains an extensive archive of photographs spanning Philadelphia's history. One of the country's largest municipal archives, it has an estimated two million photographs dating from the late 1800s. A number of different search options make it possible to find photographs from a specific time period, locale, or topic.

U.S. History
www.ushistory.org

Run by the Independence Hall Association (IHA), an organization founded in 1942 in conjunction with the creation of Independence National

Historical Park, the nonprofit's mission is to educate the public about the Revolutionary and colonial era in Philadelphia. This website does just that with detailed and interesting information about the sites and history of Independence Park.

PARKS AND RECREATION

Friends of the Wissahickon
www.fow.org

This nonprofit is dedicated to Wissahickon Park, the part of Fairmount Park in the northwest section of the city. The site offers maps, activities, and trail and event information.

BEST PHILLY BLOGS

Foobooz
www.foobooz.com

With a name derived from "food" and "booze," you can guess what this blog is all about. Foobooz keeps us up-to-date on the latest restaurant and bar openings as well as events, with original content and links to articles from other local food critics. It also features great deals around the city.

Philebrity
www.philebrity.com

Covering "Philly Media, Gossip, Nightlife & Politics," Philebrity is often irreverent and entertaining and sometimes even useful. They rely on reader tips for gossip, so they can't be taken too seriously, but it is often a fun read, and the youth-oriented arts and events listings are solid.

Uwishunu
www.uwishunu.com

"Uwishunu" is not a foreign word, but a subtly hip rendering of the words "you wish you knew," all smooshed together. The younger, hipper offshoot of the Greater Philadelphia Tourism and Marketing Corporation (www.visitphilly.com), Uwishunu offers an insider's look at Philadelphia. Written in blog form by GPTMC staff and other local contributors, it highlights the latest and greatest places to eat, drink, shop, and more. Their mission is to "enable visitors to hang like locals and locals to hang like insiders."

Young Philly Politics
www.youngphillypolitics.com

With the tagline "Progressive, Young, Philly Politics, from Small to Big," this progressive political blog offers a forum to discuss and learn about current issues with a focus on local politics but often branching out into the national level. Many of the active bloggers are passionate and knowledgeable and often have interesting things to say, and discussions are especially heated and informative around election times. Anyone can contribute by signing up for a username.

RESOURCES
INTERNET RESOURCES

A

Academy of Music: 32, 173
Academy of Natural Sciences: 29, 30, 178
accommodations: *see* hotels
Adams, John: 85
Adrienne Theatre: 178
Adventure Aquarium: 29, 86
African American Museum in Philadelphia: 169
African American Street Festival: 323
air travel: 331
alcohol: 337
Allen, Richard: 56
Amada: 30, 97, 98
American Helicopter Museum and Education Center: 275
American Swedish History Museum: 186
Amish Farm and House: 293
Amish villages: 293
Amtrak: 334
Antique Row: 224
Apple Hostels of Philadelphia: 246, 248
aquariums: 86
architecture: general discussion 325-328; Arch Street United Methodist Church 61; Athenaeum 55; Beth Sholom Synagogue 86; Bishop White House 38; Boathouse Row 67; Cathedral Basilica of Saints Peter and Paul 67; Chinatown Friendship Gate 61; City Hall 61; Comcast Center 66; Eastern State Penitentiary 68; Elfreth's Alley 51; First Bank of the United States 53; Fonthill Castle 283; Germantown 82; homes of Fairmount Park 80-85; Independence Hall 40; Lemon Hill Mansion 71; Masonic Temple 64; Merchants Exchange Building 43; Mother Bethel A.M.E. Church 56; Nemours Mansion 278; Philadelphia Museum of Art 71; Powel House 59; Rodeph Shalom Synagogue 79; Second Bank of the United States 48-49; St. Stephen's Episcopal Church 66; 30th Street Station 76; Venturi, Robert 39; Woodlands Cemetery and Mansion 78
Arch Street Friends Meeting House: 32, 49
Arch Street United Methodist Church: 61

Arden Theatre Company: 173
Art After 5: 72
art galleries: Brandywine Valley 270; Center City East 174; free 32; New Hope 282; Northern Liberties 183; Old City 168-169; Philadelphia International Festival of the Arts 321; South Philadelphia 181; *see also* museums
Articles of Confederation: 40
arts and culture: 165-186; Center City East 173-177; Center City West 177-178; Fairmount Park 184-185; festivals 319-325; fine art 328; Greater Philadelphia 186; highlights 166; Museum District 178-181; Northern Liberties and Fishtown 183-184; Old City 168-173; South Philadelphia 181-182; University City 182-183
Ashburn, Richie: 213
Ashkenazic congregation: 79
Assembly Room: 40
Athenaeum: 55
Audrey Claire: 102
Avenue of the Arts: 31, 167

B

Balboa, Rocky: 72
Baldwin's Book Barn: 275
Barbary: 160, 164
Barkley, Charles: 212
Barnes Foundation: 30, 32, 166, 178
Barns-Brinton House: 272
Bartram's Garden: 207
baseball: 208-210, 213
basketball: legends 212; Palestra 78; 76ers 210
Battleship *New Jersey*: 87
Bednarik, Chuck: 212
beer, craft: 159
Belmont Mansion: 80
Benjamin Franklin Bridge: 54
Benjamin Franklin Parkway: 30, 167; *see also* Museum District
Benjamin Lovell Shoes: 218, 231
best-of itinerary: 30-31
Beth Sholom Synagogue: 86
Betsy Ross House: 29, 30, 50
B. Free Franklin Post Office and Museum: 39
Bicycle Club of Philadelphia: 196

biking: Chestnut Hill and Manayunk
203; Greater Philadelphia 207;
Manayunk 204; Museum District
195, 196; Pro Cycling Tour 323;
Ridley Creek State Park 275;
Schuylkill River Trail 193; for
transportation 336; University City
197
Bishop White House: 32, 37
Black Walnut Winery: 274
Blue Cross River Rink: 190
Boathouse Row: 30, 67
boating: Dad Vail Regatta 319;
Delaware River 285; Old City
tours 45
Bob & Barbara's: 142, 149
BOLT Bus: 333
booing, at sports: 209
Bourse, the: 30, 93
bowling: 191, 201
boxing: 201
Brandywine Battlefield Historic Site:
271
Brandywine River Museum: 266, 271
Brandywine Valley: 269-281
Brandywine Valley Wine Trail: 274
Bridgid's: 90, 113
Buckingham Valley Vineyards: 274
Bucks County: 274, 281-288
Bucks County Wine Trail: 274
business hours: 337
business travelers: 338
bus travel: 332
B Wilk Fabrics: 225
BYOB restaurants: 102

C

Camden Riverfront: 86
Candlelight Ghost Tour: 44
canoeing: 285
Carlton, Steve: 213
Carpenters' Hall: 32, 38
carriage tours: 45
car share: 336
car travel: 332
Cathedral Basilica of Saints Peter and
Paul: 67
Cedar Grove: 81
cemeteries: Christ Church Burial
Ground 51; Gloria Dei (Old Swedes'
Episcopal Church) 75; Laurel Hill
Cemetery 79; Old St. Mary's Church
57; St. Peter's Episcopal Church 60
Center City East: arts and culture 173-
177; hotels 252-254; map 9; nightlife

145-148; planning tips 26; recreation
191-192; restaurants 100-105, 131;
shops 221-227; sights 61-66
Center City Pretzel Co.: 125
Center City West: arts and culture
177-178; hotels 256-259; map 11;
nightlife 149-154; planning tips 26-
27; recreation 193-195; restaurants
105-112, 131; shops 228-235; sights
66-67
Center Square: 301
Central Market: 266, 288
Chadds Ford: 270, 279
Chadds Ford Historical Society: 272
Chaddsford Winery: 274
Chamberlain, Wilt: 212
Chamounix Mansion: 246, 264
Channel 6 Zooballoon: 74
cheesesteaks: 31, 118, 119, 138
cherry blossom festival: 323
Chestnut Hill and Manayunk: hotels
262; map 20; planning tips 28;
recreation 203-204; restaurants 135-
137; shops 242-243
children's activities: see family
activities
Chinatown: 31, 61
Chinatown bus: 333
chocolate store: 291
Christ Church: 50
Christ Church Burial Ground: 51
Christian C. Sanderson Museum: 272
Chubby's Steaks: 31, 138
churches: Arch Street United
Methodist Church 61; Cathedral
Basilica of Saints Peter and Paul
67; Christ Church 50; Gloria Dei
(Old Swedes' Episcopal Church)
75; Mother Bethel A.M.E. Church
56; National Shrine of St. John
Neumann 79; Old St. Mary's Church
57; St. Peter's Episcopal Church 60;
St. Stephen's Episcopal Church 66
cinema: film festivals 324; Landmark
Theatres 166, 168; Old City 168;
South Philadelphia 181; University
City 182
Cira Green: 198
City Hall: 30, 34, 61
CityPASS: 37
City Tavern Restaurant: 30, 92
Civil War history: 310
Civil War Memorial: 80
Clarke, Bernie: 213
Clark Park: 198

Clay Studio: 168
climate: 299
Cliveden: 82
Clothespin: 62
colloquialisms: 318
colonial history: 300
Colonial Pennsylvania Plantation: 275
Comcast Center: 66
Comcast Experience: 66
comedy: 164
communications: 342
Concerts in the Park: 323
Congress Hall: 40
consolidation: 309
Constitutional Walking Tours: 44
Continental, the: 30, 95
craft beer: 159
Crane Arts: 169
crime: 309, 341
criminal justice system: 68
cross-country skiing: 275
Crossing Vineyards & Winery: 274
culture: 317-325
currency, U.S.: 54
Curtis Center: 51
Curtis Institute of Music: 177
customs, social: 337-338

D

Dad Vail Regatta: 319
dance clubs: 156, 164
Deck the Alley: 53
Declaration House: 38
Declaration of Independence: 38, 40, 46, 307
Delaware River: 266, 285
demography: 317
Deshler-Morris House: 83
Devil's Den: 131, 154
Dhyana Yoga: 195
dialect: 318
Di Bruno Bros.: 31, 107
Dickens, Charles: 70
Dilworth Park: 192
disabilities, access for travelers with: 335, 340
disc golf: 204
Distrito: 98, 128
Dmitri's: 102, 124
Doylestown: 283
Dream Garden mosaic: 51
drinking: 337
driving: 332, 336
Duross & Langel: 218, 227
Dutch Wonderland: 289

E

Eagles football: 210-211
Eakins Oval: 67
Eastern State Penitentiary: 30, 34, 68, 324
Ebenezer Maxwell Mansion: 82
economy: 316-317
Edgar Allan Poe National Historic Site: 32, 78
Elfreth's Alley: 51
Elkins Park: 86
Ephrata Cloister: 290
Equality Forum: 320
Erving, Julius "Dr. J": 212
Eulogy Belgian Tavern: 131, 143
events: 319-325
excursions from Philadelphia:
    Brandywine Valley 269-281; Bucks
    County 281-288; highlights 266;
    map of 268; Pennsylvania Dutch
    Country 288-296; planning tips 269

F

Fabric Row: 224
Fabric Workshop and Museum: 174
Fairmount Bicycles: 195
Fairmount Park: arts and culture 184-
    185; hotels 264; map 21; planning
    tips 28; recreation 204-207; sights
    79-85
Fairmount Water Works Interpretive
    Center: 30, 32, 70
fall travel: 28
family activities: Academy of Natural
    Sciences 29, 178; Adventure
    Aquarium 29, 86; Arden Theatre
    Company 173; best bets 29;
    Betsy Ross House 29, 50; Dutch
    Wonderland 289; Fairmount Water
    Works Interpretive Center 70;
    Franklin Institute 29, 179; Franklin
    Square 29, 53; National Constitution
    Center 29, 43; National Toy Train
    Museum 293; New Hope and
    Ivyland Railroad 282; Philadelphia
    Science Festival 321; Philadelphia
    Zoo 29, 74; Please Touch Museum
    29, 166, 184; Sesame Place 284;
    Smith Memorial Playground
    and Playhouse 29, 207; Spruce
    Street Harbor Park 29, 191; Wilbur
    Chocolate Company's Candy
    Americana Museum & Store 291
Farmicia: 96, 102
FDR Park: 200
Fergie's: 142, 145

ferries: 86
festivals: 54, 319-325
Fete Day: 53
film festivals: 324
fine art: 328
firefighting: 58, 170
Fireman's Hall Museum: 170
First Continental Congress: 38
First Friday: 32, 169
First Unitarian Church: 153, 160
Fisher Fine Arts Library: 77
Fishtown: see Northern Liberties and Fishtown
fitness centers: 192
flag, American: 50
Fleisher Art Memorial: 181
Flyers hockey: 214
Fonthill Castle: 283
food trucks: 127
Foolish Waffles: 127
football: 210, 212
Forrest Theatre: 176
Frankford Hall: 142, 163
Franklin, Benjamin: general discussion 308; Christ Church Burial Ground 51; Eastern State Penitentiary 68; Franklin Court 39; Pennsylvania Hospital 58; Philadelphia Contributionship 58; St. Stephen's Episcopal Church 66; University of Pennsylvania 77
Franklin Court: 30, 39
Franklin Court Museum Shop: 39
Franklin Institute: 29, 30, 166, 179
Franklin Mortgage & Investment Co.: 142, 149
Franklin Square: 29, 53, 301
Free Library of Philadelphia: 70
Freemasons: 64
Free Quaker Meeting House: 39
Friendship Gate: 61
Friends of Independence National Historical Park: 44
FRINGE Festival: 324
frisbee golf: 204
Fulton Theatre: 266, 289

G

Garces, Jose: 98
Garces Trading Company: 98, 101, 102
gardens: see parks and gardens
gastropubs: 131
geography: 298
Germantown: 82
Germantown Historical Society: 82

ghost tours/haunted sights: Old City tour 44; Terror Behind the Walls 70, 324
Gloria Dei (Old Swedes' Episcopal Church): 75
Good Dog: 131, 151
government: 316
Government of the People: 62
Graff House: 38
gratuities: 338
Great Depression: 312
Greater Philadelphia: arts and culture 186; map 23; planning tips 28; recreation 207-215; restaurants 138-139; sights 86-87
Great Essentials Exhibit: 40
Great Plaza: 54
Greyhound: 333, 334
Grumblethorpe: 83
gunpowder: 278

H

Hagley Museum and Library: 278
Halloween: 224
Hamilton, William: 78
Headhouse Square: 56
helicopter museum: 275
hiking: Chestnut Hill and Manayunk 203; Greater Philadelphia 207; Ridley Creek State Park 275; Schuylkill River Trail 193
Historic Fallsington: 284
Historic Germantown: 82
Historic Philadelphia Center: 44
Historic RittenhouseTown: 82
historic sights: Arch Street Friends Meeting House 49; Battleship New Jersey 87; Betsy Ross House 50; Brandywine Battlefield Historic Site 271; Chadds Ford 272; Christ Church 50; Christ Church Burial Ground 51; City Hall 61; Colonial Pennsylvania Plantation 275; Edgar Allan Poe National Historic Site 78; Elfreth's Alley 51; First Bank of the United States 53; Germantown 82; Gloria Dei (Old Swedes' Episcopal Church) 75; Historic Fallsington 284; homes of Fairmount Park 80-85; Independence National Historical Park 36-49; Lemon Hill Mansion 71; Library Company of Philadelphia 63; Longwood Gardens 271; Mother Bethel A.M.E. Church 56; Nemours Mansion 278; Old Pine Street Church 57; Old St. Joseph's

Church 57; Old St. Mary's Church 57; Pennsylvania Hospital 58; Physick House 59; Smith Civil War Memorial 80; Thaddeus Kosciuszko National Memorial 60; University of Pennsylvania 78; Valley Forge National Historical Park 276-277; Washington Crossing Historic Park 285; Waynesborough 276; West Chester 275; Woodlands Cemetery and Mansion 78

history: 299-316
hoagies: 125
hockey: 213, 214
horseback riding: 275
horse racing: 214-215
hospitals: 341
Hotel Palomar: 246, 256
hotels: 244-264; Center City East 252-254; Center City West 256-259; Chestnut Hill and Manayunk 262; Fairmount Park 264; highlights 246; Museum District 259; Northern Liberties and Fishtown 262; Old City 248-251; Society Hill 251-252; South Philadelphia 260; taxes on 338; tips on choosing 247; University City 260-261
Hub Bub Coffee: 127
Human Zoon: 204

I

ice-skating: 190, 198, 203
immigrants, historic: 309
Indego Bike Share: 196
Independence After Hours Tour: 44
Independence Hall: 30, 32, 34, 40
Independence National Historical Park: free sights 32; planning tips 30; sights 36-49
Independence Seaport Museum: 170
Independence Square: 7, 36
Independence Visitor Center: 30, 32, 36, 42, 196
indie music: 160
Institute of Contemporary Art: 32, 182
insurance, property: 58
International House: 182
International Sculpture Garden: 54
international travelers: 338
Internet services: 342
Iron Chef Jose Garces: 98
Italian Market: 122
Italian Market Festival: 320
itinerary, best-of: 30-31
Iverson, Allen: 212

J

Jamaican Jerk Hut: 102, 106
James A. Michener Art Museum: 283
Jefferson, Thomas: 38, 60
Jewelers' Row: 225
Jewish community: 79, 86, 172
JG Domestic: 98, 128
Jim's Steaks: 31, 118
jogging/walking paths: Boathouse Row 67; Laurel Hill Cemetery 80; Locust Walk 77
John Chads House: 272
Johnny Brenda's: 131, 160, 163
Johnson House: 82
John's Roast Pork: 31, 138
John's Water Ice: 125
Joseph Fox Bookshop: 218, 228
Julius Sturgis Pretzel Bakery: 291

K

kayaking: 285
Kennett Square: 270
Khmer Gallery: 183
Kimmel Center: 32, 166, 173, 174
Kinetic Sculpture Derby and Trenton Avenue Arts Festival: 321
King of Prussia Mall: 232
Koch's Deli: 125
Kohn and Kohn: 224
Kosciuszko, Thaddeus: 60
Kreutz Creek Vineyards: 274

L

La Colombe: 90, 106
lacrosse: 215
Ladies Home Journal: 51
lager: 144
Lancaster: 288
Landis Valley Museum: 293
landmarks: 302-303
Landmark Theatres: 166, 168
landscape: 298
Laurel Hill Cemetery: 79
Laurel Hill Mansion: 81
Legendary Blue Horizon: 201
Lemon Hill Mansion: 71
LGBTQ culture: general discussion 339; Antique Row 224; Center City East Gayborhood 100, 147, 252; Equality Forum 320; Giovanni's Room 221; Philadelphia International Gay and Lesbian Film Festival 324; University City Washington West 247; Woody's 142, 148
Liberty Bell Center: 30, 32, 34, 42
Liberty Brew Tours: 159

libraries: Free Library of Philadelphia 70; Library Company of Philadelphia 63; Library Hall 46; Mercer Museum and Library 284; Van Pelt Library 77; West Chester 272; Winterthur Museum, Garden, and Library 278

Lindros, Eric: 213

literature: 78, 283, 328

Lititz: 291

Locust Walk: 77

lodging: see hotels

Logan Square: 301

London Grill: 30, 114

long-term accommodations: 253

Longwood Gardens: 266, 271

LOVE: 62

Love Letter: 76

Love Park: 200

Lucky Strike Lanes: 191

M

Mac Mart: 127

Madame Saito Bed & Breakfast: 246, 251

Madison, Dolley: 49

Madison, James: 49

Magic Carpet: 127

Magic Gardens: 75

Magnolia Garden: 190

mail services: 343

Mama's Wellness Joint: 192

Manayunk: see Chestnut Hill and Manayunk

Mann Center for the Performing Arts: 184

maps: 4-23; Center City East 9; Center City West 11; Chestnut Hill and Manayunk 20; Fairmount Park 21; Greater Philadelphia 23; Independence Square 7; Museum District 13; Northern Liberties and Fishtown 19; Old City 5; Society Hill 5; South Philadelphia 15; University City 17

maritime museums: 170

markets: Central Market 266, 288; Headhouse Square 56; Italian Market 122; Reading Terminal Market 64

Maryanne S Ritter: 225

Masonic Temple: 31, 34, 64

Maxie's Daughter: 225

media: 342

medicine, history of: 58, 59

Megabus: 333

Mercato: 90, 101, 102

Mercer Mile: 266, 283

Mercer Museum and Library: 284

Merchants Exchange Building: 43

microbreweries: 159

Mint, U.S.: 54

Mitchell & Ness: 218, 223

modern history: 315

Monk's Café: 108, 131

Moravian Pottery and Tile Works: 283

Morris, Robert: 48

Morris Arboretum: 203

Morris Gallery: 32, 176

Morris House Hotel: 246, 251

mosaics: 51, 75, 283

Mother Bethel A.M.E. Church: 32, 56

Mott, Lucretia: 49

Mount Pleasant: 85

Mummers Museum: 181

Mural Arts Program: 76

Mural Mile Walk: 76

murals: 30, 76

Museum District: 30; arts and culture 178-181; hotels 259; map 13; planning tips 27; recreation 195-197; restaurants 113-114; sights 67-74

museums: Athenaeum 55; Brandywine River Museum 271; Center City East 176; Center City West 177; Chadds Ford 272; Doylestown 283; Fairmount Park 184; Fisher Fine Arts Library 77; Franklin Court 39; free 32; Greater Philadelphia 186; Hagley Museum and Library 278; Landis Valley Museum 293; Masonic Temple 64; Mother Bethel A.M.E. Church 56; Museum District 178-181; Old City 169-173; Philadelphia Contributionship 58; Philadelphia Museum of Art 71; Philosophical Hall 46; Second Bank of the United States 49; South Philadelphia 181; Strasburg 293; University City 182; West Chester 275; Wilmington, Delaware 277; Winterthur Museum, Garden, and Library 278; see also art galleries

music: Art After 5 72; Center City East 148, 173; Center City West 153, 177; Fairmount Park 184; Greater Philadelphia 186; Northern Liberties 161; Penn's Landing festivals 54; Philadelphia musicians 153; R5 Productions 160; South Philadelphia 157; University City 157; Wawa Welcome America Festival 322, 324

Mutter Museum: 31, 177

N

National Constitution Center: 29, 30, 34, 43
National Liberty Museum: 170
National Museum of American Jewish History: 172
National Park Service: 36
National Shrine of St. John Neumann: 79
National Toy Train Museum: 293
Native American history: 60, 61
Neighborhood Bike Works: 197
Nemours Mansion: 278
New Freedom Theatre: 183
New Hope: 266, 282-283
New Hope and Ivyland Railroad: 282
New Hope Winery: 274
New Jersey battleship: 87
Newlin Grist Mill: 272
newspapers: 343
New York, cheap travel to: 333
nightlife: 140-164; Center City East 145-148; Center City West 149-154; highlights 142; Northern Liberties and Fishtown 158-164; Old City 144-145; South Philadelphia 154-157; Spirit of Philadelphia cruises 45; University City 157-158
XIX: 90, 104
North Bowl: 188, 201
Northern Liberties and Fishtown: arts and culture 183-184; hotels 262; map 19; nightlife 158-164; planning tips 28, 30; recreation 201-202; restaurants 129-134; shops 239-240; sights 78-79
North Third: 130, 131

O

observatories: 193
Odunde African American Street Festival: 323
Old City: arts and culture 168-173; hotels 248-251; map 5; nightlife 144-145; planning tips 26, 30; recreation 190; restaurants 91-99, 131; shops 219-221; sights 36-55; tours 44-45
Old City Hall: 40
Oldenberg, Claes: 62, 77
Old Pine Street Church: 32, 57
Old St. Joseph's Church: 57
Old St. Mary's Church: 57
Old Swedes' Episcopal Church: 75
One Liberty Observation Deck: 193

P

Paesano's: 125
Paine's Park: 188, 196, 200
Painted Bride Art Center: 173
Palestra: 78
Paradocx Vineyard: 274
Parent, Bernie: 213
parking: 336
parks and gardens: Chestnut Hill and Manayunk 203; Fairmount Park 205; Greater Philadelphia 207; Longwood Gardens 271; Museum District 196; Physick House 59; Powel House 60; Society Hill 190; University City 198; Winterthur Museum, Garden, and Library 278
Parrish, Maxfield: 51
Parx Racing: 214
passes: 37
Patriot Harbor Lines: 45
Pat's King of Steaks: 31, 118
Peace Valley Winery: 274
Peirce-du Pont House: 271
Penn, William: Arch Street Friends Meeting House 49; baptismal font of 50; City Hall 61; city layout by 299; naming of city 306; Pennsbury Manor 284; Penn's Landing 54; statue of 62; Welcome Park 55
Penn Relays: 321
Pennsbury Manor: 284
Penn's Landing: 54
Pennsylvania Dutch Country: 288-296
Penns Woods Winery: 274
Pennsylvania Academy of the Fine Arts: 31, 32, 176
Pennsylvania Dutch culture: 290-291
Pennsylvania Hospital: 58
Pennypack Park: 207
people, the: 317
Perelman Building: 32, 74
periodicals: 343
Peters, Richard: 81
pets, traveling with: 341
pharmacies: 341
Philadelphia Contributionship: 58
Philadelphia Film Festival: 324
Philadelphia Gay News: 339
Philadelphia History Museum: 172
Philadelphia Horticultural Society: 159
Philadelphia Horticulture Center: 205
Philadelphia International Airport: 331, 334
Philadelphia International Festival of the Arts: 321

Philadelphia International Gay and Lesbian Film Festival: 324
Philadelphia Museum of Art: 30, 32, 34, 71
Philadelphia Pass: 37
Philadelphia Phillies: 208-210
Philadelphia Record Exchange: 218, 240
Philadelphia Science Festival: 321
Philadelphia Society for the Preservation of Landmarks: 44
Philadelphia Theatre Company: 176
Philadelphia Trolley Works and Carriage Company: 45, 76
Philadelphia Zoo: 29, 34, 74
Philly Beer Week: 159
Philly Bike Tour Co.: 196
Philly Brew Tours: 159
Philly Overnight Hotel Package: 247
Philly Pretzel Factory: 125
Philosophical Hall: 46
PHLASH: 37, 334
phone services: 342
Physick, Dr. Philip Syng: 59
Physick House: 59
Pitruco: 127
Pizzeria Beddia: 102, 134
planning tips: 26-29
Please Touch Museum: 29, 166, 184
The Plough and the Stars: 131, 144
Poe, Edgar Allen: 78
Polish American Cultural Center and Museum: 172
politics: 316
President's House: 34, 48
pretzels: 125, 291
Printing Office and Bindery: 39
prisons: 68
Pro Cycling Tour: 323
public transportation: 333

QR

Quaker Meeting Houses: 39, 49
R5 Productions: 160
Railroad Museum of Pennsylvania: 293
Rave Motion Pictures University City 6: 182
Reading Terminal Market: 30, 31, 34, 64
recreation: 187-215; Center City East 191-192; Center City West 193-195; Chestnut Hill and Manayunk 203-204; Fairmount Park 204-207; Greater Philadelphia 207-215; highlights 188; Museum District 195-197; Northern Liberties and Fishtown 201-202; Old City 190; Society Hill 190-191; University City 197-201

religion: 318-319
R.E. Load Baggage, Inc.: 218, 239
re-locating to Philadelphia: 253
restaurants: 88-139; best cheesesteaks 31, 118, 138; BYOB 102; Center City East 100-105; Center City West 105-112; Chestnut Hill and Manayunk 135-137; food trucks 127; Garces, Jose 98; gastropubs 131; Greater Philadelphia 138-139; highlights 90; Italian Market 122; Museum District 113-114; Northern Liberties and Fishtown 129-134; Old City 91-99; snack options 125; Society Hill 99; South Philadelphia 114-126; University City 126-129
Retrospect Vintage: 218, 238
Revolutionary War history: 306
Ridley Creek State Park: 275
Rita's: 125
Rittenhouse Hotel: 246, 256
Rittenhouse Row: 31, 82
Rittenhouse Row Festival: 321
Rittenhouse Square: 31, 188, 193, 301, 323
Ritz-Carlton of Philadelphia: 246, 254
Ritz theatres: 168
RiverLink Ferry: 86
Rocky: 30, 72
Rocky Steps: 71, 72
Rodeph Shalom Synagogue: 79
Rodin Museum: 179
Rose Bank Winery: 274
Rose Garden: 190
Ross, Betsy: 39, 50
Royal Tavern: 131, 156
rudeness: 320
Rushland Ridge Vineyards: 274
Ruth and Raymond G. Perelman Building: 74

S

Sabrina's Café: 30, 90, 115
Sand Castle Winery: 274
Sarcone's: 125
Saturday Evening Post: 51
Schmidt, Mike: 213
Schmidt's Commons: 218, 240
Schuylkill Banks River Tours: 45, 208
Schuylkill River: 70
Schuylkill River Trail: 188, 193
sculpture: Barnes Foundation 178; City Hall 62; Civil War Memorial 80; *Dream Garden* mosaic 51; International Sculpture Garden 54; James A. Michener Art Museum

283; Masonic Temple 64; near City Hall 62; Oldenberg, Claes 77; Philadelphia Zoo 74; *Rocky* 30, 72; Rodin Museum 179; 30th Street Station 77; University of Pennsylvania 77; Washington Monument 68
seasons, best travel: 28
Second Bank of the United States: 48
Second Thursdays: 169
Sedgley Woods Disc Golf Course: 204
Segway tours: 76
senior travelers: 339
SEPTA: 333
Sesame Place: 266, 284
76ers: 210
Shambles, the: 56
Shofuso Japanese House and Gardens: 205
shops: 216-243; Center City East 221-227; Center City West 228-235; Chestnut Hill and Manayunk 242-243; highlights 218; Northern Liberties and Fishtown 239-240; Old City 219-221; South Philadelphia 235-238
Sidecar Bar & Grille: 131, 152
sights: 33-85; Center City East 61-66; Center City West 66-67; Fairmount Park 79-85; free: 32; Greater Philadelphia 86-87; highlights 34; Museum District 67-74; Northern Liberties and Fishtown 78-79; Old City 36-55; Society Hill 55-61; South Philadelphia 75; University City 76-78
Silk City: 142, 160
Sister Cities Park: 197
skateboarding: 200
slavery, history of: Belmont Mansion 81; in Declaration of Independence drafts 38; Germantown 82; Liberty Bell Center 42; Mother Bethel A.M.E. Church 56; Mott, Lucretia 49; Odunde African American Street Festival 323; President's House 48
Smith Civil War Memorial: 80
Smith Memorial Playground and Playhouse: 29, 207
smoking: 337
snacks: 125
Snyderman-Works Gallery: 169
social customs: 337-338
society: 317-325
Society Hill: hotels 251-252; map 5; planning tips 26; recreation 190-191; restaurants 99; sights 55-61

soft pretzels: 125
Soul football: 211
South Philadelphia: arts and culture 181-182; hotels 260; map 15; nightlife 154-157; planning tips 27; restaurants 114-126, 131; shops 235-238; sights 75
Space 1026: 174
Spirit of Philadelphia: 45
sports: baseball 208-210; basketball 210; bowling 191, 201; boxing 201; disc golf 204; football 210-214; hockey 213, 214; horse racing 214; ice-skating 190, 198, 203; lacrosse 215; legends 212-213; soccer 215; water sports 266, 285; *see also* recreation
spring travel: 28
Spruce Harbor Park: 54
Spruce Street Harbor Park: 29, 188, 191, 203
squares, city: 301
Standard Tap: 130, 131
Starlight Ballroom: 160
Stenton: 83
Steven Singer Jewelers: 225
St. John Neumann: 79
St. Peter's Episcopal Church: 60
Strasburg Railroad: 293
Strawberry Mansion: 85
Strickland, William: 55, 60, 68
St. Stephen's Episcopal Church: 66
student travelers: 340
Subaru Cherry Blossom Festival: 323
summer travel: 28
Suzanne Roberts Theatre: 176
Swedish settlers: 75
synagogues: 79, 86

T
Tacconelli's Pizzeria: 102, 139
taxes: 338
taxis: 334, 337
temperatures: 299
Terme Di Aroma: 218, 221
terms, local: 318
Terror Behind the Walls: 70, 324
Thaddeus Kosciuszko National Memorial: 60
theater: general discussion 329; Center City East 176; Center City West 178; FRINGE Festival 324; Fulton Theatre 289; Northern Liberties 183; Old City 173
30th Street Station: 76

Thomas Bond House Bed and Breakfast: 246, 250
Tiffany Studios: 51
Tiffin: 90, 132
tiles, Mercer: 283
Tinto: 98, 112
tipping: 338
Tippler's Tour: 44
tobogganing: 275
Todd, John: 49
Todd House: 49
tourist information: 344
tours: 44-45, 76, 296
train travel: 331
transportation: 281, 331-337
travel tips: 338-341
Trenton Avenue Arts Festival: 321
Tria: 142, 154
12th Street Gym: 192
Twilight Tours: 44

U

Underground Museum: 39
Underground Railroad Museum: 81
Union soccer: 215
Union Transfer: 30, 142, 160, 161
United Artists Riverview Stadium 17: 181
University City: arts and culture 182-183; hotels 260-261; map 17; nightlife 157-158; planning tips 27; recreation 197-201; restaurants 126-129; sights 76-78
University Museum of Archaeology and Anthropology: 32, 183
University of Pennsylvania: 77
University of Pennsylvania Arena: 198
Upsala: 82
Urban Adventures: 159
U.S. Constitution: 40, 43, 308
U.S. Mint: 54

VWXYZ

Valley Forge National Historical Park: 276-277
Van Pelt Library: 77
Venturi, Robert: 39
Verde: 218, 226
Vermeil, Dick: 212
Vetri: 90, 101
Village Whiskey: 98, 142, 152
Vox Populi and Khmer Gallery: 183
Walls Fargo Center: 186
Walnut Street Theatre: 176
Washington, George: Deshler-Morris House 83; Masonic Temple 64;

Powel House 59; President's House 48; Washington Monument 68
Washington Crossing Historic Park: 285
Washington Monument: 68
Washington Square: 301
Washington Square Park: 190
water ice: 125
water sports: 285
water works: 70
Wawa Welcome America Festival: 322, 324
Wayne, Anthony: 276
Waynesborough: 276
weather: 299
Welcome Park: 55
West Chester: 272, 279
Wheatland: 293
Wheel Fun Rentals: 45, 195
White, Reggie: 212
White, Reverend William: 37, 50
White Dog Café: 90, 129
Wilbur Chocolate Company's Candy Americana Museum & Store: 291
William Brinton 1704 House and Historic Site: 275
William McIntyre Elkins Library: 71
William Penn statue: 62
William Way LGBT Community Center: 339
Wilma Theater: 177
Wilmington, Delaware: 277, 280
wine bars: 148, 154
wine trails: 274
Wing Bowl: 319
Wings lacrosse: 215
Winterthur Museum, Garden, and Library: 266, 278
winter travel: 28
Wissahickon Park: 188, 203
women travelers: 341
Woodford Mansion: 85
Woodlands Cemetery and Mansion: 78
Woody's: 142, 148
World Series championship team, 2008: 213
World War II: 312
Wright, Frank Lloyd: 86
Wyck: 82
Wycombe Vineyards: 274
Wyeth, Andrew: 271
Yakitori Boy: 142, 145
yoga: 192, 195, 197
Yuengling lager: 144
Zagar, Isaiah: 75
Zahav: 30, 95
zoos: 74

Amada: 97, 98
Amos' Place Restaurant: 294
Anthony's Chocolate House: 117
Anthony's Italian Coffee House: 117
Ants Pants: 106
Audrey Claire: 102, 108
Avalon: 279
Barbuzzo: 103
Bar Ferdinand: 130
Bayou Bar & Grill: 136
Beau Monde: 121
Bing Bing Dim Sum: 114
Black Sheep: 107
The Bourse: 93
Brandywine Prime: 279
Bridgid's: 90, 113
Buddakan: 91
Capogiro: 104
Center City Pretzel Co.: 125
Chapterhouse Café: 117
cheesesteaks: 119
Chubby's Steaks: 138
City Tavern Restaurant: 92
The Continental: 95
Couch Tomato Café: 137
Dahlak: 127
Devil's Den: 131, 154
Di Bruno Bros.: 107
Distrito: 98, 128
Dmitri's: 102, 124
El Poquito: 136
Eulogy Belgian Tavern: 131, 143
Famous 4th St. Delicatessen: 118
Farmicia: 96, 102
Federal Donuts: 115
food trucks: 127
Foolish Waffles: 127
Fork: 96
Four Dogs Tavern: 280
Franklin Fountain: 97
Fuji Mountain: 105
Garces Trading Company: 98, 101, 102
gastropubs: 131
Geno's Steaks: 118
Gianfranco Pizza Rustica: 93
Good Dog: 131, 151
Green Line Cafe: 126
Green Line on Locust: 126
Green Line-Powelton Village: 126
Hank's Place: 279
Hawthornes Café: 117
High Street on Market: 96

hoagies: 125
Honey's Sit 'N Eat: 129
Hub Bub Coffee: 127
Hungry Pigeon: 123
Isgro Paticceria: 124
Italian Market: 122
Jack's Firehouse: 113
Jake's and Cooper's Wine Bar: 136
Jamaican Jerk Hut: 102, 106
JG Domestic: 98, 128
Jim's Steaks: 118
John J. Jeffries: 294
Johnny Brenda's: 131, 163
John's Roast Pork: 138
John's Water Ice: 124, 125
Jones: 97
Koch's Deli: 125
La Colombe: 90, 132
La Famiglia Ristorante: 93
Lambertville Station: 286
Lebus: 111
Little Babies Ice Cream: 134
Lolita: 104
London Grill: 114
Mac Mart: 127
Magic Carpet: 127
Mama's Vegetarian: 112
Manayunk Brewery and Restaurant:
    137
Marigold Kitchen: 128
Marrakesh Restaurant: 123
Marra's Pizza: 123
Marsha Brown: 286
McNally's Tavern: 135
Mercato: 90, 101, 102
Metropolitan Bakery: 111
Monk's Café: 108
Monk's Café: 108
Monk's Café: 131
Morimoto: 91
Moro: 280
Moshulu: 99
Mugshots Coffeehouse & Café: 113
Nam Phuong: 125
XIX: 90, 104
North Third: 130, 131
Old City Coffee: 92
1225 Raw Sushi and Sake Lounge: 100
Osaka Japanese Restaurant: 135
Oyster House: 109
Paesano's: 125
Parc: 107

Paris Bistro and Jazz Cafe: 135
Pat's King of Steaks: 118
Philly Pretzel Factory: 125
Pitruco: 127
Pizza Brain: 134
Pizzeria Beddia: 90, 102, 134
Plain and Fancy Farm Restaurant: 294
The Plough and the Stars: 131, 144
Positano Coast by Aldo Lamberti: 95
Ralph's: 121
Ray's Café and Tea House: 101
Rouge: 109
Royal Tavern: 131, 156
Sabrina's Café: 90, 115
Sampan: 100
Sam's Morning Glory Diner: 115
Sarcone's: 125
Seafood Unlimited: 111
Shane Candies: 97
Sidecar Bar & Grille: 131, 152
soft pretzels: 125
South Philly Barbacoa: 121

SpecialTeas Tea Room and Gift Shop: 279
Sprig & Vine: 286
Standard Tap: 130, 131
Tacconelli's Pizzeria: 102, 139
Tequilas Restaurant: 108
Tiffin: 90, 132
Tinto: 98, 112
Valanni: 103
Valley Green Inn: 138
Vedge: 105
Vernick: 109
Vetri: 90, 103
Vic Sushi Bar: 106
Vientiane Café: 126
Vietnam Restaurant: 100
Village Whiskey: 98
water ice: 125
Wedge and Fig: 92
White Dog Café: 90, 129
Wm. Mulherin's Sons: 132
Xochitl: 99
Zahav: 95

Nightlife Index

A. Bar: 149
Barbary: 160, 164
Barcade: 163
The Bards: 149
Bike Stop: 147
Bob & Barbara's: 142, 149
Cavanaugh's: 157
craft beer: 159
Devil's Den: 154
Dirty Frank's: 145
Dolphin Tavern: 156
Electric Factory: 161
Eulogy Bar Tavern: 143
Fergie's: 142, 145
First Unitarian Church: 153, 160
Fountain Porter: 155
Frankford Hall: 142, 163
Franklin Mortgage & Investment Co.:
    142, 149
Garage: 154
Good Dog: 151
Good King Tavern: 155
Grace Tavern: 151
Johnny Brenda's: 160, 163
Khyber Pass Bar: 143
lager: 144
Las Vegas Lounge: 144

L'Etage: 156
Liberty Brew Tours: 159
Loco Pez: 163
McGlinchey's: 151
microbreweries: 159
Morgan's Pier: 158
New Deck Tavern: 157
Philadelphia Horticultural Society: 159
Philly Beer Week: 159
Philly Brew Tours: 159
The Plough and The Stars: 144
Pub and Kitchen: 152
Pub on Passyunk East (POPE): 155
Punch Line Philly: 164
Rotunda: 157
Royal Tavern: 156
700 Club: 158
Sidecar Bar & Grille: 152
Silk City: 142, 160
Starlight Ballroom: 160
Tattoed Mom: 156
Tavern on Camac: 147
Ten Stone: 152
Theatre of Living Arts: 157
Tria: 142, 154
Trocadero Theatre: 148
U Bar: 147

Union Transfer: 142, 160, 161
Urban Adventures: 159
Village Whiskey: 142, 152
Vintage: 148
Voyeur: 147

W/N W/N: 161
Woody's: 142, 148
World Café Live: 158
Yakitori Boy: 142, 145
Yuengling lager: 144

Shops Index

Adamstown: 294
AIA Bookstore and Design Center: 223
Anastacia's Antiques: 237
Anthropologie: 228
Antique Row: 224
Apple Store: 230
Art Star: 239
Balance Health Center: 233
Benjamin Lovell Shoes: 218, 231
Bluemercury Apothecary and Spa: 233
Book Trader: 219
Born Yesterday: 228
Boyd's: 229
Brickbat Books: 235
Buffalo Exchange: 234
B Wilk Fabrics: 225
Children's Boutique: 228
Duross & Langel: 218, 227
East Passyunk Avenue: 237
Fabric Row: 224
Garland of Letters: 235
Germantown Avenue: 242
Giovanni's Room: 221
Golden Nugget Antique Market: 286
Grocery: 224
Halloween: 224
Head Start Shoes: 231
Hideaway Music: 242
Jewelers' Row: 225
Jinxed: 239
Joan Shepp: 229
Joseph Fox Bookshop: 218, 228
Kiehl's: 233
King of Prussia Mall: 232
Kitchen Kettle Village: 294
Knit Wit: 229
Kohn and Kohn: 224
Lapstone and Hammer: 223
Lost & Found: 221
Macy's: 227
Main Street Music: 242
Manayunk: 243
Maryanne S Ritter: 225

Maxie's Daughter: 225
Midtown Village: 227
Mitchell & Ness: 218, 223
Modern Eye: 223
Moon and Arrow: 235
Norman Porter Company: 240
Old City: 220
Olde Mill House Shoppes: 294
Omoi Zakka Shop: 230
Open House: 226
Peddler's Village: 285
Penn's Purchase Factory Outlet Stores: 286
Philadelphia AIDS Thrift: 238
Philadelphia Record Exchange: 218, 240
R.E. Load Baggage, Inc.: 218, 239
Repo Records: 237
Rescue Rittenhouse Spa: 234
Retrospect Vintage: 218, 238
Rice's Market: 286
Rittenhouse Row: 231
Rockvale Outlets: 294
Salon L'Etoile & Spa: 243
Scarlett Alley: 220
Schmidt's Commons: 218, 240
Shops at Liberty Place: 232
Shops at the Bellevue: 232
South Street: 238
Steven Singer Jewelers: 225
Sugarcube: 219
Tanger Outlets: 294
Ten Thousand Villages: 225
Terme Di Aroma: 218, 221
Theory: 230
Third Street Habit: 219
Toppers Spa and Salon: 234
UBIQ: 231
Urban Outfitters: 230
Vagabond: 220
Verde: 218, 226
Via Bicycle: 237
West Elm: 226

Airbnb: 253
AKA Rittenhouse Square: 253
Alexander Inn: 252
Appel's Society Bed and Breakfast: 251
Apple Hostels of Philadelphia: 246, 248
Bed and Breakfast Connections of
    Philadelphia: 253
Bella Vista Bed & Breakfast: 253, 260
Best Western Independence Park
    Hotel: 249
Chamounix Mansion: 246, 264
Chestnut Hill Hotel: 262
Clinton Street Bed & Breakfast: 252, 253
Cornerstone Bed & Breakfast: 260
Craigslist: 253
Franklin Hotel at Independence Park:
    250
Gables: 261
Hilton Inn at Penn: 261
Holiday Inn Express Penn's Landing:
    249
Hotel Monaco: 249
Hotel Palomar: 246, 256

Independent Hotel: 253
International House: 253, 261
La Reserve Center City Bed and
    Breakfast: 253, 256
Le Méridien: 254
Loews Hotel: 254
Madame Saito Bed & Breakfast: 246,
    251, 253
Morris House Hotel: 246, 251
Penn's View Hotel: 250
Philly Overnight Hotel Package: 247
Rittenhouse 1715: 257
Rittenhouse Hotel: 246, 256
Ritz-Carlton of Philadelphia: 246, 254
ROOST Apartment Hotel: 253, 257
Sofitel: 257
Thomas Bond House Bed and
    Breakfast: 246, 250
Westin: 259
Windsor Suites: 253, 259
Wm. Mulherin's Sons: 262
Wyndham Historic District: 250

Photo Credits

Acknowledgments

To the wonderful team at Avalon Travel, thank you for consistently working to improve the Moon Handbooks' user experience to make sure it's as good as it can be.

To my highly talented and artistic sister, Molly Gavin, you have contributed to this book in every way possible, from writing to taking photos and much more—all while bringing a baby, my wonderful nephew Sergio, into the world. I simply could not have done it without you.

To my husband Damian, thank you for taking such good care of our boys during the many crazy hours I spend working. Your work is the hardest and more important of all, and no one does it as well as you do. And to my boys, Dylan and Niko, all the love in the world.

And thank you to the amazing and wonderful city of Philadelphia, which I am lucky to have grown up in and continue to call home.

Also Available

PITTSBURGH

DAN ELDRIDGE

PENNSYLVANIA

ANNA DUBROVSKY

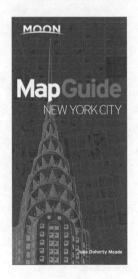

Map Guide

NEW YORK CITY

Julie Doherty Meade

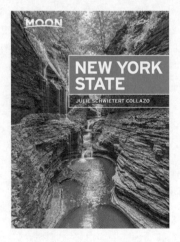

NEW YORK STATE

JULIE SCHWIETERT COLLAZO

MAP SYMBOLS

═══ Expressway	○ City/Town	✈ Airport	⛳ Golf Course
┅┅┅ Primary Road	◉ State Capital	✈ Airfield	🅿 Parking Area
┅┅┅ Secondary Road	◉ National Capital	▲ Mountain	⛏ Archaeological Site
┅┅┅ Unpaved Road	★ Point of Interest	✚ Unique Natural Feature	⛪ Church
┄┄┄ Trail	● Accommodation	⚘ Waterfall	⛽ Gas Station
┈┈┈ Ferry	▼ Restaurant/Bar	⚑ Park	Glacier
┅┅┅ Railroad	■ Other Location	🚩 Trailhead	Mangrove
═══ Pedestrian Walkway	△ Campground	🎿 Skiing Area	Reef
▭▭▭ Stairs			Swamp

CONVERSION TABLES

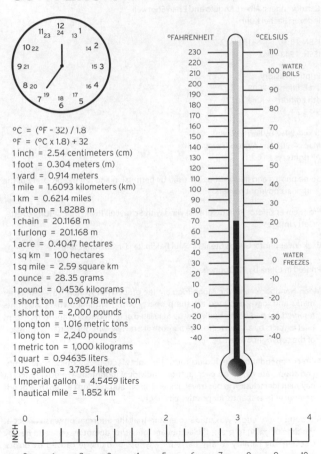

°C = (°F - 32) / 1.8
°F = (°C x 1.8) + 32
1 inch = 2.54 centimeters (cm)
1 foot = 0.304 meters (m)
1 yard = 0.914 meters
1 mile = 1.6093 kilometers (km)
1 km = 0.6214 miles
1 fathom = 1.8288 m
1 chain = 20.1168 m
1 furlong = 201.168 m
1 acre = 0.4047 hectares
1 sq km = 100 hectares
1 sq mile = 2.59 square km
1 ounce = 28.35 grams
1 pound = 0.4536 kilograms
1 short ton = 0.90718 metric ton
1 short ton = 2,000 pounds
1 long ton = 1.016 metric tons
1 long ton = 2,240 pounds
1 metric ton = 1,000 kilograms
1 quart = 0.94635 liters
1 US gallon = 3.7854 liters
1 Imperial gallon = 4.5459 liters
1 nautical mile = 1.852 km

MOON PHILADELPHIA
Avalon Travel
An imprint of Perseus Books
A Hachette Book Group company
1700 Fourth Street
Berkeley, CA 94710, USA
www.moon.com

Editor: Rachel Feldman
Series Manager: Leah Gordon
Copy Editor: Ruth Strother
Graphics and Production Coordinator: Elizabeth Jang
Cover Design: Faceout Studios, Charles Brock
Interior Design: Domini Dragoone
Moon Logo: Tim McGrath
Map Editor: Albert Angulo
Cartographers: Albert Angulo and Brian Shotwell
Indexer: Rachel Kuhn

ISBN-13: 978-1-63121-412-7
ISSN: 1942-406X

Printing History
1st Edition — 2008
4th Edition — June 2017
5 4 3 2 1